Russia's Plato
Plato and the Platonic tradition in Russian education, science and ideology (1840–1930)

FRANCES NETHERCOTT
Universities of Nijmegen/Fribourg

LONDON AND NEW YORK

First published 2000 by Ashgate Publishing

Reissued 2019 by Routledge
2 Park Square, Milton Park, Abingdon, Oxon, OX1 4 4RN
605 Third Avenue, New York, NY 10017

First issued in paperback 2021

Routledge is an imprint of the Taylor & Francis Group, an informa business

Copyright © Frances Nethercott 2000

All rights reserved. No part of this book may be reprinted or reproduced or utilised in any form or by any electronic, mechanical, or other means, now known or hereafter invented, including photocopying and recording, or in any information storage or retrieval system, without permission in writing from the publishers.

Notice:
Product or corporate names may be trademarks or registered trademarks, and are used only for identification and explanation without intent to infringe.

Publisher's Note
The publisher has gone to great lengths to ensure the quality of this reprint but points out that some imperfections in the original copies may be apparent.

Disclaimer
The publisher has made every effort to trace copyright holders and welcomes correspondence from those they have been unable to contact.

A Library of Congress record exists under LC control number:

ISBN 13: 978-1-138-74153-9 (hbk)
ISBN 13: 978-1-315-18281-0 (ebk)
ISBN 13: 978-1-138-74149-2 (pbk)

For my parents

RUSSIA'S PLATO

'Frances Nethercott, a frequent visitor to Russia, has written an important book which gives more than just a scholarly description of the reading of Plato: it offers a sensitive and important insight into Russian intellectual life in the nineteenth and early twentieth centuries. I recommend it to not only Russianists but all European intellectual historians.'
—*Constance Blackwell, President of the International Society for Intellectual History; Department of History, Birkbeck College, University of London, UK*

It is generally acknowledged by historians of ideas that Plato and the tradition he inspired occupied a privileged place in Russian nineteenth-century culture, but that this situation changed dramatically after the October Revolution when the Bolsheviks declared their preferences for the 'materialists', Aristotle and Democritus. Yet if one is to venture beyond the fairly narrow confines of the history of ideas to investigate developments in humanities scholarship and the contentious issues surrounding education in Russia, this 'hero' to 'villain' narrative turns out to be somewhat misleading.

Russia's Plato examines how Russian intellectuals, professionally engaged as historians, philosophers, philologists, and teachers of law, read, taught, and interpreted the Platonic dialogues. Bridging intellectual and institutional history, the book shows that attitudes towards Plato were far more wide-ranging than usually thought. Through the prism of Plato's reception in Russian universities, Nethercott also explores broader issues such as: the phenomenon of rupture and continuity with Russia's past traditions, and the age-old problem of Russia's relations with West European culture. Addressing such issues in light of Plato's thought, the common property of European culture as a whole, this book presents an illuminating challenge to a number of accepted opinions not only on Plato and the Platonic tradition, but also on the nature of Russia and early Soviet culture.

Frances Nethercott is senior researcher at the Centre for Russian Humanities Studies, Nijmegen, Holland, and scientific collaborator at the University of Fribourg, Switzerland.

Contents

Acknowledgements	*viii*
Translation and Transliteration	*x*
List of Abbreviations	*xi*

Introduction   1

1   The Development of Plato Scholarship in Nineteenth-Century Russia   20

From an 'Orthodox Ethics' to the Pragmatism of Reform and Counter Reform   21

Compromise and Conflict: The Scientific Community and the State   25

Developments in the Historical and Philosophical Sciences   27
History of Philosophy   27
Trends in Historiography   34

Russian Plato Scholarship   36
The 'Plato Question'   38

2   Plato and Russian Idealism: The Platonic Impulse in the Construction of a Philosophical Tradition   58

From 'Integral Knowledge' to the 'Ideal Real': The Slavophiles and their Successors   61

Plato, the 'Father of Idealism'   65
'On the Necessity and Possibility of New Principles in Philosophy' (Ivan Kireevskii)   67
'Concrete Idealism' (Sergei Trubetskoi)   71

	Plato as a 'Contemporary' of Kant	75
	Kant and Plato in the Theological Academy	76
	Plato and Kant: The 'Plus' and 'Minus' in the European Philosophical Tradition (Pavel Florenskii)	80
	Plato's Doctrine of Reason versus Kant's Theory of Experience (Pamfil Iurkevich)	82
	The Neo-Kantian Recovery of Plato	86
3	**Plato as an Impulse in Russian Philosophy of Law**	**96**
	Reforming Justice in Late Imperial Russia	97
	Teaching Justice: Between Western Science and Domestic Needs	101
	Past Philosophies for a Contemporary Science of Law: Plato and Kant as Two Paradigms in Juridical Thought	106
	Plato as a Philosopher of Natural Law/Justice	106
	Plato and/or Kant: Duty versus the Good	110
	Justifying the Common Good: From Subjective to Objective Ethics	115
	Between Plato and Kant	118
	Law, Society and the State	121
	Russian Liberalism: Nostalgia for the Ideal City?	124
4	**Russians Reading the *Republic***	**133**
	Teaching the Republic	135
	Interpreting the Republic	141
	Confronting Western Scholarship: 'Classical' versus 'Modernizing' Trends	145
	The Actuality of the Republic: *Education and the Woman Question*	148
	Plato, the Teacher (Nastoiashchii Uchitel')	148
	Sexual Equality, Solidarity, or 'Stud Farm'?	150

	A Question of Utopia-nism	156
	Terrestrial Utopia	158
	Discovering the Kingdom of God: The *Republic* as a Celestial Utopia	161
5	**A Question of Russian Platonism**	173
	Plato's Republic *in a Soviet Utopia*	174
	Plato, the 'Father of Idealism' and Soviet Historiography of Philosophy	179
	Continuity and Change in Perceptions of Plato	182
	Conclusion: Was there a 'Russian' Platonism?	184

Biographical Profiles   *191*
Select Bibliography   *207*
Index   *227*

Acknowledgements

The completion of this project would not have been possible without the Swiss Research Foundation and the Dutch Organization for Scientific Research. Their generous financial support meant that I was able to profit from several long-term stays in Moscow. This proved to be particularly important, given that many materials I needed to consult are unavailable in West European libraries. I would like to express my gratitude to the staff of the State Historical Library in Moscow for their good-natured services, and for giving me access to rare and damaged books. Above all, the trips to Russia provided many an opportunity to discuss my findings with historians, philosophers and classical scholars. Their knowledge, insights, and, in some cases, personal experience of the educational system under Stalin, was especially valuable for refining hypotheses and pursuing a line of thought, which might otherwise have been overlooked. My special thanks go to Professor Alexander Dobrokhotov for reading an earlier draft, and to members of the IVGI research team – Professors Georgii Knabe, Nina Braginskaia, Sergei Nekliudov, and Olga Vainshtein – for their comments, advice and enthusiasm when I first embarked on the topic. Equal thanks go to Professor Gennady Batygin and his collaborators at the Moscow School of Sociology and Economics. As philosophers and sociologists, their comments and questions gave fresh impetus to the project, opening up a spectrum of possibilities, which turned out to be far more than I had first imagined.

In Switzerland, I owe special gratitude to Professor Heiko Haumann and Professor Edward Swiderski. I am very grateful to them for reading earlier versions of the book, and for drawing my attention to related literature in the field. My thanks also go to Professor Alexander Haardt in Bochum, for providing an ongoing commentary of the chapters as I was in the process of writing them. Heartfelt thanks go to Dr Jonathan Sutton, and to Professor James Scanlan.

Parts of the following chapters were originally conceived as papers for conferences and colloquia held in 1997 and 1998. I would like to thank the various organizers – in particular Michel Espagne (CNRS, Paris) and Katia Dmitrieva (Institute of World Literature, Moscow), Evert van der Zweerde (University of Nijmegen), and Constance Blackwell, founder of the Society for Intellectual History (London) – for their skills in creating a forum for discussion, and for attracting the attention of a wider, non-informed public to the still largely ignored wealth of Russian culture.

Last, but not least, I would like to express much gratitude to my friends and colleagues at the Centre for Russian Humanities Studies, University of Nijmegen. Thanks to their example, I have learned that doing scientific research does not mean you have to sacrifice a sense of humour.

Translation and Transliteration

Unless otherwise stated translations are my own. Russian words have been transliterated according to the Library of Congress system (avoiding diacritical marks). With the exception of commonly occurring names, proper nouns and place names have also been transliterated according to the same system.

List of Abbreviations

Journals

RM	*Russkaia Mysl'*
SEET	*Studies in East European Thought*
TKDA	*Trudy Kievskoi Dukhovnoi Akademii*
VFP	*Voprosy Filosofii i Psikhologii*
VP	*Voprosy Filosofii*
ZhMNP	*Zhurnal Ministerstva Narodnogo Prosveshcheniia*

Other

Kn.	kniga
M. - L.	Moscow - Leningrad
Pbg.	Petersburg
Pgd.	Petrograd
SPb.	St. Petersburg
Vyp.	vypusk

Introduction

How did Russian intellectuals in the nineteenth and early twentieth centuries read Plato? Which, if any, dialogues did they prefer, and why? Were their preferences susceptible to change as the science of Antiquity progressed, opening up new horizons in interpretation? Did their interest in Plato differ in any significant way from readings in contemporary France or Germany? Studying the 'posthumous life of Plato'[1] in Russia in view of these questions is a fascinating, yet complex undertaking. Granted, at one level, just 'how' Plato was read may be answered quite simply: he was read in any number of ways – scientifically, ideologically and 'poetically'. There is little doubt that, as the 'philosopher-poet', Plato was highly congenial to romantic 'reveries of love' (*grezi liubvi*). His modern audience was inspired by the creative, artistic possibilities embedded in his notion of the Eros. 'Platonic ideology', as one Russian commentator, the historian of ancient philosophy, Aleksei Giliarov, wrote, 'is not only the most brilliant of all philosophical systems, it ranks among the best works of poetry'.[2]

Statements to the effect that Plato is 'our favourite Russian philosopher' (*nash liubimyi russkii filosof* [3]) were frequent not just in literature intended for a wider, non-specialized audience; they also found their way into more scholarly works. At his '*pro venia legendi*' lecture presented to the Moscow Theological Academy in 1908, the religious philosopher and mathematician, Pavel Florenskii, appealed to the pathos of Platonic thought, couching it in the very same expression – 'reveries of love' – as Giliarov had before him. He also seized this ceremonious occasion to proclaim the Platonic 'pedigree' of Russian 'national' philosophy: 'It was he – oh yes! – he, who gave our institution its name. And, it is surely more than a simple coincidence that it is called "academy", and not "lyceum", or "university". In taking the name we have, we consider ourselves pupils of the Athenian Academy.'[4]

Behind the drama of Florenskii's words is a grain of more serious truth. Philosophically, Plato had long been assimilated to aspects of Russian nineteenth-century idealism with its frequently strong religious overtones. Aspects of his thought were mirrored in the complex process of 'russifying' motifs of German idealism: an encounter with the *Weltseele* and *All-Einheit* was also a path of twists and turns leading back to an original Platonic metaphysics and epistemology. Indeed, nowadays, it has become commonplace to claim the importance for Russian idealism of Platonic philosophy in its neo-Platonic and Schellingian perspectives. The recovery of Plato was, to a large extent, via the tradition he inspired. But, it is also the case, particularly during the last quarter of the nineteenth century, that Plato came to occupy a place for himself in Russian scholarship, irrespective of the allegiance he inspired from his long line of successors. Numerous monographs and articles attest to the revival of Plato in light of new historical, philosophical and philological findings. Russian philosopher-philologists and historians endeavoured to reconstruct Plato's thought, paying heed to the original context in which it was developed. It is only to be regretted that, although their work in this field was of considerable importance for the 'Science of Antiquity', it has largely been overlooked by Western scholars.

For the historian of Russian culture, this scholarly output is significant in other ways. It is instructive of patterns of learning and the establishment of intellectual traditions. More specifically, it offers a key to a deeper understanding, not so much of Plato as of the Russian nineteenth and early twentieth-century intellectual world. The historical orientation of Russian philosophical enquiry alone, with its thinly concealed models of influence, offers many fruitful indications of the ways Western, particularly German, but also French, scholarship left its imprint on the constitution of a Russian intellectual tradition, especially in the second half of the century. But there are, of course, other, more telling instances of how Plato reception throws light on contemporary issues in Russia itself. One such instance concerns the official promotion of his philosophy for purposes which, regrettably, in the eyes of some, had only very little to do with the 'Science of Antiquity' itself. As the spiritual foundation of Eastern Orthodoxy, Plato and the tradition he inspired were believed to answer the needs of an Orthodox ethic. Or again, aspects of Plato's social thought (or perceptions of it, at least) were instrumentalized for the political strategies of nation building, whether it be of the Romantic or the Bolshevik kind. In both instances, it was believed that the most effective means to the aspired ends lay in consolidating Russia's and Soviet Russia's educational system. In nineteenth-century debates about what kind of schooling was best suited to Russian society, some intellectuals paid tribute to Plato and the Platonic tradition, colouring their arguments with allusions to humanism, the Renaissance. In short, in their defence of classicism as the foundation of a generalist education they worked in motifs which had once formed a part of the Plato patrimony in fourteenth and fifteenth-century Italy.[5] And, even if the early Bolsheviks rejected classicism because of its bourgeois connotations, the Plato of the *Republic*, in which he conceived of an educational programme along strict disciplinary lines, was congenial to Lenin's concern to inculcate a firm sense of loyalty to the new Soviet State in the making.

These various readings of Plato yield a *pot-pourri* of images, many of which were pieced together from select aspects of earlier Platonic revivals. As Ada Neschke suggests, these fall, *grosso modo*, into the pre- and post-Kantian periods, and are marked by a corresponding shift in accent, passing from portrayals of Plato as the religious metaphysician, to epistemologist and secular moralist.[6] Any one of these images, combined in a variety of ways, may be found in Russian nineteenth and early twentieth-century (including early Soviet) literature. Plato is depicted as the precursor of the Christian faith, a moral force. He is the originator of the doctrine of Ideas, a remarkable philosopher-poet whose imagination and creative fantasy were prized as arms against the dry scholastic heritage of Aristotelianism. Plato was also the author of an 'objective ethics', which was to be of paramount importance for Russian philosopher-jurists active at the end of the century. Yet, while it may be interesting to know 'how' Plato was read, the mosaic-like picture which emerges nevertheless begs the question why was Plato read in these ways, and what might we learn from this? To answer this question means to address cultural, social and political perspectives, which may, directly or indirectly, have shaped these readings.

Among historians today, it is usual to describe the period of Russian history beginning with the reign of Nicholas I through to the consolidation of Bolshevik rule as a process of modernization, which was often vexed, if not thwarted, by strongly voiced attitudes of conservatism and traditionalism in Court and bureaucratic circles.[7] Reform and Counter Reform, an ideology of nation building and Russification, measured liberalization and conservative reaction, the emergence of a public sphere (*obshchestvennost'*) and professions, together with variously relaxed or strict degrees of censorship, represent so many specific moments in this see-saw motion of change. Advocates of the dominant conservative politics argued that Russia's original forms of social organization, as exemplified by the peasant commune, the people's unshakeable faith in Tsar and God, or the religiously inspired nature of Russian 'national philosophy', with its motto of 'heart over reason', were all too specific for Russia's current development to be compatible with Western social and political institutions. On the contrary, those who believed that Russia's future lay in finding a place for herself within the fold of Europe made repeated bids to update the country's legal and administrative system in the hope of improving what were, in reality, the appalling circumstances of peasant daily life.

Granted, this double-edged phenomenon of modernization and traditionalism affected all walks of Russian life. However, one useful way to focus the problems incurred by attempts to update Russian society within the confines of a strong autocratic state, is, I suggest, to consider its impact on the practice of learning (education and research) in the humanities in Russian schools, and especially in the university. Given its double social and scientific status in an environment of absolute autocracy, the role of the university, both in nineteenth-century Russia and in the aftermath of the Revolution, proved, more often than not, to be a problematic issue. A preliminary examination, period by period, of the conditions under which teaching and research were carried out may usefully impart a better understanding of the various reasons for the return to and/or actualization of Plato, and, in turn, allow us to explore answers to the questions raised above – in short, what prompted Russian scholars to read Plato in the ways they did? Put another way, it is a matter of determining how far Plato reception was carried out for the sake of advancing academic values *per se*, and how far the Russian recovery of Plato formed part of a more widespread nostalgia throughout Europe for a 'humanist culture' in reaction to 'depersonalizing' science, popular in the middle years of the nineteenth century. Certainly, it is in this sense that comments to the effect that Platonism is an 'expression of high ideals and values which have been lost in the modern world with its emphasis on science', or that Platonism 'restores meaning to human existence' might be best understood.[8] But, there is also another question lurking here, namely how far was Plato scholarship in Russia motivated by, or indeed merely the consequence of, ideological and political conflicts, attesting to the absence of scientific autonomy from the public sphere?

As one nineteenth-century scientist of note, the physician and surgeon, Nikolai Pirogov, was quoted to have said, the university in Russia, was first and foremost a 'barometer of social change'.[9] By turns an important beneficiary of the reform programme, and a main target of repressive measures, the university became a catalyst of public opinion, the seedbed of revolutionary activity, as well as a leading representative of the socio-cultural values of liberalism.[10] Part of the problem was that, ever since Peter the Great, education had been traditionally considered as a legitimate sphere of state influence. The upshot was an ambiguity in relations between the 'academic intelligentsia' and the state, an ambiguity, which in turn led to further problems, among them, the double function – as experts and as bearers of public opinion – which accrued to some professors. It also created an unclear conception of science and its role in society.

Although relations between the professorial body and the state tended towards a compromise of interests, this could, and occasionally did, turn into a conflict of values. A case in point was the unresolved issue of how to modernize state power without impinging on the absolute authority of the tsar. Clearly, the state required an educated elite competent in specialized, and socially useful disciplines, such as pedagogy, law and medicine, but to achieve this it was obliged to provide the necessary conditions (scholarships abroad, privileged access to literature, professional contacts) if future scholars and professors were to fulfil their promise of service to the state. In other words, by taking expedient measures to acquire its own corps of educators, the state was putting its uncontested authority at risk.

The consequences of the state's poorly focused strategy of 'means and ends' were visible at various levels. The custom of sending future professors and schoolteachers abroad to complete their training encouraged the formation of an educated elite, perfectly at ease with the recent developments in science on a European scale. But it also unwittingly sponsored the growth of an 'ideology' among this elite – the autonomy of science. As it grew familiar with research and teaching practices abroad, Russia's community of teachers and scholars came increasingly to defend academic liberty and autonomy in collegial matters, citing their West European counterparts as an example to follow. Many believed that autonomy was the necessary precondition for the advancement of science, and that only on these grounds would it then be possible to reconcile service to the state with service to society.

Such a contest of values did, occasionally, degenerate into open conflict, sometimes leading to repressive measures by the state, anxious to curb any potential threat to its authority. Heavy censorship and control over the content of lecture courses, dismissals, or provocations leading to 'voluntary' resignations by professors count among the softer measures employed. Harsher measures – frequently documented by modern-day social historians – involved the introduction of the police into the university auditorium, and mass arrests of both professors and students on suspicion of sympathy for the Revolutionary movement.

This confusion of expediency with ideology ultimately had repercussions on the practice of learning itself. The late nineteenth century saw the emergence of alternative foyers for the advancement of science – around a journal, for example, or through the creation of scholarly societies, as well as private schools offering a more flexible curriculum.[11] As for state schools and the university which continued to bear the brunt of outside interference, it is possible to observe a marked difference in quality between the level of instruction, subject to measures of standardization, on the one hand, and research, on the other. The quality and variety of the latter attests to the ways Russian scholars saw their place within the European scientific community as a whole. At the same time, however, it is also a telling sign of their isolation, as a 'community', from Russian society at large, not least because the reach of more original contributions tended to be very limited, confined to publications in specialized journals with a small circulation, or to discussions at closed meetings of scholarly societies. Ironically, at best, they were published in foreign language journals and monographs, thus providing their authors with an entry into the European arena of scientific discussion, but cutting them off from their readers at home.[12]

To suggest that relations between the professorial body and the state were managed only under the sign of compromise or threat of conflict would not, however, be a just presentation of things. Although between each side conceptions of the social role of science differed, both the state and professors advocated the need to modernize the country, but not at the price of undermining traditional moral values. So, when, in the 1830s and again in the 1870s, the state promoted classical studies as the basis of a generalist education in the gymnasia, and as the ground course for university students reading the arts, there was a fortunate coincidence of interests at least insofar as 'means' were concerned.

The state's promotion of the study of Antiquity reflected both an ideology of education, and also a utilitarian attitude towards scholarship, which became especially blatant at the time of the Counter Reform (1884). Earlier, in the 1830s, schooling in Latin and Greek (which between 1810 and 1830 benefited from a major increase in teaching hours, placing it virtually on a par with Latin) had been combined with Russian (language, literature and history) and catechism. These subjects were privileged as the most appropriate means to inculcate a sense of national pride, of legitimating Russia's present in light of her Greco-Byzantine roots, indeed, of underscoring her difference from, if not superiority over, the Latin foundations of most West European culture. Later, in the wake of the Great Reforms in the 1860s, the study of Latin and Greek (with mathematics) once again received official blessing, but the deplorable rote learning of grammar and syntax to which gymnasium pupils were subjected, with little opening on to the ancient world in terms of its literature or history, suggests that the point in encouraging a classical education was merely to exercise the pupil's mind. Given their obvious degree of difficulty, studying these two dead languages was arguably an ideal way to do so.[13] In other words, the romantic philohellenism of the 1830s, which had been used to encourage a sense of national identity in light of the triple principle of 'Autocracy, Orthodoxy and Nationhood'[14] shifted to a more pragmatic approach to schooling. The universal qualities afforded by a classical education were to be reserved for the gymnasia elite (that is, children of the nobility, mainly), while a programme of Russification was most actively pursued in primary schools and the more technically oriented *Realschule*. Similar to the German model, from which this type of secondary school took its name, instruction in these schools focused on modern languages and science, together with Russian language, literature and history. Given that a basic knowledge of Latin was a requirement for higher education (with both Latin and Greek for the faculty of history and philology) the omission of these subjects from the *Realschule* timetable effectively blocked access to the university.

As a direct consequence of the 1884 Counter Reform statutes, university degrees in the humanities were devised with the explicit purpose of providing future schoolteachers with an adequate training in classical syntax and grammar to pass on to their future pupils in the classroom. But these measures met with an unexpected backlash – a sharp drop in the number of inscriptions to the faculty, with most students migrating to the faculties of law and medicine. Thanks to a timid initiative, taken by the professorial body itself, to include auxiliary courses on civilizational aspects of the Ancient world (history and the history of philosophy), this situation did see a gradual improvement during the final decade of the century. But the damage had, seemingly, already been done. For all their efforts to make the humanities more attractive to prospective students, the number of degrees continued to be quite low compared to other subjects. The modest proposal in question consisted in enhancing the status of secondary disciplines – philosophy in particular, a subject which, incidentally, could be studied as a major option only after 1905 – so as to provide students with more adequate tools for their tasks as secondary school teachers. Accordingly, the modified programme was devised along the lines of a general *'philosophicum'* for the first two years, and comprised compulsory instruction in Latin, Greek and the history of language, together with courses on the history of ancient Greece and Rome, and philosophy (logic, psychology and the history of ancient thought).[15] Courses in the student's chosen specialization in classical philology, history, or modern philology (viz., Russian language and literature[16]) were reserved for the third and fourth years, but interestingly, the commission also recommended additional courses in philosophy for each major branch – six hours in the history of modern philosophy for historians and students of modern philology, and a special seminar (four hours) on Plato and Aristotle for students reading classical philology.

While the character of school and university programmes certainly supports the view that, by the end of the century, study of the classics had become a *sine qua non* of being 'well educated', this emphasis on the ancients was, of course, not unique to Russia. Throughout Europe, classical studies were enjoying a revival as part of a drive to combat what was feared as the annihilating effects of scientism on the moral outlook of the youth. That in Russia this should also have counted as a leading argument in defence of a classical education provides a telling example of the phenomenon of non-differentiated arguments in face of otherwise quite distinct political and historical circumstances. In Russia, arguments employed for and against a generalist (classical) versus a specialized (technical) education, centred on modern languages and science, did little more than reproduce those once heard in Germany and France. As elsewhere, Russia, too, had her share in the quarrel between 'Realists' – with its motto of 'education for life' – and 'Humanists', for whom the principle *'humaniora*, which had once been the guiding light along the path that the Ancients had taken, should still, today, guide modern man'.[17] But, perhaps what is worth noting with respect to the Russian variant of this polemic is the way the underlying world outlook associated with the humanist position altered quite considerably as the nineteenth century progressed. Whereas in the mid-nineteenth century, defenders of the classical gymnasium (for example, the historian Timofei Granovskii, or the aforementioned Pirogov) were criticized by their adversaries as liberals and

Westernizers, in the post-reform period (1870s onwards) instruction in Latin and Greek became identified with the premises of conservatism. The upshot was dissent among classical scholars, with some (the noted philologist Vasilii Modestov, for example) becoming sceptical of the type of education for which they had once actively campaigned.[18]

Even if it is true to say that, in the eyes of certain members of the professorial body, the programme devised by the Ministry of Education and cohorts (the arch-nationalist Mikhail Katkov played a considerable role in devising the 1871 rulings leading to a disproportionate number of hours learning Latin and Greek) was flawed by a crude pragmatism, and blatantly used in support of conservative politics, it is also true to say, that its promotion did not altogether conflict with the genuine interests of other professors. For many, Antiquity was an exemplary instrument of intellectual discipline, indeed, a much needed antidote – and apparently at any price – to correct the haphazard ways in which the intelligentsia had traditionally educated itself. According to some critics, this 'bad education', typical of the Russian youth, was the regrettable consequence of having neglected to discipline the mind.[19] For Sergei N. Trubetskoi, Professor of Ancient Philosophy at the University of Moscow, the solution lay in a methodological study of philosophy in an historical perspective. For him, Greek philosophy was the school in which all European thought matured, and in this vein he reasoned that 'anyone wishing to philosophize, judge or understand more complex contemporary problems and tasks of speculation must also pass through this school'.[20]

It may be argued that the combined training in ancient history, classical philology and the history of philosophy, such as this was established institutionally, contributed to the particular profile of quite a number of leading Russian scholars active at the end of century, among them figures such Trubetskoi, Pavel Novgorodtsev, or Vladimir Solov'ev, whose research is discussed in the following chapters. More generally, it should not be forgotten that this period was to produce the generation of Silver Age poets and literati with its eminent figures Valery Briusov, Andrei Bely and Viacheslav Ivanov, all of whom had passed through the gymnasium and university in the Counter Reform period. What exactly did a future 'intelligent' study? A brief reconstruction of Sergei Trubetskoi's secondary and university instruction during the 1870s and 1880s, such as this is documented in memoir accounts and commented by his biographers, offers some clues.

Named Professor of Ancient Philosophy in 1890, at Moscow University, Trubetskoi (1862–1905) passed his gymnasium years under the sign of the 1871 ruling. The weekly timetable for the final two years was made up as follows: catechism – 1 hour; Russian language and church Slavonic – 2 hours; Latin – 6 hours; Greek – 6 hours; mathematics – 6 hours; geography – 1 hour, with no instruction in history, French or German languages. From 1881 to 1885 Trubetskoi studied at the Faculty of

History and Philology of Moscow University, years which would be capped by the conservative measures of the Counter Reform in 1884. The memoirs of Sergei's younger brother, Evgenii (1863–1920), provides an idea of the institutional lacklustre and intellectual apathy which marked their student years:

> For my brother and me, philosophy at that time was everything. (...) The university made an extremely oppressive impresssion (...). We felt at once that there was no one (...) who knew Kant, Schopenhauer, and Plato better that we freshmen.[21]

As a secondary branch, the courses Sergei followed in philosophy entailed the rudiments of logic, psychology (a philosophical enquiry into the nature of the human soul, not experimental psychology), and the history of philosophy (with the exclusion of materialist and positivist systems, banned in 1884). In addition, obligatory for all students of the Orthodox confession were courses in theology. During his undergraduate studies Trubetskoi's main teacher was M.M. Troitskii, author of a textbook on psychology which was widely used for teaching purposes along with German materials (Trendelenburg's *Geschichte der Kategorienlehre* and Prantl's *Geschichte der Logik* appear the most often in reading lists). The historian of philosophy, Nikolai Grot, who took up his post in 1886, lectured on Plato and Aristotle.

This situation was duplicated in the other main universities, all subjected to the same regime. In Kiev, Kozlov tackled 'systematic' aspects of philosophy, Giliarov, the history of philosophy. In St. Petersburg, Professor Vladislavlev read his main course in the history of ancient philosophy, and *Privat-Docent*, Aleksandr Vvedenskii, taught aspects of logic and psychology. The secondary literature on which these courses were based was just as standardized, tending to support a spiritualist line of interpretation, as suggested by the quite widespread use of works by Alfred Weber and Alfred Fouillée. But, it should also be noted, bureaucratic ignorance in matters of science sometimes created convenient loopholes which scholars seemingly exploited. Rather surprisingly, 'kosher' authorities also included writers of reputed 'liberal' politics, works by Zeller, Brandis, Windelband ranking as some of the better-known examples.[22]

Besides the opportunity granted to some promising students to complete their studies abroad (Trubetskoi, himself spent two semesters in Berlin where he studied under the philologist, Diels), a crucial part of the 'intelligent's' education was his reading outside the prescribed literature. One work that was to convince Trubetskoi of the importance of an historical problematizing of philosophy was Kuno Fischer's *Geschichte der neuen Philosophie* which he read in Strakhov's translation.[23] But such *extra curricular* reading was often little more than a chance encounter – granted perhaps fortuitous – with one or another author. Indeed, it was a custom which some professors, including Trubetskoi himself, criticized in their efforts to improve the institutional framework of learning.

Trubetskoi, who believed that scientific research should be conducted in the protected isolation of the university, tended to shirk political involvement. It was perhaps an irony of fate, then, that put him into the limelight during the heated combat between the university and the state in the years immediately preceding the 1905 Revolution. Yet, in his public-cum-political engagement with respect to the 'University Question', the position Trubetskoi defended was still that of a typical 'academist': to his mind, it was above all crucial to protect the practice of science from outside intrusion. No doubt, because of the moral integrity he showed in his stand against autocracy, but also in his endeavours to check the revolutionary fervour of certain colleagues and students, Trubetskoi's public career was finally crowned with high recognition. In September 1905 he was voted, with a wide majority, to the post of University Rector in the first free election ever to be held in Russian university history.

Although Trubetskoi was reluctant to conduct university politics, the fact that he did so was not at all exceptional for the times he lived in. It was quite usual among professors of Trubetskoi's generation to combine their role as a scholar with that of spokesman for public opinion. Of those authors whose works are discussed in this current study, the philosopher of law, Boris Chicherin served, for a short period, as mayor of Moscow, and after the somewhat abrupt ending to his career as an university professor he actively campaigned to build up the *Zemstvo* (local administration largely concerned with the welfare of the recently emancipated peasantry) by contributing to the foundation of schools and hospitals. After the Revolution of 1905, Pavel Novgorodtsev, also a professor of the philosophy of law, became Kadet member of the Duma.[24] Indeed, in the sense that professors frequently combined scholarly research with publications or conferences intended to reach a wider, non-specialized public, one could go so far as to say that the double role ascribed to the professoriate had repercussions on the practice of learning itself.[25]

The ambiguities described above with respect to the humanities generally left their mark on Russian Plato scholarship, the character of which forms the main topic in the chapters below. For sure, that Plato was acknowledged as Russia's 'favourite philosopher' or that Russian philosophy, by virtue of a constant elaboration throughout the century of key concepts such as 'integral knowledge' and 'all-unity', the 'ideal-real' may be said to be 'Platonically disposed' are statements which we come across not infrequently both in Western studies of Russian philosophy, as well as in retrospective 'histories of Russian thought' written by some of the leading figures in the pre-Revolutionary intellectual world themselves. But, if anything, such claims tend to promote a fairly homogenous portrait of Plato as a precursor of Russian metaphysical idealism, highly congenial to Orthodox spirituality. As such, it is no surprise that the study of Plato in schools and universities should have been encouraged by the state as the guardian of the Orthodox faith. But one consequence of providing an institutional framework for the study of Plato was, as I have suggested above, ultimately to allow the scientific community greater access to research methods such as these were developing abroad, particularly in Germany, where an interplay of philosophical and philological analyses of the dialogues was marked by developments in historiography more generally. The upshot with respect to Plato reception in Russia was to multiply assessments of his thought. These included not only a number of interesting evaluations from an historical-philosophical perspective, but also some innovative research in the juridical-ethical context: lectures on the history of philosophy of law provided an occasion to focus on the relation between morality and law, and the concept of justice in which Plato's thought was an important landmark.

A survey of scholarly literature (teaching curricula, textbooks, lecture courses, dissertations, review articles of recent Western literature, translations) is, therefore, instructive in a variety of ways, allowing us to confirm certain hypotheses about Plato reception in Russia, but also to challenge some of its accepted axioms. For one, the scientific production shows that while Plato scholarship in this country was certainly conducted for the sake of advancing traditional academic values, it was also carried out by dint of state directives in educational policy. Drafting lectures or textbooks, the choice of dialogues for teaching purposes had to meet requirements as set by the Ministry of Education.

Reconstructing certain readings of Plato, and the ways these shaped ulterior ones, eliciting creative reworkings, negative criticism, or a neutral rehashing of past models, may, I believe, be significant for a more comprehensive (certainly more ambitious) study of the ways in which traditions in intellectual history have been established. Certainly, through the prism of Plato reception, broader issues relating to Russian social and cultural reality come into view. The aforementioned consolidation of Russia's educational system, and the emergence of a more professional intelligentsia dedicated to scholarship and to improving Russian social life through learning count among some of these. In a different vein, determining which areas of study were favoured by scholars might throw light on other, less obviously, related aspects of Russian (and early Soviet) intellectual life. For example, historical scholarship sometimes served as a convenient vehicle to imply criticism of specific contemporary political events. In the police regime of Nicholas I, the historian Timofei Granovskii lectured on the development of political institutions in early modern France and England, the contrast between the history he was reconstructing and the reality he and his auditors lived in being all too cruelly obvious. Similarly, in the wake of the Great Reforms, it was once again predominantly historians who, by virtue of their choice of topic, or in the ways they handled their materials, passed judgement on contemporary events and change. In an atmosphere of moderate liberalization 'from above', aspects of the ancient world, such as the practice of slavery, Athenian democracy, or conceptions of the state, found a renewed actuality that was perhaps more than merely coincidental.

As an object of specialized studies, Russian Plato scholarship is, then, for the modern-day historian, revelatory of exchanges within the European scientific community as a whole, and of Russian participation in this community. As a cluster of concepts (stereotypes even) operating in various contexts (the juridical, philosophical, historical-philosophical, the poetical and political), Plato reception helps elucidate certain aspects of Russian intellectual culture, together with permanence and change in this culture with respect to practices before and after the Bolshevik seizure of power. In this regard, it becomes a matter of reconstructing the 'logic' of the readings that Russian and early Soviet intellectuals provided. This in turn raises the question of whether or not it is legitimate to speak of a 'Russian Platonism', meaning a comprehension of this philosophy which is inscribed in the historical and cultural circumstances peculiar to Russia.

In contemporary Western Plato scholarship, understanding Platonism or neo-Platonism has been a rather vexed issue, and one that is still today open to interpretation. Ada Neschke, for example, describes the traditional differences between French and German scholarship with respect to this issue. In French practice, she says, Platonism implied the philosophy of Plato itself, meaning a system comprising dialectic, physics and ethics. On the contrary, German scholars tended to put the accent on the idea of succession, or the tradition that Plato inspired. Nowadays, she observes, the two sides seemed to have come closer together, with the resulting compromise that the term Platonism 'designates, on the one hand, those elements which characterize the very essence of Plato's thought, and which, on the other, are at the origin of the tradition. It remains, she admits, for historians of philosophy to agree which elements are the most characteristic, making for an accepted understanding of the term Platonism'.[26]

Speaking very generally, the meaning that philosophers in nineteenth-century Russia ascribed to 'Platonism' suggests an amalgamation of two main sources. In their work one frequently comes across a neat unity of neo-Platonic conceptions (hypotheses of the One, the Soul and the Mind in Plotinus), such as these were assimilated to Christian doctrine and elaborated by the Church Fathers. In turn, this older 'tradition' met and was combined with a more recent recovery of Plato's thought by the German Idealists, who accentuated the importance of the Platonic doctrine of ideas. Moreover, the renewed interest in the 'original' Plato, behind the tradition, as witnessed in the work of Schleiermacher, Schelling and Hegel, prompted some Russian thinkers to follow suit, and to discover for themselves the dialogues first written in Classical Antiquity. It remains, however, that the Platonism discussed so far was common property of most European intellectuals – Russian intellectuals included – and, as such, tells us virtually nothing about a 'Russian' Platonism. Yet, already, what is interesting to note here, is the fact that the image of Plato described above appealed to certain Russian intellectuals because they believed it allowed them to mark their difference with the Western intellectual tradition, which they condemned as the product of Aristotelianism. I believe that this kind of evidence invites an enquiry from a cultural-historical perspective, in which an entire web of social and cultural circumstances peculiar to Russia's past and present, together with the intellectual biographies of individual commentators as background material, should be taken into account. Such a complementary approach may help explain the sometimes rather extravagant readings of Plato that we come across, and to determine whether (or not) Plato was somehow 'Russianized'. It is particularly this second perspective which will serve as a guideline in the current study.

Choosing to present Plato's fate on Russian soil in light of education and research has, conveniently, helped me delimit the choice of Russian authors whose works are the main object of discussion. With one major exception – Vladimir Solov'ev – they were all engaged in teaching and research in the humanities, together with law (Boris Chicherin, Pavel Novgorodtsev, Evgeni Trubetskoi, Pamfil Iurkevich and other less well-known figures) principally at the university, but also in the theological academies.[27] Both as scholars and as witnesses of the socio-political events of their times, these professors have been the object of monographs and articles by Western and Russian specialists alike, but they have not, to my knowledge, been brought together in light of assessments or use of Platonic motifs, nor indeed, in light of the amount of cross-referencing between them attesting to their involvement in active, lively debate. In this respect, the writings of the philosopher and 'journalist' (*publitsist*) Vladimir Solov'ev are of central interest. Although he abandoned an academic career soon after defending his doctoral thesis in 1881, Solov'ev never broke his ties with the university milieu. These were actively sustained through close friendships (with the Trubetskoi brothers), intellectual affinities (Novgorodtsev), and quarrels (Chicherin), just as his career as a *publitsist*, notably for the monthly *European Messenger*, brought him into close contact with specialists in history, law and literature. As the following chapters show, Solov'ev's contribution to Russian Plato reception, in terms both of his philological scholarship, as well as his interpretative studies, was quite considerable. Not only did his work serve as a point of reference and an object of debate among his contemporaries, it also became an undisputed landmark for generations of scholars working in the early Soviet period.

The period chosen – principally the last four decades of the nineteenth century with a backwards glance to the mid-nineteenth century, and an occasional eye to the early Soviet period – corresponds, in the main, to the real consolidation of Russia's educational system, together with the proper institutionalization of science. The chosen perimeters also coincide with the publication of two *Complete Works* of Plato in Russian translation, the first by Vladimir Karpov (of the Kiev Theological Academy) in 1841–1842, the second edited by Lev Karsavin, Sergei Zhebelev and Ernst Radlov, published in fifteen volumes between 1922 and 1929. But to suggest that the rise and decline of Plato in modern Russia fall within the two end points chosen in this study would, of course, be a serious underestimation of the eighteenth-century contribution to the revival of Plato studies in Russia. Suffice it to mention the translation (into a Russian heavily encumbered with Church Slavonic) of most of the dialogues between 1780 and 1785,[28] as well as the Platonically inspired writings of the Ukrainian philosopher, Grigorii Skovoroda. His reflections which he couched in dialogue form, evidently owed much to the first 'philosopher of the heart', Plato.[29]

Admittedly, then, a more complete account of Plato reception in modern Russia should also include a study of the eighteenth century. But a background interest in the development of teaching and research practices in the more secular environment of the university (or at least, less overtly religious than the seminary and theological academy) has set the perimeters of this study squarely in the nineteenth century. It should not be forgotten that the Ministry of Education in Russia was set up only in 1802, nor that, apart from the University of Moscow, which was founded in 1755, all the main Russian universities were early to mid-nineteenth century creations.[30] Moreover, as I have suggested, standardized practice in schooling was finally achieved quite late in the century, after considerable trial and error, whim even, on the part of tsars and the bureaucracy.

As the foregoing argues, endeavours to gain a better understanding of the nature of Plato reception in Russia require the optics provided by the history of interpretation and institutional history.[31] Summarizing the meaning of Russian intellectual history, Isaiah Berlin observed that 'Russia is the home of the history of general opinions, of the beliefs and general intellectual outlook of educated persons affected by the progress of the arts and sciences, and by political, economic, and social phenomena, but not necessarily involved in a professional concern with them – of the outlook of amateurs, not experts.'[32] Berlin's remarks pertain primarily to the first half of the nineteenth century, even though the phenomenon he describes was still widespread in the second half of the century. His words to the effect that government repression of free social or political activity resulted in 'the forcible canalization of the quest for self-expression and individuality (...) into the realm of thought, which, for this reason, became the opium of the civilized, their only substitute, pale as it was, for action' ring all too true. But, given the changes incurred by the Reform programme, it also seems fitting to explore aspects of Russian intellectual culture precisely as this took shape in an institutional context, and to consider the outlook of experts, not amateurs. Concentrating on the role of professors who, in their quest to defend the value of learning, were not unaffected by repressive government measures serves, then, as a complement, hopefully modifying the more usual view that Russian intellectual activity took place outside the walls of the university, and that this set of circumstances alone made for the originality and creativeness of the Russian intelligentsia. Moreover, concentrating on the institutional structuring of knowledge in an historical perspective might not only help adjust the balance with respect to the past; it is also pertinent to actual concerns in post-Soviet Russia today regarding the content and practice of a new 'humanistic' education in which recuperating and reactualizing the pre-Revolutionary tradition has been a major phenomenon. One visible sign of this phenomenon is the re-edition of pre-Revolutionary literature, including Russian-Greek dictionaries and textbooks, as well as the creation of private 'classical' gymnasia.[33]

The first chapter aims to provide the general institutional context in which Russian-nineteenth century Plato scholarship developed, caught, as it were, between the rise of the historical sciences and the heavy hand of state interference in standardizing the educational system in the name of nation building and modernization. The stages of Russian Plato scholarship are discussed with respect to the main translated *Sobranie Sochinenii* of the dialogues – those by Karpov (1841–1842 and 1863–1879), the philosopher of law, Petr Redkin (1830s–1840s and 1870s), the Solov'ev and S. N. Trubetskoi edition (1899–1903) – as well as with reference to the body of translated and original secondary literature (historical-philosophical mainly) relating to Plato and the world of classical antiquity.

The second chapter, on aspects of Russian idealism, illustrates how Plato served as a reference, resource even, in Russian philosophical culture. First, it is a matter of Plato's indirect presence in Russian thought via the tradition he inspired. Second, Plato becomes a direct, explicit reference in a number of historical-philosophical accounts of idealism. He figures as one specific moment in the development of idealism, alongside other main representatives within the tradition, making for an interplay of ideas between them. Third, chronology is dropped, and Plato is made a contemporary of classic modern representatives of idealism. In this perspective, Plato finds an interlocutor in Kant.

The third chapter deals with aspects of Russian philosophy of law. Despite restrictions placed on university instruction in philosophy (indeed, the total ban during the 1850s), knowledge about the history of philosophy was conveyed to students in the guise of the history of the philosophy of law and the 'encyclopaedia of law'. In this context, Plato was treated as a 'juridical thinker', his enquiry anchored in endeavours to determine the meaning of the good, of justice. Such an image inspired some Russian thinkers to see in him a possible prototype of the theory of natural law. More generally, Plato's philosophy prompted a reflection among Russian philosopher-jurists about the relationship to establish between law and morality. At the same time, however, the limitations of Plato's thought for modern-day preoccupations which, broadly speaking, fell into the province of liberalism, were also fairly obvious. At this point, it is once again the philosophy of Kant which enters the picture, though less as an 'interlocutor', and more as a kind of 'interface' between Plato and his Russian readers. Kant's practical philosophy highlights the problems at issue in endeavours by Russian philosopher-jurists to accommodate the rights of the individual to the social good, just as it also exposes both the pertinence and inappropriateness of the Platonic model in this regard.

In the fourth chapter I shift my approach to compare and contrast a number of reactions to a single dialogue, the *Republic*. The main issues confronted and disputed by Russian readers and which are telling of the problems still unresolved in the late nineteenth society, include the individual as citizen, his relation to the state, education and moral conduct. The choice of the *Republic* has been made for several reasons: it appeared as a set text both for students in the Historical-Philological Faculty and for students of law, a factor which allows us, therefore, to compare and contrast reactions from the perspectives of those disciplines – history, philosophy and law – which were treated separately in the earlier chapters. In the early Soviet period, the utopianism of the *Republic* was, for a short period, of symbolic importance in designs to turn the ideal city into a reality. Granted, the political and ideological objectives espoused by nineteenth-century liberals and twentieth-century communists were very different, but ironically, the secondary literature that they drew on was more often than not the same, attesting to a furtive allegiance to openly reviled past masters. Lastly, given that this dialogue brings together so many aspects of Plato's thought, a discussion of this dialogue may usefully permit us to recapitulate some of the points made in the preceding chapters, and to illustrate them in a complementary way. A final concluding chapter addresses the question of whether it is legitimate to speak of a Russian Platonism.

Notes

1   Title of a study by the Czech scholar, Frantisek Novotny (Martinus Nijhoff, The Hague, 1977).
2   A.N. Giliarov, *Platonism, kak osnovanie sovremennogo mirovozzreniia* (Moscow, 1887), p.10.
3   A. Iashchenko, author of a bibliographical study of ancient philosophy, *Russkaia bibliografiia po istorii drevnei filosofii* (Iurev, 1915), p.60. In his contribution to the *Vekhi* ('Landmarks') collection in 1909, Nikolai Berdiaev spoke of the 'Platonic lineage' of Russian philosophy, and George Florovskii, in his *Puti russkogo bogosloviia*, also referred on several occasions to Russia's 'Platonic tradition'.
4   P. Florenskii, *Obshchehelovecheskie korni idealizma* (MDA, 1908), pp.5-6.
5   James Hankins, *Plato in the Italian Renaissance*, vol.1 (E.J. Brill, Leiden, New York, 1990); Brian Copenhaver and Charles Schmidt, *Renaissance Philosophy*, in *A History of Western Philosophy*, vol.3 (Oxford, 1992).

6   Ada Neschke-Hentschke (ed.), *Images de Platon et lectures de ses oeuvres. Les interprétations de Platon à travers les siècles* (Editions de l'Institut supérieur de philosophie, Louvain, 1997), pp.xii-xviii.
7   Among more recent studies see, for example: E.W. Clowes (ed.), *Between Tsar and People. Educated Society and the Quest for Public Identity in Late Imperial Russia* (Princeton, 1991); B. Eklof, J. Bushnell and L. Zakharova (eds), *Russia's Great Reforms, 1855-1881* (Bloomington, 1994); E.H. Judge and J.Y. Simms Jr. (ed.), *Modernization and Revolution. Dilemmas of Progress in Late Imperial Russia. Essays in Honor of Arthur P. Mendel* (New York, 1992); H. Haumann and S. Plaggenborg (eds), *Aufbruch der Gesellschaft im verordneten Staat. Russland in der Spätphase des Zarenreiches* (Frankfurt am Main, 1994); B.W. Lincoln, *The Great Refroms. Autocracy, Bureaucracy, and the Politics of Change in Imperial Russia* (DeKalb, 1990); N.A. Troitskii, *Tsarizm pod sudom progressivnoi obshchestvennosti. 1866-1895 gg.* (Moscow, 1979); F.W. Wcislo, *Reforming Rural Russia. State, Local Society, and National Politics, 1855-1914* (Princeton, 1990).
8   N. Grot, *Ocherk filosofii Platona* (Moscow, 1896), pp.119-120; 174-175.
9   Cited by Pavel Miliukov in his entry 'Universitet' in Brokgaus and Efron (eds), *Entsiklopedicheskii Slovar'*, Vol. xxxiv (SPb., 1902), p.793.
10 Among the many histories of Russian education by Western authors, see: N. Hans, *The History of Russian Educational Policy* (London, 1931); P. Alston, *Education and the State in Tsarist Russia* (Stanford University Press, 1969); W.L. Mathes, 'The Origins of Confrontation Politics in Russian Universities: Student Activism, 1855-1861', *Canadian Slavic Studies*, Spring (1968), also his 'N.I. Pirogov and the Reform of University Government, 1856-1866', *Slavic Review*, 3 (1972); A. Besançon, *Education et société en Russie dans le second tiers du XIXè siècle* (Mouton-Paris-La Haye, 1974); J.C. McClelland, *Autocrats and Academics. Education, Culture and Society in Tsarist Russia* (Chicago, 1979); C.H. Whittaker, *The Origins of Modern Russian Education. An Intellectual Biography of Count Sergej Uvarov 1786-1855* (Northern Illinois University Press, 1984); S.D. Kassow, *Students, Professors and the State in Tsarist Russia* (University of California Press, 1989). On the early Soviet period see, S. Fitzpatrick, 'Professors and Soviet Power' in *The Cultural Front: Power and Culture in Revolutionary Russia* (Cornell University Press, Ithaca and London, 1992); V. Tolz, *Russian Academicians and the Revolution. Combining Professionalism and Politics* (Macmillan, 1997).
11 For example, in Moscow, L.I. Polivanov and F.I. Kreiman founded classical gymnasia with more original, stimulating curricula. In memoir accounts written by former pupils, mention is often made of their remarkable pedagogical qualities. See A. A. Nosov, 'K istorii klassicheskogo obrazovaniia v Rossii (1860-nachalo 1900-x godov)' in G.S. Knabe (ed.), *Antichnoe nasledie v kul'ture Rossii* (Moscow, 1996), p.221ff.
12 A case in point is the philologist Faddei Zelinskii (1859-1944), much of whose scholarly work on the Greek and Roman theatre, or on individual authors, was published in Germany. By contrast, his more popular writings, in Russian, were published in numerous *tolstie zhurnaly*.
13 This was the conception of P.M. Leont'ev (a classical scholar by training) which influenced the drafting of the 1871 rulings. See Nosov, op. cit., p.216.
14 *Samoderzhavie, Pravoslavie, Narodnost'* – key terms used by Count Uvarov, Minister of Education (1833-1849), in his report on education addressed to Nicolas I (in 1832, just prior to his nomination as Minister). Uvarov recommended that schooling be based on these principles, and that the study of theology and the ancient world was a propitious means to ensure the lasting effects of this new ideology on the pupil.
15 The number of hours per month are given as follows: Latin - 32 hours, Greek - 32 (24 of which for individual authors, 8 for exercises); General Introduction to Philology - 4

hours; History of Greece and Rome - 8 hours; Philosophy - 12 hours, broken down into logic (4 hours), psychology (4 hours), history of ancient philosophy (4 hours).

16 When this programme was drawn up courses in French and German language and literature were also listed as options, but at the time there was no one to teach the subject!

17 N. Pirogov, cited in E. Shmid, *Istoriia srednykh uchebnykh zavedenii v Rossii* (SPb., 1878), p.434.

18 A major point of debate in the pages of the journal *Zhurnal Ministerstva Narodnogo Prosveshcheniia* (1834-1918). For a summary, see M.M. Filippov, *Reforma gimnazii i universitetov* (SPb., 1901).

19 See A. Izgoev, 'Ob intelligentnoi molodezhi', *Vekhi* (Moscow, 1909).

20 Cited in Martha Bohachevsky-Chomiak, *Sergej N. Trubetskoi. An Intellectual Among the Intelligentsia in Prerevolutionary Russia* (Notable & Academic Books, Belmont, 1976), p.40.

21 Cited in *Ibid.*, p.29. Evgenii, one year Sergei's junior, had initially also registered at the Faculty of History and Philology, but soon after transferred to the Faculty of Law which, as I discuss in Chapters One and Three below, actually provided a more complete instruction in philosophy.

22 See the various *Obozrenie Prepodovaniia* of the Historical-Philological Faculty at Kiev, Moscow and St. Petersburg Universities published between 1880 and 1900.

23 Martha Bohachevsky-Chomiak writes that this book 'proved crucial for the intellectual and spiritual development of many Russian philosophers of Trubetskoi's generation. For Trubetskoi it opened a previously unknown world of German philosophy which went beyond the English and French authors. It made him aware of the limitations of skepticism, of the inadequacies of positivism and materialism...' op. cit., p.24.

24 For more detailed information about the university careers of the authors who figure in the present study, see below, 'Biographical Profiles'.

25 Examples of these mixed genres may be found in the writings by those authors who figure in the current study. For example, Giliarov, an enthusiast for Romantic poetry, of which he claimed Plato to be a main source of inspiration, wrote his doctoral dissertation on Plato as an historical witness of the Sophists. Zelinskii, a well-known classical philologist, is perhaps best known for his public lectures, in which he defended the role of a classical education in modern society. These were published under the general title *Antichnii mir i my* in 1905, and were almost immediately translated into several European languages. The philosopher, Vladimir Solov'ev, presents a slightly different case. Having abandoned the university lectern, he became a master in giving expression to his philosophical ideas in articles which dealt ostensibly with questions of contemporary social, political, and religious realities.

26 A. Neschke, *Platonisme politique et théorie du droit naturel*, vol. 1 (Louvain, 1995), p.2.

27 One other exception whose works are discussed here is the Slavophile, Ivan Kireevskii, active during the first half of the century. His philosophical education was largely the result of his private reading and the Moscow 'salons' he frequented.

28 Translated by Ioann Sidorovskii and M. Pakhomov of the St. Petersburg Theological Academy in four volumes, *Tvoreniia velemudrogo Platona*. All the dialogues were translated with the exception of *Timeaus*, *Sophist*, and *Parmenides*. A few years earlier, in 1777-1778, the writer Nikolai Novikov had published the translation of *Phaedo*, *Alcibiades I*, *Theages* and *Symposium* in his journal, *Utrennii Svet*.

29 See, for example, A.I. Abramov and A.V. Kovalenko, 'Filosofskie vzgliady G.S. Skovorody v krugu ego istoriko-filosofskikh interesov' in *Nekotorye ocobenosti russkoi filososkoi mysli XVIII v* (Moscow, 1987).

30 The University of St. Petersburg was founded in 1819, Kiev in 1834, pre-dated by the 'provincial' universities of Kazan and Kharkov (both founded in 1804), and the

'German' University of Dorpat (1802). Other universities include Novorossiskii at Odessa (1864) and Tomsk (1888).
31 Recent studies on the evolution of Plato interpretation in light of changing cultural practices in countries such as France, Germany, Italy and England have served as useful guidelines for this study of Plato in Russia. The collection *Philologie et herméneutique au XIXe siècle*, edited by Mayotte Bollack and Heinz Wismann (Göttingen, 1983) details the development of the humanities in Germany and France. *La naissance du paradigme herméneutique*, edited by André Laks and Ada Neschke (Lille, 1990) provides valuable information about some of Plato's nineteenth-century German interpreters – Schleiermacher, Droysen, and F.A. Wolf among them – whose theories were discussed by Russian contemporaries and near contemporaries. A recent collection of articles, also edited by Ada Neschke in collaboration with Alexandre Etienne, *Images de Platon et lectures de son oeuvre* (Louvain, 1997), confirms the view that every new epoch created its own Plato. James Hankins studies the Platonic tradition in the Italian Renaissance specifically in light of the practice of learning. Sears Jayne, in his *Plato in Renaissance England* (Kluwer, Dordrecht, 1995), describes a similar phenomenon in Tudor England. Ulriche Zimbrich's, *Bibliographie zu Platos Staat. Die Rezeption der Politeia im deutschsprachigen Raum von 1800-1970* (Frankfurt, 1994), a bibliography of readings of Plato's Republic in the German-speaking world, has served as a basis for analysing and comparing interpretations advanced by Russian nineteenth and twentieth-century commentators of the 'ideal city'.
32 M. Raeff (ed.), *Russian Intellectual History. An Anthology* (Harcourt, Brace and World, Inc, New York, 1966), pp.4-5.
33 Among the recently edited textbooks, intended for teaching purposes and published with the financial backing of the Soros Fund, quite a number treat the theme of antiquity as the cradle of European culture, to which, it is argued, Russia rightfully belongs.

Chapter 1

The Development of Plato Scholarship in Nineteenth-Century Russia

During the course of the nineteenth century, official attitudes towards Russia's educational system passed through several phases. Initially reflecting an ideology of 'Autocracy', 'Orthodoxy' and 'Nationhood' in the 1830s, state rulings later fluctuated between attempts at modernization under Alexander II in the 1860s, and staunch conservative reaction under Alexander III in the 1880s. Largely carried out in primary and parish schools situated in the non-Orthodox borderland regions of the Empire, Alexander III's programme of Russification, with its emphasis on the Russian language and Bible study, undid to a considerable extent the achievements of the early Reform years.

In the university, it tended to be the same few disciplines which, time and again, were targeted by the various measures taken. Deemed ideologically the most sensitive, the study of classics, philosophy and law was repeatedly the object of heated debate. Official state attitudes towards these subjects continually moved back and forth between paranoiac fear and excessive adoration. Depending on the moment, knowledge of the ancient world was said to betray sympathy for modern-day republicanism, or it was regarded as a sign of being 'well educated'. While certain philosophies were condemned as a dangerous challenge to the Orthodox faith, others were considered her most trusted auxiliary. In the wake of the revolutions that swept through Europe in the 1840s, law, and particularly constitutional law, was placed under suspicion as a potential threat to the ideology of nation building, and to the principles of autocracy.

The impact of these circumstances on Plato scholarship as a field of study combining the otherwise suspect perspectives of philosophy, philology, history and law, was, if anything, rather paradoxical. Perhaps, contrary to what one might expect, Plato studies actually profited from the various conflicts of interests between science and ideology. Plato was a chameleon-like foil to a series of scholarly and politico-ideological issues. 'Legitimized' as the precursor of Eastern Christianity, his philosophy met the requirements of an Orthodox (Russian) educational ethic. As the 'father of idealism' he was a privileged object of study for historians of philosophy. As the author of the *Republic* he was a source of information for historians – as well as a source of dispute among political thinkers. Additionally, one has to bear in mind the distinct objectives of education (schooling) on the one hand, and research on the other. A degree of originality in the latter (doctoral dissertations, monographs published under the auspices of the university) was offset by a striking lack of originality in the former. Granted, there were exceptions. One does occasionally come across monographs, intended for use as textbooks, in which the author gave voice to his own, sometimes rather quirky, opinions. But it remains more generally the case that the practice of familiarizing the student of philosophy with Plato's world tended to rely on models of interpretation often created by previous generations in Western scholarship, principally Hegelian inspired. By contrast, Russian Plato research properly speaking, for all its valuable insights into the 'Plato Question', as well as its critique of the more recent findings and trends in Western scholarship, was less likely to find its way into the university auditorium.

From an 'Orthodox Ethics' to the Pragmatism of Reform and Counter Reform

The immediate impact of the government-sanctioned quest for an 'Orthodox educational ethic' (usually associated with the reign of Nicholas I, though signs of this were already apparent in the latter part of Alexander I's rule) was a fairly selective endorsement of areas within the humanities deemed suitable for teaching purposes. In the university, one subject to be seriously affected by the vindication of Russian national and Orthodox values was philosophy. In the wake of the Decembrist uprising of 1825, philosophical reflection – meaning French rationalism and German idealism – was looked upon with increasing suspicion. Indeed, for certain bureaucrats, and, notably, for Nicholas I himself, it was quite simply the birthplace of potential revolutionary or terrorist action. One of two options seemed possible: either philosophy should be done away with altogether, or it should be used to promote a sense of national Orthodox pride. The curator of Kazan University, Mikhail Magnitskii, offers a telling example of an attitude that was widespread among bureaucrats and conservative-minded intellectuals during the final years of Alexander's reign:

> Unlike the mad dreams of Germans with their ideas rooted in the arrogance of the Lutheran Reformation and incorrectly called 'philosophy', we possess a healthy, pure philosophy, that which fortifies the spirit, that in which our forefathers lived happily in their devotion to God, to the Tsar. It is the

philosophy in which the saints of our Church, our marvellous compatriots, were nurtured.[1]

It was the spirit of this kind of remark which determined the fate of philosophy as a discipline over the next few decades. During the 1820s and 1830s, university instruction in philosophy consisted of rudimentary courses in logic, psychology and the history of philosophy. In 1848 it was banned altogether on Nicholas I's orders as part of an alarmed response to the revolutionary activity sweeping throughout Europe. Such measures, it was hoped, would prevent insurrections of a similar kind occurring at home. For the next fifteen years, instruction in 'philosophy', so called, was guaranteed solely in the theological academies. Courses in 'logic' and 'psychology' were taught by professors of theology in accordance with a programme devised by the Department of Religious Affairs, and carried out under its watchful eye.[2] These subjects had been exonerated from the ban because of their supposed utility. Logic, it was thought, taught the pupil 'to construct judgements correctly, and to deduce from them well-grounded arguments'. Psychology was permitted because 'the examination of the characteristics of the soul, of its aptitudes, even its passions, belongs to true enlightenment'. In short, one of the main reasons for teaching philosophy at all was to forewarn the pupil of its nefarious influence, and thereby inoculate him against any damage it might do. Accordingly, 'the purpose of teaching philosophy was to show, by enquiry, the weakness and the inability of human reason to uncover truth by its own means, independently of the supreme light of the Revelation'.[3]

However, it was not the case that all philosophical instruction reflected a religious bias. Despite state rulings on the matter, a more secular reading of philosophical texts – both ancient and modern – was practised in ways which may best be understood as a sign of cunning on the part of the professoriate to resist the heavy hand of bureaucracy in university affairs. It was, for example, not uncommon for philosophical ideas to be expounded by occupants of chairs, the title of which had little to do with philosophy. Such was the case with Schelling, whose philosophy, before it became an object of animated discussion outside the university in the 1830s, was taught by M.G. Pavlov (1793–1840) at Moscow University from the chair of agronomy and physics, while D.M. Vellanskii of the St. Petersburg Academy of Medicine reputedly expounded on Schellingian philosophy of nature from his chair of botany.[4] Another instance concerns the way the juridical sciences sometimes served as a channel for instruction in the history of philosophy. In 1835 a statute was issued with the aim to rid juridical science of any potentially nefarious political elements. In this spirit the course in 'encyclopaedia of law' (*pravo*) – originally a survey of juridical science, together with an introduction to natural law theory – was renamed the 'encyclopaedia of canons' (*zakonovedenie*). Henceforth, instruction was to be based exclusively on the legal canons as established by the *Svod Zakonov*, a codification of laws newly drafted in 1832, but which, according to the jurist and historian, Konstantin Kavelin, was flawed by the same casuistry as the early Romanov *Ulozhenie* of 1649. Neither codification accounted for the juridical principles according to which the mass of legislation had been collected and arranged. Yet, for all such constraints and obstacles, certain professors did manage to provide their students with a relatively sound juridical education. Between 1835 and 1848 Petr Redkin (1808–1891), Professor of Law at Moscow University, taught an essentially historical-philosophical course in what was supposed to be an introduction to the codified laws of the land.[5] According to memoir accounts, Redkin succeeded in combining this tedious learning by rote with an Hegelian-inspired history of philosophy and a history of the philosophy of law. By doing so, he conveyed some of his personal beliefs and enthusiasms, which were sharply at odds with the police environment of the university at that time. As his former pupil and future renowned philosopher of law, Boris Chicherin, put it:

> Thanks to Redkin's teaching we learnt to see in the State something more than merely an external form, a watchful guardian. We came to consider it as the supreme aim of juridical development, the realization of the principles of liberty and of justice in their highest union, one which, without absorbing the person, and while affording her sufficient space, guides her towards the common good.[6]

Like the study of law and philosophy, secondary-level schooling and university instruction in Latin and Greek were also a major source of controversy, especially during the reign of Nicholas I, but equally throughout the Reform and Counter Reform periods, being by turns promoted and discouraged. Conflicting attitudes towards a classical education were closely bound with conflicting perceptions of Hellenism itself, which by turn inspired great hostility and sympathy. On the one hand, the works of Greek and Roman authors were condemned as the bedrock of Republican ideas; on the other, they were seen as markers along the path towards the Orthodox faith. Russia's spiritual and cultural links with the Byzantine world not only patented her classical heritage, but, more importantly, made it possible to promote a self-portrait as the protector of true Christianity. The upshot was patriotism anchored in philohellenism.

This was the case in the 1830s and early 1840s during the Ministry of Count Uvarov (1786–1855), himself a classical scholar. At issue was the need to accommodate a general (classical) education to the requirements of national specificity (*narodnyi byt'*). To this end, Uvarov promoted the study of classical languages and ancient history, but also catechism. However, the political events of 1848 upset this vindication of classical scholarship as a source of national identity. Witnessing the social unrest across Europe, Russian conservatives noted that Latin and Greek were the languages of the Republicans, that French eighteenth-century Revolutionaries had cited Cicero and Plato. For Nicholas I, this kind of argument was sufficient to justify measures taken against what he regarded as a potential threat to his autocracy. Thus, in 1849, he ordered that instruction in Latin and Greek be reduced considerably, and between 1851 and 1854, Greek was suppressed outright. Although it was ultimately reintroduced in a handful of gymnasia scattered across the Empire, its status had radically altered to become little more than an instrument for the sake of instructing the pupil in the wisdom of the Church Fathers. Indeed, knowledge of the classics generally came to a large extent to be based on the study of Clement of Rome, St. Augustine, Tertullian, St. Irenaeus, Basil the Great, and John Chrysostom. It should be said, though, that this situation was not unique to Russia, but echoed conservative reactions throughout Europe as a whole. In France, for example, the government of Napoleon III used similar arguments so as to promote educational reforms along more conservative lines. Moreover, the literature privileged for instruction in Latin and Greek was, as in Russia, usually religious, with the Bible and the Church Fathers figuring most frequently on the reading lists.[7]

While the more liberal spirit of the new 1863 statute was to become a marker in the professoriate's subsequent attempts to secure academic freedom, juridically it was short lived. In view of the continuing student unrest which this statute had seemingly failed to curb, the Ministry of Education gradually introduced measures, during the 1870s and early 1880s, with view to excluding Seminarists, Realists, and Jews from university studies – precisely those elements which the government held responsible for social disorder. These measures, along with increased student fees and compulsory lecture attendance for those who remained, culminated in the Counter Reform of 1884. With the principle of autonomy abrogated, the university became, once again, a bureaucratically run government institution.

A direct – and at first glance surprising – consequence of the Counter Reform on university instruction in the humanities was the subordination of philosophy, along with literature and history, to the study of classical philology.[8] This move formed part of an announced programme to increase the number of teachers of Latin and Greek in Russia's gymnasia. But, underlying this policy was an ideologized, and possibly rather naive, conception of classical scholarship itself. Because of the intellectual demands it put on the pupil, and because its content was so far removed from contemporary reality, the authors of these more conservative measures, the Education Minister, D.A. Tolstoi (1866–1880) and his successor, I.D. Delianov (1882–1898), believed it might provide the much needed panacea to social unrest. In short, they saw it as an effective measure to thwart the ambitions of young 'nihilists' whose wholesale renunciation of tradition meant, among other things, rejection of a classical and humanistic education. To this end, a law passed in May 1871 dictated an increase in the number of hours to be given to Latin and Greek in the gymnasium. With the combined study of ancient Latin and Greek grammar coming to more than 40 per cent of weekly schooling hours, the number of hours for instruction in Russian language and literature was sharply reduced, while subjects, such as natural science, history, geography and modern languages virtually disappeared from the timetable, to become, instead, core subjects in the *Real Gymnasium* and the more technically oriented *Realschule*.[9] The point, though, as Bernard Pares noted, was 'as the gymnasia alone qualified for entry into the university, and as poorer scholars lacking the necessary preparation in classics could not enter the gymnasia, the universities would tend to become preserves of the well-to-do classes'.[10] Underlying this government strategy was arguably the rather naive assumption that students from well-to-do backgrounds would not associate themselves with nihilists. Moreover, this elitist view of classical scholarship, which dominated towards the end of the nineteenth century, actually incurred the loss of future students. Between 1880 and the close of the century the number of registered students at the Faculty of History and Philology dropped by two thirds.[11] Moreover, it was a decrease in numbers which, to a large extent, was due to a drop-out rate already at the secondary school level.[12] According to certain Russian commentators, some of whom were classicists themselves, this desertion was only to be expected. While they believed that classical philology (history, literature and language) was important for one's general culture, the drop in the number of students since 1885 was clearly a sign that teaching methods did not correspond to needs. In short, imposing a laborious rote learning of Greek and Latin grammars, with little opening on to the culture of the ancient world itself, was simply too much for the pupil. Such methods dulled rather than enlightened the spirits.[13]

Compromise and Conflict: The Scientific Community and the State

While this bureaucratic perception of classical studies turned out to be ill judged, in the sense that it failed to produce the desired effect of quelling student hostilities, and actually led to a decline in the number of inscriptions to the faculty, as a specialized area of research the growth in classical scholarship was, on the contrary, quite remarkable. From the last two decades of the nineteenth century onwards, the quantity of specialized literature in the field of classical languages, history, and the history of ancient philosophy increased quite considerably. Nor was it just a matter of accumulating foreign materials (grammars, histories of ancient philosophy, etc.) to be used in the classroom. Reviews and book notices published in specialized journals – *Gymnasium* (1888–1899), *Philological Survey* (1891–1902), *Hermes* (1907-1918), and the section on classical philology in the official State journal *The Journal of the Ministry of Education*

(1834–1917) – all suggest, rather, a critical awareness of the degree to which classical scholarship abroad was profiled by conflicting historical-philosophical affinities, and that Russian scholars also had their part to play in these discussions.[14] But, even this more hopeful state of affairs requires qualification. Despite what appears to have been the initiative taken by certain university professors to advance classical scholarship in Russia, the resulting changes should, nevertheless, also be understood as a direct consequence of the ideological-cum-utilitarian attitude of the state towards science, which by turns encouraged, then blocked, attempts at autonomous university organization. Part of the problem was that while the professoriate sought to reduce state interference in its activities, it still required state power to achieve its professional programmes. For its part, the state was prepared – albeit reluctantly – to concede the degree of autonomy necessary for the specific services it required of the professoriate, namely to train students in specialized medical, pedagogical, technical, and legal skills.

It was the need to provide gymnasia with qualified teachers in history, literature and classical languages that prompted the government to found, in 1867, the St. Petersburg Historical-Philological Institute. A few years later, in 1873, an agreement was signed with the University of Leipzig to create a classical philological seminar for visiting Russian students, again with an eye to training future teachers and professors. Initially directed by the well-known German scholar, Friedrich Wilhelm Ritschl, until his death in 1876, the seminar was taken over and run by his successor Justus H. Lipsius, a specialist in Greek prose and Attic law. Until its closure, in 1878, the seminar received an average of twenty to thirty Russian students a year. Among the most famous Russian students of this seminar were Faddei Frantsevich Zelinskii (1859–1944) and Ernest Romanovich Shtern (1859–1924), both of whom later gained an international reputation for their work in the field. In his research, Zelinskii worked extensively on Cicero, but he was also the author of numerous conferences and articles on cultural aspects of Antiquity more generally. As for Shtern, after his studies at both Dorpat and Leipzig, he was named Professor of Classical Philology at the University of Odessa. In 1911, however, he took the chair of ancient history in Halle, and so, like many talented scholars, left Russia altogether.

Whereas the comparatively high number of students in philology (compared with approximately five Russian students a year registered in philosophy) was to drop dramatically in the 1890s, the overall numbers of students coming to study in Leipzig continued to increase steadily. Russian students from all over the Empire, though in particular from the Baltics, went there to study law, philosophy and, in particular, medicine. Indeed, in the decade between the first revolution and the outbreak of war, almost a quarter of the students registered in the Faculty of Medicine was of Russian origin.[15] For sure, sending gifted students abroad (usually to German universities) was already a practice current in the mid-1830s (a period which produced fine scholars such as the historian Granovskii or Redkin), but the fruits of this practice were especially visible in the closing decades of the nineteenth century.

The existence of the Leipzig programme serves as one revelatory episode in the complex, often thwarted, progression of Russian science. Thanks to the direct personal contacts and exchange of ideas that it provided, the institute encouraged the emergence of a Russian 'academic intelligentsia' devoted to the advancement of learning.[16] However, once back home, the principles that these Russian scholars had come to stand for (notably a defence of university autonomy and the practice of collegiality as necessary preconditions for improving academic standards) proved, more often than not, to be at odds with the reigning politics and ideology of the tsarist regime.

It is, admittedly, no easy task to determine just how attuned Russian scholarship really was to contemporary developments abroad, and the degree to which it safeguarded an independent spirit of learning. Was its profile merely the outcome of governmental decrees, even in the sense of exploiting loopholes in the system? To answer this question many factors have to be brought into account. Apart from anything else, much, of course, depended on the charisma or scientific excellence of the individual scholars themselves.[17] All we can say for sure is that, irrespective of the nature of state intervention in matters of classical studies and the reactions it provoked among scholars, the Reform and Counter Reform periods created conditions for more and more specialization in the field. Thereafter, despite further periodical revisions of the 1884 statute right up to the First World War, the trend towards greater professionalization continued, with scholarly publications and lecture courses suggesting a continuing drive to improve academic standards very much in the spirit of the 1863 reform. This pertains not just to classical philology, but also to its annexed subjects – the history of ancient philosophy, and history. More generally speaking, study in the humanities was, as I shall discuss in more detail below, carried out in light of ongoing research – both abroad and at home, too. Together, they encouraged an attitude of professionalism in Russian scholarship. A brief account of some of the main developments in the history of philosophy and history – in Europe and in Russia – will serve to illustrate this mood, as it will also provide a useful background to a closer analysis of Russian Plato studies, helping us eventually to assess the place of Western models in Russian interpretations of Platonic philosophy.

Developments in the Historical and Philosophical Sciences

History of Philosophy

Perceptions in Russia of Plato's philosophy were to a considerable extent shaped and modified by developments in historical knowledge about philosophy more generally. As a branch of the philosophical sciences, the history of philosophy gradually gained in importance throughout Europe, particularly in Germany where, by the end of the century, it covered virtually a quarter of the lectures offered in the faculty.[18] Often written by teachers of philosophy, such publications were in the first place intended to meet pedagogical and institutional needs. But they also provided an occasion for vehiculing a combined historical and philosophical conception about the development of philosophical thought, past and present. In Germany, one obvious early authority in this domain was Hegelianism. The theory of the dialectical movement of history found an echo in the writings of a number of German historians of (ancient) philosophy. The works of Eduard Zeller (*Die Philosophie der Griechen*, 1844–1852), Friedrich Uberweg (*Grundriss der Geschichte der Philosophie von Thales bis auf die Gegenwart*, 1862–1864), and Wilhelm Windelband (*Geschichte der alten Philosophie* 1888), who reintegrated aspects of German idealism into his own brand of Kantianism, all owed something to Hegel's philosophy even as impartiality was as equally important in their work as historians and teachers of philosophy. This 'latent positivism' of a historically oriented enquiry into past philosophy also meant that studies in the domain increasingly came to draw on findings from within the historical discipline itself. One such example was Theodor Gomperz's highly popular book, *Griechische Denker*, published in 1895, a study which brought together the different perspectives of history, philology and philosophy. Granted, as his immediate critics noted, one obvious source of philosophical inspiration in Gomperz's book was the positivism of Auguste Comte and Herbert Spencer, two authors whom he quoted abundantly: Gomperz's historical account was triggered by the idea that the Greeks were the initiators of progress in humanity, on the strength of which he discussed the evolution of philosophy in terms of its relation to science. But, that said, Gomperz's personal philosophical affinities did not unduly clash with his aim to provide a book which would be useful for students.

Irrespective of the philosophical affinities of a given author, and/or his endeavours to be as neutral as possible, one major feature of the historical-philosophical narrative, such as it developed from the middle of the nineteenth century onwards, was the importance that many writers attached to the cultural conditions in which a given philosophy emerged. Even Zeller, who maintained a Hegelian viewpoint with regard to the history of philosophy,[19] conceded that the character of a given philosophy, as something which is culturally conditioned, becomes the object of historical interest. Gomperz went further in claiming that the philosophy of a people was not entirely contained within the philosophical systems of its philosophers; these systems are less than intelligible if separated from the intellectual and moral grounds in which they emerged. Windelband, in his *Geschichte der alten Philosophie* (1888) and, later, in his monograph on Plato (1899), organized his materials in a way which suggest an affinity, not unlike Zeller, with the Hegelian theory of the dialectical movement of history. But, at the same time, he signalled, against Hegel, the dependence of philosophical doctrines on the individuality of the philosopher, as well as the close interrelation between the history of philosophy and the mass of economic, political and social factors which together made up the world outlook of the ancient Greeks. For Windelband the neo-Kantian, an important aspect of historical research was its ethical dimension. To his mind, the historian's knowledge of historical events betokened a value judgement: the historian pronounces on the spiritual value of the events which compose the object of his research. Such an understanding of the historical-philosophical process is clearly present in his introduction to his book on Plato, a point that was quickly picked up by his Russian audience.[20] Here, as Windelband put it, his aim was to turn to the past:

> in order to comprehend and pay tribute to those motives and thoughts which appeal to, and ground, the social role of science in history. (...) In light of this historical development, however, nothing is so striking, instructive, nor meaningful as that which is linked with the name of Plato. In it is embodied mankind's cultural ideal to structure its life through science in a way which is exemplary for all times. Herein lies the ultimate core of his personality, and the greatest measure of his life and work, the deepest significance of his doctrine, the power of his influence across time, and his lasting importance for us today.[21]

This trend towards a broadly speaking, historical-cultural approach enjoyed an echo in Russia.[22] Indeed, given the frequency with which reference was made to the works of Zeller, Gomperz, Windelband and others, particularly as recommended secondary reading for university students, they may be said to have provided selected models, even to have served as authorities, in Russian higher education programmes. The history of their translation alone – the Russian versions and translations of Zeller and Windelband were re-edited on several occasions – bespeaks the evident need in Russia to provide students with materials, especially in the early Reform period. Extracts of Zeller's book first appeared in Russian translation in 1861, while a complete version was published some twenty-five years later under the editorial charge of Mikhail Karinskii, professor at the St. Petersburg Theological Academy.[23] Windelband's *History of Ancient Philosophy* was translated by a group of students under the supervision of Professor Vvedenskii, being edited twice in the 1890s, and once again after the turn of the century. Interestingly, the first edition also included a text by the French spiritualist philosopher, Alfred Fouillée. In doing so, Vvedenskii wanted to provide, as he put it, 'as complete a corpus of texts as possible for teaching purposes'.[24] In a book notice concerning this translation, the point was made that the decision to translate this particular work had been largely motivated by the fact that Zeller's book was too dense to be useful for teaching purposes. Moreover, the appeal of Windelband was the way he showed 'the interdependence of the history of philosophy with the general movement of the history of the ancient world'.[25]

Certainly, in the university auditorium, these authors figured among those whose works were the most frequently cited. Nor was there any significant change in this pattern right up to the First World War and Revolution. However, in terms of original research, the situation was quite different. For sure, Zeller and Windelband continued to serve as important markers for Russian historians of philosophy, but their role as models was not stable. On the contrary, their 'authority' was frequently challenged. Writing in the 1860s and early 1870s, O.M. Novitskii, author of *The Gradual Development of Ancient Philosophical Doctrines*, and S.S. Gogotskii in his *Introduction to the History of Philosophy* explicitly constructed their histories along Hegelian lines. Both authors broke down the past into two main periods, each containing three neat subdivisions established in light of what was argued to be the relation of philosophy and religion, of being and thought, and the alternating predominance of analytic or synthetic approaches to philosophical problems.[26] Accordingly, the characteristic traits of Greek thought of the Attic period were listed as reason (*razsudok*), the emergence of dialectics, and a predominantly analytic approach to the question of thought and being.[27] In the decades which followed, however, there was a noticeable shift away from this rather dry schema as successive generations of Russian historians of philosophy became increasingly reticent with respect to Hegel's philosophical account of history. S.N. Trubetskoi, for one, argued that, in treating the development of philosophy as a purely logical movement, Hegel had failed to take into account the individuality of the philosophers themselves. Nor had he reckoned sufficiently with the religious beliefs and other cultural historical influences which, together, form the body of man's intellectual production. In other words, according to Trubetskoi, Hegel had simply ignored the fact that the development of philosophy is a real historical process. Such an oversight, he said, 'could not fail to produce erroneous interpretations, and an arbitrary construction of the historical process'.[28]

Zeller, the Hegelian, was consistently a main target of Russian criticism. In the 1860s, this 'cabinet philosopher', together with his self-appointed intellectual valet, a certain Klevanov – the first to have translated long excerpts from Zeller's book for a Russian audience in 1861 – were the victims of some rather cruel, but vivacious irony, by the 'nihilist', Dmitri Pisarev, a former student of the University of St. Petersburg.[29] Zeller's book, and Klevanov's slavish reworking of it, were, Pisarev objected, of no utility for modern-day social problems. Zeller, Klevanov – Plato too – all took the brunt of Pisarev's rejection of traditional values. He went so far as to blame Plato and his cohorts, the Idealists, for the ideologization of 'abstract perfection', which he detected everywhere in contemporary high society – the *beau monde* as he contemptuously called it.

In a somewhat more matter-of-fact tone, Karinskii, who supervised the 1886 edition of Zeller's book, stated his disagreement with the weight the author had accorded certain moments in the development of Greek thought, without, though, substantiating any of his objections. Giliarov, on the contrary, went to some lengths in explaining his differences with the German 'authority'. Giliarov contended that, for all its merits, Zeller's 'objectivism' provided little real insight into the philosophical ideas of a given philosopher of the past, and to drive his point home he recalled the axiom that whereas 'the spirit vivifies, the letter kills'.[30] A case in point was Zeller's treatment of Plato. Quite simply, he had failed to capture Plato's poetic genius, precisely because of his concern to stick to the historical facts. The professor of philosophy at Kiev University, Aleksei Kozlov (1831–1901), criticized, for his part, Zeller's immanentist interpretation of Plato's theory of ideas. For Kozlov, such a reading was tantamount to claiming that ideas and things/phenomena (*veshch'*) are not two different areas of being, but one and the same: it meant that ideas constitute their essence (*sushchnost'*) in things. For Kozlov, this kind of conclusion simply ran counter to Plato's statements to the effect that ideas are neither concepts nor knowledge, but reside somehow elsewhere. They are, Kozlov claimed in fidelity to Plato, '*o sebe*' – 'of themselves' – and, as such, they must be understood as transcendent.[31] Yet another Russian commentator noted that Zeller's account of Plato's thought was refracted through the prism of his own views about philosophy as metaphysics, the upshot of which was a faulty, if not anachronistic, projection of a nineteenth-century worldview on to the Greek mind. Plato's thought was mistakenly treated as, first and foremost, a theory of ideas, only then to be broken down into the various branches of ontology, dialectics, physics and ethics. For A. Guliaev, the author of this particular criticism, Zeller had failed to see that Plato's main preoccupation was less a theory of ideas, as an ever-deepening study of the nature of man.[32]

Faddei Zelinskii criticized the relatively minor importance that German scholars in general attributed to the place of religion in the ancient Greek understanding of the world. While Zeller had spoken of a 'healthy lack of religious dogmatism' in the Greeks, Gomperz saw in religion no more than the formal expression of Greek thought, rather than the source of Greek philosophy itself. Zelinskii objected to this: in his opinion, such claims merely obscured what, for the Greeks, were clearly the distinct domains of religious representation and myth. Personification of nature, or fetishism were not, as Gomperz had argued, sources of religion in general, but only of religious representation. As Zelinskii saw it, myths were related to 'philosophical' questions about the cause and aim of the universe. This in turn meant that, in its mythological dimension, Greek religion was in fact already philosophy, or, at least, that out of which philosophy was to grow organically. In light of his argument Zelinskii recommended that the chapters of Gomperz' book be organized differently, and that the problem of the relation between religion and philosophy, as a crucial component in the development of Greek thought more generally, be given more place in the German scholar's account than it currently occupied.[33]

Paradoxically, it was openly voiced hostilities, which occasionally provided the strongest grounds to go ahead with the translation, or re-edition, of a given work of Western scholarship. A case in point concerned the second revised translation, in 1892, of a 'history of philosophy' by the positivist and amateur philosopher, George Henry Lewes. The translator, a certain Chuiko, claimed that, through his translation, he hoped to provide an example to Russian readers of what philosophy should not be.[34] It is hard to say whether Chuiko's words were intended in all earnestness, or whether it was a ploy to re-edit a highly popular book, which, otherwise, would never have passed muster with official censors, nor, indeed, with idealist philosophers. What is certain is that Lewes' popularity among Russian youth in the 1860s, when it was first translated (in 1866), had incurred sharp reaction from certain members of the established professorial corps keen to (or expected to) uphold idealist and spiritualist orientations in philosophy. The translation, in 1882, of Alfred Weber's *Histoire de la philosophie européenne* (first published in 1871) is one such example of endeavours to check the fad for positivism. The translation of Weber's book grew out of a seminar at Kiev University, and was undertaken by two of Professor's Kozlov's students.[35] In his foreword to the translation, Kozlov spoke of the book's utility as a teaching aid for courses in the history of philosophy, and of its complementarity to the 'histories' of Baur and Schwegler.[36] It was also, he added, a healthy antidote to Lewes. Kozlov, who saw in Lewes a dangerous influence on young Russian intellectuals, appealed to Weber, proponent of 'concrete spiritualism', as a healthy panacea to the nefarious pathos embedded in Lewes's writing.[37] But what most attracted Kozlov was the fact that, unlike Lewes, whose aim as a positivist was to do away with philosophy for the sake of science, Weber had argued for the unity of, and the link between, philosophical systems in their historical development. He had demonstrated to his readers that 'these various systems may be co-ordinated into a whole (...), and that, as we advance in our clarification of philosophical questions, we may hope all the more for a synthesis of systems'.[38] In his declared affinity with the French historian of philosophy, Kozlov also accommodated his portrait of the Platonic world outlook to their joint spiritualist and pluralistic conceptions. Roughly in the same period, Kozlov had himself been working on Plato as part of his lecture courses, and had published a monograph (for his Master's degree) on the subject.[39] For Kozlov, Weber's 'concrete spiritualism' designated a supreme reality which stands above the plurality of things: it is a reality comprised of the good, justice, duty, the ideal. He summarized this view as a 'spiritual reality', which 'together with entities (*sushchestva*), individuals, atoms serving as its organs, forms a living unity. It is divided, broken down, only by **abstraction**'.[40] Clearly appealing to a like-mindedness with Weber, Kozlov similarly depicted the world as an infinite plurality of spiritual substances interacting with one another. What he meant in calling his own philosophy 'panpsychism' was that the principle of pluralism (the infinite plurality of separate spiritual entities) does not nullify the unity of the world, since all substances are linked to the central substance, or God. Accordingly, his underlying philosophical position shaped his summary of the Platonic worldview:

> [T]he essence of the world is made up of transcendentally existing ideas; their reflection (*otobrazhenie*) is in things. Ideas compose a system which, as a whole, constitutes the Good, its chief attributes – beauty, truth and harmony – being reflected in the world. Thus the world is a cosmos, a beautiful and harmonious world.[41]

All in all, criticism of the kinds mentioned above suggests priorities in Russian scholarship – an appeal to religious and historical-cultural factors, together with an anti-positivism – which, occasionally, were at odds with its Western counterparts. For sure, some Russian scholars had long been aware of the dangers of crudely assimilating the Western intellectual tradition to cultural circumstances, which, by their very nature, did not lend themselves to brute copying. In the early Reform period Novitskii had already made this point in a reply to Chernychevskii's unmitigated criticism of his book on the history of Greek religions. Whereas in Germany, Novitskii wrote, materialism did, indeed, have an historical significance as an extreme opponent to Hegel's idealism, 'what meaning can it possibly have for us when all it signifies is just one of many provisory solutions to a philosophical question (the relation of thought and being), the process in which we have never taken part, and which constitutes the historical task of another nation, not our own?'[42] While, by the end of the century, this sense of cultural difference – for scholars at least – had become less acute, it was still implicitly, and sometimes explicitly, the cause for criticism of Western scholarship. Recall Zelinskii's and Giliarov's reticence with respect to Zeller, a reticence which is tinged with irony if one bears in mind that Zeller's book continued to be one of the most frequently cited works recommended as background reading for students studying philosophy and classical philology. Nor was it unusual for a student examination to be based on selected Western secondary literature – a case in point being Windelband's monograph on Plato.[43] Despite the increase in national literature in the field of the history of (ancient) philosophy, recourse to foreign models of interpretation remained a lasting practice among the Russian professoriate.

Trends in Historiography

The last third of the nineteenth century saw a growth in literature drawing on political, social, and economic data about the ancient world in order to reconstruct not only patterns of philosophizing, but, perhaps more ambitiously, to grasp the 'Greek mentality' or 'world outlook'. In Western Europe, both historians of philosophy and historians – Grote and Burnet in England, Fustel de Coulanges in France, Gomperz and Windelband, as we saw, in Germany – had begun addressing social, economic and ethical questions in ancient Greece to this effect. Thus, what had formerly been a predominantly historical-criticist approach, relying heavily on textual sources, gradually gave way to perspectives engaging socio-economic data, together with material relating to customs, institutions and the like.[44] Russian scholars, for their part, responded to this shift, not only by translating and commenting the findings of their Western counterparts,[45] but also by producing original research of their own. Ultimately, such developments saw the gradual emergence of other, more specialized branches within the 'science of Antiquity'. In Russia, strong fields of research came to include archaeology, numismatics and epigraphy, and, by the end of the century, work in these highly specialized areas had produced some interesting findings relating to the presence of Greek communities in southern Russia.[46]

The trend towards more empirical methods in historical research both altered and enriched the specialist's perception of the ancient world as an object of study. Moreover, underlying much of this new kind of historical research was an attitude which consisted in using knowledge about the past as a means to gain a deeper understanding of contemporary society. German historical literature of the period provides some quite notable examples of this approach. Known to an educated Russian audience, works by Robert Pöhlmann (his famous *Geschichte des antiken Kommunismus und Sozialismus* [1893–1901]), Eduard Meyer, and, later, Wilamowitz-Möllendorff were frequently cited for their attempts to explore and highlight the direct links between the modern and ancient worlds. Granted, Russian readers were often critical of a tendency they detected among these authors to modernize the past for the sake of the analogies they were seeking to defend. But few were unwilling to acknowledge the provocation that these anachronistic interpretations signified. Besides presenting a fresh – if inaccurate – approach to the past, they were especially important as a challenge, inciting their readers to confront present-day realities in a new way. Pöhlmann's account of Plato, in which he endeavoured to balance the interests of the individual with those of the state, or Karl Kautsky's *Die Vorläufer des neueren Sozialismus* (1895) were frequently commented on by Russian contemporaries in light of this double reference. And after the October Revolution – for a few years at least – specialists continued to read such works for the insights they unwittingly provided into the nature of the new Soviet society in the making.[47]

In Russia, a number of historians and philologists produced more 'popular' studies of their own about the classical world, likewise basing their approach on supposed parallels between the past and present. One announced aim here was to render the contemporary world more intelligible through the prism of Antiquity.[48] But a closer reading of some of these articles and public lectures suggests that there was another important issue at stake, namely to advance the cause of a classical, 'humanistic' education, the proper appreciation of which had, in the eyes of some Russian scholars, been abused by government strategies to use education as a means to stratify the various classes ('estates') within Russian society as rigidly as possible. In his series of public lectures, which appeared under the general title *The Ancient World and We* in 1905, Zelinskii vindicated a classical education by reminding his audience of the cultural correspondences between the ancient and contemporary worlds. To his mind, Antiquity had a threefold significance. First, it formed the object of a science 'which, if not always correctly, is most often called classical philology'. Second, it was an integral part of the intellectual and moral culture of modern-day European society. Third – and herein lay the point that Zelinskii was making – it figured as one of the subjects covered in the gymnasium curriculum. For Zelinskii, the wealth of Antiquity was manifest from any one of these angles. Regrettably, though, 'each one of these obliges the connoisseur to advocate a point of view, which is diametrically opposed to that most commonly held in today's, and particularly Russian, society'.[49]

For scholars like Zelinskii, the values they believed had been espoused by the ancients, and which they were seeking to reinvest with significance for the modern world, were embodied in the single figure of Plato. Plato appeared as the humanist, a moral force, but it was his role as an educator which seems to have most fascinated his modern-day proponents. In an outburst of enthusiasm for Alexander II's educational reforms, Vladimir Karpov predicted a chance for what he called a 'Russian humanism'. He imagined – or hoped – this would be the fruit of a 'classical' education, the kind, he said, designed to 'refine and elevate the mind'. And, he noted, it was Plato and the original Humanists who had first seen in an educated elite the best chances for political and moral reform. 'As in the past', Karpov wrote, 'when Platonic philosophy inspired the Renaissance in Western Europe, so today, the regain of interest in Plato which we are witnessing might be the beginning of a Russian humanism.'[50] This sentiment was reiterated in various contexts and guises. Drawing a portrait of Plato as a 'philosopher of the heart', it was as much Aleksei Giliarov's purpose, like Zelinskii and Karpov, to stress the importance of a 'moral education'. In this vein he called for the return of humanism in order to combat the recent wave of materialism which, in his eyes, had threatened to reduce notions such as 'beauty', or 'love', to physiological laws, the sorry consequences of which were, as he put it, 'the loss of aesthetic dreams and moral convictions'.[51] But whether for all the Russians who studied him Plato really was the ultimate symbol of a 'humanist culture', remains, for the moment, an open question.

Russian Plato Scholarship

Judging by the quantity of literature dedicated to Plato in Russia it would seem, as I suggested at the outset, that philosophical and philological studies in this field actually profited from the curious conflict of ideological and scientific interests described above. This is understandable: given that it was said to have inspired the teachings of the Greek Fathers on which Eastern Christianity was nurtured, it was a mere step forward (or backwards, rather) to vindicate Platonic philosophy as the primordial source of Russian Orthodox spirituality. It was, arguably, in this spirit, that the charter of the Moscow Theological Academy, issued in 1814, had singled out Plato as the 'pillar of authentic philosophy.' His thought was believed to comply with the charter's recommendations that instruction in philosophy be guided by humility before the truth of Christian doctrine. This situation altered very little throughout the first half of the nineteenth century. Both in the university, but particularly in the theological academies, a Christianized Plato continued to be the privileged object of philosophical education and a subject of commentary in the various theological journals.[52]

The image of Plato as the generator of the Eastern spiritual tradition partly relied on an opposition with the rationalizing tendencies of Western philosophy, which was said to have grown out of the Aristotelian tradition. As I shall discuss in the next chapter, this theme was quite widespread among Russian intellectuals – Karpov and the Slavophiles among them – who were openly critical of the current state of philosophical affairs in Germany. This attitude was especially marked in the first half of the century. On the contrary, by the end of the century, insisting on the spiritual opposition between Plato and Aristotle and their legacies had given way to a relation of greater complementarity. This shift in perception no doubt reflected the more secular views of certain scholars in tune with Western developments, but it can also be pinpointed to the government's newly revised policy on education. In the conservative atmosphere of the 1870s and 1880s, the Ministry of Education once again sought to restrict philosophical instruction (indeed, even banning authors of materialist or positivistic orientations), and by 1884, the year in which a new university statute appeared, materials used for courses in the subject clearly reflected the classical revival commended by Tolstoi and his successor, Delianov:

> Philosophical disciplines may be taught [i.e. as optional subjects] in the various universities. They encourage the student's curiosity. However, obligatory for all students is a basic knowledge of Plato and Aristotle, because their works contain the principles, still relevant today, of all subsequent philosophical development. Indeed, philosophical terminology may to a great extent be understood only on the strength of a basic familiarity with the works of these thinkers.[53]

The decision to teach philosophy as a branch for a degree in philology meant that in the three main universities of St. Petersburg, Kiev and Moscow, Plato, together with Aristotle, became 'patented' objects of study. Selected Platonic dialogues (particularly *Gorgias*, *Meno*, sometimes extracts from the *Republic*) were taught in alternation with works by Aristotle (*Metaphysics* and *Ethics* notably). Individual dialogues were studied from a philological point of view, while the main lines of Plato (and Aristotle's) thought formed the content of general courses on the history of ancient philosophy. A significant number of such courses were published.[54] Once coupled with Aristotle within the framework of a combined philosophical and philological instruction, the study and resulting perceptions of Plato gradually became more complex and diversified. The ideological opposition between Plato and Aristotle as generators of two radically different ways of thinking now came to represent just one of several possible dimensions of Plato studies. But while, as I shall endeavour to show in the following chapters, the impact of these government measures, whether intentionally or unwittingly, was certainly to create conditions for a wider range of assessments of Platonic philosophy, this is not to say that these new findings totally supplanted the image of Plato as a precursor of Christian morals. As late as the 1880s and 1890s, the preference for certain individual dialogues, especially for use in the gymnasium, moreover the frequency with which the translations of these dialogues were revised and commented, attests to an enduring predilection for a Christianized reading of Plato. *Crito, Apology, Phaedo*, which counted among the favourites for teaching purposes in secondary schools, is a striking choice given that it was precisely these dialogues which had been privileged in the early Christian and Renaissance revivals of Platonic philosophy.[55] For the Church Fathers and nineteenth-century Russian schoolteachers alike, the biographical information in *Crito* and *Apology* concerning the trial and death of Socrates invited obvious comparisons with the trial and death of Christ. *Phaedo* had, since Cicero, been known as the dialogue containing Socrates' autobiographical account of how he turned away from natural philosophy to ethics, while, much in the same vein, the theme of the immortality of the soul expounded in *Gorgias* (a dialogue which, if translated with less frequency, was often commented on in university seminars) was in tune with Christian doctrine.

As we can see, Plato studies were promoted with the blessing of the state, both on ideological and utilitarian grounds. Ideologically, a Christianized Plato corresponded well to Orthodox spirituality. More pragmatically, the State, as I have said, counted on the services of a classically trained elite, namely to fill schools with more competent teachers. Analysing the content, structure, and language of Plato's dialogues therefore fitted neatly with the official endorsement of classical studies as a means to improve educational standards – and, hopefully – to prevent student riots.

The 'Plato Question'

To suggest that Russian readings of Plato followed a linear progression, moving from a predominantly patristic perspective in the first half of the century through to more secular readings of his thought, combining the horizons of philology, philosophy, and history in the post-Reform decades, would be to oversimplify matters. It was rather the case that by the end of the century any numbers of options, including a reading of Plato through the prism of Christian morality, were available.

The coexistence of quite different paradigms of interpretations may be traced through a brief reconstruction of the ways in which Russian scholars addressed the Plato Question. The problem of authenticating dialogues and establishing their true chronology was a central topic discussed in each of the three main editions of 'Complete Works' published in the nineteenth century, beginning with Karpov in the 1840s through to the Solov'ev-Trubetskoi edition at the turn of the twentieth century.[56] The criteria they brought to bear in their endeavours to answer the question are, on the one hand, instructive of the intellectual climate in which they worked, but, on the other, warn the historian against the temptation of drawing too homogenized a portrait of these intellectuals as a scientific community. For example, the translation by the professor of philosophy at the Kiev and St. Petersburg Theological Academies, Vasily Karpov (1798–1867) yields a portrait of Plato as a precursor of Christian doctrine. In retrospective studies, this view of his thought as one which was readily assimilable to the 'living philosophy' of the Slavophiles is often considered as highly representative – perhaps the most representative – of the general character of Plato scholarship in Russia. But there was, already in the period when Karpov was working, another major line of interpretation, which we find exemplified in the translations and commentaries of the philosopher of law, Petr Redkin. Unlike Karpov, Redkin situated Plato in the context of the historical development of the ethical foundations of law and politics. In doing so, he provided a starting point for a reflection about Plato's role as an originator of the theory of natural law. In other words, in the slightly more secular environment of the university Plato became a subject of juridical science. Moreover, what is worth retaining in this context is that the quantity of original Russian literature (published lecture courses, but also monographs) on the history of the philosophy of law both predated and outranked the quantity produced by Russian historians of philosophy.[57]

'If one were to name just one philosopher who enjoyed pride of place in [Karpov's] sentiments, then it would be Plato, that immortal idealist of antiquity, who reaped so much praise from our renowned Fathers of the Church':[58] Karpov's two-volume translation first appeared (at his own cost) in 1841-1842. A second revised and extended edition, in six volumes, was published between 1863 and 1879.[59] Karpov's tireless labours as a translator and commentator combined a committed personal interest in Plato with his evident sympathies for the (official) state ambition to promote a national cultural identity. He believed that, as a source of Eastern Christian doctrine to which the Russian Orthodox tradition belonged, Plato's philosophy provided the grounds on which Russia might build a national philosophical tradition, one freed of the imprint of Western influence. Indeed, in his preface to the second edition he spoke about the need to eliminate the influence of Western science which had dominated in Russia since the penetration, in the seventeenth century, of ancient philosophy in Latin translation. Karpov wanted to exploit what he regarded as the natural affinity between Russian (Slavonic) and Greek, and to this end he endeavoured, where possible, to transcribe proper names in accordance with the rules of Slavonic, and thereby, as he put it, 'purify the Russian language of that which is alien and incompatible with it'.[60]

Karpov's image of Plato as the precursor of Christianity contained a number of traits which were fairly typical for the period. He drew parallels between the dialogues and the writings of the Church Fathers and the New Testament, both in terms of formulation, as well as with respect to the main themes of Plato's thought. These Karpov singled out as God, the soul and man's moral activity. 'Even Plato's most abstract reflections', he wrote, 'are constantly penetrated with the spirit of deep religious conviction, and are always connected to the idea of the supreme good.'[61] To Karpov's mind, Plato's portrait of God as the Good, as outside time and immutable corresponded perfectly to the Christian conception. He even went so far as to call Plato a 'monotheist', the fact that he spoke of the 'gods' being a mere verbal convention of the times he lived in.[62] Platonic psychology was, if not entirely, then, in many respects, similar to the teaching of the Holy Scriptures concerning the nature of the soul. According to Plato, as Karpov read him, the human essence is made up of two natures, the mortal and immortal, the irrational and the rational. But in certain dialogues he evoked man's tri-part nature of spirit, soul and body. To illustrate his point Karpov alluded to Socrates and Glaucon's description of the triple animal, which outwardly has the image of man.[63] The appetites of the multi-headed monster and the lion-like qualities of the beast may be taken together as representing the uncontrolled, instinctive life of the sensible or the mortal, whereas man's reason places him in the realm of the immortal. Karpov suggested that examples of a similar shift in emphasis, between the double and triple nature of the human essence, might be found in Paul's epistles to the Thessalonians and to the Corinthians. But perhaps, more important for Karpov's thesis was that Plato's portrait of man contained the seeds of the Christian teaching of 'Godmanhood', according to which man is said to be created in the image of God. Moreover – if only by way of contrast – Plato's condemnation of man for yielding to his physical and emotional needs provided further proof of what constitutes man's higher nature. And, even if, on the subject of the immortality of the soul, Plato was prepared to admit more than the Christian doctrine (here Karpov had in mind Plato's theory of transmigration), Karpov argued that this 'quirk' in no way diminished the force of his arguments.

For Karpov, it was the ethical dimension of Plato's philosophy which brought him closest of all to Christianity. Two main points guided his vision of man's moral behaviour as a whole which he projected on to his reading of Plato: sin as a consequence of the soul's immersion in the body (the allegory of the Fall), and love marking a striving towards divine likeness. Love is at once man's awareness of his sinfulness in his earthly existence, but also the desire to compensate for his weakness by coming as close as possible to divine beauty in which the highest truth and highest good are identical.[64] In short, for Karpov, Plato's philosophy in its entirety bore witness to an underlying conviction that everything great and beautiful on earth is the accomplishment of God's will.

This reading of Plato comforted Karpov's understanding of what philosophy should be. Its task, as he described it elsewhere, was to reconcile the interests 'of human nature with the laws of faith, and the conditions of life in the Fatherland'.[65] But it also allowed him, and others – notably authors of Slavophile tendencies – to insist on an opposition between Plato and Aristotle. If Plato was the precursor of Eastern Christianity, then Aristotle's heritage, it was argued, was the scholastic thought of the medieval West, and, more generally, of the rationalizing tendencies in modern Western philosophy, culminating with contemporary German idealism:

> With the onset of science in Western societies, theological scholasticism, which had once governed so many minds, began to lose its hold, and nowadays has totally disappeared. On the contrary, Christian philosophy, which inspires the mind with faith, has always been attentive to life. And so the supreme designs of Plato's genius, thanks to their proximity to dogmatics and especially to Christian ethics, were destined to thrive not in schools or textbooks, as was the case of Aristotle, but to enter the very core of real life (*domashnie obshchestva*), and, by means of correct philosophical research, guide the minds of Christians towards the truths of faith and of moral good.[66]

In his historical-philosophical courses about law (in which he never actually got beyond antiquity), Redkin read long extracts from Plato,

Aristotle and Cicero, which he had translated himself. These lectures, which he initially gave to third and fourth-year students at the University of Moscow in the 1830s and 1840s, were at the origin of his major work in seven volumes, *Lectures on the History of the Philosophy of Law in Connection with the History of Philosophy in General*, published half a century later in 1889–1891, just prior to his death. By the time of publication, however, Redkin had, as his closest biographers noted, undergone a shift in his philosophical orientation from Hegelianism to positivism. Indeed, the introductory lectures which comprise the first volume betray a tension, a wavering back and forth, between declared Comtian affinities and a spontaneous recourse to Hegel's concepts and method.[67] But this factor did not diminish the work's value as a source book, with extensive commentary of selected classical texts as illustrations of different ethical theories, and of their bearing on questions of law and the state. In this respect it may be said to constitute a second, fairly comprehensive translation of Plato into Russian.[68]

In general, Redkin endeavoured to limit himself to a presentation of Platonic thought, resisting, as far as possible, any personal critical evaluation. Even so, his comments did bring to view the difficulties for contemporary juridical science to accommodate the consequences of Plato's theory of the state to a modern world outlook. For liberal thinkers, such as Redkin, and especially the generation of legal philosophers who followed him – Korkunov, Chicherin, Novgorodtsev, E.N. Trubetskoi among them – whose main preoccupations fell into the province of the rule of law and the question of individual civil rights, Plato's project for an ideal city was clearly untenable. Even if this did not mean an outright rejection of his ethics as a whole, the obstacles they encountered in trying to match Plato's vision of a well-ordered state with their own theories of 'objective ethics' certainly contributed to a widespread attitude of ambivalence. At issue here was the unresolved dilemma, how best to reckon with the conflicting two-sided image of Plato, the brilliant philosopher-poet on the one hand, but a rather suspect political thinker on the other? Russian authors would suggest a variety of solutions to this problem.

As a translator and commentator, Redkin's aims were radically different from the Orthodox bias which coloured Karpov's interpretation. Redkin wanted to situate Plato's social ethics within a broader historical-philosophical framework, and thereby provide as neutral and objective (albeit Hegelian inspired) an account as possible of those concepts which, from the standpoint of the philosophy of law, were of crucial interest – truth (*pravda*) and justice (*spravedlivost'*) in relation to society and the state, but also as part and parcel of the more general problems of morality (*nravstvennost'*). Thus, Redkin's more sober account served as a corrective to the pathos embedded in Karpov's almost blind admiration of his idol. Whereas Karpov saw in Plato's understanding of the good a personal God, Redkin simply dismissed this as the error of projecting modern worldviews onto the past. Even if Plato frequently talked about the divine 'he never sought to accommodate these religious views to his theory of ideas, nor did he even attempt to show that they might be reconciled, combined (...). Plato was concerned primarily with ideas, alongside which he set the divine as the mythical form of the ideas of the good'.[69]

Irrespective of their different reasons for translating Plato, the philological apparatus that both Redkin and Karpov used is, if anything, telling of their knowledge of (and dependence on) Western models of scholarship. Karpov, recall, claimed that because of its natural flexibility and its etymological links with ancient Greek, the Russian language was more than equal to the linguistic challenge of rendering ancient Greek into modern Russian. But whatever he claimed, it remains that Karpov's translation and commentary relied quite heavily, like Redkin's, on recent philosophical and philological developments in Germany and France. Both authors referred to Schleiermacher, Ast, Stallbaum and Victor Cousin.[70] Karpov's organization of the dialogues depended very much on the critical-philological method developed by Schleiermacher, and Redkin too, in his opening bibliographical remarks, reserved his highest praise for the same author, even though he did not, in the end, adopt these same criteria in his own organization of the dialogues. The reason for this is quite simple: given that the final version of his monograph postdated Karpov's by some twenty years Redkin was able to draw on more recent models of interpretation.

Taking his cue from Ast and Schleiermacher, Karpov classified the dialogues into three groups according to the main themes or problems discussed: the 'Protagorean' (dialogues concerned predominantly with questions of ethics and politics); the 'Parmenidean' (theory of ideas); the 'Phaedrus' (nature of beauty).[71] Somewhat differently, Redkin arranged the dialogues with respect to what he called the 'gradual historical-genetic development of philosophy'. In this regard he referred to the work of Steinhart and Müller (1850–1873), who had broken down the dialogues into five groups corresponding to the main phases of Plato's assumed philosophical development: first, the Socratic, that is 'accusatory' dialogues, written essentially in agreement with Socrates' point of view, and 'accusatory' in the sense that they set out to show the failings in the views of the Sophists; second, the transitional period comprising those dialogues which bear witness to a shift from the Socratic to the dialectical dialogues; third, the dialectical, Platonic dialogues, properly speaking; fourth, dialogues written in maturity; fifth, 'Platonistic' dialogues, a term used to refer to the remaining or doubtful dialogues, written if not by Plato himself then by his pupils.[72] Clearly, this, broadly speaking, chronological order suited Redkin's need to reconstruct Plato's personal philosophical trajectory as a whole, and, from this perspective, to situate his views on justice and the state.

As the century advanced, Plato scholarship, particularly in Germany, began to draw more and more on the combined methods and findings in history, philosophy, and philology. In doing so, it gradually supplanted the purely philosophical-systematic criteria worked out by Schleiermacher. Such developments in philological scholarship are well reflected in the Solov'ev-Trubetskoi translation and commentaries (1899, 1903) which are, undoubtedly, by far the most interesting of the three sets of Complete Works discussed here. Their commentaries attest the degree to which the dating and the authenticity of the various dialogues had become one of the most central issues in Plato scholarship. Moreover, they show how an interest in the person of Plato himself, as a means to understand both his thought and the intellectual environment of his times, was also of growing importance.

At the end of his life Solov'ev invested considerable energies not only in translating the early 'Socratic' dialogues (a project which he undertook jointly with his brother, Mikhail Sergeevich, and his colleague Sergei N. Trubetskoi), and in writing commentaries, but also in addressing, in an unusual way, the still far from resolved 'Plato Question'. This massive undertaking, apart from anything else, bears witness to Solov'ev's considerable talents as a classical philologist.[73] It is also interesting to note that the translation project had actually been suggested to him much earlier, in 1882. At that time, his friend, the poet Afanasii Fet, had urged Solov'ev to give 'Plato to Russian literature' (*dat' russkoi literature Platona*), a plea which, in all likelihood, carried with it an implicit criticism of Karpov's outdated and somewhat tendentious translation. Solov'ev, however, was less enthusiastic, seeing little point in such an undertaking. Arguably, one reason for turning down Fet's proposal was that, in the early 1880s, Solov'ev's views on Platonic philosophy reflected his still deep intellectual attachment to the Slavophile world outlook: Platonic philosophy served as a mere prelude to the enduring significance of Christian teaching. 'Like Platonism', Solov'ev wrote in a lecture dating from the early 1880s, 'Christianity originates in a rejection of reality, but it was not a denial of reality as that which is untrue (Plato's case), but as that which is against morality, is evil.' Christianity, he believed, engendered the 'birth of the new man' (*rozhdenie novogo cheloveka*).[74] In a letter, dated 18 September 1881, addressed to Bestiuzhev-Riumin, director of the St. Peterburg *Kursy* where Solov'ev had been lecturing on ancient philosophy, he proposed for the forthcoming semester a course on 'Platonism and Christianity', his intention being, Solov'ev added, 'to include remarks on Aristotle, the Stoics etc., insofar as their ideas completed Plato's philosophy, and entered the fabric of neo-Platonism.' Shortly after sending this letter, however, he abandoned a teaching career altogether.[75]

By the late 1890s, Solov'ev's views on Slavophilism had evolved, prompting him to take distance from his former mentors, and to seek new intellectual allies among the more liberal-minded intelligentsia. In this period he also returned to Plato, discovering in him a means to recover his own philosophical interests, which, regrettably, for too long he had neglected for the sake of engaging in ideological and 'political' battles with officialdom. Solov'ev described this mood change very well himself in his preface to the first volume of translations:

> With the accumulation of life experience, albeit without any essential change in my convictions, I came to doubt more and more the usefulness and feasibility of those external designs (*zamysli*) to which my so-called 'best years' had been given. Disappointment in this meant returning to philosophical study, which for so long had been relegated to second place. Moral philosophy, with which I began this renewed study, inevitably led me to the fundamental theoretical questions of knowledge and being. And so, in 1897, some fifteen years after the aforementioned conversation [with Fet] I was irresistibly drawn to Plato, and immersed myself once again, but more deeply than before, in that ever fresh flow of youthful thought, the first to have recognized itself as philosophy. And what better way to master philosophical works, especially those of the ancients, than by translating them from the original into one's mother tongue.[76]

As a translator and philologist, Solov'ev proposed some rather unusual interpretations which were at the centre of debate among his colleagues.[77] In one essay, he affirmed, contrary to accepted opinion, Plato's authorship of *Alcibiades I*, claiming, moreover, that Plato had reworked his text at least three times, corresponding to the various stages of his philosophical development. Solov'ev attempted to substantiate his argument by saying that the heterogeneous elements of the dialogue (ethical reflection, Socratic monologue and discussion of the incorporeal soul as the true essence of man) corresponded to the various stages of Plato's philosophical development, and he set out to defend his view by comparing the dialogue with the authenticated *Laws* and *The Republic*.[78] In another, controversial article, he refuted the authenticity of *Protagoras*. To his mind, the eudemonism defended in this dialogue did not correspond to the philosophical positions either of Socrates, or of Plato, but rather that of another pupil, Aristippus, whose more favourable disposition towards the Sophists was quite different from the hostility expressed by Plato.[79] While it is true that these interpretations were largely rejected by contemporary Russian specialists at meetings of the Philosophical Society in St. Petersburg where they were discussed, it remains the case that Solov'ev's quite personal reading of Plato inspired respect from successive generations of both Russian and Soviet Plato scholars. Long after his death, scholars considered Solov'ev's work in this field as an important marker in the development of Russian Plato scholarship. Indeed, Solov'ev's translations and commentaries were esteemed by some as the finest example of Plato scholarship in the Russian language. In their 1923 edition of translations, Zhebelev, Radlov and Karsavin spoke of Solov'ev as 'a profound thinker, an exemplary stylist with a distinctive poetic turn of mind', concluding that he was 'to a great degree congenial to Plato'.[80]

Although only the first two volumes of a projected seven-volume edition were ever published – the 'Socratic dialogues' in 1899, and the 'Socratic battle' in 1903 – the critical apparatus Solov'ev provided in the preface to the first volume is sufficient to show his approach. First, he recapitulated the key phases, as he saw it, in the development of the 'Plato question' such as these were represented in German and English scholarship, from Schleiermacher to George Grote and Teichmüller.[81] Next, he announced his own criteria for assessing the various stages of Plato's thought:

> In order to understand Plato's intellectual biography correctly – which necessarily throws light on the internal connection and natural order of his dialogues – one should, first of all, address the much ignored fact, that, all influences on him apart, Socratic or otherwise, we find in Plato, the mature and independent thinker, two very different, albeit genetically linked, worldviews. If it is usual to speak of Plato as an idealist, then it is appropriate to call the first of these worldviews 'estranged' (*otreshennii*) or 'pessimistic' idealism, the second 'positive' or 'optimistic' idealism.[82]

The first, 'in the world resides evil', was a vision which dictated the philosopher's retreat from practical, social questions for the sake of theoretical reflection. One consequence of this dichotomy between the quest for truth and a rejection of the realities of life was the radical dualism which ran through much of Plato's work: spirit/body, rational thought/sensible perception, true being (*istinno-sushchee*) and phenomena. A quite different picture, however, emerges from the second worldview: the world harbours good. As an embodiment of truth, human society acquires positive significance, and the philosopher finds his rightful place among men as a lawgiver and ruler.

For Solov'ev, the immediate task set by these quite different expressions of idealism was to establish ways in which to bring them together, and thereby to uncover an overall coherence in Plato's philosophy. Like his German counterparts, he admitted the need for a unifying principle, both in order to grasp the overall meaning of Plato's thought, together with the place to be accorded to each individual dialogue within the entire body of works. But unlike the more usual practice of seeking this unifying principle in light of philosophical and/or linguistic criteria, Solov'ev sought to combine these with a story about (what he imagined) Plato's personal, emotional life experience to have been, and what elsewhere he called Plato's 'life drama':

> It is of course clear that Plato's dialogues express his philosophical interests, the philosophical labours of his mind. But it is equally obvious that the nature of these philosophical interests themselves depend on the personality of the

philosopher. For Plato, philosophy was above all a vital problem. And, for him, life was not a peaceable succession of days and years dedicated to intellectual labours (the case of Kant, for example), but a profound, complex drama which engulfed his entire being. The unfolding of this drama (...) is reflected and immortalized in the dialogues. So, there we have it – Plato himself, hero of his own life drama. Such is the true principle affording unity to Plato's works, the order of which is then naturally determined by the unfolding of this drama.[83]

Solov'ev singled out two crucial moments which, to his mind, allow us to determine the true chronology of the dialogues: the death of Socrates, and Plato's 'erotic crisis'.[84] It was precisely in Socrates' lawfully executed, but morally unjustifiable condemnation to death that Solov'ev saw the key to Plato's theoretical turn. In the 'Preliminary Outline' he referred to the fact that 'Plato's metaphysical doctrine about intellectual contemplation (*umstvennoe sozertsanie*), ideas and the ideal cosmos are usually interpreted as stemming from a purely theoretical investigation concerning the nature of cognition', and made the bold claim: 'this view is historically incorrect.'[85] For Solov'ev, Plato's dualism and abstract speculation were largely the response of a philosophical mind to a moral question: how was the killing of Socrates, a righteous man, possible? His answer, as Solov'ev read him, is that it was possible and natural because the world in which it happened, was, quite simply, not the real world. In other words, Plato's rejection of practical, vital tasks in favour of pure speculation occurred on moral soil. On the strength of this observation Solov'ev singled out a cluster of dialogues in which theoretical concerns, albeit stemming from the moral, come into their own: *Meno* (on the teachability of virtue in relation to the nature of knowledge), *Phaedo* (on immortality and ideas, or forms as objective essences), *Theaetetus* and *Parmenides*. In connection with this he drew attention to another complementary theme in these and other dialogues (*Cratylus, Sophist, Gorgias*), written, he believed, in the same period, namely, the nature of philosophy and the philosopher's vocation as a pure theoretician.[86] Solov'ev labelled this phase of Plato's philosophy 'negative idealism'.

The turning point in Plato's thought to positive or 'practical' idealism was, according to Solov'ev, only partly motivated by strictly theoretical considerations. More importantly, it should be understood as the outcome of Plato's experience of what Solov'ev termed 'the pathos of personal love'.[87] In *Sophist* and *Parmenides* Plato shows how 'true being', the 'real' (*sushchee*) should be understood not as a 'single unity', but rather as that which embraces its opposite, meaning that it is at once 'one' and 'many', the 'same' yet 'other'. However, for Solov'ev, although this conception of true being made possible a union between true being and non-being, thereby marking acceptance of the visible phenomena of the real world, it nevertheless failed to account satisfactorily for the real foundation in which such a union may be said to exist. To Solov'ev's mind, the key to understanding Plato's path towards 'positive' idealism, that return to the world which his philosophy ultimately took, is provided by his account of the erotic principle, so masterly evoked in the *Symposium* and *Phaedrus*. Interestingly – or perhaps intriguingly – Solov'ev chose to read Plato's description of the Eros less as the fruit of theoretical speculation than as an expression of the philosopher's own personal life experience, even though, as Solov'ev admitted, there was no biographical evidence to corroborate this view. For Solov'ev, it was Plato's discovery of the pathos of personal love, irreducible to either one or the other realm of the spiritual or the corporeal, which rendered his former pursuit of otherworldly perfection meaningless.

Besides being the hero of *Symposium* and *Phaedrus* – two dialogues which, according to Solov'ev, marked the apogee of Plato's philosophical and creative genius – the Eros also served as an organizing 'principle' for the 'Plato question'. In Solov'ev's reading, the appearance of the Eros heralded Plato's leap back into the world, but also foretold the final breakdown in his life experience – the second part of the philosopher's life drama or 'tragedy', as Solov'ev called it in the *Outline*. Thanks to his discovery of the Eros, Plato turned to human society in view of the positive role afforded to the community of philosophers within it, namely to seek a remedy to the evil which exists in the world (the phase of 'positive idealism', to which Plato gives expression in *Philebus, Republic, Timaeus, Critias* – Solov'ev's projected sixth volume of translations). The problem, though, for Solov'ev – and herein lay the tragedy – was that the consequences of this new task on the form Plato's socio-political views ultimately took were in the end detrimental to his original, Socratic, philosophy, viz., the quest for the good and the truth. Instead of correcting the anomalies of ancient Greek life such as they existed, Plato contented himself with a vindication of the total authority of the state over man. By approving the practice of slavery, accepting the distinction between Greeks and Barbarians, and by dint of counselling the positive value of war, Plato merely encouraged such anomalies. Finally, his disillusionment after the utopianism of the *Republic* (*Laws* – the subject of the projected final volume 'the Downfall of Idealism') was, for Solov'ev, irrefutable proof of the folly Plato had committed. Not only did Plato's entry into the world betray his political naivety, worse still, he also betrayed his spiritual master, Socrates. This unhappy ending brought Solov'ev to an equally pitiful conclusion: Plato's particular life history, such as it had become immortalized in his life's work, should justly be called the 'tragedy of humanity'.

Solov'ev's somewhat idiosyncratic account of Plato's personal tragedy was one of the last pieces he wrote before his untimely death in 1900. Indeed, for Solov'ev specialists, his interpretation throws as much light on the drama of his own life as it does on his announced object of study. There was, as François Rouleau has suggested, an undeniable personal empathy on Solov'ev's part with his author. He found himself confronted by a similar failure to unify speculation and politics. In Plato's case this failure originated in the impossibility to remain true to the principles and example of Socrates, whereas for his Russian interpreter, it was the failure of his theocratic projects which was in question.[88] One might be tempted to ridicule the significance that Solov'ev attached to the erotic principle by reading it in light of his own recent failures in love. Soviet and Western critics alike have noted that the *Drama of Plato's Life* was written in the wake of a 'last intense, but somewhat ridiculous infatuation' for Sophia Martyovna, and in the immediate aftermath of a rejected proposal of marriage (1896) to his lifelong love, and newly widowed, Sophia Khitrovo.[89] Whatever truth there is in this, it is certainly tempting to bear it in mind when Solov'ev goes on at some length (in the *Drama*) about Plato's 'erotic crisis' and the appeal of 'Platonic love'! More seriously perhaps, Solov'ev's remarks about a kind of 'transcended Eros' which he developed in response to the Platonic Eros may be understood in terms of his personal expression of Christian faith: we might say that Eros finds its answer in Agape.[90] In resituating Eros in the context of his ideas relating to Godmanhood, Solov'ev endeavoured to 'save' Plato, turning the unpalatable pagan ideas into something more congenial. Plato's Eros, Solov'ev contended, can be considered as an inchoate understanding of Godmanhood, only Plato failed to see the logical consequences of his idea, i.e., its double spiritual-corporeal dimension, and the possibility of what Solov'ev called 'the resurrection of mortal nature in view of eternal life':

> Just as it is impossible for the divine to restore man as a spiritual-corporeal being without man's participation in this (...), it is equally impossible for man to create by his own efforts a *surhumanité* (...). It is clear that man cannot become divine uniquely by the effective power of divinity itself, by that which does not 'become' but which exists eternally. It is also clear that, from its very beginnings, the path of the spiritual – which unites perfectly the feminine and the masculine, the spiritual and the corporeal – is necessarily the union or interaction of the divine and the human, in other words, it is a divino-human process.[91]

Despite the highly personal colouring of Solov'ev's commentaries, the categories he introduced to describe the various stages in Plato's philosophical development – negative idealism, positive idealism, Eros – came to operate as markers in subsequent Russian and early Soviet Plato studies. Both Evgenii Trubetskoi and Pavel Novgorodtsev (in his lectures *Sokrat i Platon,* read at the Courses of Higher Education for Women in 1901) adopted this breakdown of the dialogues. In his introduction to the Russian translation of Windelband's book on Plato (1909), Professor Zhakov followed Solov'ev's scheme of 'negative' and 'positive' idealism, and likewise offered an account of Eros as the force which reconciled Plato with life. A. Jashchenko's bibliographical study of ancient philosophy, published in 1915, also used Solov'ev's categorization as headings to organize his presentation of the secondary literature in his section on Plato. And again, much later, at the time of more relaxed censorship in the early 1960s, when the well-known classical scholar, Aleksei Losev, rescued Plato from oblivion by re-editing the dialogues, he as it were, surreptitiously reinstated those terms which, for specialists, had a Solov'evian ring to them. However, as far as the actual order of dialogues was concerned, subsequent translation attempts, notably those edited in the 1920s, as well as the Asmus and Losev edition of the 1960s (an edition, which, incidentally, was re-edited in the early 1990s) paid little heed to Solov'ev's template, and even less to the arguments which had prompted his arrangement of texts. The editors of the early Soviet edition, Radlov, Karsavin and Zhebelov, for example, modelled their translation, together with the order of the dialogues, on the Burnet five-volume edition (Oxford, 1899–1907), while the later, Soviet version, arranged the dialogues according to what by the mid-twentieth century had become, so to speak, 'standard practice.' But all of them did, nevertheless, pay tribute to Solov'ev's unfinished enterprise, applauding his concern to provide materials to meet with the growing philosophical interests and needs of an educated reading public. Moreover, they presented, like Solov'ev, an image of Plato as a 'spiritual guide for truth seekers' (*uchitel' iscushchikh*). As the editors Zhebelev and Radlov put it, Plato had long since become worthy of humanity, his indisputable historical importance and his genius as a writer making him a thinker for all times.

*

Today, most historians of Russia would agree that the striking progress in Russian humanities scholarship in the closing decades of the nineteenth century was, to a great extent, due to more sustained interaction and exchange with the European scientific community as a whole. Most, I think, would also agree that there was, nevertheless, a lingering tension within the Russian scientific community itself between the different objectives of research and education, especially as the latter had continually to bear the brunt of *ad hoc* state measures, even in periods of relative political stability. One unresolved difficulty that seems to have taxed certain Russian intellectuals was that striving for originality in historical and philosophical research was quite simply at odds with pedagogical expediency which required that they draw heavily on available foreign literature, despite what might have been reservations with respect to the nature of the materials they taught from. For the historian today, this coexistence of foreign and national literature, and the random use of both complicates the task of justifying, or refuting, claims to the effect that

Russian scholarship – in this instance Russian Plato scholarship – was in some key respects distinct from the patterns of interpretation developed by Western counterparts. It was, however, a question frequently posed, openly and implicitly, by Russian scholars themselves in their attempts to research aspects of Plato's philosophy in the light of questions asked within the framework of Russia's intellectual and cultural past and present. It is precisely these factors of an historical-cultural dimension, besides the purely historical-philosophical, which need to be borne in mind once we come to analyse more closely the role of Plato as a source of inspiration for Russian nineteenth and twentieth-century thinkers.

Notes

1   Speech read before the Imperial Society of History and of Ancient Russia at the University of Moscow in 1825. Published in *Chtenie v Imperatorskom Obshchestve Istorii I Drevnosti Rossiiskikh pri Moskovskom Universitete*, IV (Moscow, 1861), pp.160-161.
2   See Gustav Shpet, *Ocherk razvitiia russkoi filosofii* (Petrograd, 1922), rpt. in *Russkaia Filosofiia* (Moscow, 1991), p.479. On the history of educational reform in Russia more generally, see, for example: P. Miliukov, 'Universitety v Rossii' in Brokgaus and Efron (eds), *Entsyclopedicheskii Slovar'*, Vol. xxxiv (1902), pp.788-803; B. Glinskii, 'Universitetskie ustavy (1755-1884)', *Istoricheskii Vestnik*, Jan-Febr. (1900), pp.324-351, 718-742; M.M. Filippov, *Reforma gimnazii i universitetov* (SPb., 1901); V.S. Solov'ev, 'Gosudarstvennaia filosofiia v programme Ministerstva Narodnogo Prosveshcheniia' (1885) in *Sobranie Sochineniia*, vol.2 (Moscow, 1989), pp.175-184; V.I. Vernadskii, *Ob osnovaniiakh universitetskoi reformy* (Moscow, 1901); P. Novgorodtsev, 'Institutions of Higher Education before the War', in *Russian Schools and Universities in the World War* (Yale Univ. Press, New Haven, 1929), pp.133-153. On the question of Russia's modernization and its effects on creating a more professional 'academic' intelligentsia, see E.W. Clowes (ed.), *Between Tsar and People: Educated Society and the Quest for Public Identity in Late Imperial Russia* (Princeton University Press, 1991); A. Besançon, *Education et société en Russie dans le second tiers du XIXè siècle* (Mouton-Paris-La Haye, 1974). Among the more recent studies on this question see: Ben Eklof (ed.), *School and Society in Tsarist and Soviet Russia* (New York, 1993), and Trude Maurer, *Hochschullehrer im Zahrenreich*, Beiträge zur Geschichte Osteuropas, Band 27 (Köln, 1998).
3   I. Chistovich, 'Istoria St. Peterburgskoi Akademii' (SPb., 1857). Quoted in Shpet, op. cit., p.371.
4   See F. Copleston, *Philosophy in Russia: From Herzen to Lenin and Berdyaev* (Notre Dame, 1986), p.22.
5   On Redkin see Nikolai Korkunov's entry in *Biograficheskii slovar' professorov i prepodavatelei Imperatorskogo St.-Peterburgskogo Universiteta za istekshuiu tret'iu chetvert veka ego sushhcestvovaniia (1868-1894)*, vol.2 (SPb., 1896-1898). See also the memoirs by Boris Chicherin in *Moskovskii Universitet v vospominaniiakh sovremennikov (1755-1917)* (Moscow, 1989), pp.375-382.
6   Boris Chicherin, quoted in A. Koyré, *Etudes sur l'histoire de la pensée philosophique en Russie* (Paris, 1950), p.115.
7   See A. Chervel, *Les auteurs français, latins et grecs aux programmes de l'enseignement secondaire de 1800 à nos jours* (Paris, 1986), p.12.

8 All these subjects were taught in the Faculty of History and Philology, which, as part of the overall reorganization of the university in the 1850s and 1860s, replaced what had previously been called the Philosophical Faculty.
9 M.M. Filippov, *Reforma Gimnazii...* (SPb., 1901), p.30.
10 B. Pares, *A History of Russia* (London, 1926; rpt. 1965), p.420.
11 Pavel Miliukov gives the following percentages: 1880 – 11, 3%; 1885 – 9, 8%; 1894 – 5, 2 %; 1899 – 3, 9%. Miliukov, 'Universitet'. op. cit., p.799.
12 Filippov gives the following figures for 1893: of a total of 62, 674 pupils 11,987 (18, 8%) dropped out, and transferred to other schools. Filippov, op. cit., p. 31.
13 V. Modestov, 'Mesto klassicheskoi filologii sredi nauk istoriko-filologicheskogo fakul'teta i eia prepodavanie', *ZhMNP*, 12 (1889), pp.1-16.
14 See, for example, Prof. A.N. Giliarov, *Istochniki o Sofistakh: Platon kak istoricheskii svidetel'* (Kiev, 1891), and his 'Trudy po istorii grecheskoi filosofii (za 1892-1896)', *Universitetskie Izvestiia*, 6 and 12 (Kiev, 1896), pp.53-72, 211-226 (Giliarov discussed works by Zeller, Uberweg, Windelband, Burnet, Gomperz, Milhaud, Scott, Bernard, Ch. Huit); V.N. Buzeskul, 'Kharakternie cherty nauchnogo dvizheniia v oblasti grecheskoi istorii za poslednee tridtsatiletie', *RM*, 2 (1900), pp.58-79 (on Grote, Pöhlmann, and Meyer); N.Stelletskii, 'Neskol'ko kriticheskikh zamechanii po povodu mneniia nemetskogo filosofa F.A. Lange o sravnitel'nom znachenii dlia razvitiia nauki vzgljadov Protagora i Platona na poznanie', *Vera i Razum*, Vol.II, pt.II (1894), pp.156-180. (In this article, Stelletskii took Lange's *History of Materialism* to task. Lange had argued that Protogaras' theory of knowledge was more propitious to the development of science than Plato's.)
15 Compare figures given for the academic year 1889-1890 (medicine, 5 Russian students of a total of 872; philosophy, 5 out of 58; philology 7 out of 168), and for the academic year 1911-1912: medicine - 208 Russian students out of a total of 614; philosophy 26 out of 259 and philology 4 out of 621. (Figures are taken the *Personal-Verzeichniss der Universität Leipzig* for the years in question).
16 Concerning the 'ideology' of the academic intelligentsia, see J.C. McClelland, *Autocrats and Academics. Education, Culture and Society* (Chicago, 1979), pp.57-113.
17 See, for example, A. Besançon, *Education et société en Russie...*, who illustrates this point with reference to a number of individual scholars.
18 Between 1820 and 1860 there was an increase in lectures in the subject from 9% to 23%. See U.J. Schneider, 'The Teaching of Philosophy at German Universities in the Nineteenth Century', *History of Universities*, vol.XII (Oxford, 1993), pp.197-338; see also his 'Bibliography of Nineteenth Century Histories of Philosophy in German, English, and French (1810-1899)', in *Storia della Storiografia*, 21 (1992), pp.141-169.
19 'The history of philosophy has its own system of laws, in so far as the various attempts to solve philosophic problems of knowledge do not merely follow an external, more or less accidental, order. One problem, rather, grows out of another by an inner necessity, and one system draws another after it by way of progress or completion, contradiction or contrast.' E. Zeller, *Die Philosophie der Griechen*, 3 vols. (Tübingen, 1844-1852). Cited from the abridged English translation by L.R. Palmer (Cleveland and New York, 1963), p.18.
20 See the foreword to the Russian translation of Windelband's *Platon*, translated from the fourth German edition (SPb., 1909). Professor Zhakov presented Windelband as a neo-Kantian working along axiological lines: 'Platon i ego znachenie v istorii filosofskoi mysli', p.5.
21 Windelband, *Platon*, cited from the 6th edition (1920), p.2.
22 Examples of Russian (generalist) histories of philosophy in this vein include: M.M. Filippov, *Filosofiia deisvitel'nosti. Istoriia i kriticheskii analiz nauchno-filosofskykh mirosozertsanii ot drevnosti do nashikh dnei*, 2 vols. (SPb., 1895-1896); M.V. Bezobrazova, *Kratkii obzor sushchestvennykh momentov istorii filosofii* (Moscow,

1894); L.E. Obolenskii, *Istoriia mysli. Opyt kriticheskoi istorii filosofii* (SPb., 1901); V.N. Speranskii, *Obshchestvennaia rol' filosofii. Vvedenie v istoriiu politicheskykh uchenii* (SPb., 1913). Textbooks for instruction in the history of philosophy at the theological academies include: M. Ostroumov, *Obzor filosofskykh uchenii* (Tambov, 1878; Moscow, 1880); N. Markov, *Obzor filosofskykh uchenii* (Moscow, 1880 /2nd ed. 1881/); M.E. Sokolov, *Kratkaia istoriia filosofii* (Simbirsk, 1880); N. Strakhov, *Ocherk istorii filosofii* (Kharkov, 1893 /2nd ed. 1910/); I. Nazar'ev, *Kratkaia istoriia filosofii* (Voronezh, 1895); I.P. Solov'ev, *Kurs istorii filosofii* (SPb., 1913). For 'Histories of Philosophy' with particular reference to the classical period see: S.N. Trubetskoi, *Istoriia drevnei filosofii*, 2 vols. (Moscow, 1906 /2nd edn. 1912/); M.I. Karinskii, *Lektsii po istorii drevnei filosofii* (read to students at the SPb. Theological Academy) (SPb., 1889); Zelenogorskii, *Ocherk iz istorii drevnei filosofii* (Kharkov, 1908); A.I. Vvedenskii, *Lektsii po drevnei filosofii* (SPb., 1912). Some noted examples of translated literature include: A. Schwegler, *Geschichte der Philosophie im Umriss*, (Stuttgart, 1848), translated by a group of students under Iurkevich's direction in 1864; George Henry Lewes, *The History of Philosophy from Thales to Comte*, London, in 3 edns: 1857, 1868, 1872, translated into Russian twice (SPb., 1866 /2nd rev. trans. 1892/); W. Bauer, *Geschichte der Philosophie für gebildete Leser, zugleich als Einleitung in das Studium der Philosophie*, (Halle, 1863), translated under the title *Istoriia Filosofii v obshcheponiatnom izlozhenii*, edited by M. Antonovich (SPb., 1866); F.A. Lange, *Geschichte des Materialismus und Kritik seiner Bedeutung in der Gegenwart* (1866) was translated from the 3rd German edn. by N.N. Strakhov (SPb., 1881), and again in 1899-1900 under the editorship of V.S. Solov'ev; Fr. Kirchner, *Katechismus der Geschichte der Philosophie. Von Thales bis zur Gegenwart* (Leipzig, 3 edns: 1877, 1884, 1896), was translated under the simpler title *Istoriia Filosofii* by V.D. Vol'fson (SPb., 1895); M. Brasch, *Die Klassiker der Philosophie. Von frühesten griechischen Denkern bis auf die Gegenwart*, 3 vols. (Leipzig, 1884-1885) was translated as *Razvitie Filosofskoi Mysli. Filosofskie ucheniia ot drevne-grecheskogo perioda do nashikh dnei* (SPb., 1885); Hans von Arnim, *Die Europäische Philosophie des Altertums* (Leipzig, 1909) was translated by S.I. Povarnin as *Istoriia antichnoi filosofii* (SPb., 1910).
23 A. Klevanov, *Obozrenie filosofskoi deiatel'nosti Platona i Socrata (po Tselleru)* (Moscow, 1861). Klevanov simplified Zeller for the sake of a nonspecialist Russian readership. He also included, as a supplement, four articles by Victor Cousin. The second edition, translated by a certain M. Nekrasov, and edited with foreword by M. Karinskii was entitled *Ocherk istorii grecheskoi filosofii Tsellera* (SPb., 1886).
24 Windelband, *Istoriia drevnei filosofii*, translated by students of the Vysshie Zhenskie Kursy under the direction of Professor Vvedenskii (SPb., in 3 rev. edns: 1893, 1898, 1902).
25 See *Filologicheskoe Obozrenie*, V, kn. 1 (1893), pp.24-25; Windelband's *Platon*, was translated from the second edition by Al. Grombakh (SPb., 1904), and, again, from the fourth edition by I.V. Postman, with a foreword by Prof. K. Zhakov (SPb., 1909); Th. Gomperz, *Grecheskie Mysliteli* was translated from the second German edition by E. Gertsyk and D. Zhukovskii, under the direction of S. Zhebelev, 2 vols. (SPb., 1911-1913). For a review notice of the German original published in 1893 see Zelinskii, *Filologicheskoe Obozrenie*, VI, kn.1 (1894), pp.17-22.
26 O.M. Novitskii, *Postepennoe razvitie drevnikh filosofskikh uchenii*, 4 vols. (Kiev, 1860-1861); S.S. Gogotskii, *Vvedenie v istoriiu filosofii* (Kiev, 1871).
27 O.M. Novitskii, op. cit., vol.1, pp.39-41.
28 S.N. Trubetskoi, 'Istoriia Filosofii' in Brokgaus and Efron (eds), *Entsyclopedicheskii Slovar'*, Vol. xiii(a) (SPb., 1894), pp.508-510.
29 D. I. Pisarev, 'Idealizm Platona. Obozrenie filosofskoi deiatel'nosti Sokrata i Platona, po Tselleru; sostavil *Klevanov*' (1861) in *D.I. Pisarev: Sochineniia v shesti tomakh*, t.1 (SPb., 1894), pp.257-280.

30 A.N. Giliarov, 'Trudy po istorii grecheskoi filosofii (za 1892-1896)', *Universitetskie Izvestiia*, 6 (Kiev, 1896), p.60.
31 A.A. Kozlov, *Metod i napravlenie filosofii Platona* (Kiev, 1880), pp.191-192.
32 A. Guliaev, 'Kak Platon ponimal svoiu filosofiiu?', *Vera i Razum*, vol.II, pt. II (1897), pp.1-27.
33 F. Zelinskii, review notice of Gomperz, *Griechische Denker*, vol.1 (Leipzig, 1893), in *Filologicheskoe Obozrenie*, Vol.VI, kn. 1 (1894), pp.17-22.
34 George Henry Lewes, *Istoriia filosofii ot nachala eia v Gretsii do nastoiashchego vremeni*, 2 vols., trans. by V. Chuiko (SPb., 1892). A similar example is provided by Solov'ev's translation of Friedrich Lange's *History of Materialism*. In his editorial foreword, Solov'ev stated quite clearly his reservations with respect to the author's neo-Kantian standpoint.
35 Alfred Weber, *Istoriia evropeiskoi filosofii* (1871) translated from the second French edition by I. Linnichenko and VI. Podvysotskii under the editoral direction of A.A. Kozlov (Kiev, 1882).
36 F.C. Baur, *Das Christliche des Platonismus, oder Sokrates und Christus* (Tübingen, 1837); A. Schwegler, *Geschichte der griechischen Philosophie* (Tübingen, 1859).
37 A.A. Kozlov, preface to *Istoriia evropeiskoi filosofii* (A.Weber).
38 Ibid.
39 Kozlov, *Metod i napravlenie filosofii Platona* (Kiev, 1880).
40 Kozlov, preface to *Istoriia evropeiskoi filosofii*.
41 Kozlov, *Metod i napravlenie...*, p.203.
42 Novitskii, op. cit., vol. 4, p.x.
43 *'Platon' po knige Windelbanda. Otvety na dva pervykh bileta programmy po istorii filosofii prava, prof. P.I. Novgorodtseva* (Moscow, 1909). This text is a simplified recapitulation of Windelband's monograph on Plato as taught by the philosopher of law, Pavel Novgorodtsev.
44 George Grote, *Plato and the other Companions of Socrates*, 2nd ed. (1867); John Burnet, *Early Greek Philosophy* (1892), Fustel de Coulanges, *La cité antique* (Paris, 1864). Other similar examples include the works of Paul Tannery and G. Milhaud (on ancient science). In Germany, historians working on social-political and moral-philosophical aspects of the Greek world include Robert Pöhlmann, Georg Adler, K. Belloch, Friedrich Jodl. (For exact titles see below note 44.) In Russia, some of the most noted historians working in this direction include: V.G. Vasilevskii (1833-1899), for his 'Politicheskaia reforma i sotsial'noe dvizhenie v drevnei Gretsii v period ee upadka' (1869); M.S. Kutorga (1809-1886) *Istoriia Afinskoi Respubliki* (SPb., 1848); V.P. Buzeskul (1858-1931), *Istoriia Afinskoi Demokratii* (SPb., 1909). On Russian historians of ancient Greece and the introduction of new historiographical methods, see V.P. Buzeskul, 'Kharakternye cherty nauchnogo dvizheniia v oblasti grecheskoi istorii za poslednoe tridcatiletie', *RM*, 2 (1900), pp.58-79. Also his 'Razrabotka grecheskoi istorii v Rossii', *Annaly*, 4 (1924), pp.139-153, and *Vseobshchaia istoriia i ee predstaviteli v Rossii v XIX i nachale XX veka*, 2 vols. (Leningrad, 1929-1931). See also: M.N. Tikhomirov, M.A. Alpatov, and A.L. Sidorov (eds), *Ocherki istorii istoricheskoi nauki v SSSR*, vol.2 (Moscow, 1955), chp 5, #2, 'Izuchenie antichnoi istorii.'
45 The titles in Russian translation did not always correspond to the original, nor was it unusual for the translated work itself to be an abridged version of the original. For example: P. Tannery, *Pour l'histoire de la science hellène* (Paris, 1887) appeared in Russian as *Pervye shagi drevne-Grecskoi nauki*, translated by N.N. Pol'nova and S.I. Tsereteli under the direction of Profs. Radlov and G.F. Tsereteli, with a foreword by Prof. Vvedenskii (SPb., 1902). G. Adler's *Geschichte des Sozialismus und Kommunismus von Platon bis zur Gegenwart*, vol.1 (Leipzig, 1899) was translated as *Istoriia Sotsializma i Kommunizma* (SPb., 1907), and later under the title *Iz istorii obshchestvennykh uchenii*, edited by Prof. V.N. Speranskii (SPb., 1913). Robert

Pöhlmann's *Geschichte des antiken Kommunismus und Sozialismus* (Munich, 1893-1901) was edited, with a foreword by M. Rostovtsev (SPb., 1910). An earlier essay by Pöhlmann, his 'Grundzüge der politischen Geschichte von Griechenland', first published in J. Müller (ed.), *Handbuch der klassichen Altertumswissenschaft*, vol.3 (1889), appeared in Russian as *Kratkii ocherk grecheskoi istorii* (Moscow, 1890). This article was later revised under the title *Griechische Geschichte und Quellenkunde*, and in this form was translated in two Russian editions (SPb., 1908, 1910). Fustel de Coulanges' *La cité antique* (Paris, 1864) appeared as *Grazhdanskaia obshchina antichnogo mira*, trans. E. Korsh (Moscow, 1867). A second translation, edited by Prof. D.N. Kudriavskii, appeared in St Petersburg in 1906. F. Pollock's, *Kurze Geschichte der Staatslehre* (Leipzig, 1893) was translated as *Istoriia politicheskykh uchenii* (SPb., 1897). Other major works of translated Western scholarship include: P. Janet, *Histoire de la science politique dans ses rapports avec la morale*, translated from the third edition by A. Vasil'ev (SPb., 1871 /2nd Russian edn. 1878); K.J. Belloch, *Griechische Geschichte*, 2 vols. (1893-1897), trans. M. Gershenzon (Moscow, 1897-1905); John-Pentland Mahaffy, *A History of Classical Greek Literature* (1880), trans. Aleksandra Veselovskaia (Moscow, 1883. F. Jodl, *Geschichte der Etik in der neueren Philosophie*, 2 vols. (Stuttgart, 1889), ed. V.S. Solov'ev (SPb., 1896-1898).

46 See V.P. Buzeskul, *Vseobshchaia istoriia...*, vol.1; M.N. Tikhomirov, M.A. Alpatov, and A.L. Siderov (eds), *Ocherki istorii istoricheskoi nauki v SSSR*, vol.2.
47 For a more detailed discussion see below, Chapters Four and Five.
48 Besides F. Zelinskii's *Antichnii mir i my*, mention should be made of V.P. Buzeskul's *Antichnost' i sovremennost'. Sovremennye temy v antichnoi Gretsii* (SPb., 1913; Moscow, 1924) and A. Giliarov's *Platonism, kak osnovanie sovremennogo mirovozzreniia*, (Moscow, 1887).
49 Cited from the German translation: Th. Zelinskij, *Die Antike und wir*, trans. E. Schoeler (Leipzig, 1905), p.1.
50 V. Karpov, *Sochineniia Platona*, vol.1, 2nd ed. (1863). Introduction.
51 A.N. Giliarov, *op. cit.*
52 See the various lecture courses published by the academies, as well as the publication of articles and monographs largely based on these courses. See also *Obozrenie predmetov, naznachaemykh dlia otkrytogo ispytaniia studentov Moskovskoi Dukhovnoi Akademii* (Moscow, 1856). In the Reform and Counter Reform period, see, for example, monographs and articles by the 'theological' historian of philosophy, P.I. Linitskii, notably his 'Platon-predstavitel' idealizma v drevnei filosofii', *TKDA* (1868), 'Nravstvennye i religioznye poniatiia drevnikh grecheskikh filosofov', *TKDA* (1870-1872), and his *Uchenie Platona o bozhestve* (Kiev, 1876). See also, A. Derevitskii, 'Iz Istorii grecheskoi etiki: literaturno-filosofskie ocherki', *Vera i Razum* (Khar'kov, 1886). For further discussion of Plato in the theological academy see below, Chapter Two.
53 Cited in V. Vanchugov, *Ocherk istorii filosofii, samobytno-russkoi* (Moscow, 1994), p.177.
54 Among the most frequently cited works on Aristotle are: M.I. Vladislavlev, *Logika, obozrenie induktivnykh i deduktivnykh priemov myshleniia i istoricheskie ocherki logiki Aristotelia, sholasticheskoi dialektiki, logiki formal'noi i induktivnoi* (SPb., 1872, 2nd ed. 1881); S.A. Zhebelev, *Grecheskaia politicheskaia literatura i 'Politika' Aristotelia* (SPb., 1911). For a more complete list, covering some twenty pages, see Iashchenko, *Russkaia Bibliografiia*. Monographs on Plato which grew out of university lecture courses, and/or dissertations include: N. Ia Grot, *Ocherk filosofii Platona* (Moscow, 1896); A.A. Kozlov, *Metod i napravlenie filosofii Platona* (Kiev, 1880); S.N. Trubetskoi, *Metafizika v drevnei Gretsii* (Moscow, 1890); A.N. Giliarov, *Grecheskie Sofisty, ikh mirovozzrenie i deiatel'nost' v sviazi s obshchei politicheskoi i kul'turnoi istoriei Gretsii* (Moscow, 1888); also his *Istochniki o Sofistov. Platon, kak istoricheskoi svidetel'. Opyt istoriko-filosofskoi kritiki* (Kiev, 1891).

55 *Crito* was published in new and revised translations in 1832, 1861, 1870, 1876, 1879, 1884, 1885 (twice) 1895, 1898, 1900, 1901, 1903, 1910, 1913; *Apology* (1861, 1870, 1875, 1880, 1884, six times during the 1890s, 1904, 1913); *Phaedo* (1804, 1861, 1874, 1887, 1891, 1892, 1893, 1895, 1896, 1898, 1900). Set texts for university students in the Faculty of History and Philology tended to be one or more of the following dialogues: *Gorgias, Symposium, Timaeus, Parmenides, Theaetetus*, extracts from the *Republic*.

56 A fourth Complete Works – *Polnoe sobranie tvorenii Platona v 15 tomakh*, edited by the 'Old Professors' E.L. Radlov, S.A. Zhebelev and L.P. Karsavin (Pg: Academia, 1923-1929) – largely followed the criteria as established by Solov'ev, rejecting Karpov. It should be noted that, although all the planned fifteen volumes of this last translation existed in manuscript form, only a few of them were actually ever published: I - *Euthyphron, Apology, Crito, Phaedo*; IV - *Parmenides, Philebus*; V - *Symposium, Phaedrus*; IX - *Hippius I, Hippius II, Ion*; XIII - *Laws* (bks i-vi); XIV - *Laws* (bks vii-xii). See: V.P. Buzeskul, *Vseobshchaia Istoria i ee Predstaviteli v Rossii*, Vol.2, p.146.

57 For a list of some of the most often quoted publications in the history of philosophy of law, see below, Chapter Three, note 16.

58 Cited from Karpov's obituary, *Pamiati V.N. Karpova zasluzhennogo professora Sanktpeterburgskoi duhovnoi akademii* (SPb., 1868).

59 The first edition contained translations of *Protagoras, Euthydemus, Laches, Charmides, Hippius Minor, Euthyphron, Apology, Crito, Phaedo, Meno, Gorgias*, the two *Alcibiades*. The second edition (4 volumes published in 1863, with volumes 5 and 6 published posthumously in 1879) contained all the dialogues with the exception of *Laws* and *Letters*. The first bout of reviews, dating from the 1840s, referred relatively little to the quality of the translations themselves, tending rather to focus on an image of Plato as a 'vital thinker', as the generator of much needed values (humanism, prowess and *obshchestvennost'*) which were sorely wanting in present-day society. In short, Plato was represented as a healthy alternative to the cabinet philosophizing of contemporary Europe. See: *Sovremmenik*, vol.25 (1841), pp.41-42; *Maiak*, vol.2, bk.IV (1842), pp.153-193; *Otechestvennie Zapiski*, vol.20, pt.6 (1842), pp.62-63, and vol.24, pt.6, pp.29-35. Towards the end of the century, however, with the appearance of new editions by a variety of philosophers and philologists, reference to Karpov's linguistic and literary skills became rather more disparaging. See, for example, S.P. Kondrat'ev, *Germes*, 2 (1908), pp.171-173, who contended that all Plato's artistry was lost in Karpov's translation. In their foreword to vol.1 of their *Polnoe sobranie tvorenii Platona v 15 tomakh*, S. Zhebelev and E. Radlov simply dismissed Karpov's translation as 'unreadable', and his philological apparatus 'outmoded'.

60 Already in his foreword to the first edition of 1841, Karpov had contended that the beauty of Plato's language had been deformed in the Latin translations. But, basically, all he did, himself, was to substitute an i for an e in certain letter combinations (for example, Demosthenes becomes Dimosthenes).

61 V.Karpov, 'Sochineniia Platona, perevedennye s grecheskogo i ob'iasnennye professorom Karpovym', *Strannik*, t.2, no. 6, pt.3 (1864), p.83.

62 As Karpov put it: 'It is possible to deduce Plato's monotheism from the sole fact that in his Republic he considers monarchy as the most perfect and rational form of government'(!) ibid., p.89.

63 *Republic*, IX, 588.

64 Karpov, *Strannik*, pp.108-109.

65 Karpov, *Vvedenie v Filosofiiu* (SPb., 1840).

66 Karpov, *Strannik*, p.74.

67 See Korkunov's entry on Redkin in *Biograficheskii Slovar'*....

68 Redkin translated and discussed the following dialogues: *Ion, Hippius Major, Hippius Minor, Alcibiades I, Laches, Protagoras, Meno, Apology, Crito, Georgias, Politicus,*

Republic and *Laws*. For a discussion of Redkin's conception of legal and moral norms in the light of a Platonic impulse see below, Chapter Three.
69 P. Redkin, *Iz lektsii po istorii filosofii prava v svjazi s istoriei filosofii voobshche*, vol.3 (SPb., 1889-1891), pp.299-300.
70 Russian translations of German scholarship in the first half of the century include Ast, *Obozrenie istorii filosofii*, translated by a certain Vershinski (SPb., 1831); Heinrich Ritter, 'O zhizni i tvoreniiakh grecheskogo filosofa Platona' in *ZhMNP*, pt.10 (1836), pp.486-512, and a compilation, 'Vzgliad Platona na nauku filosofii (po Ritteru)', *ZhMNP*, pt.13 (1837), pp.265-301. As for Schleiermacher, some of his works were translated towards the end of the century, and a revived interest in him came with the Russian translation, in 1915, of Dilthey's biography.
71 This criterion was subsequently disqualified by Radlov and Zhebelev in their 1920s edition of the translated dialogues, just as it was by philological scholarship in general.
72 The corresponding order Redkin gives is: 1: *Ion, Hippius Major, Hippias Minor, Alcibiades I, Lysis, Charmides, Laches, Protagoras*. 2: *Euthydemus, Meno, Euthyphron, Apology, Crito, Gorgias, Cratylus*. 3: *Parmenides, Theaetetus, Sophist, Politicus*. 4: *Phaedrus, Symposium, Phaedo, Philebus, Republic, Timaeus, Critias, Laws*. 5: *Alcibiades II, Menexenus, Theages, Rivals, Clitophon, Hipparchus, Minus, Epinomis*.
73 The texts Solov'ev wrote on Plato between 1897 and his death include: 'Platon' in Brokgaus and Efron (eds), *Entsyclopedicheskii Slovar'*, vol.xxiii(a) (1898); 'Zhizn' i proizvedeniia Platona (Predvaritel'nyi ocherk)', in *Tvoreniia Platona*, vol.1 (Moscow, 1899) – essentially the same text with some revisions; *Zhiznennaia Drama Platona*, 1898; commentaries to individual dialogues: *Theages, Alcibiades I, Alcibiades II, Ion, Laches, Charmides* (vol.1); *Lysis, Hippias Major; Protagoras* (vol.2), and an afterword to volume 1, 'O pervom otdele platonovykh tvorenii'.
74 Quoted from a lecture read at the *Vysshie Zhenskie Kursy* in March 1881. See *V.S. Solov'ev. Sochineniia v dvukh tomakh* (Moscow: Pravda, 1989), p.34.
75 *Sobranie Sochinenii Vladimira Sergeevicha Solov'eva: Pis'ma*, vol.3 (Brussels: Zhizn' s Bogom, 1970), p.34.
76 *Tvorenie Platona, perevod c grecheskogo Vl. Solov'eva. Predislovie*. Cited in *Sobranie Sochinenii Vladimia Sergeevicha Solov'eva*, vol.12 (Brussels, 1970), p. 360 (henceforth *SS, XII* and page reference). Solov'ev translated four of the dialogues in volume one (*Theages, Alcibiades II, Ion, Charmides*), the other three were translated by his brother, Mikhail Sergeevich.
77 Solov'ev's originality may be illustrated with respect to his criteria for the organization and inclusion of some 'doubtful' dialogues in the first two volumes. Whereas Redkin followed Steinhart and Müller (1850-1873) in grouping as 'Socratic' the dialogues *Ion, Hippias Major, Hippias Minor, Alcibiades I, Lysis, Charmides, Laches, Protagoras*, Solov'ev included 'doubtful' dialogues in this category (*Theages, Alcibiades II*) on the grounds of what he argued to be their 'Socratic world view' (the case of *Alcibiades II*), or because he claimed to find traces of the mature Plato in them (*Theages*). But, somewhat strangely perhaps, Solov'ev also included certain other dialogues in his edition (a case in point in volume I being *Laches*), even though the nature of historical events hinted at in the text led him to query Plato's reputed authorship.
78 V.S. Solov'ev, 'Iz zametok o dialogakh Platona', *VFP*, 47 (1899), pp.146-159.
79 V.S. Solov'ev, 'Ob avtore dialoga Protagora', *VFP*, 53 (1900), pp.357-380.
80 *Polnoe sobranie tvorenii Platona v 15 tomakh*, vol.1, p.4.
81 Schleiermacher's theory (1817) (adopted by Karpov) was that between the dialogues there is an internal link. Ast (1816) argued that the link between the various dialogues was not the abstract unity of a preconceived plan, but emerged organically from the interrelation of independent individual moments. Karl Hermann (1838) suggested that Plato's philosophy betrayed a variety of influences other than that of Socrates. Eduard Munk (1857) attributed an all-determining importance to Plato's relationship with

Socrates, on the strength of which he defended what he called a 'natural' as opposed to a 'temporal' order of dialogues. George Grote (1865) claimed that Plato's philosophy did not bespeak any one particular worldview. Rather his ideas were a symptom of what he called 'no personal Plato, no common characteristic'. Finally, Solov'ev mentioned the novel proposal put forward by Gustav Teichmüller (1876). The latter argued that Plato should be seen less an abstract theoretician as a 'philosopher-*publitsist*', meaning that the dialogues should best be read as a commentary on contemporary moral and social issues.

82 V.S. Solov'ev, 'Zhizn' i proizvedeniia Platona. Predvaritel'nii ocherk', *Tvorenie Platona...*, vol.1, p.18.

83 Cited and translated from the French edition *Le drame de la vie de Platon* in *Vladimir Soloviev. Le Sens de l'Amour*, trans. B. Marchadier, intro. F. Rouleau (Sagesse chrétienne, Paris, 1985), p.108.

84 In light of this, Solov'ev organized the dialogues in the following way: Volume I contained the 'Socratic' dialogues: *Ion, Alcibiades I, Alcibiades II, Lysis, Charmides, Laches, Theages*; volume II, 'The Socratic battle', contained dialogues pertaining to the 'Socratic cycle' in the broad sense, namely, those in which Socrates' struggle with the Sophists is depicted (*Hippias Major, Hippias Minor, Protagoras, Apology, Crito, Euthyphron, Euthydemus*). The remaining projected volumes were to be organized as follows: III – 'The Principles of Platonism': *Gorgias, Meno, Phaedo;* IV – 'Relinquished Tasks' (*Otreshennye Zadachi*) containing important dialogues – *Cratylus, Theaetetus, Sophist, Politicus, Parmenides* – even if their authenticity was disputed; V – 'Eros', a volume which was to comprise just two dialogues, *Phaedrus, Symposium*, but which, for Solov'ev, marked an all-important turning point in Plato's philosophy; VI – 'Positive Idealism': *Philebus, Republic, Timaeus, Critias;* VII – 'The downfall of idealism', a final volume dedicated to *Laws*. See 'Preface', pp.V-XII.

85 *SS, XII*, pp.386-387.

86 Ibid., p.389.

87 Ibid., p.390.

88 François Rouleau, however, rightly respects the limits of affinity between the intellectual and personal biographies of the two thinkers: 'Ce qui sera rupture et même reniement dans la vie de Platon sera assumé religieusement par Solov'ev. Dans l'ordre de la spéculation, l'immense refonte du système de pensée trouvera chez Solov'ev une nouvelle cohérence et un équilibre dans ses conceptions apocalyptiques (à condition de bien comprendre l'apocalypse, qui – dans la Bible comme chez Solov'ev – est une rigoureuse récapitulation de toute l'histoire antérieure autant que la dramatique révélation de son terme). Dans l'ordre de la sexualité, chez Solov'ev le tourment (...) aura un terme : une difficile et douloureuse sublimation conduit à un apaisement final.' V. Solov'ev, *Le sens de l'amour*, intro., F. Rouleau (Paris, 1985), pp.12-13.

89 A. F. Losev, *Vladimir Solov'ev i ego vremiia* (Progress, Moscow, 1990), p.90, 94.

90 On the theme of Eros, Solov'ev distinguished five paths of love, from the lowest negative paths (of hell and physical attraction) moving up through what is essentially the human, positive experience of eros (marriage, procreation, as well as the path of asceticism), culminating in the supreme path of love, which is both the sign of rebirth, and of the divine. This in part echoes comments Solov'ev had made in *Smysl Liubvy* (1892-1894).

91 *Le Drame* ..., p.161.

Chapter 2

Plato and Russian Idealism: The Platonic Impulse in the Construction of a Philosophical Tradition

The degree to which Russian nineteenth-century idealist philosophy was imbued with the spirit of Platonism may be suggested by tracing the genealogy of a cluster of interrelated notions derived from the leitmotif of 'integral knowledge' (*tsel'noe znanie*). Obviously, though, much depends on what is meant by the term 'Platonism' itself. If it is a question of the strict 'letter', then one need not look very far to see that the philosophical concerns of the Wisdom Lovers, or the early Slavophiles in the 1820s and 1830s were quite remote from the doctrine of ideas, and the dialectic – those salient features of Platonic philosophy, which Schleiermacher, for one, had identified. If, however, one means by Platonism the underlying spirit of Plato's philosophy, his quest for knowledge of truth and the good, and 'the wondrous vision of beauty itself', it becomes, on the contrary, tempting to seek a Platonic impulse in the philosophical and religious ideals which dominated early nineteenth-century Russian thought. Yet, once again, a note of caution is in order, since it is unlikely that Plato himself was actually the direct source of inspiration. Neither the Slavophile theory of integrality, in which they 'anchored' their own quest of true knowledge, nor, indeed, their elaboration of associated notions – 'living knowledge', 'believing reason' (an expression originally derived from Jacobi) – owed anything, consciously at least, to the Platonic doctrine of ideas, even as the latter itself is said to have required an attitude of 'something approaching religious faith, or mystical experience'.[1] More often than not, knowledge of Plato was prompted, and ultimately governed by the transformations that his thought had undergone in its long course of successive revivals. In other words, in a culture intent on promoting itself as the guardian of true Christianity, Plato was obliged to play second fiddle to his spiritual and intellectual progeny – early Christian and Byzantine thinkers.[2] Still, for all these notes of caution sounded above, there are grounds, which I shall explore in more detail below, to suggest that these leading motifs of Russian idealism were 'Platonically disposed' after all. Their authors' silence with respect to the distant source of inspiration is sometimes cause for suspicion, not least because they spent considerable energies in denouncing quite vociferously Plato's 'miscreant' successor and rival – Aristotle.

In the wake of the Great Reforms, this situation altered quite dramatically. The predilection for a Christian Platonism, and silent tribute to Plato himself which characterized the spirit of Russian idealism in the first half of the nineteenth century, was gradually offset by historical-philosophical reconstructions of idealism, which paid Plato perhaps even more than his due. Plato, the 'Father of the Idealists',[3] was openly cited as a model for the future course of idealism, such as some Russian thinkers hoped it might develop on home ground. This belief was not infrequently bolstered by arguments to the effect that, in Germany, idealism had reached an impasse: following Hegel, the only options for the future development of philosophy were positivism, materialism, or worse, scepticism.[4] Of course, sentiments of this kind were first and foremost to be found in programmatic statements made by *publitsisty*, or in public speeches. In the polemical context of the *Landmarks* debate (1909), for example, Nikolai Berdiaev argued that Russian philosophy had a distinctive strain, which harked back to the classics of Greek and German thought, and out of which a new, 'Russian' philosophical tradition had begun to grow: 'In it, the spirit of Plato and the spirit of classical German idealism are still alive.' That said, however, Berdiaev was quick to point out that German idealism, particularly in the abstract and rationalistic form it had taken in Hegel's philosophy, failed to answer the needs of Russian thinkers in their quest for a mystical complement (*vospolnenie*) to the accent placed on reason (*razum*) in European philosophy, 'the consequence of which has been to lose sight of living being'. Berdiaev summed up his position as follows:

> I think that concrete idealism, in connection with a realistic attitude to being, may serve as the foundation of our national philosophical creativity. It may provide the conditions for a national tradition in which we are so sorely wanting.[5]

Programmatic statements of this kind were not exclusively the stuff of essayistic reflections. University professors, too, occasionally gave vent to what we might call a 'philosophical patriotism' in works ostensibly intended for teaching purposes. Somewhat outlandishly, Pavel Florenskii compared Plato's philosophy to 'a fragrant rose, growing in the dark earth: it is the shining bright daughter of black chaos'.[6] Professor of Philosophy, Nikolai Grot, at Moscow University concluded an otherwise objective textbook presentation of the main lines of Plato's thought by taking an unambiguous stand on the matter:

> His theory of the eternal and the all-abiding (*predvechnoe*), of the spirit, which is neither born nor dies, but rather falls into slumber then awakens; his theory of oblivion and remembrance – all this should find an appropriate evaluation in idealism to come, and especially in Russian philosophy, which is so alien to the prejudices of West European philosophy, prejudices, which, over the centuries, have both shaped and hindered the further development of idealism.[7]

A decade later, Nikolai Losskii reiterated similar hopes for the future of Russian philosophy in his doctoral dissertation:

> Until now, Russia has not known its own independent history of philosophy. It has never had a successive growth of philosophical systems, as was the case in ancient Greece or in Germany. We hope that mystical idealism (i.e. in the Platonic sense of the word 'idealism'), which already counts quite a number of representatives in Russia, will show itself capable of assuring such an organic growth and development.[8]

Running through statements of this kind was a concern to assert the identity of idealism in Russia in respect of the relation to be established between ancient Greek and modern German variants of idealism. Just how Russian thinkers endeavoured to determine this relation, and what they drew from it in terms of a reflection upon the course of Russian philosophy will be discussed in more detail presently with respect to a choice of authors. Suffice it to mention here that the various endeavours by successive generations of Russian thinkers to determine the relation between ancient and modern variants of idealism, and, in the process, arrive at a definition of Russian idealism, took principally two forms: first, in the guise of historical-philosophical narratives, and second, in more systematic, theoretical accounts. In neither case, however, was it just a matter of a purely historical, or an entirely systematic reconstruction of past philosophy. It was equally as much a concern to reintegrate past philosophy into modern-day categories, thereby making for a curious, yet enriching cohabitation of the contemporary with the non-contemporary. In this vein, Professor Zhakov singled out Kant and Hegel as the two thinkers whose ideas were the most comparable with Plato. With his worldly dialectics, Hegel had managed to set in motion Plato's realm of ideas, while Kant owed his 'transcendental prototype' and the transcendent idea to the example of Plato.[9] This cohabitation of the past and present is naturally more evident in texts which explored the possibilities of juxtapositioning selected aspects (idea, ethics, notably) in the philosophy of Plato and a latter-day successor. No longer the stuff of history, Plato was treated as a living contemporary, as an active partner in discussion. In this regard it is striking that Russian commentators should have privileged Kant as Plato's main interlocutor across time. Setting off Plato against Kant in the name of a religiously inspired philosophy was the task that a number of nineteenth and early twentieth-century Russian thinkers set themselves. Vladimir Karpov, Pamfil Iurkevich, Pavel Florenskii, Solov'ev, Vladimir Ern were among those who brought the two thinkers together, albeit to draw from the confrontation quite different conclusions. Their attitudes towards Kant ranged from outright hostility (the case of Karpov, Florenskii and Vladimir Ern) to more mitigated ones (Iurkevich, Solov'ev, as well as S.N. Trubetskoi). Correspondingly, while those hostile to Kant tended to accentuate the differences between the two philosophers, others, with less pronounced likes and dislikes, were inclined to seek points of overlap bringing Plato and Kant closer together. But, whatever the attitude, it was a matter of a reconstruction, in which Plato was no longer an author of a past philosophy, but a contemporary providing viable solutions to actual philosophical problems.

From 'Integral Knowledge' to the 'Ideal Real': The Slavophiles and their Successors

The notion of integral knowledge (*tsel'noe znanie*), most often associated with Ivan Kireevskii (1806–1856),[10] was developed by bridging two sources of philosophical inspiration: the *Naturphilosophie* of Schelling and Greek patristics. While the young Kireevskii had seen in Schelling a means to combat the rationalism of the French encyclopedists, which had predominated in late eighteenth-century Russia,[11] his discovery, in the 1830s, of the writings of the Church Fathers led him to re-qualify this initial wave of enthusiasm for contemporary German idealism. In Basil the Great, Gregory of Nyssa (also John Chrysostom), Kireevskii believed he had found Schelling's precursors, a discovery which in turn persuaded him that a new wisdom (philo-sophia or *liubomudrie*) could be drawn from Russian life and her religious tradition. In the Church Fathers, Kireevskii encountered a theory of knowledge grounded in the Biblical conception of man as body, soul and mind/spirit. Authentic knowledge accounts for all the dimensions that make up human existence – the material, the intellectual and the spiritual, or divine. Inspired by this he went on to develop a theory of 'integral knowledge' which was to become instrumental in his ultimate disavowal of rationalism.

For Kireevskii, the rationalism endemic to West European philosophy had resulted in the one-sided development of man's cognitive faculties. On the contrary, true, integral knowledge, which consisted in surmounting reason, managed to safeguard the harmonious unity of the spirit. As Kireevskii understood it, knowledge betokened the progressive realization by the person of his 'integrity' (*tsel'nost'*), his essence (*sushchnost'*). Freed from the limitations imposed by intellect alone, integral knowledge connoted the inseparability of knowledge and life. Indeed, for Kireevskii, there was finally no major distinction between knowledge (*znanie*) and 'conscious awareness' (*soznanie*). Knowledge not only merged with his idea of the conscious life, it became synonymous with the life of the spirit. In other words, to insist on man's inner integrality was to restore his spiritual values, and to recall the reality of his freedom and his intelligence.

Clearly, the Slavophile theory of knowledge and philosophy of man were run through with a deeply moral reflection, one consequence of which, at a more formal level, was to blur distinctions between the various branches within philosophy as a discipline more strictly speaking, such as it was taught – if only nominally – in the university.[12] Arguably, this was deliberate. The integral whole permitted a harmonious fusion of all the spheres of epistemology, ethics and social philosophy, precisely those domains which the Slavophiles felt had been wrenched apart in contemporary Western philosophy, and, by the same token, separated from the whole.

In roughly the same period, and apparently without knowledge of his Slavophile contemporaries, Professor Vladimir Karpov, in the St. Petersburg Theological Academy, developed a theory of what he called 'philosophical synthetism'.[13] Just as for man, there are three paths into the world – sensations which exhibit sensible reality, ideas linking us with the metaphysical sphere of being, and spiritual contemplation bringing us into contact with the divine – so too, he argued, the world should be broken down into three tiers of the sensible, the metaphysical and Absolute being. With the harmonious fusion of these three principles in man's soul, 'everything is built into one infinite cosmos, and with one accord the song of the Almighty resounds'.[14] But, beyond the similarities with his Slavophile contemporaries, the spirit – indeed, the phrasing – of Karpov's appeal to the true and the good suggest his indebtedness to the example of Plato. In his *Introduction to Philosophy*, he wrote:

> All our knowledge is grounded in the idea of the true and the good. (...) And the idea of the unconditional true and the good, this 'image of the infinite and the eternal in our soul', is understood inseparably from the idea of its object, the supreme Essence, which leaves its imprint of the eternal truth and the eternal good on its creation – man and the world. This not only has a moral significance (as the rationalists held), but also a theoretical one. It is not only subjective, it is objective as well.[15]

In this tribute to the ancient Greek vision of the cosmos, and indeed, to some of the key motifs of Platonism (the image of the infinite and the eternal in our soul, the idea of the true and the good), Karpov was not simply citing his philosophical affinities. He used this and other occasions quite purposefully to mark his differences with the trends of contemporary German philosophy, which, to his mind, had committed the cardinal error of separating the theoretical and practical dimensions of philosophy. Precisely this separation highlighted what Karpov believed was a fundamental incompatibility between German rationalism and Russian Orthodoxy. Without the guidance of religion, and more specifically, that of Christianity, he contended, philosophy introduces 'folly into science and a moral infection into society'. For Karpov, there could be little room for doubt that it was the philosophy of Kant which was ultimately responsible for this folly. Indeed, he accused Kant of ignoring the fact that:

> not only the mind in all its forms, but also the whole person is nothing other than a synthesis of the Omniscient Creator. Consequently, he forgot that the answer to the question [concerning the nature of human knowledge] must be sought not in mental activity, but in accordance with the conditions of man's being which are dictated by faith, and which, in light of faith only, provide the basis for solving philosophical questions.[16]

In a long article dating from 1860, Karpov once again took issue with Kant, this time endeavouring to demolish, point by point, the main lines of his philosophy. Appealing to the worldview of the ancient Greeks, on to which he grafted his own Christian values, Karpov claimed that the hollowness of Kant's theory of moral law begged to be filled with the divine law, that law, as he put it, 'which leaves its indelible imprint on the heart, urging man to act for the sake of God's will'. But, he cautioned, even the pagan thinkers had understood that morality implies deeds, and cannot remain an empty formula.[17] Karpov's underlying point here was that, by separating the domains of theoretical and practical philosophy, modern German (meaning Kantian) philosophy had betrayed the Socratic and Platonic example. Rallying to his chosen authorities, Karpov took up the Platonic idea of knowledge as virtue, opposing it – if not always explicitly, then certainly transparently – to Kant:

> The point of knowledge is not the theoretical development of the mind, but to guide the combined forces of the soul – mind, feeling and the will – in a harmonious way towards the 'supreme aim', the divine, that which finds its reflection in the human being, and which manifests itself in truly good deeds, or virtue.[18]

As a young man, Vladimir Solov'ev also took issue (managing to avoid some of the pathos of Karpov's remarks) with recent Western philosophical practice. At that time, his views were profoundly marked by his attachment to Slavophilism. For Solov'ev, the autonomy of 'theoretical philosophy' (what he called 'abstract knowledge') and the autonomy of ethics ('abstract moralism') should be seen as signs of having fallen away from integral wholeness, the consequence of which was conflict, disunity and chaos. The task of philosophy, therefore, was one of reintegration. At issue was the need to recover the spiritual unity, which, to his mind, Western thought had squandered in its quest for 'abstract principles' and by dint of having driven apart the theoretical and ethical dimensions of philosophy. Moreover, like the Slavophiles and Karpov, Solov'ev held the view that knowledge is rooted in faith. Indeed, more generally, this fideistic perception of the world was to serve as an important resource in attempts to resolve the tangled problem left by transcendental idealism, namely, the problem of affirming the existence of the external world, the 'other', and hence, that of reflecting about the nature of the relation between subject and object.

Solov'ev's metaphysics of All-Unity was clearly indebted to the original Slavophile concept of integrality. He contended that the human being belongs to the integral wholeness, and can become aware of its reality from within by a kind of innate immediate perception (intuition or faith).[19] In Solov'ev's words, the goal of integral knowledge is:

> man's inner integration with true being, and whose material are the facts of human experience in all its forms – above all mystical experience, followed by inner or psychic experience, and, finally, external or physical experience. Its basic form is intellectual insight or the intuitive perception of ideas, systematized with the help of purely logical or abstract thought; its active source, or causative principle, is inspiration, that is, the influence of higher ideals upon the human spirit.[20]

Running through this Slavophile-Solov'evian 'anti-epistemology' was a religiously inspired world outlook – a 'unity in multiplicity' – in the spirit of which Solov'ev spoke variously of 'World Soul', or 'Sophia' as a living force, mediating between God and the world. Undoubtedly, the meaning that Solov'ev attached to Christianity was a highly personal one, and as Andrzej Walicki suggests, the immediate source of the notions he employed may be pinpointed to Leibniz and Schelling. That said, however, Solov'ev's elaboration of his worldview was arguably just as much a distant echo of the ancient (Greek and Gnostic) cosmological idea, according to which plurality was regarded both as a falling away from unity and also the cause for returning to unity in God or the Absolute (being, oneness, the good).[21] In addition to Walicki's observation, we might say that Solov'ev's account of the 'World Soul' was also an implicit reaffirmation of the importance of Plato's thought as a source of inspiration in the writings of Plotinus and the Church Fathers, to whom both he, as well as the Slavophiles and the 'Academy' philosophers Karpov and Iurkevich before him, had openly appealed in defence of religious philosophy. Thus, while relatively few explicit references were made to Plato himself on this particular issue, there was arguably little need to do so, since the authorities that Solov'ev and others more readily acknowledged was evidence enough of a type of thinking that could be described as 'Platonically disposed'. Only much later, in the 1890s, did Solov'ev himself, finally define the World Soul explicitly in terms of its Platonic colouring.[22]

For the generations following the initial wave of Slavophilism, in the 1830s and 1840s, the central motifs of integrality, integral knowledge, personhood, freedom and unity found their place in continuously renewed attempts to speak about immediate knowledge of the real and the metaphysical foundations on which knowledge is built. But, unlike the Slavophiles who made relatively little direct reference to Plato himself, preferring instead to draw on the tradition he inspired, this later generation of philosophers – including Solov'ev, especially in his writings dating from the 1890s – more readily combined references to those authors said to subscribe to the Platonic tradition (Plotinus notably) with a closer reading of the original dialogues themselves (in particular Plato's cosmology as set out in the *Timaeus*). In short, it would seem that the growth of Plato scholarship towards the end of the nineteenth century in Russia, and throughout Europe, had left its mark on philosophical research. As a result, Plato became more frequently acknowledged as a direct source of inspiration – although not to the point where he might be said to have eclipsed his successors. Quite the contrary: in elaborating their theories of 'organic wholeness' (most often associated with Semën Frank and Nikolai Losskii), Russian thinkers repeatedly coupled references to the Platonic 'World Soul' with references to its various historical permutations (*akeraiotes*, Christian totality, *Alleinheit*, *Ganzheit*).[23]

Plato, the 'Father of Idealism'

If it was the case that, with respect to theories of integrality, references to Plato continued to be as indirect as they were direct, this is arguably less so when it came to more comprehensive overviews of idealism. The view of Platonic idealism as being thoroughly imbued with a sense of the real made its author, for many latter-day commentators, a proponent of 'extreme or radical realism'. This interpretation, moreover, served a number of Russian historians of philosophy – Solov'ev, Radlov, Kozlov, among them – in their attempts to counteract more recent developments in philosophical idealism, as well as to identify 'national' traits within Russian philosophical culture itself. Kozlov, proponent of 'pan-spiritualism', discussed at some length the question of which term – idealism or realism – was finally best suited to define the philosophy of Plato, and came out strongly in favour of realism. But he went on to qualify this by adding that, insofar as Plato did not identify the real with matter he might also legitimately be called the 'forefather of philosophical spiritualism'. As he phrased it:

> Plato's philosophy is, first of all, *naive realism*, given his account about the correspondence of knowledge and being. Second, it is *rationalism*, because of the importance Plato gives to reason, and its activity, thought. Third, it is

apriorism, given that the cognitive subject constructs knowledge through its own efforts. Fourth, it is *pluralism,* because the real is conceived as a multiplicity. Fifth, it is *spiritualism,* because the real is neither spatial nor material, and, sixth, it is *aesthetic eudemonism,* because the ultimate aim (...) is full possession of beauty, truth and harmony.[24]

In a short article written for the Brokgaus and Efron encyclopaedia, Solov'ev summarized the main stages in the development of idealist philosophy. To begin with, he wrote, there was Platonic or a dualistic type of idealism grounded in a radical opposition between two spheres of being – the world of contemplated ideas, of eternal and true essences, and the world of sensible phenomena, of the transient or elusive. This second, phenomenal realm has neither inner force nor quality. But that said, it does possess a basis which is independent of the world of ideas, namely matter, understood as something between being and non-being. Solov'ev saw in this a 'residue of realism'.[25] Once set against his account of modern idealism, where, on the whole, Solov'ev was far more critical, this particular observation becomes rather significant. Neither Hegel nor his predecessors within the framework of transcendental idealism, he claimed, had managed to satisfy what he called a 'deeply rooted concern about the reality of the external world and our knowledge of the world':

> For Kant, the world not only exists, it possesses a fullness of content, but one which necessarily remains unknown (...). With Fichte, reality is transformed into an unconscious frontier, which impels the transcendental subject, or the 'I' to create its own, fully ideal world. With Schelling this 'external barrier' is swallowed up in the dark *Urgrund (Ungrund)* within the creative substance itself, understood as neither subject nor object as such, rather it is the identity of both. Finally, Hegel abolished the last remnants of external reality (and anything to do with the universal process) for the sake of, and in defence of, the unconditioned immanent dialectical self-revelation of the absolute idea.[26]

Still, for Solov'ev, the Hegelian solution failed to account for what he called the 'truths of human existence and of life in the world'. To achieve this was, to his mind, precisely the best vindication of idealism. It was imperative, he believed, 'to confront the effective, practical realization of the absolute idea (...).'[27] In much the same spirit Solov'ev had objected to the Hegelian absolute in his doctoral dissertation, *Critique of Abstract Principles* (1880). It is a negative principle, derived from a process of renunciation (thesis to antithesis):

> Such a negative all-unity (...) cannot be the principle of truth. All-unity may be such a principle only in a positive sense, not as that which is contained in everything, but rather as that, which contains everything within it (...). The all-unity, as the real form of truth, cannot exist uniquely for and in itself (*sama po sebe*), because form without content is unthinkable (...) The all-unity presupposes the unconditional reality of that of which it is the form,

namely the all-unified. Therefore, it should be defined not as 'true thought', but as 'true-being'.[28]

It should be said, however, that, Solov'ev's preoccupation with concrete human reality not only marked a reaction to Hegelianism. It, admittedly, also distanced him from the Platonic concept of the *eidos* which excludes all individuality, a point of difference which would become all the more acute once Solov'ev (and others) tackled Plato's 'social philosophy'.[29]

Both in the nineteenth century and in the Soviet period, it was usual to label Plato's philosophy as 'Greek', or 'objective' idealism, the latter term chosen with respect to Plato's account of the objective, autonomous existence of ideas. Writing in the Soviet period, Aleksei Losev nuanced this traditional view by labelling Platonic idealism 'ancient objective idealism'. In doing so, he wanted to highlight the fact that Plato's idealism admits of the independent existence of matter. According to Losev, Plato was a typical Greek whose mental portrait of the cosmos and the gods always had a tactile, tangible, or solid quality to it.[30] By presenting Plato in this way, Losev was arguably cleaving to, reinforcing even, the interpretation that had inspired Solov'ev to speak about a 'residue of realism'. More generally, Losev's remarks about Plato coincided with a view held by some of the leading pre-Revolutionary philosophers about the 'Russian philosophical tradition' which they had endeavoured to build. Writing in emigration, Nikolai Losskii identified this in terms of a preoccupation with the knowable real. 'A keen sense of reality', he wrote, 'as opposed to regarding the contents of external perception as mental or subjective, seems to be a characteristic feature of Russian philosophy.'[31]

Endeavours to find a solution to what was generally acknowledged as a crisis in philosophy after the collapse of Absolute Idealism, and which Solov'ev had singled out for criticism in his brief account of described above, underscored quite a number of nineteenth-century 'histories of philosophy'. Below, I shall illustrate this point with reference to two authors, Ivan Kireevskii and Sergei Trubetskoi. For both thinkers, Platonic thought exercised an obvious appeal, but whereas Trubetskoi, in texts dating from the 1890s, openly endorsed this, indeed built it into his own theory of 'concrete idealism', Kireevskii, writing in the 1850s made no explicit reference to Plato whatsoever, even as his rather reductionist account of the history of European philosophy relied quite blatantly on a view of the dichotomous spiritual and philosophical heritage of Plato's and Aristotle's thought.

'On the Necessity and Possibility of New Principles in Philosophy' (Ivan Kireevskii)

For Kireevskii, it was essential to close the gap between the profane and religion, which, to his mind, the Renaissance and the Reformation had originally caused, and which Descartes and Kant had widened. In an unfinished text entitled 'On the necessity and possibility of new principles in philosophy' (1856), he sought a solution to this problem from a historical-philosophical perspective. The target of his criticism was not so much rationalism *per se*, as the form it had taken in Western philosophy:

> The concept of reason, such as it has been elaborated in the most recent philosophy and finds its expression in the Schellingian-Hegelian system, would in no way oppose the concept of reason which we find in the writings of the Church Fathers, if it weren't for the fact that this concept has since been vested with the supreme power of knowledge. The consequence of this false claim (...) is to reduce the reach of truth to the domain of rational and abstract knowledge.[32]

This observation, together with remarks concerning the division between philosophy and religion, underscored the main thrust of Kireevskii's outright condemnation of all Western philosophical culture as little more than the unilateral development of logical reason. The main consequence of this, he added, was the moral destruction of the person and of society.

Kireevskii traced the history of Western thought as a direct line leading from Aristotle down to Hegel, passing through the doctrine of the Roman Catholic Church, scholasticism and the Reformation along the way. This simplified development allowed him to exaggerate parallels between the originator of Western thought, Aristotle, and its modern-day champion, Hegel:

> The mind of Western man seems to have a particular affinity with Aristotle. From its very beginnings, West European intellectual culture (*obrazovannost'*) has been sympathetic to his thought. (...) True, Hegel took another path, independent of Aristotle's system, yet his final conclusions, together with his basic position regarding the relation of reason (*um*) to truth, brought him close to Aristotle. Hegel may have constructed another system, but he did it in such a way that Aristotle would have done so himself, had he lived in our times (...). The voice of the modern world resounds with an echo of the world of the past.[33]

In short, Kireevskii accused Aristotle of being the root cause of the pre-eminence of rationalism in West European philosophy, and, ultimately, of the split between religion and philosophy. His system corrupted all of western life by inverting the order of values; it 'split up the integrality of spiritual consciousness, and transferred the source of man's most intimate convictions away from the aesthetic and moral, to the abstract consciousness of "rationalizing reason".'[34] Undermining all tenets other than those of rational logic, Aristotle's philosophy destroyed any drive capable of raising man above his personal interests. The moral spirit collapsed. All the mainsprings of inner authenticity (*samobytnost'*) weakened. This, in turn, left its traces on the subsequent development of philosophy in its relation to religion. As ratiocination (*rassudochnost'*), philosophy reached its fullest, independent development with the rise of Protestantism, a stage marking the passage from the narrow concept of *Verstand* (*ratio*/judgement, *rassudok*) to the more englobing notion of *Vernunft* (intelligence, mind/spirit, *intellectus*, *razum*). For Kireevskii, these two expressions of reason corresponded to the underlying character of the Roman and Protestant Churches respectively, though in its most recent development, namely in the philosophies of Schelling and Hegel, *razum* had come to 'draw its knowledge (...) not from abstract concepts, but from the very root of self-consciousness, where being and thought are conjoined in absolute identity (*bezuslovnoe tozhestvo*)'.[35]

Although abstract idealism had found its most complete expression in Hegel, it was Schelling, rather than Hegel, that Kireevskii selected in this text as marking the real end point of modern German philosophy. His choice to do so was in part motivated by Schelling's own criticism of Hegel, which Kireevskii obviously shared, but also by an evident sympathy for the later Schelling's, albeit vain, attempts to find a solution to philosophical problems in religion. Kireevskii fully agreed with Schelling in his assessment of Hegel's philosophy as 'thought incapable of attaining the real', and that, by contrast, 'authentic rationality, far from being reduced to a logical mechanism, ought to integrate all the wealth of the real.' By not doing so Hegelian philosophy remained one-sided.[36] But, at the same time, Kireevskii was aware of the problems that Schelling himself had created and left unresolved. While he had demonstrated the implausibility of rationalism, he nevertheless failed in his attempt to construct a new system. Convinced by the necessity of divine revelation preserved in tradition, Schelling had grasped the need for living faith as supreme reason (*razumnost'*), and thereby came to address the question of man's relation to God. But Schelling's tragedy, as Kireevskii saw it, was that he failed to measure fully the value of his findings in the Church Fathers, even as he had already wisely rejected both Protestantism and Roman Catholicism for want of an adequate solution to his quest:

> In the Holy Fathers Schelling sought expressions of theological dogma, but did not appreciate their speculative conceptions of reason, nor the laws of supreme cognition (*poznavanie*). And so, lacking the inner character of 'believing thought', the positive side of Schelling's system, which already had relatively little success in Germany, had even less chance in Russia.[37]

As a culture steeped in its own 'wisdom of the believer' (Kireevskii's words), and endowed with a rich tradition of spiritual thought handed down from the Fathers, it was to be expected that Russia would more severe than other nations in her criticism of Schelling. But, on the other hand, as 'a country where a man, after an initial bout of youthful enthusiasm for an foreign system, has the chance to return to the fold of a more fundamental rationality (*sushchestvennaia razumnost'*) (...), one which is in full accord with his (his country's) historical specificity,' Russia might, in the end, be more sympathetic to the problems Schelling had confronted, even though he proved to be unequal to the task he had set himself.[38] Kireevskii concluded, somewhat surprisingly, that German philosophy, such as it had developed in the late system of Schelling, might, after all, be a fruitful starting point in Russia, if only to serve as a useful catalyst in an independent quest for the integral consciousness of believing reason. By 'believing reason' Kireevskii meant thought related to 'life in faith', and which lays bare the inner experience of that life. It is not a function of detached cognition, but rather, as we saw earlier, the intelligent discovery of the integral person, bringing together the entire range of man's faculties – the cognitive, aesthetic and the volitional.[39]

Kireevskii's highly reductionist account of the history of philosophy is as interesting for what was left unsaid, as for what was actually said. One obvious lacuna is his silence with respect to Plato. This silence was not due to ignorance of the Platonic dialogues. Kireevskii, who had studied under Schleiermacher in Berlin for a semester in (1830–31), certainly knew his, as well as Victor Cousin's translations. Indeed, in a letter dated 3/15 March 1831, he openly praised the theologian and philosopher highly, saying that he could 'in no way be classed among superficial thinkers, not least because of his remarkable translation of Plato, the best that exists, along with Cousin's (...)'.[40] By not including Plato in the Western European philosophical tradition, he was arguably protecting him for the sake of the Byzantine and patristic tradition that he inspired, and in which the Slavophiles saw their spiritual heritage.

Kireevskii had made this point more explicitly in an article written four years earlier. By virtue of having taken her religion from Byzantium, Russia, he claimed, was the true successor of Greek Antiquity. Moreover, Greek thinkers themselves, he suggested, had shown a marked preference for Plato over Aristotle because:

> Plato's method of thought is one of greater wholeness in terms of the movement of the mind; there is more warmth and harmony in the speculative activity of reason. The relationship that existed between the two ancient philosophers repeated itself in the rift that later occurred between the philosophy of the Latin world (in scholasticism) and that spiritual philosophy which we find in writers of the Eastern Church, and which is especially evident in the Holy Fathers, writing after the fall of Rome.[41]

It is tempting to say that, for Kireevskii, there was seemingly little need to turn to Plato himself, because his thought was already present, deeply embedded (albeit transformed) in the religious philosophy of the Church Fathers. Inspired by Plato, the Church Fathers had gone further in considering that the path to true knowledge requires a 'conversion', or a progressive 'purification' such as this is taught in the Bible. In much the same spirit, Kireevskii argued that knowledge of the divine truth requires that we rid ourselves of all the accoutrements of a one-sided, over-intellectualized culture. Knowledge of the divine truth is the fruit of authentic philosophy. As he put it:

> Divine truth is not embraced by the grasp of ordinary reason, but demands higher, spiritual knowledge, which is acquired not by means of external scholarship, but by the interior integrity of being. That's why man seeks true, divine thought where he thinks to encounter pure integral life, imparting the integrity of reason. He does not seek it in what is to be had from a school-bookish education.[42]

'Concrete Idealism' (Sergei Trubetskoi)

> In its protest against the 'dialectic of reason' the philosophy of Kireevskii wishes, in the first place, to be 'concrete'. To this end, it seeks a reconciliation of all man's forces, in other words, a recovery of the person who, alone, is capable of communicating with reality in its totality.[43]

François Rouleau's comment might just as equally apply to Trubetskoi, for whom the notion of the 'concrete' was central. Indeed, not unlike Kireevskii, Trubetskoi criticized the Western European philosophical tradition from this perspective, though rarely was his 'protest' as virulent as Kireevskii's, especially in the latter's mature writings.

In his major, most personal piece of research, *The Foundations of Idealism* (1896), Trubetskoi constructed a theory of what he called 'concrete idealism'. Using a historical-philosophical framework, he designated the term both a corrective to recent predecessors (Kant and Hegel notably) within Idealism, but also as a statement of his own, personal adherence to the tradition as such. At issue for Trubetskoi was the status of reason as a source of knowledge. While he admitted of the universal laws of reason, according to which we establish links within the world of phenomena, he wanted to modify this essentially Kantian position by arguing that will, sense perception, and faith as well, are equally sources of knowledge, each with different, yet complementary functions. Knowledge, he argued, is the fruit of empirical experience conditioned by the *a priori* laws of our perception. Reason establishes the lawful (*zakonomernaia*) connection between phenomena. But faith also has a role to play in this, precisely as that moment which allows us to affirm the reality of the entities and beings (*sushchestva*) that we think of and apprehend.[44]

One striking feature of Trubetskoi's argument is the way he blended philosophical and non-philosophical terminology. While, on the one hand, the philosophical vocabulary took its cue from the language of transcendental and absolute idealism, on the other, the non-philosophical – words such as 'conviction', 'acknowledgement', 'belief' – were presumably included because their power of conviction appealed to hope, if not common sense. With this in mind we may recapitulate Trubetskoi's claims. If nothing other than concepts and ideas (*Vorstellung, prestavlenie*) existed, he contended, then our definition of the real (*sushchee*) as that which is thought and appears would be an exhaustive one. But, 'in as far as we *acknowledge* (*priznaem*) that there exists something which is irreducible to our thought and perception, namely an aggregate of real entities (*sushchestva*) outside us', then to define the *sushchee* as an idea or representation, or as the simple object of thought and senses is no longer adequate:

> Real beings outside us are not 'things in themselves'. They appear to us, are thought by us. And at the same time we *believe* (*verim*) that they exist in and of themselves, independently of our thought or senses.

Posing the intractable problem about human knowledge of the external world, Trubetskoi begs that we admit of faith:

> Recognition (*priznanie*) of the reality of external phenomena and especially of independent self-determining (*samobytnykh*) living beings (...) – acceptance or recognition of such a reality does not find a requisite logical grounding in our sense perceptions alone, nor in our abstract thought. It is an act of faith, the third factor in cognition. The *sushchee*, therefore, is defined not only as an object of the senses and thought, but also as an object of faith (...). Such a concurrence of faith, senses and thought compounds our recognition of real entities, whose existence is independent of us, yet at once interrelated with our own. Put another way, this coincidence of faith, senses and thought affords an awareness of the *sushchee* as a concrete being, as an objectifying 'self-sameness' (*samost'*) within itself.[45]

Besides the positive meaning that Trubetskoi attached to the term 'concrete', there is little doubt that he was also using it to more polemical ends, namely as a means to criticize the idealism of the German classics. In particular, he wanted to demonstrate his differences with the 'abstract idealism' of Hegel. But, as such, Trubetskoi's challenge consisted in little more than turning some of the leading tenets of Hegelianism, so to speak, upside down. Whereas Hegel started out from his concept of pure being, Trubetskoi began with the concrete real (*sushchee*), meaning reality which pre-exists any thought about it. He rejected outright the identity of thought and being, contending that philosophical enquiry cannot be without presuppositions, as Hegel claimed. Thirdly, as we saw in the foregoing, Trubetskoi defended the place of faith in our knowledge of the world. In short, his aim was to oppose 'panlogism' with a theistic worldview.[46]

Trubetskoi's 'reply' to Hegel, namely that only concrete unity, unity in diversity, explains to us the co-relation of thought to the real, meant, among other things, a reluctance to accept the view that nothing outside thought is conceivable.[47] Moreover, like Kireevskii and Solov'ev, Trubetskoi wanted to safeguard the person (*lichnost'*) which he believed had been annihilated in Hegel's absolute idealism. Cautioning against this he wrote:

> German idealism avers the absoluteness of a universal, supra-individual (...) principle in everything: the absoluteness of abstract logical categories which govern the universe; the absoluteness of unconscious nature, of the generic principle together with the total annihilation of transient individuals (*prekhodiashchie individy*); the absolutism of the state.[48]

For Trubetskoi, the 'concrete' interaction between the I and the non-I, between spirit and nature, subject and object, presupposed a basic unity in their diversity, a universal encompassing of the spirit with its opposite, of thought with the reality of existence.[49] In this sense he stood very much in line with the Slavophiles, whose insistence on the (rather vague) term of 'faith' Trubetskoi seems to have shared. His views also brought him close to the philosophy of reintegration, developed by his immediate contemporary and friend, Solov'ev. In his *Critique of Abstract Principles*, Solov'ev had argued that the 'all-unified real' (*sushchee vseedinoe*) is irreducible to experience or logic alone, and that it grounds our full interrelatedness with the world. Accordingly, true knowledge is grounded in mystical or religious perception, and from this 'our logical thought derives its unconditional quality of reason (*razumnost'*), while our experience is vested with a sense of unconditional reality'.[50]

Irrespective of the authorities that Solov'ev may have been referring to, or arguing with here (in this instance it was, once again, Hegel), the underlying 'pathos' of his words is redolent of a nostalgia for a world harmony once envisaged by the ancients. Much the same might be said of Trubetskoi. In his discussion of the findings in modern German philosophy, he constantly backtracked to the ancients, fluctuating between Platonic cosmological motifs, on one side, and the theories of Kant and Hegel, on the other. Certainly, as a means to tackle the perennial questions about our knowledge of the real, the history of philosophy was for Trubetskoi highly pertinent. His account of the concrete *sushchee* provides just one example of a curious 'recasting' of certain motifs from within the historical development of idealism in light of a world outlook, which paid special tribute to Greek philosophy and religion. His presentation of the 'World Soul' in a text written in the 1890s, but published posthumously, provides another example of an implicit encounter between the ancients and the moderns, a paradoxical echo of ancient Greek cosmology in recent philosophical developments:

> In order to explain the sensible forms of things, a non-material principle is presupposed (a sensed object presupposes a sensing subject); the world is thinkable only if one accepts that, at its basis lies an *objective thought*, or idea, which constitutes both the content and development of the former. This objective thought may be perceived by the world, it may realize itself, become embodied in the sensible forms, only on the presupposition that the world is an 'animated' and 'thinking' (*razumnoe*) living being (*sushchestvo*). It is animated by a single soul, by one subject of sense and thought: *in short, this is Plato's theory of the world soul*, which apprehends ideas and embodies them in nature.[51]

While it would be an overstatement to say that Trubetskoi was simply setting off the Greeks against the Moderns and stating his preferences, one finds instances where it does actually appear to be little more than that. The ancient tradition of a universal principle as the basis both of the world and of human reason, and thereby a precondition of the objectivity of human cognition, clearly served him in his attempt to answer Hegel all the while remaining within the fold of rationalism. Rejecting Hegelian philosophy as a reduction of reality to a logical idea, Trubetskoi turned to Plato, whose theory of ideas or forms with its strain of realism clearly appealed to him. For, by ideas or forms Plato meant – as Trubetskoi understood it – objective essences, an independent, essential reality. Moreover, Plato's 'special' principle of the 'World Soul', as the basis of sensible nature and of finite consciousness, had allowed him to admit of the existence of the real, that which Hegel could not do. For Trubetskoi's own view of the inter-relatedness of the real this was of cardinal importance. As he put it:

> Alongside an ideal principle, both he (Plato) and Aristotle recognized another principle distinct from it. Hegel with his panlogism did not admit of anything 'other', nothing apart from pure thought, and that's why essentially, he was unable to explain the passage from thought to reality, other than by way of an anti-logical contradiction.[52]

In their historical-philosophical reconstructions of idealism, both Kireevskii and Trubetskoi drew on images of Platonic philosophy. Kireevskii, by dint of his silence with respect to Plato, reinforced the 'anti-Western' ('anti-rational') character of 'authentic' Russian philosophizing. Trubetskoi, on the contrary, very explicitly referred to Plato, as it were pitching him against his modern-day, German successors. To Trubetskoi's mind, in the history of philosophy Plato marked an important turning point as the first to have seen in the absolute an eternal and immutable principle. But more than that, he also understood it as the source of universal movement, of creative living forces.[53] Finally, Trubetskoi openly praised Plato before all other philosophers for the nature of his philosophical enquiry, inviting us to recognize, 'the historical rightness of Plato and his victory, not only in the name of one or another philosophical theory, but, in the name of philosophy itself in the Socratic spirit'.⁵⁴ Given the circumstances in which Trubetskoi and his peers were working, this last remark is especially poignant. Referring to the Socratic principle, which Plato inherited, of free enquiry, animated by a faith in the 'reason of truth' was also a distressing reminder of the fact that Russian officialdom had done much to stifle the spirit of free enquiry.

Plato as a 'Contemporary' of Kant

What we might call the 'Platonic strain of Russian idealism' suggests itself in the type of philosophical enquiry that Russian philosophers tended to engage in. It has frequently been noted that, rather than investigating the nature of our cognitive faculties – thereby addressing questions to do with the 'how' and 'what' of knowledge – Russian thinkers and philosophers often anchored their speculations in a set of attitudes about the existence of the world and of man's place in it. As such, their preoccupations arguably brought them closer to the realm of Greek metaphysical thought than to the concerns of critical idealism. This philosophical temperament emerges quite clearly in respect of attempts to confront, whether in order to compare or to contrast, aspects of Plato and Kant's theory of knowledge.

In an article written after the publication of *The Foundations of Idealism*, Sergei Trubetskoi endeavoured to defend his theory of concrete idealism against criticism of 'mysticism'.⁵⁵ Here, in this more programmatic statement, Trubetskoi dropped the historical-philosophical approach which he had used in his book, and momentarily brought Kant and Plato together as two thinkers who not only complemented each other, but also, in view of their complementarity, had, he claimed, inspired his own position. Kant's theory of time and space reinforced Trubetskoi's leading idea concerning the interconnectedness of phenomena, just as it echoed, he believed, the Platonic idea of the cosmic World Soul which brings everything into a related whole. Trubetskoi wrote:

> I regard the world as an animated whole. And one of the decisive proofs in favour of this is, to my mind, Kant's theory of the nature of time and space, precisely because it bespeaks (...) the existence of a universal, world englobing sensibility (*chuvstvennost'*). If the subject of this *chuvstvennost'* can be neither an individual being nor Absolute being, then we are obliged to admit that its subject may only be a psycho-physical being, as universal as time and space, and which, like time and space, is not vested with the attributes of Absolute being. In other words, we are dealing here with Cosmic being (*sushchestvo*), or the world in its psychical grounding – that which Plato once called World Soul.⁵⁶

Trubetskoi was far from being alone in bringing Plato and Kant together in a non-historical context. Other Russian intellectuals, writing before and after him, also privileged the two philosophers as interlocutors across time. Yet, just why this should have been the case may be due to a double set of factors, the first of which is related to the peculiarities of Russian cultural and institutional history, while the second falls into the province of the history of ideas and philosophy, more properly speaking.

Kant and Plato in the Theological Academy

As the guardian of philosophical idealism – both ancient and modern – the role played by the theological academy throughout the nineteenth century was a highly important one. Compared to the university, instruction in philosophy here was quite extensive. With a programme covering logic, metaphysics, moral philosophy, history of ancient and modern philosophy, its importance was second only to theology.[57] Emphasis was also given to the study of classical languages, a fact which was propitious for what was also an interest in ancient philosophy, and in the first place, Plato. In other words, teaching and research within the academies brought together two spheres of philosophical interest. As George Florovsky suggests, it was here that a tradition of philosophical instruction, very much anchored in work on the classics 'first responsibly encountered German idealism'.[58] However, if, at the beginning of the century the coexistence of these two quite different paradigms – philosophy in the spirit of religious truth as exemplified by Platonic thought, and German idealism above all identified with the philosophy of Kant – was feasible, their complementarity would gradually be transformed into a source of conflict as conservative reaction in the court of the tsar began to take its toll on the system of education more generally.

'When I entered the academy in 1820', N.I. Nadezhdin recalled, 'complete translations (in manuscript) of Kant's *Critique of Pure Reason*, Bouterweck's *Aesthetics*, Schelling's *Philosophy and Religion*, and others could be found greedily copied by young men assembled from all corners of boundless Russia.'[59] Nadezhdin tells how the students ran a 'learned discussion' society. The members of the group 'philosophized, argued, assisted one another in understanding Kant's teaching, toiled over the translation of technical terms in his writings, and critically examined the systems of his disciples'.[60] Yet Nadezhdin's enthusiasm for contemporary German idealism was seemingly at odds with the spirit of the Moscow Academic Charter, issued some six years earlier in 1814, and which represented the official stand on philosophical instruction in the Academy. The Charter had stated that 'anything not in accord with the true reason of Holy Scripture is in essence falsehood and error, and must be mercilessly refuted'.[61] It reminded the philosophy teacher of the importance to be 'inwardly certain that neither he nor his students ever think they see the light of higher, true philosophy, unless it be sought in the doctrines of Christianity.' The statute therefore recommended for teaching purposes the

Holy Scriptures, Plato – the author of 'authentic philosophy' – and his 'followers in ancient and modern times'.[62]

The underlying spirit of these rulings, drafted as they were under the auspices of the state-controlled Holy Synod, both mirrored and augured the pietist and mystical mood to which Alexander I was to become increasingly prone in the second half of his reign, a period marked by the 'Holy Alliance' (a pact signed with Prussia and Austria after the defeat of Napoleon, and which invoked the Holy Trinity). Politically, one of the consequences of Alexander's retreat from politics into mysticism was to encourage a reactionary clamp down on hopes for democratic reform. In 1812, projects for the tentative introduction of a constitutional monarchy were abandoned. Its initiator, Mikhail Speranskii, was dismissed, while greater responsibility in ministerial affairs ultimately passed to the 'brutal, rude' General Alexis Arakcheev, 'a Martinet of the worst sort'.[63] Matters of education and religion fell to Prince Golitsyn, a figure who, already prior to his nomination as Minister of Education in 1816, enjoyed the double privilege as president of the influential, pietist inspired 'Bible society' and as the tsar's civilian procurator of the Holy Synod. Once named Education Minister the two, previously distinct spheres of education and religion were brought together and placed under his charge. As Nicholas Riasanovsky and James Billington have both noted, it was during Golitsyn's service as Minister of Education and Religious Affairs that the universities fell prey to heavy purges and censorship. A case in point was the University of Kazan. Its curator, Mikhail Magnitskii, went to crude extremes in his attempts to crystallize a surge in national self-consciousness in the wake of Russia's victory against Napoleon. Capitalizing on what was already a religiously tinged reaction among intellectuals and public figures against the rationalism and scepticism of the Enlightenment's *philosophes*, Magnitskii ordered that all books associated with the 'Age of Reason' be removed from the university library, and replaced by a large quantity of Bibles.[64] As Riasanovsky put it, this particular centre of learning was turned into a kind of 'monastic barracks'.

Needless to say, endeavours by such obscurantists and pietists as Magnitskii and Prince Golitsyn to ensure fidelity to God and the Tsar by imposing a system of learning based almost exclusively on the Bible, were poorly conceived and, inevitably, failed to produce the desired results. Moreover, it should not be forgotten that the extreme form of bureaucratic opportunism and philosophical obscurantism such as this was exemplified in the figure of Magnitskii, was actually more the exception than the rule, even though some form or other of it was to reappear in court circles throughout the nineteenth century. According to Billington, Magnitskii produced an 'original Orthodox' species of counter-revolutionary theory, which, in the 1830s, was refined and codified by Uvarov as the official ideology of the Russian Empire.[65] A classicist by training, and an ambitious administrator by profession, Uvarov implemented throughout the Empire an education programme which brought together study of the ancients and catechism. In doing so, he had finally succeeded in standardizing a practice which he had already introduced in the St. Petersburg region much earlier, in 1811, while serving as curator there.

If anything, Uvarov's promotion of a generalist education for gymnasium pupils in St. Petersburg, or Magnitskii's recommendations to Golitsyn that the University of Kazan 'be sentenced like a criminal and razed to the ground' for harbouring 'heretical German philosophy'[66] are indications, quite simply, of the amount of confusion and lack of clear-sightedness that governed in the latter part of Alexander's reign. It stands in sharp contrast with the 'police regime' of Nicholas I, which, in some ways, marked a return to greater sobriety. Ultimately, Alexander's closest advisers all lost their influence as high ranking officials, but the nationalism and social conservatism that they had engendered out of a kind of personal elated mysticism, was to become more indelibly rooted, standardized so to speak, throughout most branches of Nicholas' administrative machine. Thanks to Uvarov's role as minister and adviser to the tsar, the educational system in Russia began to be consolidated. On the other hand, however, because of the ideology of 'Autocracy, Orthodoxy, Nationhood' that he coined, any dissent from the system was to be tolerated less and less.

Returning to philosophical and religious instruction in the theological academy, just how far the official stance, such as this developed from the beginning of the century to the height of Nicholas I's reign, affected the actual content of the courses themselves is quite difficult to assess with any precision. Not least among these difficulties is the fact that what precisely was meant by 'Plato's ancient and modern successors' as counselled by the 1814 Charter was open to interpretation, and, indeed, seems to have been interpreted in a variety of ways. Nadezhdin's recollections, for example, suggest a degree of resistance, albeit among a privileged elite which was limited in numbers, against the explicit requirement of loyalty to Orthodox-inspired thought.

On the surface, at least, there was a sharp difference between Nadezhdin's enthusiasm for critical philosophy in the early 1820s and Karpov's caricature of Kant as a typical expression of the Protestant mind, which he devised in the 1840s. Kant, he claimed, is subjectivistic, relativistic, withholding any definite views about the transcendent. While, according to Karpov, Kant may have 'stunned the intellectual world with the rigour of his methods and the rightness of his deductions', his philosophy had also left its mark by dint of its barrenness, its aridity and its vacuity. It was 'nothing but a fine skeleton assembled from purely logical concepts'.[67] In seeking a purely intellectual answer to the question of how synthetic cognition is possible *a priori*, Kant forgot that 'not only the mind in all its forms but also the whole person is nothing other than a synthesis of the Omniscient Creator.' Consequently he forgot that 'the answer to the question must be sought not in mental activity, but in accordance with the conditions of man's being which are indicated by faith, and that it is faith which provides the basis for solving philosophical problems'.[68]

Karpov's hostility towards Kantian philosophy was nourished by a priority to defend the 'truth' of Orthodoxy, understood as the profession, by the heart and mind in concert, of Christian faith. To this end, his presentation of Kant focused on an image of the 'two worlds' Kant, an approach which was to become fairly common in Russian assessments of transcendental idealism where, essentially, it was a matter of defending faith and revelation against philosophical speculation. Otherwise, Russian critics took cruel pleasure in playing on an image of Kant's intellectual dryness – a product of the Protestant mind, they argued. Yet, paradoxically, this overt criticism also began to operate as a, so to speak, covert form of influence, if only because such expressions of hostility towards Kant and other representatives of contemporary German philosophy necessitated extensive study of his philosophy. For, how else would it be possible to justify the condemnation demanded by Magnitskii and Golitsyn, and seemingly still expected from Uvarov? Indeed, the ends to which refutations of Kant's philosophy were supposedly intended were sometimes rather ambivalent or obscure. According to I.M. Skvortsov (1795–1863), professor at the Kiev Theological Academy, Kant was a nefarious influence, but who, despite himself, had reinforced a theistic worldview on three accounts, on the strength of which he therefore merited study. First, Kant had demonstrated the insufficiency of human reason in knowledge of supra-sensible things; second, the impossibility of grounding ethics on psychological factors of any kind; and third, the depravity of man imprisoned in his empirical nature.[69] Whatever the case, whether openly attacked or covertly praised, Kant ranked as one of the main objects of philosophical discussion in an atmosphere of censorship which marked so much of Nicholas I's reign. In lecture courses, or articles published in the Academy journals, such factors arguably contributed to a direct or implicit confrontation between Kant and Plato.[70] Moreover, it was a confrontation which was highly significant, for they were believed to encapsulate two opposed orientations within the history of philosophy – the anthropocentric and the theocentric.

Setting Plato off against Kant in the name of an Orthodox-inspired philosophy was a task undertaken by several nineteenth and early twentieth-century Russian thinkers – Vladimir Ern, Florenskii, Sergei Bulgakov, Iurkevich, Solov'ev, as well as Karpov whose philosophical preferences, as we have seen, left little room for doubt. Like Karpov, they insisted on sharp oppositions between the two types of thinking. Ern, for one, coined this in terms of 'ratio' and 'logos'. The former, identified as the transcendental subject, and what Ern called the 'rationalizing unbodily I', was the keystone of the metaphysical and gnoseological individualism of Descartes, Kant, Hegel and neo-Kantianism, he said. Since this amounted to no more than a formal 'schema of judgement' it was entirely indifferent to mythological, poetic, or religious-mystical experience. By 'logos', on the contrary, Ern meant the doctrine of the divine logos, the source of thought and being which Parmenides, and Plato, had first discovered, and which was later developed by the neo-Platonists and the Church Fathers.

Pavel Florenskii, for his part, stated the opposition in quite unequivocal terms, expressing his hostility to Kant in the name of the traditional Platonism of European metaphysics to which he claimed allegiance:

> Two names, like two crises in the life of one individual, demarcate the ages of European thought. Plato and Kant. Two watersheds separating the unknown beginnings of philosophy, lost in the cosmogonies of dim antiquity, from its end, nested in an as yet unexplored future.[71]

But the opposition between Plato and Kant, which all these authors recognized and explored in various ways, did not always mean an outright denunciation of Kant for the sake of Platonic philosophy, and especially the neo-Platonic tradition he inspired. Unlike Florenskii's outright rejection, Iurkevich insisted on a relationship of protagonist (Plato) and foil (Kant), the conclusions that Kant drew about the nature of our experience serving merely as the starting point for Plato's enquiry into the nature of reason.

Plato and Kant: The 'Plus' and 'Minus' in the European Philosophical Tradition (Pavel Florenskii)

Florenskii expressed his fundamental dislike for Kant in a number of texts written in different periods, but perhaps gave vent to his most striking condemnation in a lecture entitled 'Cult and Philosophy' (1918).[72] Here he not only opposed the doctrines of Plato and Kant, but went so far as to contrast what he imagined their lives and personalities to have been, the result being a rather crude caricature of both men. I shall return to this second aspect presently.

Florenskii's main argument in this and other lectures in a series on the 'Philosophy of Worship' concerned the primordial importance of cult, or worship, in our understanding of the world. He contended that, for an appraisal of philosophy to be of any worth, it should, first and foremost, test the nature of its relation to the phenomenon of human devotion:

> Neither thought, nor theoretical enunciation, or fickle command determine our understanding of the world at its core, at its source, but cult – negatively and positively. Where there is no worship, there is subjective reverie like autumn leaves swirled around by gusts of wind (...). On the contrary, contact with worship rouses the soul from its reverie, compelling it to move towards self-determination. And no matter the degree to which philosophy has fallen into partiality, nor how much effort it takes to say 'yes' or 'no' instead of

something in between, it always comes to a point where either a 'yes' or a 'no' is compulsory – as cult.⁷³

It was this view of philosophy which governed Florenskii's account of Kant, the devil (*velikii lukavets*). Florenskii broke down the main points of Kant's theoretical philosophy into phenomena 'in which nothing appears'; noumena which are accessible to the mind, 'but are otherwise incomprehensible'; the 'thing in itself', 'which turns out to be in no way "in itself", nor a thing, but merely concepts in the mind'; pure intuitions, 'space and time, which, however, cannot be conceived of as pure'.⁷⁴ In short, Kantian philosophy slips evasively between the 'yes' or the 'no' which cult demands.

In some respect, Florenskii conceded, it was only to be expected that Kant, as a Protestant, should have been ignorant of cult, if not loath to it. Yet Florenskii insisted on a paradox here, namely that while fighting cult for the sake of speaking about the possibility of knowledge/science, Kant's manner of philosophizing merely betrayed the degree to which he depended on it. To bear out his observation Florenskii turned to Plato, whose philosophy was not only imbued with a sense of cult, but was also the unavowed model for the Kantian worldview:

> Should you take the trouble to confront Kant and Plato's philosophical worldviews (*zizhneponimanie*) point by point, you would immediately see the simplicity of Kant's recipe. All the while keeping Plato's terminology (noumenon, phenomenon, idea), Kant took over Plato's worldview, except that he merely turned the plus sign in front of it into a minus. All the plus signs became minuses, and the minuses plus signs with respect to the Platonic standpoint. That's how Kantianism came about.⁷⁵

Whereas for Plato, 'phenomenon' is sensation (*predstavlenie*), and refers to the sensible world, for Kant, it is sensation, representation, and refers to sense experience; whereas for Plato, the truly knowable (*istinno-poznavaemoe*) is the idea, for Kant the truly knowable is only the phenomenon. And again, when it came to the problem of antinomies: for Florenskii, Kant's use of this term was no less than a profanation of the meaning afforded to it by Plato in his dialogues. Plato's 'passion for the dialogical form, alone, is proof of the antinomial nature of his thinking'. Before anything else, his dialogues should be seen as an 'artistic dramatization of the antinomies'.⁷⁶

> Plato and Kant go together like a seal and its imprint. All that is in the one is in the other, but the convexity of the one is the concavity of the other, the void of the other. One is a plus, the other a minus.⁷⁷

Unlike Kant, Plato's thought is 'culto-centric'. It is a philosophy of cult, of worship lived and thought through by a profound and wise thinker. Plato's gaze, touching the depths of the human spirit, turned outwards towards the object. Kant's gaze, apparently so intrigued by external experience, in fact was entirely given to pure subjectivity. A case in point is the 'idea'. Florenskii saw in Plato's theory of the ideas the key to his entire philosophy. They are, he suggested, instruments in the cognition of the authentic real, but they are also the known reality itself. In other words, ideas are the most subjective of all that exists, but also the most objective. They are ideal, but they are real, he claimed.[78] Whereas for Plato, as Florenskii read him, the 'idea' was the ontological root of thought, vanishing into the depths of myth, for Kant it was merely a 'problematic expansion of reason'. Ideas in Kantian philosophy are the necessary preconditions of true knowledge, but are not in themselves objects of experience. The real, as a thing in itself, is unthinkable. Rather, it is presumed by critically self-knowing reason. Quite differently for Plato, and his Russian successors, ideas are the prototype of what is most real, attainable by reason. They are the true foundations of the being of the real. It was precisely this kind of interpretation of the Platonic idea which Sergei Bulgakov, for example, was later to build into his theory of Sophiology. According to this theory, the created world exists, illuminated by the world of ideas. But for Bulgakov, the point here was to acknowledge his indebtedness to Plato, and he did so willingly: 'There you have the greatest, the most meaningful, and most important truth about the world, the essence of the cosmodicy of Platonism.'[79]

Obviously, as a methodological account of the process of cognition (*poznavanie*) – which Florenskii scathingly called a modern-day tower of Babel – the Kantian perspective on philosophy was simply anathema.[80] An enquiry into the how and what of knowledge could scarcely satisfy his own very different priorities with respect to philosophy, which he took to be 'inseparable from dialectics, from the penetrating gaze'. For Florenskii, philosophy signified 'a mental deepening and "living through" (*vzhivaniia*) of reality, an unending search for truth'. It is 'an urge which is inherent in every man'.[81]

Plato's Doctrine of Reason versus Kant's Theory of Experience (Pamfil Iurkevich)

Writing some fifty years earlier, Pamfil Iurkevich (1827–1874) had asked a similar question, though his answer was rather less exuberant: How is it possible that Kant and Plato should have arrived at such radically different accounts of the world when the nature of their enquiries were so similar? 'It is remarkable', he noted, 'that in his claims about the subjectivity of our cognition, or – what comes to the same – the subjectivity of our experience, Kant took the same path that Plato had chosen (in the *Theaetetus*) in order to prove that our knowledge (*poznanie*) is not confined to a range of sensations, but that it is knowledge of truth itself.'[82] Plato had argued that sensations are subjective, and he ascribed truth to the knowledge (*znanie*) which the soul forms within itself. For him, the supra-sensible ideas of being are in essence truths which make objective experience and common sense possible. Kant (in his transcendental deduction of categories) likewise proved that something may be known in a universally valid way, and therefore admitted as an object (*predmet*) once sense perceptions are worked through by the cognitive subject, meaning that an objective unity is conferred on them by the categories of reason (*rassudok*). In Iurkevich's words:

> [Kant's] theory of universal, primordial, and immutable consciousness, or his theory of the categories as forms which are independent of individual – or any – experience, and which ground the universally valid, objective relation of representations match, point for point, the argument in *Theaetetus*, namely that the soul's knowledge is to a large extent independent of experience and the empirical states of the individual subject, and that experience, along with common sense as his necessary fellow companion, is possible only as a consequence of this knowledge.[83]

That Kant and Plato, in view of these promising similarities, should have come to represent in the history of philosophy two, fundamentally opposed, standpoints on theoretical and epistemological problems is the puzzle that Iurkevich endeavoured to solve. His answer, unlike Florenskii's, however, was to insist less on an opposition as on a fleeting moment of contiguity. To Iurkevich's mind, Kant's theory of experience was valid only because of the truth of Plato's theory of reason. The point at which their views converged, albeit immediately to diverge again, concerned the question of the categories. According to Iurkevich, Plato started out from that point of common sense at which Kant arrived. Plato asked: may the world, which is given to us, or thrust upon our consciousness, be kept intact strictly in thought? He considered that objects given in experience do not fully express the content of ideas. Rather, they are no more than images or schemes of authentic being conceived in the ideas. Accordingly, objects of experience are merely phenomenal categories. If it is true that Plato considered objects of experience as phenomena in an objective sense, that is, as incomplete and limited expressions of the truth of reason, then, in this sense, as Iurkevich reasoned, he did not seriously contradict Kant, for whom the objects of experience were phenomena constituted out of the functions of the sensible and cognizing subject. According to Iurkevich, Plato began his metaphysical research from the conviction which Kant himself, many centuries later, aptly coined in the phrase 'the schemata of sensibility restrict the categories, that is, they limit them in conditions which lie outside the understanding'.[84] The difference between them is that, whereas Kant held that the universal validity of our cognition in the sphere of possible experience depends on this sacrifice of reason, on its being limited by an extraneous element, for Plato, all universally valid cognition is related to reason unhampered by outside influence and effective only in the ideas.[85]

In view of this argument, Iurkevich then went on to select a number of points which, he believed, bore out his main hypothesis, namely that Kant's account of the world of phenomena ended where Plato's account of the world of ideas began. By the same token, however, he was, obviously, using the occasion to take issue with Kant in the name of the Platonic philosophy that he clearly preferred. For Iurkevich, Kant's view that objects are given to us in sense perception, that 'sensibility makes for understanding' had long since been challenged, indeed defeated, by Plato's theory that all knowledge (*poznanie*) is knowledge of the supra-sensible, that, on the contrary, 'understanding makes for sensibility'. Iurkevich's chosen affinities emerge quite clearly in the following remark:

> Objects are not so much given (*dany*) in sense perceptions as presented as tasks (*zadany*) to the understanding. Sense perceptions 'incite' reason to these tasks, and the solution of these tasks, in accordance with the content of the ideas, is the birthplace of the real world (*predmetnyi mir*). For example, becoming aware that in front of us is a thing (*veshch'*) of a definite colour, form and size etc., is precisely the outcome of the solution to such a task. Awareness (consciousness) is conditioned by questions concerning the essence of the thing (...), it comes about through an effort of the understanding to cognize (*poznat'*) the idea of the thing. Sensibility (...) motivates (*povod*) questions about the essence of a thing, attends (*soprovozhdaet*) this idea, or this ideal object, with imagination (*obrazy fantasii*). Nevertheless, as an unseen thought (*nevidimaia mysl'*), the ideal object is the bearer of qualities of sensibility, of, for example, these definite colours, scents and so on. Already here, we see how far Kant undermined his theory, because he neglected to take as his starting point that which Plato had regarded as an irrefutable truth, namely the principle of identity and general concepts. Instead, Kant chose to focus instead on the derivative and remote categories of thought.[86]

For Iurkevich, then, a major point of confrontation concerned Kant's transcendental deduction and Plato's theory of identity, being and the universal. Kant was convinced that, once it is proven that objects of experience are phenomena, and not things, then the employment of the categories as universally valid and necessary becomes self-evident. Plato, quite differently, held that the simplest and most basic ideas, in and through which an object is given to thought are identity, being and the universal:

> No matter how great the sensation that images of colours or figures afford us, the knowledge that these colours or figures exist (*est'*), that each of them is identical with itself, but different in relation to one another, finally, that each belongs to a kind (*prichastna vidu, obshchemu poniatiiu*), – all this is knowledge (*poznanie*), without which experience is impossible. (...) But Kant,

in his analysis of the understanding (*razum*) evaded this 'abc' of metaphysics, hoping to substitute it with the forms of space and time, what he called the sources of cognition (...) No doubt they are the sources of cognition, but only for the understanding endowed with immediate knowledge of metaphysical truth.[87]

On the strength of these and other selected moments of comparison, Iurkevich contended, much to Kant's disadvantage, that no single definition in his theory of experience refuted the possibility of a metaphysics of the supra-sensible. On the contrary:

Kant's theory of experience (...) is the discovery and brilliant development of a single, unconditional metaphysical truth, namely that reason, in working through sense data in accordance with its ideas, may recognize and cognize only the appearance of things. But when, as Plato claimed, conscious reflex (*soznatel'nyi refleks*) subjects the appearance of things to a critique, and seeks that which may be retained by pure reason as its object, then, from this point onwards, we are dealing with knowledge of the very essence of things. Not only do these two tenets not contradict one another, on the contrary, the latter served as a principle for Kant himself. Furthermore, the undeniable validity of this principle gave him the means to speak about the forms, conditions and laws according to which the sensible-rational subject engages in the act of cognition, and acquires knowledge of things such as they are, not as they appear, or present themselves to us.[88]

*

As a contest of theoretical (epistemological) positions, Florenskii's and Iurkevich's preference for Plato leaves little room for doubt. Kant was by turns rejected outright, or used as a foil to Plato, putting questions before problems for which Plato had already found the solution. As Iurkevich put it, Kant's philosophy was completed by Plato. Yet, in declaring his allegiance to Plato, Iurkevich was at the same time, as Sergei Levitskii and others have suggested, 'Platonizing Kant', that is, presenting Kant through the prism of the questions raised by Plato in the *Theaetetus*.[89] Moreover, he was arguably also 'Christianizing Plato'. This tendency is perhaps more obvious in a slightly earlier text, 'Ideia', published in 1859. While the definition Iurkevich gave of the idea took Plato as its acknowledged source, his underlying purpose was to assimilate it to a Christian worldview. He wrote:

If philosophy endeavours to explain the phenomena before us, or the world revealed to us in and through ideas, if it regards the phenomena of the world as revelations, or as the embodiment of thought, if, for philosophy, the idea is the source, the ground, the law and type of phenomenal reality, then, in this sense, philosophy is endeavouring to explain or ground that special worldview, the source of which may be found in every human soul, and which is necessarily presupposed in the religious and moral life of humanity.[90]

Statements of this kind offer an insight into what, perhaps, had really motivated the otherwise academic exercise of comparing and contrasting two leading figures within the European philosophical tradition. The hostility that Florenskii expressed towards Kant, his sense of affinity with Plato, has prompted some recent commentators to characterize Russian thought more generally in terms of a preoccupation with 'truth in itself', meaning a type of enquiry anchored, not so much in philosophical 'autocentric' concerns, as in 'theocentric' yearnings. Anatoly Akhutin has aptly termed it as a quest to uncover the 'shining light of revealed truth':

> Where Kant's pure (theoretical) reason is suspended, as it were, in the air of unsubstantiation, Russian thinkers find an absolute supra-rational foundation and 'remember' that they have always been standing on it already.[91]

According to Akhutin, such a rejection of the 'autocentric' nature of Kantian (and generally, Western) thought meant that Russian thinkers – certain Russian thinkers, if not all – tended to leave philosophy behind to become 'theosophists', 'sophio-sophists' and theologians instead. For sure, the relation between Kant and Plato, such as it was depicted by the authors whose works have been discussed in this chapter, consistently highlights – granted, to different degrees – a tendency among Russian thinkers towards metaphysical idealism, together with a realism in epistemological questions. Moreover, their comparisons often point to what, perhaps, was for many, the one major sticking point in the heritage of Kantian thought itself, namely the unknowability of the thing-in-itself. Sergei Trubetskoi, for one, dismissed the '*Ding an sich*' as one of the main, and potentially most dangerous, weaknesses in Kant's philosophy: 'If the concept of the "*Ding an sich*" is opposed to the concept of phenomenon', he argued, 'then this means that a phenomenon is no less than a "thing outside itself".' For Trubetskoi, the point was that 'phenomenal reality, just like consciousness, is grounded in a universal metaphysical principle'.[92]

The Neo-Kantian Recovery of Plato

By the end of the nineteenth century a confrontation between Kant and Plato in Russian philosophical studies was, arguably, just as much the consequence of the overall growth in philosophical production as it was a sign of the need to do battle with secular philosophy in the name of Russian spirituality. In this later period, translations and commentaries of both ancient and modern philosophy increased considerably. Just as Russian Plato scholarship began developing quite markedly, so too, did the study of

Kant. The *Critiques* and other works were translated, and commentaries of the main lines of his thought published. Moreover, it is worth noting that, quite often, the authors of these translations and critical studies were philosophers and historians of philosophy whose research otherwise included monographs or articles on Plato. Kozlov, author of *Method and Orientation in the Philosophy of Plato* (1880), also published a *Genesis of Kant's Theory of Time and Space Genezis* (1884). Vladimir Solov'ev wrote a long article on Kant in the 'Brokgaus and Efron' encyclopaedia (1895), and, together with N.Ia. Grot, translated the *Prolegomena* (1889). Grot, himself, besides his *Outline of Plato's Philosophy,* which he published in 1896, wrote several articles on Kant, virtually all of them dating from the 1890s. Giliarov, who wrote several pieces on Plato, his openly acknowledged favourite author, took issue with Kant and Kantianism in a monograph entitled *The Essence, Meaning, and History of Philosophy,* published just after the October Revolution. Evgenii Trubetskoi, Professor of Law at Kiev and Moscow Universities, first wrote his *Plato's Social Utopia* in 1908, and quarrelled with Kantianism in his *Metaphysical Presuppositions of Knowledge: An Attempt to overcome Kant and Kantianism,* a decade later. And, as for Florenskii, for all the contempt he expressed for the reviled symbol of the Enlightenment, he, too, edited a translation of one of Kant's works.[93]

The increase in monographs and articles in Russia about the two authors may have been prompted by the neo-Kantian recovery of Plato in Germany, most often associated with the work of Windelband, Hermann Cohen and Paul Natorp. Understanding Plato and Kant in light of neo-Kantian interpretations was an approach adopted by a number of Russian philosophers active in the decade prior to the First World War. They drew on contemporary neo-Kantianism, building aspects of both its theoretical and ethical dimensions (as exemplified by the two schools of Marburg and Baden) into their own original research.[94] And while Florenskii's own personal attitude to the neo-Kantians may have been no less detrimental than it was towards Kant himself (he accused the Marburgers of dislocating the spirit, of running away from faith and falling into the trap of superstition[95]), for other Russian contemporaries, Windelband's monograph on Plato, and Natorp's *Platons Ideenlehre* (first published in 1903) provided an occasion to turn Plato into the 'Kant' of antiquity, or inversely to 'reinvent' Kant as the Plato of modern times. As Professor Zhakov put it in his preface to the revised Russian translation of Windelband's *Platon*:

> Kant's *a priori* nature of the mind corresponds to the recollection of the ideas. The ideas residing in the 'kingdom of the beyond', above 'the vault of the skies' correspond to Kant's '*Ding an sich*' (...) Plato's theory of knowledge, which surmounted sensualism, together with his theory of ideas, constitute those summits of idealism which were developed further in Kant's critique and in Hegel's panlogicism.[96]

One of the better-known instances of an encounter in Russia between Kant and Plato in the context of a neo-Kantian recovery of both authors concerns the international journal, *Logos*. Founded with the help of Heinrich Rickert, it was published in Germany (1910–1933) and in Russia by the Moscow publishing house Musaget (1910–1914). While its appearance in Russia reflected a growing interest for contemporary academic philosophy, at issue was an underlying ambition to provide what was generally accepted as the neo-Platonic impulse of Russian (religious) philosophizing with more solid theoretical underpinnings. This point was explicitly stated in the editorial comment to the first Russian issue.

One of the most virulent attacks in Russia against the journal and its Russian editors, Fedor Stepun, Sergei Hessen and Emil Metner, was voiced by Vladimir Ern. Defending the 'ontologism and thorough personalism' of Russian philosophizing, with its origins in 'logicism' mentioned above, Ern sharply criticized mainstream Western philosophy which, he contended, was given exclusively to rationalism and impersonalism.[97] In his openly declared hostilities, Ern radicalized the differences between the defenders of an indigenous philosophical style and Russian adepts of the *Logos* programme. The polemic was, however, short-lived, and these sharp differences gradually gave way to cross-influences stemming from the two camps. Stepun abandoned his former interest in predominantly methodological questions for an enquiry into the nature of being, the absolute. Hessen began elaborating a theory of 'metaphysical mysticism', and later, in emigration, turned his interest to a theory of law in which he readily acknowledged his indebtedness to Plato.[98] At the same time, moreover, the leading German contributors to the journal, Georg Mehlis and Richard Kroner, were also beginning to leave their footholds in Kantianism, ultimately to embrace, as some commentators have suggested, mystical and religious philosophy close to neo-Platonism.[99] And when the revised second edition of *Platons Ideenlehre* came out in 1921, it seemed to some of its readers that its author, Natorp, had also taken the same path. According to Losev, Natorp had abandoned his earlier Kantian standpoint to provide an interpretation of Plato which was now far more in keeping with the spirit of neo-Platonism.[100] A similar observation prompted Semën Frank to describe the philosophical mood of the early 1920s more generally as one marked by a conversion of the Kantian categories into 'objective' or 'Platonic' idealism.

While reactions to Plato and Kant were principally inspired, if not governed, by arguments concerning the nature of 'philosophizing', they were also shaped by opinions concerning the personality of the philosopher himself, behind the theories he espoused. Russian readers were seemingly as much intrigued by the life of Plato (and, of course, his leading *dramatis persona* in the figure of Socrates) as they were by his philosophy. Their comments suggest that they welcomed a view of philosophy as something which is inseparable from a way of life. They therefore tended to idolize

Plato as the philosopher *par excellence*. On the contrary, it was quite usual to portray Kant, the person, as some kind of narrow-minded *'Fachidiot'*. For Iurkevich, the fact that Plato's idea was also a poetic idea made for the remarkable value of his philosophy as a whole. Florenskii's sympathy for Plato against Kant depended on a series of rather blatant and crude oppositions:

> Plato is an aristocrat, Kant a plebeian, a snob who sought the company of upper-class society. Plato is a poet, who at once fought against, yet was inspired by, the erotic pulse. Kant is dry, alien to Eros, a eunuch who spent his time worrying about day-to-day comforts, the pleasures of the table, and status.[101]

Writing just after the outbreak of the First World War, Vladimir Ern even went so far as to suggest that Kant's breakdown of the world into noumena and phenomena was pertinent for an understanding of the nature of German military aggression as, what he termed, the *'Wille zur Macht'*.[102] An evident sympathy for philosophical thought which bears the imprint of a personal life experience and engagement seems also to have guided distinctions that Russian thinkers tended to make quite readily between authentic and 'taught' philosophy. Kireevskii, we saw, dismissed school-bookish philosophy for the sake of pursuing the path to integral knowledge, that knowledge which demands the inner integrity of being. More then half a century later, Florenskii reiterated the same distinction, and cited Plato as his model for authentic philosophy. Platonism is rooted in the 'earthy' (*pochvennyi*) good of human beliefs, he said. Precisely because of its attachment to the soil (*pochvennost'*) his thought is eternal. Plato 'is not the product of school philosophy, but the flower of a people's soul, nor will his colours fade so long as this soul lives'.[103]

*

I suggested at the beginning of this chapter that certain Russian intellectuals were keen to safeguard the future development of idealism, which they felt had been endangered by the 'absolute' idealism of Hegel, as its last major expression. If this is the case, it becomes clearer why they repeatedly juxtaposed Plato, Kant, as well as Hegel, in both historical and systematic accounts of philosophy. Tackling Kant, and Hegel, by turning to the 'Father of Idealism', Plato, they were not simply appealing to tradition as a means to combat latter-day philosophical deviants, but were also, and sometimes primarily so, endeavouring to secure the place of Russian philosophy within this same tradition. These remarks pertain above all to a widespread rejection among Russian philosophers of the phenomenalist aspects of Kant's theoretical philosophy. As Zhakov put it:

> As the belief that there exists a world of ideas which is more beautiful and more just than our visible universe, Platonism is the single greatest thing which inspires philosophers, giving them strength to overcome the inertia of our earthly experience.[104]

However, once Russian thinkers addressed the question of ethics, and the associated topics of law and justice, the opposition between Plato and Kant underwent a significant change. Kant's engagement with the problem of moral law, together with his critique of the faculties of judgement in which he affirmed the existence of the *Ding an sich*, and came to stress a purposefulness (*tselesoobraznost'*) in the world prompted some Russian commentators to call him precisely 'the Plato of our times'. As I shall discuss in the next chapter, the ethical dimension of Kant's philosophy found a more positive response in Russia, especially among certain juridical thinkers such as Boris Chicherin, Pavel Novgorodtsev, but also Solov'ev in his major work, *The Justification of the Good*. Plato's theory of knowledge as the good encountered the Kantian categorical imperative as part of attempts by Russian legal and religious philosophers alike to understand the relation between law and morality, and to consider how best to achieve the common good. True, on the surface, such a tendency to pair Plato and Kant as two spokesmen of law and justice is rather puzzling. One might be tempted to think that the Platonic example, alone, should have sufficed, requiring no updating or complement from Kant, if only because Plato's interest in the nature of reality, for its own sake, was met by an exhortation 'to tend one's soul', to practise courage, justice and kindness. Unifying the metaphysical and ethical sides of philosophy was, as we saw in this chapter, upheld as an important goal by certain Russian thinkers. If this is true, one might wonder why they needed Kant, when Plato already provided the model they wanted to emulate. And yet – particularly at the close of the century – Russian intellectuals seemingly did require a Kantian optic to guide their assessment of Plato as a moral philosopher. Moreover, the upshot was a paradoxical one. Adopting a Kantian perspective resulted in driving a wedge between the theoretical and ethical dimensions of Plato's thought, and ultimately left some Russian readers less than entirely enthusiastic for a philosopher, whose place in the pantheon of Russian culture had, so far, never been challenged.

Notes

1 W.K.C. Guthrie, *The Greek Philosophers. From Thales to Aristotle* (Harper and Row, New York, 1960), p.90.
2 See, for example, the various 'histories of philosophy' by Russian authors such as Zenkovskii, Radlov, Shpet, Losskii, Florovskii (details given in the general bibliography). In Western scholarship, see in particular: A. Walicki, *The Slavophile Controversy: History of a Conservative Utopia in Nineteenth Century Russian Thought*

(Oxford, 1975), as well as his *A History of Russian Thought from the Enlightenment to Marxism* (Oxford, 1980). See also: F. Rouleau, *Ivan Kiréievski et la naissance du slavophilisme* (Namur, 1990); A. Koyré, *La philosophie et le problème national en Russie au début du XIXe siècle* (Paris, 1929); also his *Etudes sur l'histoire de la pensée philosophique en Russie* (Paris, 1950); E. Müller, *Russicher Intellekt in Europaïcher Krise. Ivan V. Kireevskij* (Köln-Graz, 1966); F. Copleston, *Philosophy in Russia: From Herzen to Lenin and Berdyaev* (Notre Dame, Indiana: Search Press / University of Notre Dame/, 1986).

3   So called by Professor Zhakov in his introduction to the Russian translation of Windelband's *Platon* (1909).
4   S.N. Trubetskoi, *Osnovaniia Idealizma* (Moscow, 1896), cited in *S.N. Trubetskoi: Sochineniia* (Moscow: Mysl', 1996), p.594.
5   N.A. Berdiaev, 'Filosofskaia istina i intelligentskaia pravda', *Vekhi* (1909), cited from the 1991 edition (Moscow: Pravda), pp.26-27. The expression 'concrete idealism' is an implicit reference to Sergei Trubetskoi, who first introduced it in his book *Osnovaniia Idealisma* (1896) in response to the absolute idealism of Hegel. For a more detailed discussion of this text see below, pp.71-75. The reference to 'ontological realism' most probably refers to Losskii's endeavours at the turn of the century to construct a theory of knowledge in which he aimed to restore the status and validity of ontology, a field of philosophical enquiry which had previously been ignored in the methodological preoccupations of late nineteenth-century positivism and neo-Kantianism.
6   P. Florenskii, *Obshchechelovecheskie korni idealizma*, p.32.
7   N. Ia. Grot, *Ocherk filosofii Platona* (Moscow, 1896), p.185.
8   N. Losskii, *Obosnovanie intuitivizma* (SPb., 1908), pp.193-194. By 'Platonic idealism' Losskii meant the duality of the ideal and the real which he built into his own philosophy of 'ideal-realism'. For Losskii, 'ideas' are the intelligible model, or blueprint, of the sensible world. The unnamed 'representatives' of this current that Losskii alludes to included Semën Frank, as well as Sergei Bulgakov for his *Svet Nevechernii*. Losskii's use of 'mystical' is intended as an echo of the philosophy of Schelling, which Losskii labelled 'mystical rationalism'.
9   Zhakov, op. cit., p.20.
10 Together with Aleksei Khomiakov (1804-1860), author of the principle of *sobornost'*, an idealized vision of Orthodoxy as 'unity in freedom'. With respect to the question of integrality, however, I have chosen to limit my remarks to Kireevskii.
11 Early in his career, Kireevskii frequented the 'Lovers of Wisdom' (1820-1825), a group of young intellectuals which was animated by Prince Odoevskii. Odoevskii was a key figure in the introduction of Schelling into a non-university milieu.
12 See the *Obozrenie prepodovaniia nauk* of the Universities of Kiev, Moscow and St. Petersburg, for this period, which, at the time of the 1835 statute, broke the subject down into 'ethics', 'psychology', 'history of philosophy', 'logic'.
13 See his *Vvedenie v filosofiiu* (SPb., 1840).
14 *Vvedenie v filosofiiu*, cited in Zenkovskii, *Istoriia russkoi filosofii*, vol.1, pt.2 (Leningrad: EGO, 1991), p.114.
15 *Vvedenie v filosofiiu*, pp.106-111.
16 'Vzgliad na dvizhenie filosofii v mire khristianskom i na prichiny razlichnikh eia napravlenii', *ZhMNP*, vol.92, 11, pt.II (1856), p.190. Cf. T. Nemeth, 'Karpov and Iurkevich on Kant: Philosophy in Service to Orthodoxy?' in *SEET*, vol.45, no.3 (1993), pp.169-211.
17 'Filosofskii ratsionalizm noveishchego vremeni', *Khristianskoe Chtenie*, 5 (1860), p.467.
18 Karpov, *Khristianskoe Ctenie*, 1893, cf. Nemeth, op. cit.
19 See Copleston, op. cit., pp.218-219.

20 Solov'ev, *Philosophical Principles of Integral Knowledge* (1877). Cited in A. Walicki, *A History of Russian Thought from the Enlightenment to Marxism*, pp.378-379.
21 Cf. Walicki, ibid., p.381.
22 See 'Mirovaia dusha', in Brokgaus and Efron (eds), *Entsiklopedicheskii Slovar'*, vol.xix(a) (1896), pp.518-519.
23 In his *Predmet znaniia* (1915), for example, Frank combined references to *Timaeus, Parmenides, Sophists*, with Plotinus, Augustine, Nicolas of Cusa.
24 Kozlov, *Metod i napravlenie filosofii Platona*, p.203.
25 V. Solov'ev, 'Idealism', Brokgaus and Efron (eds), Vol.xii(a) (1894), pp.796-797.
26 Ibid., p.797.
27 Ibid.
28 Solov'ev, *Kritika otvlechennykh nachal*, cited in *Vl Solov'ev. Sochineniia* (Mysl', Moscow, 1990), pp.680-681.
29 See below, Chapters Three and Four.
30 See Losev's entry on Plato in the Soviet philosophical encyclopaedia, *Filosofskaia Entsiklopediia*, vol.4 (Moscow, 1967), pp.262-269. For further comment on Losev see below, Chapter Five.
31 N.O.Losskii, *History of Russian Philosophy*, trans. N. Duddington (London, 1952), p.403. Interestingly, Losskii concluded this comment with the following observation: 'The Slavophils already urged that our knowledge of reality was immediate, unfortunately they described such knowledge by the misleading term "faith".' Losskii's remark suggests that Russian philosophy should be free of some of its stereotypes. Ibid.
32 I. Kireevskii, 'O neobkhodimosti i vozmozhnosti novykh nachal dlia filosofii' in *I.V. Kireevskii: kritika i estetika* (Moscow: Iskusstvo, 1979), p.325.
33 Ibid., pp.303-304.
34 Ibid., pp.307-308.
35 Ibid., p.316; p.327.
36 Cf. Rouleau, op. cit., p.161.
37 Kireevskii, 'O neobkhodimosti...', pp.331-332.
38 Ibid.
39 Rouleau, op. cit., p.215. See also A.V. Akhutin, 'Sophia and the Devil: Kant in the Face of Russian Religious Metaphysics', *Soviet Studies in Philosophy*, Spring (1991), p.74.
40 Cited in Rouleau, op. cit., p.275.
41 Kireevskii, 'O kharaktere prosveshcheniia Evropy i ego otnoshenii k prosveshcheniiu Rossii' in *I.V. Kireevskii: kritika i estetika*, pp.271-272.
42 Kireevskii, 'O neobhodimosti...', p.320.
43 F. Rouleau, op. cit., p.214.
44 S.N. Trubetskoi, *Osnovaniia Idealizma* (1896) in *S.N. Trubetskoi: Sochineniia* (Moscow: Mysl', 1994), pp.667-670.
45 Ibid., p.651; p.669.
46 Cf P.P. Gaidenko, 'Konkretnyi Idealizm S.N. Trubetskogo in *S.N. Trubetskoi: Sochineniia*, pp.3-41.
47 Elsewhere in the same text, Trubetskoi qualified this position as 'metaphysical socialism' (p.700), a term which Berdiaev, for one, was to quick to pick up. See his contribution to the *Vekhi* collection in 1909.
48 S.N. Trubetskoi, *O prirode chelovecheskogo soznaniia* (1890) in op. cit., p.489.
49 Cf. M. Bohachevsky-Chomiak, *Sergei N. Trubetskoi: An Intellectual Among the Intelligentsia in Prerevolutionary Russia*, pp.44-49.
50 Solov'ev, *Kritika otvlechennykh nachal*, cited from *Sochineniia v Dvukh Tomakh*, vol.1 (Mysl', Moscow), p.589.
51 *Uchenie o Logose v ego istorii: filosofsko-istoricheskoe issledovanie* (1906), cited in op. cit., p.66.
52 Trubetskoi, *Osnovaniia Idealizma*, p.626.

53 Trubetskoi, *Metafizika v drevnei Gretsii* (1890). Cf. M. Bohachevsky-Chomiak, op. cit., pp.37-45.
54 S.N. Trubetskoi, commentary to the Russian translation of *Euthydemus*, in *Tvorenie Platona*, vol.2 (1903), pp.267-286.
55 The criticism was launched by the philosopher-jurist, B. Chicherin, in an article entitled 'Sushchestvo i metody idealizma,' *VFP*, 37 (1897), pp.185-238. Trubetskoi's reply, 'V Zashchitu idealizma', appeared in the same issue, pp.288-327. Cf. Gaidenko, op. cit., p.28.
56 Ibid. Cited in Gaidenko, pp.28-29.
57 See the various *Obozrenie Prepodovaniia* published annually by the academies.
58 G. Florovsky, *Ways of Russian Theology*, Part Two, trans. Robert L. Nichols (Notable & Academic Books, 1987), p.7.
59 Quoted in Florovsky, p.6.
60 Ibid. See also A. Abramov, 'Kant v russkoi dukhovno-akademicheskoi filosofii' in *Kant i Filosofiia v Rossii* (Moscow, 1994), p.82. A bibliography of Russian translations and commentaries of Kant's philosophy mentions a published translation dating from 1803 (*The Fundamental Principles of the Metaphysics of Morals*) and a second dating from 1804 (*Observations on the Sensations of the Beautiful and the Sublime...*). Otherwise, the bulk of published translations and commentaries (other than those published for internal use by the theological academies) date from the 1860s onwards, the first published translation of the *Critique of Pure Reason* appearing in 1867 only. See 'Bibliograficheskii spisok izdanii I. Kanta i literatury o nem (1803-1918)', compiled by L.S. Davydova and B.V. Emel'ianov, in op. cit., pp.248-270.
61 Cf. Florovsky, op. cit., p.5. For an account of philosophical instruction in the St. Petersburg Academy (which had issued a charter along similar lines in 1809) see archpriest Vl. Mustafin, 'Filosofskie dispiliny v S.-Peterburgskoi Dukhovnoi Akademii', in *Bogoslovskie Trudy. Iubileinyi Sbornik* (Moscow, 1986), pp.186-191. See also: A. Abramov, 'Filosofiia v duhovnykh akademiiakh (traditsia platonizma v russkom dukhovno-akademicheskom filosofstvovanii)', *VP*, 9 (1997), pp.138-155.
62 Ibid. See also I. Chistovich, *Istoriia Sankt-Peterburgskoi Akademii* (1857), cited in G. Shpet, *Ocherk razvitiia russkoi filosofii* (Petrograd, 1922) in *Russkaia Filosofiia*, p.371.
63 N. Riasanovsky, *A History of Russia* (New York, 1963), p.353.
64 Ibid. See also James H. Billington, *The Icon and the Axe* (New York, 1966); Alexandre Koyré, *La philosophie et le problème national...* (Paris, 1929).
65 Billington, op. cit., p.290ff.
66 Ibid., p.292.
67 Karpov, *Vvedenie v filosofiiu*, p.66.
68 Karpov, 'Vzgliad na dvizhenie filosofii v mire khristianskom i na prichiny razlichnikh eia napravlenii', *ZhMNP*, vol 92, 11 (1856), p.190.
69 Cf. Abramov, op. cit., p.83.
70 Some of the more noted examples on the philosophy of Kant include: P.I. Linitskii, *Ob umozrenie i otnoshenii umozritel'nogo poznaniia k opytu* (Kiev, 1881); also his *Osnovnye voprosy filosofii: opyt sistematicheskogo izlozheniia filosofii* (Kiev, 1901); Karpov, 'Filosofskii ratsionalizm noveishego vremeni', *Khristianskoe Chtenie*, pt.1 (1860), pp.501-550; M.I. Karinskii, *Lektsii po istorii drevnei filosofii, chitannie studentam SPb. Dukhovnoi Akademii v 1888/9g* (SPb., 1889); A. Kirilovich, 'Uchenie Kanta o Tserkvi', *Vera i Razum*, (Khar'kov, 1893); V. Kudriatsev, 'Metafizicheskii analiz ideal'nogo poznaniia', *Vera i Razum*, 1888; P.V. Tikhomirov, *Vechnii mir v filosofskom proekte Kanta: Ocherk* (Sergiev Posad, 1899), and his *Istoriia filosofii, kak protsess postepennoi vyrabotki nauchno obosnovannogo i istinnogo mirovozzreniia* (Sergiev Posad, 1899).
71 P. Florenskii, 'Kosmologicheskie antinomii Kanta' (1908), cited in A. Akhutin, op. cit., p.78.

72 The other texts include 'Kosmologicheskie antinomii Kanta' (1908); 'Obshchechelovecheskie korni idealizma' (1909); *Stolp i utverzhdenie istiny* (1914).
73 'Kul't i filosofiia' (1918) in *Bogoslovskie Trudy*, 17 (1977), p.122.
74 Ibid., pp.122-123.
75 Ibid., p.124.
76 See *Stolp...*,vol. 1/i (Moscow: Pravda, 1990), p.156; pp.158-159.
77 'Kul't i filosofiia', p.126.
78 *Obshchechelovecheskie korni idealizma*, p.30.
79 S. Bulgakov, *Svet Nevechernyi* (1917). Cited in Ahutin, op. cit., p.79.
80 'Vstupitel'noe slovo' (1914). Cited in *P.A. Florenskii*, vol.1/ii (Moscow: Pravda, 1990), p.820.
81 Ibid., p.823.
82 P. Iurkevich, 'Razum po ucheniiu Platona i opyt po ucheniiu Kanta' (speech delivered in January 1866 at Moscow University) in *P.A. Iurkevich: Filosofskie Proizvedeniia* (Moscow: Pravda, 1990), pp.500-501.
83 Ibid., p. 503.
84 Iurkevich's quotation would seem to be an abridgement of the following: 'But although the schemata of sensibility serve thus to realise the categories, it must strike everybody that they at the same time restrict them, that is, limit them by conditions foreign to the understanding and belonging to sensibility.' Quoted from *Critique of Pure Reason*, trans. F. Max Müller (New York: Doubleday & Company, 1966), p.126.
85 Iurkevich, op. cit., pp.512-513.
86 Ibid., pp.509-510.
87 Ibid., p.516.
88 Ibid., p.520.
89 Cf. Nemeth, 'Karpov and Jurkevic on Kant: Philosophy in Service to Orthodoxy?', in *SEET*, vol.45, 3 (1993), p.211.
90 'Ideia', in Iurkevich, op. cit., pp.14-15.
91 A. Akhutin, *op. cit.*, p.78.
92 S.N. Trubetskoi, *Metafizika v drevnei Gretsii*, p.27.
93 *Physical Monodology*, translated from the Latin (1905). See 'Bibliograficheskii spisok...' in Abramov, op. cit.
94 Witness, for example, the interplay of Kantian, neo-Kantian (especially Natorp), and Platonic references in Semën Frank's *Predmet Znaniia*.
95 Florenskii, 'Filosofiia i Kult', p.129.
96 Zhakov, op. cit., p.14; p.17.
97 V. Ern, 'Nechto o Logose, russkoi filosofii i nauchnosti: po povodu zhurnala *Logosa*', *Moskovskii Ezhenedel'nik*, nos.29-32 (1910). The *Logos* episode in Russian intellectual history, together with the polemic it provoked with Russian thinkers associated with the publishing house *Put'*, whose aim, the editorial board declared, was 'the philosophical rediscovery of Eastern Orthodoxy, and of its applicability in the contemporary world' has been discussed in some detail by a number of Russian and Western specialists. See, for example, M. Bezrodnyj, 'Zur Geschichte des russischen Neukantianismus. Die Zeitschrift *Logos* und ihre Redakteure', *Zeitschrift für Slawistik* 37 (1992), pp.489-511; A. Abramov, 'O russkom kantianstve i neokantianstve v zhurnale *Logos*' in *Kant i Filosofiia v Rossii*, pp.227-247; M. A. Meerson, '*Put'* against *Logos*: The Critique of Kant and Neo-Kantianism by Russian Religious Philosophers in the Beginning of the Twentieth Century', in *SEET : Neo-Kantianism in Russian Thought*, vol.47, nos. 3-4 (December 1995), pp.225-243.
98 Cf. A. Walicki, *Legal Philosophies of Russian Liberalism* (Clarendon Press, Oxford, 1987), pp.404-470.
99 Cf., Meerson, op. cit., p.240.

100 Ibid. In an article on Ernst Cassirer written in the late twenties, Losev also claimed that in his last work, *Die deutsche Philosophie der Gegenwart in Selbstdarstellungen* (Leipzig, 1921), Cassirer had completely revised his epistemology in the light of neo-Platonic ontology. Cf. Meerson, ibid., p.241.
101 Florenskii, 'Kul't i filosofiia', p.126.
102 See his 'Sushchnost' nemetskogo fenomenalizma', in *Mech i Krest* (Moscow, 1915).
103 Florenskii, *Obshchie korni...*, pp.7-8.
104 Zhakov, op. cit., p.16.

Chapter 3

Plato as an Impulse in Russian Philosophy of Law

Running through much juridical thought in late nineteenth-century Russia were repeated attempts to establish the moral and legal rights of the individual, and to square these with the interests of the state. In many respects, this kind of thinking had been encouraged by the era of reform inaugurated under Alexander II. Certain intellectuals hoped that the changes introduced into the educational and judicial systems would help ensure the lasting success of perhaps the most decisive reform at that time, namely, the emancipation of the serfs. It was crucial, they believed, to recognize the civil status of the peasant population, but to do so meant having to educate the population at large to respect the law, to admit of its normative value. Associating law and morality formed an important component in legal thought throughout the late imperial period. At issue was the need to overcome a deep prejudice against 'law', which many identified with the arbitrary practice of the state, by somehow locating it in the moral realm. It is precisely in this context that both the Platonic idea of law/justice and the good, as well as the Kantian categorical imperative served as important references for Russian juridical thinkers.

In some respects, it is no surprise that Plato should have figured as a positive reference in Russian juridical science, but, in others, it was rather paradoxical. Given that his philosophy already enjoyed pride of place in the official pantheon of national literature, it might only be expected that Plato's name should have figured as often as it did in the teaching programmes of the Faculty of Law. Moreover, in view of the historical perspective in which lecture courses in the philosophy of law were generally read, it is no surprise that the Platonic notion of justice should have comprised an important early chapter, as, indeed, it did. That said, however, once philosopher-jurists endeavoured to evaluate the relevance of Plato's thought for modern-day society, his status as a 'positive reference', prized over his later successors, proved to be more problematic. Most agreed that Plato's role in contemporary theories was minor, and in need of the complement – or rectification – provided by post-Enlightenment philosophy. Once again, it fell to Kant to act as a sort of interface between Plato and his Russian readers. Kant's practical philosophy highlighted the problems at issue in endeavours by Russian philosopher-jurists to accommodate the rights of the individual to the social good. It also allowed them to appreciate the real extent to which the Platonic model of social justice could serve in their own projects to create a modern Russian society.

Reforming Justice in Late Imperial Russia

The hopes raised by the Judicial Reform in 1864 were short-lived. Calls by more liberal-minded jurists, '*publitsists*', and philosophers to admit of the inviolable dignity of the person, or the immutable value of law, tended to fall on deaf ears, their projects to improve the judiciary system along Western European lines, more often than not, thwarted by social practices and attitudes which simply resisted any bid to introduce change. Opponents to the reform process, moreover, were often quick to see the flaws in the reform programme itself, once parts of it were put into practice. The obvious immediate difficulties in instituting a just legal procedure with adequately trained judges and an impartial jury prompted its critics to call for a return to the pre-reform tradition of closed courts trials. To a point this is understandable. Given that judges were now invited to decide cases 'on the basis of their conscience, as well as the law', all sorts of deviations from the spirit of an ideal legality were imaginable. On paper, at least, the strict, formalized rules by which judges had been bound prior to the reform, obliged, as they were, to apply the law 'in accordance with their exact and literal meaning, without any change or expansion' did, in the eyes of some, have the advantage of sparing executors of justice from assuming the heavy burden of moral responsibility.[1]

Other major difficulties, at the centre of polemics among specialists in civil and criminal law, involved assimilating aspects of customary law, according to which the peasantry had been traditionally tried by their elders, to a new civil law code, applicable for one and all. In practice, as documented in eyewitness accounts, this occasionally led to even worse discrimination between the peasants and the rest of society. A case in point concerns the regional *volost'* law courts, which continued to enforce corporal punishment, but only when it was a matter of infractions committed by peasants.[2] Consequently, the *volost'* courts, which, anyway, were used mostly by former serfs, came to stand for separateness, as opposed to equality before the law. Indeed, this lingering disparity in dispensing justice was all the more exacerbated by the fact that, despite the programme of emancipation, the peasantry continued to be tied to the commune. It was only with Stolypin's agrarian reform in 1906, which granted the peasantry the right to private ownership, that members of this 'estate' (*soslovie*) finally acquired legal rights equal to those of other social classes.

While advocates of the ideal of legality may have been appalled by this kind of discriminatory practice, its survival after the 1864 legislation provides a clear illustration of resistance to reform on two fronts. On the one hand, conservative bureaucrats, gentry, as well as certain intellectuals, wanted to maintain a paternalistic relationship with the rural population. On the other, part of the peasantry itself was unwilling to change its longstanding customs, and continued to dispute minor issues on the basis of local tradition. And if government policy was, at best, poorly focused and mismanaged, in practice it betrayed a deep-seated reluctance to live with a fairer legal system. One of the most significant countermeasures dating from the period of conservative rule under Alexander III was the introduction, in 1889, of the office of land captaincies. Officials were appointed from the gentry directly by the Ministry of the Interior in order to exercise bureaucratic supervision over the peasants. Moreover, they received vast judicial powers, and thus, contrary to the 1864 legislation, justice and administration were, once again, brought together and placed under the control of a single state representative. Hopes, therefore, to transform the Russian people into a more just and modern society were quickly thwarted.

Setbacks of this kind prompted reflection among the initiators and proponents of reform on other means of pursuing their goals. One way involved rhetoric aimed at reminding the reading public of all-but-lost high ideals, and to suggest that the original momentum of reform might still be recovered. To this end, professional jurists and *publitsisty* produced monographs designed to commemorate the spirit of the 1864 judicial reform. They published 'secular hagiographies' of some of Russia's leading judges and advocates, as well as transcripts of defence speeches (*sudebnie rechi*) as telling examples of how justice should, and could, be carried out 'in accordance with their conscience, as well as the law'.[3] Otherwise, attempts to promote a respect for law were argued out in *publitsistika*, with intellectuals of different camps engaging in their own private battles as to its meaning and application. Yet, this public sphere in which intellectuals were able to present their various viewpoints was, of course, very limited. Moreover, there was a major problem lurking in these quarrels which no one could easily resolve, namely, the huge discrepancy that existed between appeals to admit of classical juridical definitions of the person – as self-determining and with a right to property – and the meagre relevance of such definitions to a society in which only a very small percentage of the population answered the criteria of 'civil subject'.

This web of circumstances should be borne in mind when we consider the nature and gradual consolidation of a 'legal culture' in late nineteenth-century Russia. One of the leading questions asked by both theoreticians and practitioners of law alike was how best to motivate change in Russian judicial practice? It is interesting to observe that, while they did certainly base their arguments for legal progress on recent transformations, both at home and abroad, there was a strong tendency, as some recent commentators have noted, to ground a legal culture of the future in abstract metaphysical arguments, in natural law theory and idealism.[4] Countless times one comes across statements to the effect that 'law that would not rely upon the strength of morality, would in vain support itself by means of compulsion alone'.[5] Insisting on the importance of a morally/legally grounded 'personal principle' (*lichnostnoe nachalo*) was a central point in Pavel Novgorodtsev's writings, and one which directly guided his views about the nature of society. He, for one, repeatedly reminded his readers that 'the concept of society has no other ethical significance than the one it receives from the principle of personality'.[6] For the reader today, appeals of this kind to admit of a moral/legal consciousness, are all the more poignant given the lingering social injustice of which these intellectuals were all too well aware, and which they did, when chance allowed, criticize openly. Boris Chicherin, whose understanding of law entailed, in the first place, the free self-determination of the individual, denounced slavery, serfdom, the caste system and class divisions – so many obstacles standing in the way of this – as no less than immoral. Vladimir Solov'ev, in particular, frequently singled out for criticism acts of social and moral injustice which he saw being perpetrated against peasants or minority ethnic groups. Yet, while his own vindication of a 'personal principle' as a basis on which to establish the common good (viz., the foundations of an 'objective ethics' that both Solov'ev and Novgorodtsev were working on in this period) should certainly be applauded, it remains that late nineteenth-century Russian social reality was sharply at odds with these conceptions. Indeed, it is tempting to go so far as to suggest that the facts of everyday life simply undermined the credibility of such projects.

In the absence of a properly open forum of debate other than journals, which themselves were frequently subjected to surveillance, or censored, it was in the university lecture hall that the task of inculcating what we might call a 'legal consciousness' in young students of law, history and philosophy was, ultimately, to see more positive results. This is not, of course, to say that the university had always been a privileged forum of free discussion. On the contrary, some of the prejudices which had developed among Russia's educated public were in part due to an education programme which, because of the restrictions imposed on it, actually encouraged an attitude of 'legal nihilism', as Walicki put it. For Slavophiles, and, later, anarchists and Bolsheviks, law signified the whims of the tsar carried out by his bureaucratic henchmen. 'Law' was, therefore, to be distrusted as an instrument of oppressive authority. It was a distrust, moreover, which brought many intellectuals to the romantic and rather anarchic opinion that 'law' and 'freedom' were two contradictory notions.[7] However, as I shall argue in more detail below, a more thorough grounding in law – its history, practice and philosophical foundations – which was introduced and consolidated during the reform period, did help combat the prejudices against legal (civil) order which lingered in society at large.

During the reign of Nicholas I, instruction in law, like philosophy, had been subject to heavy censorship. A statute passed in 1835, ostensibly to reorganize the cathedra within the faculty, led to the creation of courses which were highly dogmatic and practical in character.[8] With the chairs of philosophy, history and political economy removed to form the first section of the Philosophy Faculty, instruction in the Juridical Faculty concentrated henceforth on state law, 'customary law' (*narodnoe pravo*) and Russian law (broken down into civil, criminal, commercial and canon law).[9] Courses in what had previously been called 'encyclopaedia of law' were renamed '*Zakonovedenie*', and involved, as memoir accounts confirm, rote learning of the Codified Laws (*Svod Zakonov*). In 1849, as a reaction to the revolutionary events which had assailed most of Europe, instruction in state law (*gosudarstvennoe pravo*) was also suspended on Nicholas I's orders. It was believed to be a potentially dangerous source of insurrectionary activity.[10] The single exception to these constant modifications in juridical education concerned Roman law, which was taught without interruption throughout the century. Indeed, one cannot help but note a certain irony here given that it was precisely Roman juridical excellence that Slavophile writers identified and condemned as the root cause of Western rationalism.

One might well imagine that the pragmatic manner in which law was taught prior to the reforms, with its aim to prepare students for their future state service as 'jurist-bureaucrats' (*iurist-chinovniki*', as Miliukov called them[11]), did little to enhance trust in legal institutions. On the contrary, it arguably encouraged the attitude of legal nihilism that Walicki describes. The Slavophiles believed that, given the peace-loving nature of the Russian people and their deep faith, theirs was a nation which could dispense with law. Political and/or civil rights were simply incompatible with spiritual freedom. As Konstantin Aksakov expressed it:

> The Russian nation/people (*narod*) is a non-state nation, that is, it does not strive for state power, does not want political rights for itself, it does not even possess the seeds of national lust for power. The Russian nation, devoid of any political element, has detached the state from itself and does not want to govern. Not wishing to govern, the nation/people has given the government unlimited state power. In exchange, the Russian nation gives itself moral freedom, the freedom of life and the spirit.[12]

This attitude was also fostered by the State. The 'official' historians of Russia and her literature, Mikhail Pogodin and Stepan Shevyrev, both of whom taught at Moscow University in the 1830s and 1840s, presented a deep-seated passivity, together with an implicit trust in the tsar as the holder of truth, as the most positive virtues of the Russian people. The people could, therefore, they argued, dispense with law.[13] Such a seemingly endemic distrust of law was, moreover, an enduring one, and not just a sign of reaction to the police regime of Nicholas I. Writing in 1904, Lev Tolstoi condemned outright the significance of law in the name of absolute moral values, claiming that social betterment may come about only through the religious and moral perfectioning of individual people. On the contrary, political agitation, which, to his mind, merely enticed people with the illusion of social improvement, tended, if anything, to put a stop to true progress, and to drive his point home he singled out the constitutional states of France, England, and America as examples of 'illusionary progress'.[14]

It has been suggested that, underlying this 'legal nihilism' was a tendency – indeed, one borne out by educational practice in the first half of the century – to confuse law (*pravo*) with positive or codified laws (*zakon*). The upshot was to ignore the distinctions which, from a juridical-philosophical perspective, exist between the two notions.[15] Attempts to correct this juridical short-sightedness was a task the generation of philosopher-jurists, active in the post-Reform period, set itself. They believed that it was important to bring students of law to understand the difference between law as a normative principle and codified law (*zakon*), moreover, that it was crucial to inculcate an appreciation of the unshakeable moral foundations of law (*pravo*).

Teaching Justice: Between Western Science and Domestic Needs

It was in the period of Reform that the prestige of the Juridical Faculty in the leading universities began to grow. As early as the 1870s, philosopher-jurists such as Redkin, Nicolai Korkunov, Chicherin, Iurkevich, Novgorodtsev and Evgeni Trubetskoi, began producing original literature in the field.[16] This is quite noteworthy if one considers that, professors in the Faculty of History and Philology continued to rely quite heavily on foreign scholarship, both translated and in the original languages. It was only in the following decades that they began to produce more original studies of their own. Henceforth, instruction in law consisted in three main branches: Roman law, encyclopaedia of law and the history of the philosophy of law. Yet, judging by the nature of the accompanying textbooks, published lectures and recommended secondary literature, the latter two courses were as philosophically generalist as they were intended to be juridically specialized. This practice was all the more current with the renewed cutback in philosophical instruction at the time of the Counter Reform, when, in the words of the historian Pavel Miliukov, the Faculty of History and Philology was turned into little more than 'a special school for ancient languages, with history and literature as additional subjects'.[17]

Between the time Redkin and Iurkevich first made their appeal to recognize the value of law in the 1870s to the moment Novgorodtsev published his *Crisis in Contemporary Juridical Consciousness* (1909), Russian teaching and research in the philosophy of law had become scientifically quite diversified, with scholars defending a variety of different approaches. Suffice it to mention Petrazycki's intuitive theory of law, or Novgorodtsev's updating of natural law, or again Bogdan Kistiakovskii, whose work on the socialistic foundations of law marked a break with the individualist premises of law which had characterized the work of earlier thinkers such as Chicherin or Korkunov. Yet running through these different approaches, and, irrespective of the polemic that sometimes divided their various proponents, were a number of common motifs, the origin of which stemmed from the emphasis repeatedly given to the distinction to be observed between codified law and the ideal nature of law. Chicherin stated this quite categorically:

> In no way should law and a people's obligations be established without knowing what, as such, a law is, where its source lies, and what demands derive from it. This principle is closely tied to the human person, for which reason it is necessary to study the nature of man, his qualities and significance.[18]

Understanding the meaning of law was prerequisite to the study of a host of related issues. These included the nature of the person (*lichnost'*) as a legal and/or moral entity endowed with civil rights, and, by extension, the problem of accommodating her legal and/or moral freedom to the equally important issue of ensuring social well-being (*blago*). In short, it was a matter of determining a just relation between the individual and the state. Although predominantly discussed in a theoretical way, these questions also spilled over into more obviously 'political' themes, such as constitutionalism, and rule of law. Granted, the latter was to become the subject of more open debate after the 1905 Revolution. Correspondingly, in this later period, the scope of instruction in law broadened quite considerably, to include courses such as 'the history of political theory', or 'the origins and the development of constitutionalism'.[19] Moreover, the growth in specialized branches of law relating more directly to legal practice – civil law, criminal law, international law, commercial law, civil court procedure and canon law – is a telling sign of how radically the university atmosphere changed in just a decade.

In their attempts to develop a juridical consciousness through education, philosopher-jurists commented the current state of the juridical science itself, together with its recent developments in Western Europe. In this regard Russian scholars tended to single out two main currents, neither of which, however, seemed to answer priorities at home. First, the Historical School of law (associated with Savigny), which saw in law the expression of a given people, or nation, seemingly undermined the ideal nature of law. Legal positivism, the second main current to be mentioned as one which dominated in the latter part of the nineteenth century, had, to the minds of many Russians, unwarrantedly severed the link between morality and law. Any number of textbooks, written by Russian juridical thinkers, offered a critique of the current situation in the juridical sciences. Iurkevich, for example, compared the idea of law as the expression of a particular nation's spirit – the position of the historical school – to a rejection of the universalist ambitions of the Christian worldview, and, sadly, he added, to the revival of a 'parochial' pagan world outlook. His main objection from a juridical point of view was that historical law proceeds from the particular to the general. On the contrary, 'the principles of life should not be fortuitous; they should be grounded not only in factors of a partial nature, but in the universal principles of reason'.[20] Chicherin also sharply criticized juridical positivism, especially as this was epitomized in Ihering's account of law as the 'politics of coercion' (*politika sily*).[21]

In Russia, then, it would seem that the problem of law needed to be posed differently. To this end, virtually all philosopher-jurists sought models or authorities in past philosophy. Some, such as Chicherin and Kavelin, also studied Russian history as a means to establish the right foundations for a modern-day state respectful of the law. For Chicherin, who, early in his career, had studied Russian history in light of her juridical institutions, it was necessary, given the course that Russian history had taken since Ivan III, to admit of a strong benevolent state, and only from within this structure vindicate individual civil rights. His combined theoretical and historical interests prompted his call for a 'strong hand' (*tverdaia ruka*), a strong state (*vlast'*), empowered to safeguard state unity, yet also 'liberal measures' (*liberalnye mery*), designed, he said, to protect the rights of the citizen.[22] With respect to the latter, he rigorously distinguished between the spheres of morality and law, cleaving very much to the Kantian distinction of positive and negative freedom.

Chicherin's manner of addressing this particular problem of 'civil rights and duties' was, if anything, the exception rather than the rule. Among contemporary philosopher-jurists (if not among practising lawyers who occasionally wrote theoretical articles on law) it was more usual to inculcate a sense of the value of the rule of law by appealing to the moral dimension of law, thereby insisting far more than Chicherin on the interrelationship of law and morality. In much the same vein, their views on the nature of society were, also, frequently motivated by a reflection about the relation between the individual person/citizen and the state in terms of law and/or morality. Paradoxically, such appeals to ground law in morality were actually not so remote from attitudes to the law among the peasantry, which traditionally spoke of crime and punishment in terms of 'sin' (*grekh*) and 'sympathy' (*zhalost'*). Though, surely no more than coincidental, it is tempting to imagine that the world outlook underlying rural customs might, indirectly, have played a role in the theories that certain jurist-philosophers were elaborating in the lecture hall and in their *kabinet*. All else aside, such calls to reinforce the moral dimension of law fitted well with the religious pathos according to which the commune elders administered justice.

*

A rapid overview of lecture courses written relatively early on in the reform period attests to an awareness among philosopher-jurists of the need to distinguish between law as an ideal principle (*pravo*) and *jus positivum* (rendered in Russian as *zakon*). In his introductory lecture (published in 1889, though originally drafted in the 1870s), Petr Redkin identified the latter with a 'command theory' of law, and set this off against what he called an inexhaustible belief, both among men and society at large, in a higher law, independent of positive law established by the will of a community. This ideal principle is both the source of all positive law, as it is also a yardstick, according to which the worth of positive laws may be evaluated.[23] Anxious to enhance the scientific value of law as a discipline, Redkin defined the subject of his proposed lecture course as 'the historical development of scientific thought about law (*pravo*), together with the related notions of truth (*pravda*) and justice (*spravedlivost'*)'. In addition, he regarded it as 'the scientific study of society and the state in which law comes to expression'.[24] Given the urgent need to train lawyers in a country with such a poorly developed legal system, grasping this last point, Redkin added, was especially important 'for us in Russia'.

Writing at roughly the same time, Pamfil Iurkevich also stressed the need for an 'education to juridical consciousness', in which the accent would be given in the first place to theory rather then practice:

> Up to now, the law code in Russia has been applied arbitrarily, like some sort of holy writ, unlike in England, for example, a country where, although lacking a law code as such, the law is applied in a humane way. That's why we so urgently need a Juridical Society, for, despite the fact that it is possible to study law in the official spheres of circuit courts or under Justices of the Peace (*okruznoi sud* or *mirovaia kamera*), the problem remains that law is still considered in a purely formal way. On the contrary, a juridical society would analyse law from within the framework of science. Nowadays, only in this sense, as a science, is law really important for us.[25]

In the course of their lectures on the philosophy of law, both professors addressed, from an historical perspective, the relation of law to morality. Iurkevich, the theologian, was quite explicit about this relation. For him, 'the task of the philosophy of law as a discipline is to show the vital link between the various possible forms of law and their moral ideas'.[26] In this regard he singled out Plato, seeing in his philosophy an original vindication of the ideal 'moral person' (*moral'naia lichnost'*), and of her role in grounding laws. With her capacity to distinguish actions which depend on necessity from those which depend on virtue, the moral person is, for Plato, as Iurkevich read him, 'the immutable source of law (*zakon*)'.[27] The ideal moral nature, was, Iurkevich believed, central to what may be said to constitute Plato's theory of natural law/justice, a theory, which 'engages all those necessary, obligatory forms of human relations (i.e. man's relation to God, to the external world, to himself, and to others). Failure to meet these demands is a form of evil'.[28] In this sense, Iurkevich saw Plato as an original proponent of natural law, meaning law vested with a 'moral essence', but which, in order to be grasped requires, as Iurkevich put it, a mass of knowledge, and religious convictions. Natural law may only be sought at the very highest levels of human nature. It requires man's striving for the good. It is a positive force, which is presupposed in every social order:

> All our positive laws are grounded in the idea of natural law as a force. Every form of government, community life, marriage, etc., is in essence merely the realization of this idea.[29]

Embedded in this kind of statement were a number of issues, which continued to preoccupy Russian intellectuals at the turn of the century. Endeavours to understand the nature of society through the prism of the morality/law problem, with 'natural law' grounded in transcendent values, arguably betokens a radically pre- and anti-modern mentality. That said, one might suggest that the Plato of the *Gorgias* (the rights of the stronger versus justice at all costs) and the *Republic*, in which he explored the essence of justice, and envisaged a social order respectful of just relations between its members, was of an interest to his Russian readers, that, perhaps, was more than incidental. Certainly, Plato's conception of politics as social ethics appealed to some juridical thinkers. Novgorodtsev and Solov'ev both referred to this in their own efforts to pass from a 'subjective' to 'objective' ethics, the task they set themselves being to 'complete' the (Kantian) principle of ethical individualism with a concept of social development. While they accepted that the aim and foundation of morality lay in the person, they also argued that her development occurred in circumstances created by the social environment. At this level, at least, it is understandable that they should have welcomed Plato for posing the political question in terms of how best to construct the state in relation to questions about the nature of man, morality and justice.

Past Philosophies for a Contemporary Science of Law: Plato and Kant as Two Paradigms in Juridical Thought

In discussions among Russian commentators about the relation between law and morality, duty and the good, it was almost inevitable that the philosophy of Kant should be evoked. Attitudes with respect to Kant ran from a fundamental acceptance of Kant's idea of moral duty grounded in human reason (the case of Chicherin, notably), to an outright rejection prompted by religious convictions (the example of Karpov). Generally speaking, most recognized and applauded Kant as the philosopher who had made the common ethical foundation of law and morality explicit in the categorical imperative. Yet, despite this major contribution to practical philosophy, they regretted that Kant did not provide solutions to problems concerning the moral foundations of society. In reaction to Kantian subjectivism (and the division between the private and public spheres that this connoted), Russian readers turned instead to Plato. Regarded as the proponent of the ideas of the good and justice, Plato seemed to offer principles of order relating both to the inner world of the human soul and to the social sphere as well. Consequently, in working out theories of an ideal legality it was not uncommon for Russian thinkers to offset two governing principles identified with each of these two philosophers, and which clearly marked the distance between them – the theory of 'duty' (*dolg*) originating in the Kantian categorical imperative, and the theory of 'the good' (*dobro*), which most immediately associated with Plato.

Plato as a Philosopher of Natural Law/Justice

The portrait of Plato to emerge in Russian histories of the philosophy of law is one which highlighted his contribution to the development of the idea of (social) justice. A usual procedure consisted in first identifying the main lines of Plato's philosophy as such, then to focus on his ethical theory and its immediate relevance to the construction of the social good, and in some cases, to the prevention or correction of social disorder. Redkin characterized Plato's thought in terms of a two-sided, theoretical and practical concern, each side corresponding to a particular realm of enquiry: knowledge of the *sushchee*, and the problem of virtue. The latter, to Redkin's mind, was particularly pertinent to the modern-day theory of criminal law. Given his understanding of virtue as the moral perfection of the soul, Plato, according to Redkin, considered punishment not in terms of revenge (an eye for an eye), but as a 'moral necessity based on the principle of correction and deterrence (*ustrashenie*)'.[30] It is an edifying means to purify the soul of base instincts. For Redkin, this attitude towards punishment was embryonic to the thinking which underscored contemporary theories of correction, prevention, as well as state security. For both Plato and his modern-day successors, protection of the state necessitated capital punishment. Both advocated that the state be rid of irremediably nefarious people, either by capital punishment or by expulsion. These stern measures are proposed on the grounds that, for the people concerned, it is better to die than to live:

> In this kind of thinking we see the beginnings of a fourth theory of criminal law. It is an absolute theory, according to which evil, as the denial of good, and the illegal (*nepravo*) as the denial of *pravo* should themselves be revoked in the name of the very essence of law (*sushchnost' prava*). For, evil is not true being (*istinnoe-sushchee*). Only the good is true being. Evil is shame (*porochnost'*), non-being (*nesushchee*).[31]

A second major feature that Redkin singled out for discussion concerned the importance Plato attributed to the virtue of justice as such (in Russian rendered in the combined terms of *pravda* (truth), *spravedlivost'* (justice), *pravednost'* (rightfulness). Plato, Redkin commented, likened this to the nature of the soul, which, in its perfection, manifests beauty, finesse, harmony, unity. In turn, the harmony and unity of heterogeneous elements are crucial to the principle of order, both with respect to the human soul, and also in relation to the political order of the city. In other words, for Plato, as Redkin presented him – as did most Russian commentators – the idea of law and justice is inextricably bound to the idea of 'order' understood as an aim towards which all human communities strive. On this point it should not be forgotten, as some contemporary specialists have indeed noted, that, for the Ancients, law/right had not yet acquired the meaning of a socially sanctioned rule. This was, rather, the hallmark of modern juridical thought. Somewhat differently, law implied the content of a rule, and, as such, was termed 'justice' or a 'just order'.[32]

In his lecture course entitled *The Political Ideals of the Ancient and Modern Worlds*, Novgorodtsev argued that Plato's understanding of the essence of justice represented an important moment in the development of the theory of natural law.[33] The meaning of justice in the life of man and of the state was, Novgorodtsev claimed, already a central issue for Plato in the early dialogues, *Apology*, *Crito*, and the *Gorgias*. Plato, who, as Novgorodtsev reminds his readers, did not distinguish between the terms 'just' and 'law' (*pravo*), tended to speak of 'natural justice' (*estestvennaia spravedlivost'*, as Novgorodtsev renders it). Against his contemporaries, the Sophists, Plato had contended that natural law/justice precedes, or serves as the foundation of positive laws (*zakony*). Moreover, the idea of justice is not simply contained in the idea of legality or written laws as his contemporary rivals claimed, but stems from the province of the ideal. As such, it is an affirmation of the quest of the good. In Novgorodtsev's terms, Plato set out to show that 'the foundations of justice are inextricably linked with the ideal world order, that the ideal of truth-justice (*pravda*) constitutes a vital force, which reveals itself in the destiny of a people'.[34]

How well-founded was Novgorodtsev in making Plato the first author of natural law? Ultimately this is a question for professional theoreticians and historians of the philosophy of law to decide. Still, it is interesting to note a coincidence between Novogorodstev's arguments and those of more recent scholars attracted by the image of a 'natural law Plato'. Ada Neschke, for one, has taken issue with accepted opinion, which ascribes the origins of natural law to the Pre-Socratics, the Sophists and the Stoics, by suggesting that their views did not amount to a comprehensive theory as such. This she attributes to Plato as 'une pensée qui, non seulement fonde le droit positif dans un droit naturel, mais aussi cherche à établir un ordre juste dans la communauté politique. Cette recherche d'un ordre juste s'exprime dans la question de savoir ce qu'est une bonne loi'.[35] And she identifies the source of the Platonic conception of law and justice in the following way:

> Le juste a son origine et son domaine dans la nature des choses (*fisis*). Par conséquent, Platon s'attelle à analyser la nature des choses, à savoir la nature de la cité, de l'âme humaine, et du monde entier, ce dernier comprenant la nature du sensible et celle de l'être parfait.[36]

As for Novgorodstev, he discerned the very same meaning and practice of law/justice in the criticism that Plato launched against the eudemonistic conception of justice defended by Callicles in the *Gorgias*. Novgorodtsev summarizes Plato's standpoint in the following manner:

> Happiness and justice do not consist in the fact of satisfying one's own inclinations indiscriminately, nor in striving to have more than others, but rather in trying to exercise (or avoid a lack of) self-control, to respect equality 'which both among the gods and among men has great significance'.[37]

According to Novgorodtsev, by answering the Sophists in this way, Plato was advocating a supreme norm, which poses limits on the individual lives of people, as well as on their relations with one another. As he understood it, this marked a first attempt to forge the principle of natural justice, a principle which is a universal imperative rule, and yet is vested with a certain content in the sense that Plato sought to establish what it is that constitutes justice:

> Natural law is not only defined as an unconditional norm of life and as a fulcrum of social relations. An attempt is also made to establish its content by linking it to the principle of equality, and by bringing it to bear on the principles of community (*obshchenie* – association), friendship, moderation and justice, those principles, notably, which serve as the foundations of the moral world order.[38]

Plato, we know, went on to develop this idea of higher justice in the *Republic*. Summarizing the famous account of a just state in which the harmonious relations between classes mirrors man's soul as a balanced (just) interrelation between reason, will and feeling, Novgorodtsev drew the conclusion that 'justice is something which stems from nature':

> Just and unjust actions are to the soul what healthy and poisonous foods are to the body. Certain strengthen the soul, others infect it with disease, and this happens precisely because such is their very nature (*svoistvo*). Such, therefore, is their likely impact on man (...). In this way, Plato makes his case that justice and injustice exert an influence on man's soul in and of themselves, due to their very nature (...). Unlike the Sophists, Plato presents justice as natural law (...) derived from the deeper foundations of the order of the world, and bearing a real inner force.[39]

According to Novgorodstev, and, indeed, many scholars since, thanks to his conception of a healthy soul based on the correct balance of parts – reason, will and desire – Plato convincingly resolved this particular controversy with the Sophists. He succeeded in closing the gap between nature and law: 'The healthy and natural soul will contain no conflict within it, it will inevitably express itself in acts which are lawful and just.' As Novgorodtsev read him, Plato attributed relatively little importance to the imperative character of justice (with the exception, of course, in the *Laws*). Instead, he focused on the essence of justice, understood as harmonious order, in which the good finds its true justification. Indeed, in posing the question of the essence of justice, of law (*pravo*), and of a good law code (*zakony*), Plato complemented, by virtue of the difference, an understanding of law in which greater emphasis would ultimately be given to its regulative dimension. By this, Novgorodtsev had in mind the concept of natural law such as this developed in the wake of Enlightenment philosophy. In its more modern formulation, natural law gradually became identified with the 'inalienable rights of the individual', as a vindication of the autonomous, absolute significance of the individual which remains unaltered in any political structure. More than a call for a better law code, natural law came to mark a protest by the individual against state absolutism. The professor of law at Kharkhov University, a certain Fateev, gave the following, fairly typical, description:

> The rights of the person (...) were discovered by thinkers in modern times, the first to have spoken about natural law and natural states (*sostoianie*). Referring to the natural law doctrine, these 'writer-individualists' showed that equality and freedom are more primordial (*iskonnee*) than either the practice of corporate class (*soslovnykh*) privileges which grew up in the Middle Ages, or the emergence of state absolutism (...). This view of law, which takes as its starting point the individual, and which bases law and the state on principles

of natural law, culminated with the French Revolution – that is, in a politics of liberal individualism.⁴⁰

Given its ultimate development in modern thought, there was, as indeed Novgorodtsev was aware, a potential conflict of interests between, on the one hand, a view of natural law as a formal, universal rule, closely associated with the Kantian categorical imperative, in short as something required (*Sollen, dolzhenstvovanie*), and the ancient (Platonic) conception which tended to identify justice/law as the good. This, in turn, had less to do with obligations or rules, but inferred, rather, an aim to be achieved. In this sense, natural justice connotes a certain content (a harmonious order in human relations), and as such, becomes a model to imitate, to be put into practice.⁴¹ It was precisely this 'Platonic' view of law and of a lawfully ordered state which inspired several philosopher-jurists – professional and amateur alike – in their attempts to fill the vacuum which had been left by the purely formal principle of the Kantian moral law.

Plato and/or Kant: Duty versus the Good

Karpov's sharp criticism of the categorical imperative was based on what he considered to be the fundamental 'anti-Christian' and egotistical spirit of Kantian thought. The second formulation of the categorical imperative was, to his mind, decisive proof of this. For Karpov, '*Act as to treat humanity, whether in your own person or in that of any other, always at the same time as an end, and never merely as a means*' flew in the face of the meaning of human existence. 'Moral beings', he protested, 'have to go forward, serving one another.' Only in this way would the foundations of society be strengthened:

> Each human being is to be understood precisely as a means, in service to others. Accordingly, all people are conceived of as one big family, joined together by the law of mutual love, which, in its very essence, is a living sacrifice. For, in the words of the Apostle (I Corinthians X 22–25) 'Each of you ought to study the well-being of others, not your own.'⁴²

Much more in line with Kant (in the *Metaphysical Elements of Justice*), Chicherin believed that natural rights could be reduced to one – freedom – understood, that is, as independence from the constraints of another's will. Insofar as it is compatible with the freedom of everyone else in accordance with a universal law, freedom, Kant argued, and as Chicherin agreed, is the one and sole original right belonging to every human being by virtue of his humanity. Likewise, for Chicherin, freedom is an ever-present element of law, although its legally sanctioned limits (i.e. of *zakon*) might change in relation to historical and social conditions. Accordingly, Chicherin formulated his conception of law as a 'juridically determined freedom':

'pravo est' (vneshnaia) svoboda cheloveka opredelennaia zakonom.'[43] But while, for Chicherin, law is inseparable from freedom (a view which was totally at odds with the Slavophile credo), he clearly restricted its reach to mean 'negative' or 'external' freedom, and from this perspective drew attention to the fundamental differences between law and morality. To his mind, law involved the rules to be observed by free individual agents. In this respect, freedom refers to man's external freedom in his relation with other free individual agents. Morality, on the other hand, provides the norms for man's unbounded inner freedom as positive self-determination. In this inner realm of freedom, actions are carried out not on the basis of reciprocal coercion, but voluntarily (*dobrovol'no*). In constructing his argument, Chicherin explicitly took his cue from the Kantian moral law, according to which moral injunctions are not conditioned by extraneous aims, but are determined purely formally, by the concept of unconditional and universal obligation (*dolzhenstvovanie*) (wherein, in fact, Kant admitted of 'feelings' of respect, duty). 'As an abstract rational principle', Chicherin wrote, endorsing Kant, 'the moral law determines inner thoughts only.' Only here, in the inner realm, may it be an unconditional claim, because it is only here that man is entirely self-determining. Whence the radical difference between morality and law. The latter determines external volitional relations, the former – inner motives:

> *Pravo* is related to obligation. The moral law throws light on this relation, for respect towards man, as a rational being, requires this. But the moral law goes further: it requires that man be given not only that which accrues to him on the grounds of juridical laws, but also that which befits him according to the moral law. In this consists inner truth.[44]

Chicherin's concern to demarcate the boundary between morality and law was to a degree prompted by what he regretted as the current tendency to do precisely the opposite. As he saw it, morality which tries to institutionalize itself by legal means risks turning into little more than an instrument of immoral and lawless oppression. The same would also be true of law, he feared, should it encroach on the realm of morality. To Chicherin's mind, the moralizing jurists advocating legislation on matters of morality, contributed, willy-nilly, to the destruction of the autonomy of the personality, the cornerstone of both morality and law.[45] Even so, he did recognize a meeting point between morality and law, and acknowledged a degree of reciprocity between them:

> Though, in essence, moral law is unconditional, as such it is formal. It acquires content from without, and this content requires adaptation. Coming to realization in the external world, the moral law has to conform to the circumstances and laws of this world, just as man, in order to master nature has to submit to its laws. In this covenant between the moral and the

empirical resides the perfection of life, that which constitutes the aim of humanity. Here morality and law come together.⁴⁶

For his views which, overall, stemmed from a double Kantian-Hegelian attachment, Chicherin was a rather isolated figure among juridical thinkers in late nineteenth-century Russia. Most of his 'philosopher-jurist' contemporaries went further in redressing the balance between law and morality, tending to highlight more the close interrelatedness of the two concepts, rather than to insist on their difference. Novgorodtsev summarized this relation succinctly in terms of reciprocity and unity. Moreover, his comments signal the importance of this relation in terms of their ultimate goal – the fulfilment of the good. In this sense, he may be said to be moving between Kantian and Platonic perspectives:

> Insofar as both law (*pravo*) and morality refer to the sphere of the ideal and of the ought (*dolzhnoe*), they cannot be grounded in completely separate principles. This would mean that the human ideal is double. Both morality and juridical law (*zakon*) address, in equal measure, the inner existence of man, his will. And, even if they may differ in partial matters, in temporary results, this does not rule out the fact that their ultimate goals are one and the same. Both law (*pravo*) and morality are governed by the principle of the person (*licnost'*). Albeit operating differently in one or the other sphere, she brings them together in view of the ultimate aim, namely the realization, in life itself, of the idea of the good.⁴⁷

Addressing the question of the relation between morality and law, the specialist of Roman law, Veniamin Khvostov, took his cue, like Chicherin, from Kant, but like Novgorodtsev, his remarks also bear witness to a shift in affinities, once he set the relation between law and morality in terms of an ultimate goal. In a lecture series on ethics, which he read at the Courses of Higher Education for Women in St. Petersburg, much of Khvostov's account was an obvious reconstruction of Kantian philosophy. The moral ideal, he began, concerns, first and foremost, man's obligation to himself: 'Each and every one of us should cultivate his character under the guidance of the moral ideal.'⁴⁸ Besides this moral duty to ourselves, we should also practise this towards others, and towards society at large, which, for its part, exists in terms of a relation of obligation to its members. We should not forget that the person is not only an instrument of social aims, but also an end in herself. Society, therefore, has to provide each and every member with the chance to serve his or her own personal wealth: 'this marks the moral end limit of social influence (*vozdeistvie*) over the individual.'⁴⁹ And, as if there could be any doubt as to the source of Khvostov's argument, here he concluded with the following remark:

> The value of morality resides, as Kant correctly pointed out, in its autonomy, insofar as each of us performs a duty in accordance with a free exercise of

will, prompted by his or her convictions. Alongside morality there is *pravo*, meaning a set of norms for which the supreme authority of state power stands, and which in turn, vests these norms with a compulsory, heteronomous character.[50]

Although Khvostov readily acknowledged his indebtedness to Kant on the question of moral autonomy, it was nevertheless the case that its reach was, finally, too limited to enable him to tackle a set of problems which he had posed at the outset of his chapter on the law/morality problem. Once again, like so many of his peers, the fundamental issue that Khvostov wanted to explore from the perspective of the philosophy of law was how best to accommodate individual legal and moral rights to the common good. To answer this question, he turned to the 'amateur philosopher-jurist', Vladimir Solov'ev, visibly approving the latter's endeavours to provide the state and law with a moral foundation, even as – or, precisely because – it meant querying the purely formal principles of Kantian practical philosophy. By way of a solution, Solov'ev had tried to invest the categorical imperative with a 'content'. His views concerning the moral underpinnings of society not only set the stage for his quarrel with Kant, but also guided his enquiry into the nature of the common good. To this end he insisted, far more than Chicherin had, on the moral dimension of law. For him, it was important to complete the purely formal principle of ethical individualism with a theory of social development which is, first and foremost, morally grounded. As for Khvostov, in passing from Kant to Solov'ev, he was, so to speak, confronting two paradigms – that of duty (Kant), and that of the good, identified with the Platonic tradition, and co-opted by its Russian adherents.

Solov'ev had actually begun analysing the relation between law and morality in *Critique of Abstract Principles* (1877–1880). In this early work he relegated the significance of law to a negative function, seeing its purpose as that of imposing limits. This viewpoint which, although not entirely unlike Chicherin's (who endorsed this distinction), brought him close to the Slavophiles, whose disdain for law in the name of love the young Solov'ev clearly shared. However, when in 1894 he returned to this text with the intention of revising parts of it for a new edition, Solov'ev's ideas on the question had undergone such a change that he ended up writing a new book instead. The result was *Justification of the Good* (1897).[51] In this last, major work, Solov'ev reflected about the meaning of law, the state, and their moral foundations in light of his belief in the absolute moral value of the good. His point in arguing for the moral value of juridical institutions, and their significance for moral progress, was to convince his reader that, for the development of freedom and morality, a well-organized (*blagoustroennoe*) society is required. Without this, he believed, morality remains an empty, abstract notion. Accordingly, from this perspective Solov'ev explored the relation between morality and law, and while he still admitted of their differences, it was less a difference of nature as one of degree, not unlike the difference, he suggested, which exists between notions of 'absolute' and 'relative'. Each presupposes the other. As such, they are inextricably bound.[52]

In contrasting the unlimited character of moral claims (*trebovanie*) with the limited, specific nature of the juridical, Solov'ev proposed the following definition: '*pravo* is a compulsory demand for the realization of a definite minimum of good, or for a social order which excludes certain manifestations of evil.'[53] Law is directed towards the attainment of a minimum good, its purpose is to eliminate evil, whence its fundamentally restrictive character. It mediates between the interests of personal liberty as a condition of human dignity, and those of the common good, the security of all, guaranteed on the strength of restrictive laws (*prinuditel'nye zakony*). Moral law alone cannot do this, because the 'antisocial instincts' which inhabit certain members of society would always be indifferent to its demands. This task falls to the 'law of constraint' (*zakon*) which Solov'ev took to be a necessary condition of moral perfection in the sense that it is required by the moral principle, though without being a direct expression of it. It is rather *pravo*, which acts as a fulcrum between the two 'moral' interests of personal freedom and the common good. In Solov'ev's words:

> The demand for personal freedom presupposes, for its realization, the restriction of that freedom, should it, at a given moment in the development of humanity, turn out to be incompatible with the existence of society or with the common good. These two interests, seemingly opposed from the perspective of abstract thought (...), accord fully with each other, however, in reality, and it is law (*pravo*) which is the fruit of their union.[54]

Accordingly, Solov'ev formulated the function of *pravo* as 'the necessary balance, maintained by constraint, between two moral interests, that of personal liberty and the common good'.

Solov'ev illustrated the moral dimension of *pravo* in a fairly intriguing and paradoxical way, arguing that certain positive laws (those which admitted of capital punishment, for example), should be abolished, not so much out of a sense of human compassion, as one might imagine, but because such laws failed to meet the moral criteria 'inscribed' in the notion of *pravo*. Punishment by outright suppression of supposed criminals (capital punishment, life sentences) was, he argued, wrong from a juridical point of view, because it upsets this balance of moral interests between personal freedom and the common good, which *pravo* is meant to uphold. Obviously, for Solov'ev, 'the common good is *common* precisely because it includes the good of *every* individual person without exception; otherwise it would be the good of the majority'.[55] Or again:

> The common good must, in one way or another, be the good of this man. But, should he be deprived of the possibility of free action, that is, deprived of the possibility of the good, then the good ceases to be a good for him. By becoming a partial interest, the good loses the right to limit personal freedom (...). Here we see (...) how moral claims coincide fully with the essence of law. In general, although law, in exercising constraint so as to guarantee a minimum good, differs from morality in the strict sense, through its very practice of constraint it actually respects the demands of morality, and must in no way enter into conflict with the latter. This is why we can be sure that, should a positive law be at odds with the moral consciousness of the good, then, *a priori*, this law no longer meets the essential requirements of law (*pravo*) itself.[56]

In other words, as an interstice between morality and positive law, *pravo* conjoins with morality to test the validity of codified laws. On the basis of this argument, Solov'ev believed that the moral dimension of *pravo* should always be accounted for in the elaboration of laws.

Justifying the Common Good: From Subjective to Objective Ethics

> The moral law cannot remain an abstract norm: it should find its realization in the external world (...). For us, it is especially important to note that this link between an unconditional moral principle and the world of real relations requires that we complete the principle of ethical individualism with a concept of social development. The aim and the foundation of morality is the person, certainly, but the development of the person occurs in circumstances created by the social environment. The moral law, therefore, cannot be indifferent to these circumstances.[57]

In reflecting upon the moral/juridical foundations of society, Russian intellectuals sometimes tried to counter, substitute even, the Kantian theory of the moral law of the autonomous will with a moral norm for the community (*obshchenie*) as a whole. Solov'ev, for one, was suspicious of a philosophy which, in face of the realities of human existence, persists in understanding the moral principle as one devoid of any content. As he saw it, the consequence of this exaggerated formalism was to reduce morality to a postulate, instead of viewing it as that which is determined by the idea of the good.[58] Indeed, his objection to what he regarded as excessive trust in the findings of science prompted him to call, somewhat disparagingly, Kant's practical philosophy a 'moral chemistry'.[59] But, that said, Solov'ev's own solution to the problems left unresolved by Kant arguably betray a dependency on the authority he was supposedly challenging. All he did was turn the Kantian principle on its head, and, not unlike Florenskii's 'plus and minus' signs which he later attached to Plato and Kant, translate the 'prose of Kant' into the 'poetry of Plato'. Thus, he argued, morality is autonomous precisely because it is not an abstract formula suspended in air, but contains within itself all the conditions for its realization. For Solov'ev, morality referred intrinsically to the existence of God, and the immortality of the soul. 'God and the soul', he wrote, 'are not postulates of the moral law, but are the directly creative forces of moral reality.'[60]

As Novgorodtsev saw it, the underlying reason for Kant's formalism was the division he had drawn between phenomena (realm of necessity) and the thing in itself (the realm of freedom). Inevitably, this meant that his endeavours to state the autonomy of the moral principle, freed from the chains of necessity, led him to situate it beyond the reach of the real world. As an expression of the sheer capacity of will, Kant's concept of moral freedom amounted to a pure ideal of morality. While, of course, highly laudable, the 'lofty inner life of the spirit', alone, should not be the only place where the moral will finds an anchorage. On the contrary, Novgorodtsev objected, 'the moral will seeks its realization in the world, in the establishment of harmony between the ideal and reality'. In this 'living reciprocity' with the world, the moral will is strengthened, it grows, developing its goals and ideals: 'Such is the necessary passage from subjective to objective ethics, namely ethics which endeavours to resolve the problem of the actual implementation of moral norms in view of real life circumstances.'[61]

In a programmatic article, entitled 'Moral Idealism in the Philosophy of Law' (1902), Novgorodtsev paid tribute to the ancient Greek worldview as a moral impulse in current attempts to rethink the meaning of law in the wake of nineteenth-century historicism and sociologism. He wrote:

> If we turn to the great representatives of Greek thought, to Plato and to Aristotle, in order to learn the lesson they drew from their own observation of the Greek states, we find one and the same conclusion: abstract principles of equality and freedom alone are not enough to establish harmonious social forms. This requires the more solid fastenings of life in society – friendly association, brotherhood, renunciation of private interests, and their subordination to higher aims (...). [F]or both thinkers, the ideal of social justice meant having to complement the abstract principle of law with new moral content.[62]

In the same text he addressed, once again, the problematic legacy of the Kantian split between the 'is' and 'ought' (*bytie/dolzhenstvovanie*), this time, however, lending a good deal of pathos to the solution he proposed:

> Nowadays, our task is to seize the link between these two domains in view of their ultimate harmony (...). Here we are entering the realm of metaphysics (...) from which the moral task, and, especially, natural law derive their greatest support. These metaphysical foundations give moral constructs their strength, just as they make hopes unshakeable before disappointments or transitory failures. Whatever the disappointment or failure, in aspiring to the supreme good, in becoming aware of the moral law, we end up by liberating

ourselves from the illusory hold of phenomena in the name of a joyful recognition of absolute principles.[63]

Couched in the pathos of these words destined for a wider public are a number of Platonic stereotypes. Turns of phrase such as 'in quest of the supreme good', or the distinction Novgorodtsev draws between the transient nature of phenomena and absolute values were among the features which constituted the hallmark of Platonism in Russia as everywhere else. A decade later, in his courses on political theory, Novgorodtsev openly acknowledged Plato as a 'moral impulse' in his own theories, reminding his audience of the deeply moral thrust of Plato's teaching, and that, in modern times, it still served as an example to emulate. This was especially true, he believed when, at stake was the consolidation of the ideal foundations of society, its moral regeneration:

> By reaching into the essence of the human spirit, Plato was able to find the sources of inner and infinite gratification – those sources which are the inalienable property of man under all conditions and in any situation, regardless of whether he lives in the midst of great social prosperity, or in the wreckage of its sad decline. This is precisely what gives his idealist contemplation its special meaning. It explains even better why epochs and generations so different from one another all took from this system the moral foundations for their own convictions and beliefs.[64]

To be sure, both Solov'ev and Novgorodtsev welcomed Kant's theory of the autonomy of the will for its role in opening up new horizons in moral and political thought. Moreover, as is clear from many of the preceding quotations, both of them borrowed much of their conceptual apparatus from Kant's system. It remains, though, that the latter's formalism neither met nor answered their own personal projects to speak about 'objective ethics', 'social ideals', or the 'good'. Obliged to look elsewhere, they were seemingly attracted by the Platonic worldview with its promise of a just order and harmonious relations among members of an ideal community. That said, however, one should be wary of drawing conclusions too swiftly. While it might be tempting to think that they found a solution in Plato, this is not entirely true. Confronted by two conflicting paradigms of thought as exemplified in the philosophies (or an image of them) of Kant and Plato, Solov'ev and Novgorodtsev seemed to prefer Plato, the moral teacher, to Kant, the subjectivist. But this, in turn, only trapped them in the dilemma of having to reconcile the positive image of Plato, as a moral example, and the negative one – that of social philosopher. His conception of the state, as the supreme manifestation of the good was a troubling one for modern readers, because it risked losing sight of the moral autonomy of the individual, precisely that key element which philosopher-jurists – including Novgorodtsev and Solov'ev – were so keen to defend. Shortly after Solov'ev's death, Novgorodtsev paid his friend and colleague a tribute for his role as a 'philosopher of law', stressing the point that, as a 'critique of abstract principles', and as an attempt to 'justify the good', Solov'ev's task was diametrically opposed to Kant's.[65] That said, it was important for Solov'ev, as Novgorodtsev rightly observed, to retain one fundamental principle of Kantian practical philosophy in his own project to construct a social ideal, namely to defend man's freedom and his rightful status as an end in himself, never a means. There is no possible justification, Solov'ev wrote, to treat human beings as a means only, to sacrifice them for the benefit of other people, or even for the sake of the common good.[66]

Between Plato and Kant

The Platonic impulse in Russian theories of law was, as we have seen, repeatedly offset by the acknowledged importance of Kant. Iurkevich, Novgorodtsev and Solov'ev all identified Plato's philosophy with the quest for truth and justice. Even Chicherin saw in the Greek understanding of truth (*pravda*) as a principle of order – both of social order and of the human soul – a forerunner of the modern, Kantian concept, which, he claimed, likewise described a correlation between the social and the individual.[67] But, in Chicherin's case, as a self-professed Kantian, this comparison merely gave extra ballast to his generally hostile attitude towards Plato, allowing him to condemn the ancient philosopher in the name of the Kantian principles he openly upheld. According to Chicherin, Plato had simply failed to account for human dignity. On the contrary, Kant's entire moral philosophy was governed by respect for the human being:

> Although [Plato] imagined a structure well suited to human nature, it remains that freedom is entirely sacrificed for the sake of the aims of society (...). In due tribute to Plato, his lasting achievement was to have raised the state to the eternal ideas of truth and the good. Unfortunately, in the name of these very same principles he wanted to unify all of life in a way which was contrary to man.[68]

Novgorodtsev continually vacillated between Kant and Plato, in some ways trying to use Plato as a corrective to the theory of natural law which, in its modern formulation, had become very much identified with the philosophy of Kant. In doing so, however, he was arguably modernizing Plato, reinventing him as a defender of personal liberty: Plato became the Kant of antiquity. In this spirit, Novgorodtsev declared that it was in the inner life of man that Plato sought a solution to the degradation he saw in the world around him:

> It was here, in the depths of the spirit, that he found a wealth of strength and aspirations, before which all else seems insignificant. In enhancing his

idealism in bright, dazzling forms, he bequeathed ideals and dreams to a thousand generations, inspiring them with the belief that these dreams and yearnings contain a supreme truth, incomparably more important that the trite realities of society.[69]

Novgorodtsev was, of course, aware of a conflict of values between the ancient and modern conceptions of man in society. For Plato, as Novgorodtsev pointed out numerous times in his various courses on ancient philosophy, the individual was not an end in himself: the sense of existence was afforded exclusively by the harmonious order of the city-state. But, for all his awareness of the problems bequeathed by Plato in this regard, Novgorodtsev nonetheless tried to accommodate him to the modern worldview – a worldview which, as he admitted, had found its most powerful expression in the individual moral freedom advocated by Kant. And, as if hoping to eliminate the distance between their philosophies, he even entered the murky waters of empathizing with what he imagined to be the person of Plato himself. Although Plato did not believe in the person, nevertheless, 'thanks to the incomparable gifts of his own personality he somehow, despite himself, appealed to a belief in the (...) fundamental strengths manifest in the spirit of the individual'.[70] In this respect, Novgorodtsev might be said to be constructing a Plato in tune with the individual-centred visions underlying much modern, Enlightenment philosophy:

> Plato sought consolation in some of the most profound principles of the spirit, in that inner possession of man which no authority can touch, and no decline of society can destroy. There, in the depths of the spirit he found a wealth of power and drive, compared with which everything else seemed insignificant. The state will collapse, but the individual personality (*lichnost'*) remains; it remains in the fullness of its aspirations. It must create a new world in and of itself.[71]

Just as Novgorodtsev could be accused of modernizing Plato, in ways not unlike contemporary neo-Kantians in Germany, he was also tempted to 'socialize' Kant. In this spirit, Novgorodtsev suggested that Kant's individualism was not as extreme as it might first appear:

> The categorical imperative concerns the individual person, certainly, and yet it sets such demands on her, demands which originate from the idea of the supreme objective order. This double character of the categorical imperative is expressed wonderfully in the principle of the autonomy of the will, which conjoins the subjective moment with the objective. That is why this principle is of such major importance for the problem of the relation of the individual to society.[72]

The immediate source of Novgorodtsev's argument here, however, was not so much Kant himself, as an interpretation advanced in an early text by Solov'ev. Solov'ev had claimed in a very matter of fact way that, if the categorical imperative is to be understood as universal, this necessarily presupposes many agents. If the rules governing my activity are to be universal, then obviously, there should be other actors too, for whom these rules also have meaning.[73] Seemingly attracted by the Kantian belief in freedom, albeit frustrated by what they perceived to be his extreme formalism, Novgorodtsev and Solov'ev tried to accommodate Kant on their own terms. But the result was not terribly convincing, and, in the end, their attempts to hammer out a theory of an 'objective ethics', with its difficult task of convincingly completing the principle of ethical individualism with a concept of social development, meant that neither the Kantian nor the Platonic option was plausible. Their reluctant admiration for Kant was offset by their enchantment with Plato, even as they balked at the consequences of his scheme. Novgorodtsev, for example, remarked that past philosophies, prior to Kant, had tended to fluctuate between two views of society in relation to the individual, neither of which answered present-day concerns to guarantee the interests of both without compromising one or the other. Either society marked an external limit to individual freedom, or it figured as an all-inclusive principle, absorbing everything. The upshot was either to base association (*obshchenie*) on the arbitrary views (*usmotrenie*) of a number of individuals, the consequence of which was to deny the inner and independent value of association, or, on the contrary, to proclaim society as the ultimate and unconditional instance reigning above man, a view which ultimately undermined the independent worth and significance of every single one of us.[74] Against this, Kant's defence of moral freedom signified a major turning point in the history of philosophy, as both Novgorodtsev and Solov'ev readily admitted. Novgorodtsev also applauded Kantian philosophy insofar as he saw it as an eloquent warning against the temptation of turning social ideals into so many utopias. In his view, given the purely formal character of the supreme moral criterion, Kant had successfully excluded the possibility of an unconditional moral content which might lay claims to being eternally recognized. All that Kant meant by 'eternal' was, rather, the requirement for reason to be in accord with itself, and that man be true to his rational and moral nature.[75]

Novgorodtsev clearly welcomed the anti-utopian character of Kant's thought. Indeed, he saw it as a much-needed corrective to the 'utopian' ideas rooted in, for example, contemporary theories of socialism. But, for all that, it remained the case that Kant's formalism was the greater obstacle, and this, ultimately, made it impossible for Novgorodtsev to endorse his philosophy unconditionally. All the more so when it came to a reflection on law and the state, an issue which interested Novgorodstev so deeply. Indeed, it was from this perspective that Novgorodtsev was most critical of the Kantian heritage. To be true to himself, Kant had no option other than to undermine his standpoint from the outset. As Novgorodtsev repeatedly reminded his reader, the notions of 'law' and 'state' are not the abstract ideals of private existence, but 'life' and 'reality'.[76] As for Solov'ev, his highly personal solution to the problem of the individual and the social was to relate it to the overall moral purpose of human existence 'precisely in the ultimate *justification* of the good given in our conscience and in our good will'.[77] Statements of this kind prompted Solov'ev's friend and colleague, Sergei Trubetskoi, to seek parallels between Solov'ev and Plato. Responding to Solov'ev's reading of the dialogue *Protagoras*, Trubetskoi summarized the importance of Plato's ethical views as a 'justification of the good', exactly the same idea, he added, that had prompted Solov'ev to construct an 'objective ethics'. Only it was Plato who was the first to have set himself such a task.[78]

Law, Society and the State

The theories and world outlooks sketched above invite the question, how did Russian philosopher-jurists (at least those discussed here) envisage a well-ordered society/state with law and/or morality as its foundation? Part of the problem was that the state/society itself was conceived in a variety of ways – as an irreducible whole, or unity, with the individual members that compose it, or in terms of its ultimate goal, where 'goal' might signify 'attainment of well-being' (*blago*), but equally the 'realization of the good' (*dobro*). For Novgorodtsev, it was a question of a social ideal grounded in the primacy of the 'personal principle', and of a harmonious reciprocity between them. Both – the individual and the totality of relations – were to be grounded in moral consciousness (a supreme moral command – *velenie*). It was in these terms that Novgorodtsev defined natural law. Time and again throughout his career he argued that 'society is a union of individuals' (*litsa*), and that the significance of society is wholly determined by the quality of the units which compose it. If we deprive even one individual (*litso*) of moral value, 'we deprive the totality of individuals of that same moral value, and conversely, in recognizing the moral value of individuals, we must also recognize the moral value of the union of individuals'.[79]

Chicherin, the Kantian-Hegelian, contended that society is made up of potentially conflicting elements: rights and obligation, freedom and law. For society to be just (*pravil'noe*), these elements need to harmonize, and it is this which represents the ultimate goal of society. Chicherin believed that the goal of every society is a certain well-being (*blago*):

> It is intrinsic to society, drawing its origins from the very nature of society itself, being none other than the realization of this nature in the real world. It is an ideal goal, fusing together the diverse elements of society into an

organic whole. Thanks to this internal, vital link, society is an organism. While power (*vlast'*) affords it an external, initial unity, the ultimate aim of society gives it a definitive, internal unity.[80]

For Chicherin, '*blago*' connoted 'well-being', a notion derived essentially from the Kantian pledge to do good. This latter, recall, recognizes the unconditional, fundamental basis of one's own personal freedom, while at the same time, being equally respectful of the individuality of other free beings. It is evidently quite different from the meaning that Solov'ev afforded his idea of the 'good' when he argued that the moral significance of society is determined by the religious or mystical principle in man, and that members of society do not represent an end limit for one another, but rather an inner complement, 'each for the other, in a free unity of spiritual love'.[81] Unlike Chicherin, Solov'ev understood the good (*dobro*) in terms of an harmonious order given in advance of human action, with human reason as a constructive principle. In his ideas for a free theocracy, Solov'ev conceived of the ultimate aim of society as a spiritual union, or Church. It is tempting to see in his underlying concern for social harmony, evoked in terms of the good, a nostalgia for the Platonic worldview, such as this was inherited and still operative in the late Middle Ages. Worldly being is the Good; there is a hierarchy of perfection in nature, such that any natural law is in fact grounded in transcendent values/principles, and ultimately grounded in the One. But ironically, in the late nineteenth century this kind of worldview would, for many, be redolent of utopianism, with which only very few would wish to be associated.

Prior to 1905, discussing the idea of a 'rule of law' state was, of course, a sore point for conservative bureaucrats, not to mention the tsar himself, whose prerogative to issue '*ukaz*' not only put him above the law, but also blatantly undermined the stability of laws issued in accordance with a concept of legality grounded in *pravo*. Any open debate was enough to provoke the closure of a journal should such issues be raised. Circumstances of this kind may explain why, in the difficult years of Counter Reform, philosopher-jurists placed so much emphasis on the question of civil rights and citizenship in light of discussions focusing on *pravo* and morality, while hesitating to tackle – at least openly – the more thorny issue of political rights and representation in light of specific, concrete considerations. In an atmosphere of censorship and suspicion it is perhaps understandable that bids were repeatedly made to recognize that primacy of morality qua *pravo* over laws (*zakon*) where the function of the latter referred to the 'external', institutional dimension of society. Unfortunately, in the eyes of many Russians, historically, laws (*zakony*) had simply been a tool of oppression. Thus, only very few dared, or cared, to take up the issue of rule of law in terms of its possible application in Russia. In the main, discussions were restricted to the theoretical concerns of academia, or were forced underground. There were, of course, exceptions. Chicherin ventured to develop views on 'the constitutional question' in a number of pamphlets circulated (but not published) in the 1860s and 1870s. The professor of law at St. Petersburg University during the 1890s, Nikolai Korkunov, worked on the problem of *zakon* and *ukaz*, and in doing so implied sharp criticism of the tsar's divine rights, as well as his peers in the juridical profession itself, who also tended to identify one with the other. According to Korkunov, by doing so they simply obscured the meaning of law.[82]

On the eve of the 1905 revolution, Novgorodtsev published an article in which he expressed hopes for a 'self-limiting' state (*gosudarstvennoe samoogranichenie*), grounded in natural law, the obligatory character of which is afforded by a supreme moral command. Only such a state, he believed, would respect the equality and freedom of the members who compose it. In his view, this 'rule-of-natural-law state' would be sanctioned by supreme norms to which it must submit, and from which, in turn, it would derive its justification and principles of governance. In relation to these norms, the state is merely an instrument – not the creator – of laws. It is a lawgiver, not a lawmaker. And, while it determines the form of *pravo*, in the sense that it devises instructional structures, ensures the separation of bodies of power, and so on, the content of *pravo* is, as Novgorodtsev put it, 'peremptorily (*vlastno*) determined by life, and finds its highest sanction in moral consciousness'.[83] The state, he contended, is not just 'government', or 'power', it is a 'co-operative unity of the people as a whole'. The state finds its source, its 'vital roots' in personal consciousness. Hence a neat reciprocity, mutual requirements which are met: 'Safeguarding and establishing the state (...) is at once to safeguard the living human person: it is a confirmation of, and concern for, the man and the citizen within every individual.'[84]

In his bid to admit of the personal principle as a grounding factor for the state, Novgorodstev was aiming to overcome a general and lingering tendency to regard the relation between state and people/society in terms of opposition, between a 'we' and an 'it'. But, disappointment after the first Revolution in what was shortly to prove an unsuccessful constitutional experiment in Russia led Novgorodtsev, the Kadet, to speak of an 'exaggerated respect' for the 'rule of law'. Granted, his criticism was aimed not so much at the concept of 'rule of law' as such; rather it expressed regret that in contemporary theories the notion of *pravo* had lost sight of its moral basis. Novgorodtsev still hoped that the current revival of natural law, both in Germany and at home (in the figures of Evgenii Trubetskoi, V.M Hessen, besides himself), would prove propitious for ensuring a just and stable society. Otherwise there was a risk that hopes, if not satisfied, might turn into idle dreams, an unrealizable ideal of social harmony, or, if you prefer, a nostalgia for the ideal city.

In his assessment of the ancients, Novgorodtsev had singled out for positive praise the stress that both Plato and Aristotle had placed on the moral foundation of society. He suggested, moreover, that the importance they attached to this was in part due to their actual experience of Athenian life which was sharply at odds with their ideals. For Plato, the state's task is to preserve justice among its members. Once people are just then laws (*zakony*) will correspond to *pravo*, and the state will be grounded in something higher than law (*pravo*). It will be grounded in justice. In other words, in the realm of human relations, the supreme manifestation of the idea of the good is the state; for it is a perfect organism into which individual persons enter as members.[85] In his own theories, Novgorodtsev was urging much the same thing:

> The experience of the nineteenth century has shown that law alone (*pravo*) does not have the force to bring about the complete transformation of society. And while, for some, this experience has become the grounds to argue that we can dispense with law altogether, for others, it is proof of the need to complement law with new principles, to broaden its content, so that it meets the needs of contemporary European society, which today requires more than the rule of law state has so far provided. (...) The rule of law state is not the crown of history, nor is it the ultimate ideal of moral life; it is no more than a tributary factor, operating as one partial element, among others, within the broader web of moral forces. From this it follows that law, in relation to the plenitude of moral demands, is an extremely poor, insufficient means to give body to the purity of moral principles.[86]

But, despite the distant Platonic ring to Novgorodtsev's words, just how far Plato really was a viable solution here is open to question. Not least because, for those Russian readers, including Novgorodtsev, who otherwise endorsed his idea of social justice, the ideal city, as such, was horribly reminiscent of the hierarchical structure in which they actually lived, and were anxious to change.

Russian Liberalism: Nostalgia for the Ideal City?

In the writings of the Russian philosopher-jurists discussed in this chapter, it is not difficult to identify a number of traits typical of liberal thinking, understood, that is, as a socio-cultural phenomenon, rather than in terms of strict political policy. There are moments in their social philosophies which come close to a view of liberalism understood as a system in which priority is given to securing the civil and political rights of the individual. The accent that Chicherin placed on the idea of individual freedom, together with the importance he attached to private ownership of property as a guarantee of civil rights, or Novgorodtsev's arguments to the effect that society is grounded in the principle of the individual figure as some of these. Or again, Solov'ev's argument against capital punishment was not unlike the liberal tendency to humanize the practice of criminal law, the logic of which stemmed directly from its overall conception of the role of social institutions as that of protecting the subjective rights of the individual. In turn, this basic task allotted to institutions refocuses the kind of relation that exists between the individual and the state. Victor Leontovitch describes it as follows:

> Liberalism does not presuppose that man is always good, or that his will is always directed towards the good (...). This is why liberalism requires that objective juridical and state orders be created, capable of checking and involving the will of each individual. For this reason also, it approves social institutions or structures which have a disciplinary function. But for all that, liberalism is none the less individualist, because man, as an individual, always comes first, while social institutions or entities are justified uniquely on the strength of maintaining the rights and interests of the individual, and of providing the conditions within which he may realize specific goals.[87]

Despite the presence of identifiable 'traits of liberal thinking' in Russia which closely echoed certain leading tenets of liberalism in Western Europe, it has been repeatedly, and correctly, pointed out that the historical foundations on which these were based, and out of which they had developed were all too obviously missing. Leontovitch singles out two decisive moments: the Church in Russia was never sovereign, as was the case in the Medieval West; nor had Russia known a feudal system of government. Arguably, these historical differences had an impact on the way Russian intellectuals thought about liberalism, and on the distinctive accent they were to give it. Whereas in the West, liberalism had an essentially negative connotation, in the sense that it set out to abolish eighteenth-century absolutism and the police state, in Russia its appeal consisted much more in the positive example it afforded as part of attempts to construct a social ideal. Albeit anchored in the idea of the primacy of the individual, in Russia this was not necessarily intended as a means to check absolutism, but rather to conjugate the interests of the individual with those of the state. In other words, both Russia's past and present were too much at odds with the preconditions necessary for liberalism really to take root. Certain Russian juridical thinkers were aware of this, and made a point of the difference. For one, Chicherin's 'etatist liberalism', in which he tried to combine strong power with liberal measures, reflected his view that the tradition in Russia of a strong centralized state was the unavoidable outcome of historical and geographical factors, and could not (nor should) really be altered. The emphasis on balancing individual interests and the common good (or the state), rather than grounding the state on the primacy of individual principles underscored much of Solov'ev's social and moral philosophical studies, too. In Novgorodtsev's tribute to him after his death, he summarized his friend and colleague's social ideal in the following terms:

> The state has as its function to maintain, by means of constraint, an equilibrium between the private (*chastnie*), self-interest of its members, and to set limits on egotistical usurpation of power. Without this 'protection' (*okhrana*), society cannot exist. However, it remains that the aim of history is not merely to guarantee man's existence, but to provide him with the means to ensure a dignified life, a dignity which is grounded in an inner moral solidarity. This means that the best form of government is that which eliminates to the greatest degree possible all forms of evil, and which gives as free a rein as possible to those forces which propel society towards its future ideal well-being.[88]

Much the same may be said of Novgorodtsev himself. Although he championed the notion of a 'personal principle', his point was not to oppose it to the interests of the state, but to conjugate the interests of the two sides. In the end, though, the ideals that these Russian intellectuals expressed had to account for the social and legal reality around them. It was a reality which obliged them to content themselves with the development principally of civil rights (and only later, after 1905, political liberty) within the framework of traditional institutions. This perhaps explains the 'conservative', 'sober' but also, paradoxically, the utopian character of the socio-political views they defended. For some, it was above all a matter of safeguarding the fabric of the state from a revolutionary cataclysm that led them to urge the importance of a well-structured juridical order, whence a certain conservatism. Listing the topics debated at meetings of the Moscow Juridical Society, the historian, Alexander Kizewitter, wrote that these included problems of government. Discussions 'bore directly on those hopes nurtured in the public sphere, namely that the Russian state be set on the new rails of a rule of law (*pravovoi stroi*) and political freedom.' Kizewitter admitted that the period of Counter Reform had been one where social interests were abandoned, and where revolutionary utopianism had begun to take hold in the political underground. But it was also a period, he added, in which 'the constitutional idea, the idea of political progress grounded in legality (*pravomernost'*) did not die.' That it did not die was largely thanks to the efforts of that group of Moscow professors who worked tirelessly to explain and make known constitutional ideas.[89]

Certainly, an awareness of social injustice had a real part to play in the formulation of the solutions that these intellectuals provided. Their bid to admit of a true understanding of the meaning of law, and of the social good was often prompted by the injustice that they saw around them. Recall Chicherin's outright condemnation of slavery, feudalism, of the caste system, in short, of any infringements imposed on the free self-determination of individuals. All of this stood in stark contradiction with the theory of moral claims (*trebovaniia*) he defended.[90] But there was a tragic irony lurking here. Despite their efforts, any proclamation of equal rights as natural rights, any call for constitutionalism was not only seen as a threat to autocracy, it was flagrantly undermined by a legal practice which continued, despite the reform process, to deny the peasant population rights equal with the rest of society. That hopes and reality were so blatantly out of kilter may have led to the projection of ideals far removed from the nature of the actual social fabric, ideals which risked engendering a tendency to ignore social reality, despite what might have been claims to the contrary. The limited public space in which intellectuals could air their views (university lecture halls, society meetings, *publitsistika*, polemics between Slavophile and Westernizer sympathizers), and the fact that they were denied the possibility to translate them into action via the formation of political parties and so forth, may well have contributed to this phenomenon. Although much of what Solov'ev wrote was, indeed, triggered by signs of social injustice that he saw still being perpetrated in Russia, his views were, in the main, elaborated and refined through personal (intellectual) quarrels with his contemporaries – first with the Slavophiles, whose views had influenced him as a young man, and, later, in the stand he took against Tolstoi's outright hostility to any idea of law for the sake of moral values. Besides undermining any eventual political aptitude in the Russian people, this attitude, Solov'ev believed, ran counter to the objective principles of truth (*pravda*) and the good. Yet, paradoxically, in the very way he couched his response to Tolstoi, Solov'ev may be seen to be sacrificing liberal principles for an all-embracing metaphysics, the Platonic elements of which made for a somewhat uncomfortable marriage with the principles of individualism, and, by extension, with liberalism, which he otherwise advocated. Albeit calling for the recognition of civil rights, at the same time Solov'ev advocated their voluntary renunciation for the sake of the interests of the State (even though the interests of the latter were, supposedly, to consist in protecting the liberty of the former). Solov'ev wrote:

> That man should be subordinated to society is coherent with the absolute moral principle, which does not sacrifice the particular to the universal, rather it closely unites them. In exchange for giving up her unlimited freedom (at any rate uncertain and unreal), the person receives a true guarantee of her determined, or rational, freedom.[91]

Moreover, Solov'ev endorsed the idea of an all-inclusive control by the State in which, rather than separating administrative, judicial and executive powers, à la Montesquieu, it was a matter of their ultimate unification through their combined services to the common good, to a supreme authority vested with all the positive rights of the social in its entirety.[92] It falls to this supreme unity, the State, as the incarnation of law (*voploshchennoe pravo*) to safeguard a harmonious relation between 'the organizing principle, the system of bodies or instruments of organizational activity, and the totality of elements to be organized'.[93]

The appeal that liberal principles may have exercised on writers such as Solov'ev seems, then, to have run up against a preference for the philosophical and theoretical underpinnings of unity, integral wholeness, in short motifs which hark back to the Platonic worldview, whether or not reinforced by the Hegelian *Rechtsstaat* model with its vision of a modern, centralized state as the incarnation of human rational consciousness. Chicherin, certainly, based his 'etatist' interpretation of Russian history along these Hegelian lines, while many contemporaries, even though they criticized Hegel (and Plato) for treating the individual merely as a transient phenomenon, nevertheless preached that the individual achieves liberty only through the state. Of the authors discussed here, this was certainly the case of Solov'ev, and a similar kind of thinking may be found in some of Novgorodtsev's earlier writings.[94]

The host of social and intellectual circumstances described above almost inevitably facilitated the utopian character of so much political and social thought in Russia. Projects in which hopes for a better future were nurtured may be said to contain, willy-nilly, a strain of utopianism, and this, regardless of a given author's political affinities, or his concern to distance himself from Plato's original plan for an ideal city. An analysis of a selection of readings by liberal, socialist and Bolshevik intellectuals – most of them active in the university milieu – of Plato's ideal city, the subject of the next chapter, should highlight, in a complementary way, some of the problems within Russian political culture. In addition, by dint of the fairly widespread ambivalence with respect to Plato, author of the first utopia, our account may serve to pinpoint some of the overlaps and close similarities actually existing among those political factions which, otherwise, were eager to state their differences.

Notes

1   For literature on the judicial reform, see, for example: Peter H. Solomon, Jr. (ed.), *Reforming Justice in Russia, 1864-1996. Power, Culture, and the Limits of Legal Order* (New York, London: M.E. Sharpe, 1997); Jörg Baberowski, *Autokratie und Justiz. Zum Verhältnis von Rechsstaatlichkeit und Rückständigkeit im ausgehenden Zarenreich 1864-1914* (Frankfurt am Main: Klostermann, 1996); Harold Berman, *Justice in the USSR*, revised ed. (New York, 1992). The problematic history of the judicial reform is well-documented in specialized journals dating from the reform period itself (*Iuridicheskii Vestnik, Zhurnal Grazhdanskogo i ugolovnogo prava, Zhurnal Ministerstva Iustitsii*), as well as in generalist *tol'stye zhurnaly*, such as the 'liberal' *Vestnik Evropy*.
2   K.K. Arsen'ev, 'Tsarstvovanie imperatora Aleksandra III-go' in his *Za chetvert' veka (1871-1894). Sbornik Stat'ei* (Pgd., 1915), p.611.
3   See, for example, K.K. Arsen'ev (ed.), *Glavnye deiateli i predshestvenniki sudebnoi reformy* (SPb., 1904). In much the same vein, the 'complete works' by leading proponents of reform and legal thinkers, as well as judges, were published, together with biographies to commemorate their careers. See, for example, D. Korsakov, *Konstantin Dmitrievich Kavelin. Ocherk zhizni i deiatel'nosti* (SPb., 1896); *Sochinenia V.D.*

Spasovicha (SPb., 1890-1900); *Sbornik statei N.M. Korkunova (1877-1897)* (SPb., 1898). A.F. Koni, a well-known judge, had various *'Sudebnye Rechi'*, correspondance, and memoirs published during his lifetime.
4   Solomon, op. cit. See also R. Wortman, *The Development of a Russian Legal Consciousness* (Chicago and London, 1976) A. Walicki, *Legal Philosophies of Russian Liberalism* (Oxford, 1987).
5   The words of the lawyer, Vladimir Nabokov, written in 1898. Cited in Jane Burbank, 'Legal Culture, Citizenship, and Peasant Jurisprudence: Perspectives from the Early Twentieth Century', in Solomon, op. cit., p.93.
6   Novgorodtsev, *Vvedenie v filosofiiu prava* (Moscow, 1922), p.66. Quoted in V.N. Zhukov, 'The Social Philosophy of P.I. Novgorodtsev', in *Russian Studies in Philosophy*, vol.33, no.3 (Winter 1994-95), p.39.
7   A. Walicki, *Legal Philosophies...*, p.17ff.
8   Cf. P. Miliukov, 'Universitet', op. cit., p.791.
9   The two sections of the Philosophy Faculty existed up to the 1850s when the Faculties of History and Philology, and Mathematics and Physics were created.
10 Instruction in state law was resumed in 1858. For an account of the atmosphere in the faculty during the reign of Nicholas I, see: *Moskovskii Universitet v vospominaniiakh sovremennikov (1755-1917)* (Moscow: Sovremennik, 1989).
11 Miliukov, op. cit.
12 Quoted by Novgorodtsev in 'Ideia prava v filosofii Vl.S. Solov'eva', *VFP* (1901). Cited from the English translation in *Russian Studies in Philosophy* (Winter 1994-95), p.54. See also Walicki, op. cit., chapter one.
13 M. Pogodin (1800-1875) lectured on history, and S. Shevyrev (1806-1864) on prose and poetry at Moscow University during the 1830s and 1840s, that is, at the height of the 'Nation, Orthodoxy, Autocracy' ideology.
14 Cited in Novgorodtsev, *Krizis sovremennogo pravosoznaniia* (Moscow, 1909), p.4.
15 Cf. Walicki, op. cit., and the numerous introductory courses entitled 'History of the Philosophy of Law' dating from the 1860s onwards, some of which are discussed in this chapter.
16 Authors and works most frequently recommended for courses in the period beginning in the 1870s up to 1910 included: Boris Chicherin, *Istoriia politicheskikh uchenii*, 5 vols. (Moscow, 1869-1902), and his *Filosofiia Prava* (Moscow, 1900); A. Bershadskii, *Lektsii po istorii filosofii prava* (SPb., 1890); Evg. Trubetskoi, *Lektsii po entsikopedii prava* in various editions as of the 1890s); Nikolai Korkunov, *Lektsii po obshchei teorii prava* (1904); Pavel Novgorodtsev, *Konspekt k lektsii po istorii filosofii prava* (Moscow, 1908), and the Pole, Lev Petrazickij, *Teoriia prava v sviazi s teoriei nravstvennosti* (SPb., 1909-1910), also his *Vvednie v izuchenie prava i nravstvennosti* (SPb., 1905). The most frequently cited foreign authorities, some of whom were translated into Russian, include: Paul Janet, *Histoire de la science politique dans ses rapports avec la morale*, 2nd ed. (Paris, 1872), translated under the title *Istoriia gosudarstvennoi nauki*; Henry Michel *L'idée de l'Etat* (1895); Karl Hildenbrand, *Geschichte und System d. Rechts und Staatsphilosophie* (Leipzig, 1860); J.S. Stahl, *Geschichte der Rechtsphilosophie*; Ludwig Gumplowicz, *Grundriss der Sociologie* (1885). Also noteworthy is the inclusion of French and German generalist histories of philosophy, such as those by Windelband, Fouillée (*La science sociale contemporaine*, 1880), Stampel, Kuno Fischer, or A. Weber as recommended reading for students of law.
17 Miliukov, op. cit., p.799. A second effect, as attested by the figures, was a sharp drop in the number of students registered in the Arts, and a steady increase in student inscriptions to study law. Miliukov, ibid., gives the following percentages for law for the years 1880, 1885, 1894, 1899 as 22.3%, 30.2%, 36.9%, 43.1% respectively. It was only with the appearance, during the first decade of the twentieth century, of talented *Privat-Docenty* in philosophy – Losskii, Frank, Ivan Lapshin, Sergei Povarnin, Gustav Shpet and others, that instruction in philosophy finally improved, attracting more students.

18 Chicherin, *Filosofiia Prava* (1900), pp.1-2.
19 Recommended literature for these courses included authors such as the political historian Robert Pöhlmann, and Maxim Kovalevskii (his *Proizkhozhdenie sovremmenikh demokratii*, 4 vols. (Moscow, 1895-1897).
20 P. Iurkevich, 'Istoriia filosofii prava. Vvedenie' (archive material of lectures read at Moscow University (1872-1874), and published for the first time in 'Rukopisnoe nasledie Pamfila Iurkevicha', *Filosofskaia i Sotsiologicheskaia Mysl'*, 3-4 (Kiev, 1996), pp.42-43.
21 Chicherin, *Filosofiia Prava*, p.8.
22 Chicherin, *Neskol'ko sovremmenikh voprosov* (1862), and *Konstitutsionnyi vopros v Rossii* (Moscow, 1878).
23 Redkin, 'Predmet i soderzhanie Istorii Filosofii Prava' in *Lektsii po istorii filosofii prava...*, vol.1. (SPb., 1899), p.215.
24 Ibid.
25 Iurkevich, op. cit., p.63. A Juridical Society had been set up under the auspices of Moscow University in 1862, and in St. Petersburg in 1877. In Kiev, where Iurkevich addressed this issue, an analogous society was also founded in 1877.
26 Iurkevich, op. cit., p.52.
27 Ibid., p.63.
28 Ibid., pp.64-65.
29 Ibid. See also K.A. Kuznetsov, Professor of Law at Odessa, who, in his course on the *Republic* and *Laws*, written half a century later, made much the same point. Kuznetsov claimed that Plato makes a clear distinction between an ideal law order, understood as something immutable, eternal, which men are summoned to take on as such, and codified law (*zakon*) which, on the contrary, being created by the hand of man, is adopted in good faith. K.A. Kuznetsov, *Platon. Vvedenie v analiz 'Gosudarstvo' i 'Zakonov'* (Odessa, 1916), p.15.
30 Redkin, *Istoriia filosofii prava*, vol.3, p.324.
31 Ibid., p.325.
32 Ibid., p.327ff. Cf. Ada Neschke, *Platonisme politique et théorie du droit naturel : contributions à une archéologie de la culture politique européenne* (Louvain: éd. de l'Institut supérieur de Philosophie, 1995), p.221.
33 P. Novgorodtsev, *Politicheskie idealy drevnego i sovremmenogo mira*, 2 vols. (Moscow, 1910-1913). For his discussion of Plato's dialogues, see, in particular vol.2, pp.21-96. Part of the text entitled 'Uchenie Platona o estestvennom prave: *Gorgias*, kak pervyi ocherk nachal estestvennogo prava u Platona', was first published separately under the title 'Uchenie Platona o estestvennom prave' in the *Filosofskii Sbornik* dedicated to Lev Lopatin (Moscow, 1912), pp.282-290. Quotations are taken from this earlier version.
34 P. Novgorodtsev, 'Uchenie Platona o estestvennom prave', 1912, p.283.
35 Neschke, op. cit., pp.74-75.
36 Neschke, ibid., pp.87-88.
37 Novgorodtsev, op. cit., p.285.
38 Ibid.
39 Ibid., p.289.
40 Prof. A. Fateev, *Istoria obshchikh uchenii o prave i gosudarstve* (2nd ed. Kharkov, 1909), p.18. See also Novgorodtsev, 'Nravstvennii idealizm v filosofii prava: k voprosu o vozrozhdenii estestvennogo prava' in *Problemy Idealizma* (Moscow, 1902), pp.295-296.
41 Cf. Neschke, op. cit., p.134.
42 V. Karpov, 'Filosofskii ratsionalizm noveishego vremeni' in *Khristianskoe Chtenie*, 5 (1860), pp.472-473.
43 Cf. Walicki, op. cit., p.131; p.138. See also V.D. Zork'in, *Chicherin* (Juridecheskaia Literatura, Moscow, 1984), p.29 ff.
44 Chicherin, *Filosofiia Prava*, p.175; pp.198-199.

45 Chicherin, *Filosofiia Prava*, p.87; *Mistitsizm v nauke*, p.95. Cf. Walicki, op. cit., pp.146-147.
46 Chicherin, *Filosofiia Prava*, p.223.
47 Novgorodtsev, 'K voprosu o sovremennykh filosofskikh iskaniiakh' (1902-1903).
48 V.M. Hvostov, 'Nravstvennost' i pravo' in *Ocherki istorii eticheskikh uchenii* (SPb., 1912), p.268.
49 Ibid., p.269.
50 Ibid.
51 Parts of this new work originally appeared in separate issues of the journal *Vestnik Evropy* (1894-1897). Also, in 1897, Solov'ev published a shorter text, *Law and Morality*, containing revised excerpts from both the *Critique...* and *Justification....* Clearly, Solov'ev's return to the problem of law and its moral foundation is suggestive of the importance that he attributed to the subject. My quotations are taken from the revised French edition (Slatkine, Genève, 1997).
52 Solov'ev, *La Justification du Bien*, p.364.
53 Ibid., pp.371-372.
54 Ibid., pp.373-374.
55 Ibid., p.378.
56 Ibid., p.397.
57 Novgorodtsev, 'Nravstvennii idealizm v filosofii prava: k voprosu o vozrozhdenii estestvennogo prava' in *Problemy Idealizma* (Moscow, 1902), p.292.
58 Solov'ev 'Kant' in Brokgaus and Efron (eds), *Entsyclopedicheskii Slovar'*, vol.xiv (SPb., 1895), p.332.
59 *La Justification du bien*, p.157.
60 Ibid., p.160.
61 Novgorodtsev, 'Nravstvennaia problema filosofii Kanta' (Moscow, 1903), p.24; p.22.
62 Novgorodtsev, 'Nravstvennii idealizm v filosofii prava...', p.283.
63 Ibid., p.296.
64 Novgorodtsev, *Politicheskie idealy...*, vol.2 (1913), pp.95-96.
65 Novgorodtsev, 'Ideia prava v filosofii Vl.S. Solov'eva', *VFP*, no.6 (1901), pp.112-129.
66 Cf. Walicki, op. cit., p.195.
67 Chicherin had in mind the second formula of the categorical imperative, according to which others should be treated as an end and not as a means. Moreover, this implied, he argued, that we should also be an end unto ourselves. *Filosofiia Prava*, p.200.
68 Chicherin, *Politicheskie mysliteli drevnego i novogo mira* (Moscow, 1897), pp.23-25.
69 Novgorodtsev, *Sokrat i Platon...* (Moscow, 1901), pp.71-72.
70 Novgorodtsev, *Politicheskie idealy...*, vol. 2 (1913), p. 96.
71 Ibid., pp.95-96.
72 Novgorodtsev, 'Nravstvennaia problema...', p.26.
73 Solov'ev, 'Formal'nyi printsip nravstvennosti (Kanta) – izlozhenie i otsenka s kriticheskimi zamechaniiami ob empricheskoi etike.' Solov'ev first worked on this text in the 1870s. It was later incorporated as an annex to *Opravdanie Dobra*. Cited in *Solov'ev. Sochineniia*, vol.1 (Moscow: Respublika, 1996), p.428.
74 Novgorodtsev, 'Nravstvennaia problema...', p.26.
75 Novgorodtsev, 'Nravstvennii idealizm v filosofii prava...', pp.287-288.
76 Novgorodtsev, 'Nravstvennaia problema...', p.24.
77 Solov'ev, *Justification du bien*, pp.172-173.
78 S.N. Trubetskoi, 'Protagor Platona v sviazi s razvitiem ego nrastvennogo ucheniia', in *Tvoreniia Platona*, vol.1, p.389.
79 Novgorodtsev, *Vvedenie v filosofiiu prava* (Moscow, 1922), p.66.
80 Chicherin, *'vlast', zakon, svoboda, obshchaia tsel'*, in *Istoriia politicheskikh uchenii*, vol.1 (Moscow, 1869), pp.6-8.
81 *Kritika otvlechennikh nachal*, in *Vladimir Sergeevich Solov'ev*, vol.1 (Moscow: Mysl', 1990), p.589.

82 N.M. Korkunov, *Ukaz i Zakon* (SPb., 1894). See also his 'Obshchestvennoe znachenie prava' (pamphlet) (SPb., 1891). On Korkunov see A.I. Ekimov, *Korkunov* (Moscow, 1983).
83 Novgorodtsev, 'Gosudarstvo i pravo', *VFP*, 75 (1904), p.510.
84 Ibid., p.535.
85 Cf. S. Zhebelev, 'Grecheskaia politicheskaia literatura i 'Politika' Aristotelia', postface to the Russian translation of Aristotle (Moscow, 1911), pp.381-465 (on Plato, see pp.426-440).
86 Novgorodtsev, *Krizis sovremennogo pravosoznaniia* (Moscow, 1909), pp.15-16.
87 Victor Léontovitch, *Histoire du libéralisme en Russie*, (1957), cited from the French translation (Fayard, Paris, 1986), p.19.
88 Novgorodtsev, *Solov'ev, kak filosof prava*, cited in *P.I. Novgorodtsev* (Pressa, Moscow, 1991), p.531. Novgorodtsev based his summary on his reading of Solov'ev's *Natsional'nyi vopros* (1891).
89 A.A. Kizewetter, *Moskovskii Universitet i ego traditsii: Rol' Moskovskogo Universiteta v kul'turnoi zhizni Rossii* (Prague: Den' russkoi kul'tury, 1927), pp.13-14.
90 Chicherin, *Filosofiia Prava*, p.203.
91 Solov'ev, *La Justification du Bien*, p.380.
92 Ibid., p.381.
93 Ibid., p.382.
94 Comments to this effect may be found in Novgorodtsev's programmatic statement of 1902 (p.283), and also in an earlier study, *Kant i Hegel' v ikh ucheniakh o prave i gosudarstve: dva tipicheskikh postroeniia v oblasti filosofii i prava* (Moscow, 1901).

Chapter 4

Russians Reading the *Republic*

It has become commonplace to say that Plato's philosophy found its most consummate, if somewhat perplexing, expression in his dialogue, the *Republic*. Throughout its long history of interpretation, Plato's project for an ideal legislation has been continually subjected to conflicting assessments. With many treating him as a forerunner of utopian communism and, in the twentieth century, of totalitarianism, some endeavoured to transpose his conception of the state as the embodiment of justice to the principles of a Christian theocracy. And, while certain philosophers may have seen him as a fruitful interlocutor for modern-day pedagogical theories, thereby pointing to Plato's actuality, for certain historians, the dialogue was in the first place an interesting document, providing insight into the moral and political decline of the Athenian world in which Plato lived.

Just why the *Republic* provoked such mixed feelings, from sympathy to outright hostilities, may, initially, be appreciated if one is to bear in mind the difference between, on the one hand, a reading of the dialogue in which at issue was an attempt to grasp and to rehabilitate Plato's underlying intentions, and to situate these in relation to the main lines of his philosophy as a whole, and on the other, a reading designed to elaborate on the consequences of his 'ideal state' for present-day society. While the first approach sometimes led readers to question the coherence between his social philosophy and his metaphysics, it was particularly the second kind of reading which prompted the extremes of excessive praise, or, alternatively, profound contempt, the 'utopian' label being brandished so as to undermine the credibility of his schemes.

Both types of reaction may be found in Russia. For idealist philosophers and religious thinkers in particular, otherwise so inspired by Plato, the logical consequences of Plato's theory of ideas, or of his dualism on his conception of the state was, to say the least, cause for confusion as how to evaluate his philosophy as a whole. At best, it meant a fairly selective reading of the dialogues, sometimes involving a valiant attempt to defend Plato's noble qualities and high ideals, in short, having to insist on those qualities which could be argued to be valid for all times. Or, it meant making allowances for those aspects of Plato's views which were at odds with post-Enlightenment conceptions of the person, of her civil and political rights, and of her relation to the state. A usual procedure here consisted in contextualizing Plato's philosophy, suggesting that it be taken as part and parcel of the ancient world outlook, an approach not infrequently adopted by philosopher-jurists and historians endeavouring to reconstruct the patterns of Athenian social and political practice more generally. At worst, if no allowances of this kind were made whatsoever, then Plato's conception of an ideal state was almost inevitably the target of abuse, his ideas denounced as 'communism of the most vulgar kind' (Solov'ev), contrary to human nature (Chicherin), 'retrograde' (Novgorodtsev), proof of his 'fanaticism' (Kozlov). And, as for those who already detested him anyway, the *Republic* provided an eloquent warning against the temptation of putting idealistic theories into practice. Pisarev, the self-avowed Nihilist, ruthlessly attacked Plato for having tried to do so, especially given that the result was so pitiful. How could he possibly have understood historical and political reality when he so evidently despised the individual factors which make up the empirical world?[1]

Nor did this ambivalence in attitudes towards Plato, as the author of the *Republic*, undergo any radical change once philosophers and historians in the early Soviet period contributed their own assessments of the dialogue to Plato scholarship. Despite the increasing demands of the newly instated Bolshevik ideology for intellectuals to cleave to the official Marxist-Leninist conceptions of the state and of social organization, early Soviet scholarship did not altogether stand in stark, black-and-white contrast to the pre-Revolutionary attitudes towards Plato just mentioned. On the contrary, Soviet scholars continued to base their arguments on the same Western scholarship as had the previous generation, indeed, not infrequently arriving at the same conclusions. This is generally true with respect to evaluations of Plato as a 'typical ancient'. That he, or indeed, any of the ancients, should admit of slavery, or that his attitude should be so elitist, his communitarian principles being limited to the soldiers and the guardians, were so many features of his world outlook which were regretted by most modern readers. Of course, before and after the Revolution there were differences in attitudes which reflected given political and ideological affinities. As one might expect, Marxist thinkers tended to read Plato through the prism of class analysis and socio-economic formations. Generally speaking, pre-Revolutionary scholars attributed less importance to the question of the class struggle, and whereas most – but not all – of them found the implications of Plato's remarks on sexual equality quite reprehensible, the early Soviets welcomed him as an emancipator from bourgeois prudery, even as a distant precursor of Engels' theory of the family. In short, Plato had declared the way open to the 'winged Eros'.[2]

In order to assess the place of the *Republic* in terms of overall Russian as well as early Soviet perceptions of Plato (to be treated in more detail in the next chapter), I shall begin with a brief account of the history of the Russian translations of the dialogue, together with the critical literature (philosophical and historical) that readings of this dialogue generated. A preliminary overview of lecture courses and accompanying textbooks allows us to isolate a number of key themes which seemed to have most preoccupied Plato's Russian nineteenth and early twentieth-century interpreters. In the broadest terms they may be described as Plato's conception of the state and its relation to the individual, the character of Platonic communism, Plato as educator (*nastoiashchii uchitel'*), the consequences, socially and morally, of the equality between men and women he envisaged, utopianism. As I said at the outset, sometimes it was a matter of reconstructing Plato's arguments in order to determine their coherence with his metaphysics and ethics. Otherwise, certain specific issues raised in the dialogue were viewed through the prism of modern-day values, a procedure which, inevitably, made the degrees of compatibility and conflict between ancient and modern worldviews all the more visible. Plato served as an interlocutor, or sounding-board, with respect to a number of contemporary socio-political and economic questions. For some commentators, the problem of the division between rich and poor that Plato despised foretold of the nefarious effects on society of capitalism, and of the need for the class struggle. His warnings against the cult of unlimited individual freedom were a just caution against anarchic tendencies in contemporary democracies, which, some argued, also had their origins in a 'cult of the individual'.[3] The degree to which Plato could be a viable interlocutor in contemporary discussions extended to cultural concerns, too, namely the pertinence of his views on education for nineteenth and twentieth-century pedagogical theories, while sympathizers and opponents of the emerging 'Woman Question' found support or threats to their opinions in Plato's conception of a sexually egalitarian society.

Teaching the *Republic*

Compared with dialogues like *Apology, Crito,* or *Phaedo,* the frequency with which *Republic* was translated and retranslated was actually rather low, and indeed, post-dated revised translations of most other dialogues. After a first translation attempt in 1805, the dialogue was published as an individual work more than a century later, in 1916, by K.A. Kuznetsov, Professor of Philosophy of Law at Odessa University. Kuznetsov also published a monograph (originally a lecture course) on the dialogue that same year.[4] Subsequent translations – both of the entire dialogue, or long extracts – all date from the early Soviet period.[5] In the main, references for teaching purposes throughout the late Imperial period continued to be taken from Karpov's translation (despite frequent criticism of its poor quality and contrived Russian) with German, and/or Latin versions cited as recommended reading. Otherwise, Russian-language editions of the dialogue consisted of extracts bearing on specific themes with education, the third estate, Plato's views on art ranking among the most frequently discussed topics. Again, in the early Soviet period, this practice was to become particularly prevalent. Moreover, it revived certain pre-Revolutionary critical editions, together with some pre-Revolutionary scientific production, one noted example being extracts bearing on Plato's pedagogical views.[6]

Given the growing specialization within the various disciplines of the human sciences in the closing decades of the nineteenth century, presentations of the *Republic* by philosophers, historians and legal thinkers reflected, as one might expect, the nature of the discipline they represented. But this is not to say, however, that there was no overlapping or cross-referencing between disciplines. On the contrary, in their reconstructions of Athenian society, historians in particular relied quite heavily on the interpretations provided by contemporary Russian philosophers and philologists, a practice which, however, is unsurprising if one bears in mind that quite often courses in ancient history were read from the chair of classical philology.[7] Indeed, most studies, irrespective of whom they were written by, endeavoured to reconstruct the social background to the dialogue. In this respect the role of Western scholarship, especially those studies marking defiant changes in historical interpretation (Robert Pöhlmann's much debated *Geschichte des antiken Kommunismus und Sozializmus*, 1893–1901 or the social-democrat Karl Kautsky's *Vorläufer des neuen Sozializmus*, 1895) certainly played a crucial role in Russian presentations and evaluations of the work at the turn of the century. However, despite the incursion of new ideas and new methodologies, many Russian scholars were often reluctant to relinquish the long 'established' interpretations of those German authorities active during the middle years of the nineteenth century, among them Hegelian-inspired writers, such as Zeller and Uberweg. Up to the First World War, and even afterwards, both authors were possibly the most frequently cited names in Russian literature intended for teaching purposes.

For students reading philosophy and classical philology, the *Republic* did occasionally feature as a set text in the programme for a given year, studied in both the original Greek and after Karpov's 1860s translation. But its length was no doubt prohibitive for an in-depth study of the entire work, and for students majoring in classical philology, obliged to take courses in both Aristotle and Plato, it was the shorter dialogues (*Phaedo*, *Philebus*, *Phaedrus*, *Theaetetus*, *Timaeus*) which featured more frequently on the reading lists for a given academic year. Correspondingly, courses in the history of ancient philosophy tended to append discussion about the *Republic* to an overview of Plato's ethics, while most attention was given to explaining his theory of knowledge and metaphysics. In his *Course in the History of Ancient Philosophy*, Sergei Trubetskoi followed, somewhat typically, this procedure of situating the *Republic* within the broader context of ethics, suggesting that the work be understood primarily as a theory of justice, an ideal shamefully belied, he added, by the conduct of Athenians in fifth-century Greece.[8]

In discussing the dialogue in light of its double ethical and social dimensions, Trubetskoi was implicitly referring to a problem which had preoccupied German scholars at the beginning of the nineteenth century: should the *Republic* be read primarily as a theory of justice, or as a theory of the state? Another issue of interpretation, which Trubetskoi touched on in his presentation, and one to which other Russian authors would return, concerned the argument that the asceticism demanded by Plato's communitarian principle anticipated the medieval Christian call for withdrawal from the world (meaning the self-denial as practised in monastic life) as the most fitting way to attain to the supreme, divine good. This general comparison was taken further. The organization of European medieval society, with its clergy (bearers of the divine truth), knights and princes (with their worldly swords at the service of the spiritual authority), and the peasants (engaged in trade or working the land) echoed quite closely the well-defined roles attributed to the classes of guardians, warriors and artisans in the Platonic state.

For students studying law, analysing the *Republic* (often in conjunction, or alternating with Aristotle's *Politeia*) formed an important part of their course work within the broader framework of the history of the philosophy of law. Indeed, knowledge of the dialogue was required for examination purposes, as attested by the publication of model answers to questions.[9] Issues treated by professors reading these courses tended to bear on the problem of the Platonic conception of the individual within the state. Redkin introduced his students to this topic in the following terms:

> For Plato, the individual is first and foremost a citizen. For this reason Plato did not develop a theory of 'subjective' ethics as such, but situated his ethical views in relation to his conception of the state as that which provides the framework for an objective ethics – meaning a complete theory of the supreme good, wellbeing, virtues, and moral obligations (...). Both the moral perfection of the individual and the perfection of the state structure and governance stem from one single principle, namely that of truth (*pravda*) and justice (*spravedlivost'*), which Plato took to be the supreme aim of both the individual and the state in their respective activities.[10]

While Redkin endeavoured to balance the interests of the individual-citizen and those of the state, other commentators were less neutral. Chicherin accentuated the total absorption of the individual by the state, claiming that Plato had taken the regimentation of private life further than any other thinker. While Plato's greatest merit was to have invested the state with the eternal ideas of truth and the good, the sore point was that 'in the name of such principles, he wanted to consolidate daily life in ways which totally contradict human nature'.[11] A host of other intellectuals and scholars followed suit in the criticism they directed at Plato's social plan. Evgenii Trubetskoi and Solov'ev both stated in no uncertain terms that Plato neglected the individual, and that the consequences of this neglect were as ruinous to his political theory as they were detrimental to the message of his philosophy as a whole.[12] Novgorodtsev held similar views, even though, as I argued in the previous chapter, these were offset by his assimilation of an image of Plato, as the protector of spiritual values, to his own social philosophy grounded in the 'personal principle'. Admittedly, the upshot was a rather uncomfortable coexistence of conflicting paradigms.

Quite differently again, others went so far as to argue for signs of individual freedom in Plato's ideas about state organization, which, albeit unwittingly, actually heralded the principles and practices of the Enlightenment. Maxim Kovalevskii attributed to Plato a view of governance grounded in a prototype theory of the rule of law (*pravovoe gosudartsvo*) in the sense that, for Plato, as Kovalevskii read him, law (*zakon*) is to operate as a principle by which everyone, including the high dignitaries, is bound.[13] Kuznetsov presented Plato as a forerunner of the idea of a 'social contract', and, ultimately, of 'constitutionalism'. 'In Plato', he wrote, 'we see the state in its emergence, for each one of us is not a self-contained entity, but requires the mutual exchange of "many things". This principle of exchange is precisely one of "contractual relations" (*dogovornoe*).'[14] In this sense, Kuznetsov argued, Plato may be said to have attributed a certain degree of freedom to the individual person:

> Perhaps the strongest argument against the view 'that the person is submerged in the polis' is the one which bids us to recognize that the polis, the whole (*tseloe*), is not so much an alien entity, towering above its constituent parts, but merely the 'sum total of those parts' (...). The idea of the state as a 'person' as something apart from those persons (*litsa*) who compose it did not exist in Plato's times (...). Least of all does Plato forget the 'individual persons' who make up the state. And, even if, from our point of view, they live on top of one another (*tesnovato*) within the confines of the city-state, it is not so much the 'whole', in which the person is said to be entirely submerged, which is responsible for this impression, as the phenomenon of 'overcrowding' experienced in daily life – neighbours meddling with everyone and everything![15]

Given the atmosphere of intellectual freedom which nourished Plato's thought, for Kuznetsov it was unthinkable that he might have had designs to turn his fellow citizens into tools for the sake of advancing state interest – 'Enchain another's soul!? Would not this be in total contradiction with the spirit of Socrates' teaching?'[16]

Kuznetsov's underlying concern here was to uncover those traits in the *Republic* which, albeit still inchoate, were to underscore much modern political philosophy beginning in the sixteenth, and especially in the seventeenth and eighteenth centuries. In doing so, he was also projecting motifs of Enlightenment and early modern thought back on to Plato. His claim that, like his 'distant progeny', Thomas Bacon (in *The Catechism*), or John Hooper, Plato had also endeavoured to distinguish between 'power' and 'freedom', between 'governors' and the 'governed', in short between 'public' and 'private' persons, is just one example of this. In the end, though, despite his rather bold attempt to update Plato, Kuznetsov was brought up against the difficulty of convincingly squaring the 'means and ends' of Plato's project. Indeed, it was a difficulty which most modern readers uncovered, leaving them uncertain as how best to accommodate what they otherwise recognized as praiseworthy ideals. The problem for many, was that, quite simply, in order to realize his noble plan Plato resorted to tyrannical methods, and thereby turned himself into the Machiavelli of his times: 'Tyranny – that's precisely what he fell back on in the name of his ideal state. The least ideal was turned into the most ideal. Just try finding anything better than that!'[17]

Virtually all commentators, irrespective of the discipline they represented, supplied some historical background, whether this be an outline of the various forms of rule such as they existed in the classical period, or an attempt to recreate those personal biographical elements – the impact of Plato's stay in Syracuse on his political views, notably – deemed important for a proper grasp of Plato's reactionary solutions. 'Professional' historians, researching specific aspects of Athenian political and cultural reality, would include the *Republic* among their source materials.[18] Many worked extensively on the social and political development of the Greek community (*obshchina, obshchestvennost'*), or the question of slavery in the ancient world, as well as education.[19] But, studying the past also presented an occasion to allude to more recent developments in Russian history, such as the reform process, or the role of the peasant commune. R.Vipper, Professor of History at Moscow University, went so far as to graft terms such as 'feudalism' and 'serf emancipation' onto his study of daily life in Attic Greece, and in a short piece on Socrates and Plato, spoke of the former as an 'organizer of a sectarian, anti-state *obshchina*', and likened the second quite simply to the 'Grand Inquisitor'.[20]

A number of studies bearing telling titles such as *The Ancient World and We, Antiquity and Modernity,* or again titles to the tune of 'an ancient philosopher on contemporary themes' provide examples of a tendency to modernize the past for the sake of throwing light on the more proximate issues of Russian social and cultural life.[21] Intended for the public at large, these essays and conferences also show knowledge of concepts and historiographical methods which, for the most part, may be identified with authors of modernizing trends in history, in particular Robert Pöhlmann and, later, after 1910, Ulrich Wilamowitz-Möllendorff. Known for the way they projected terminology relating to contemporary conceptions of state (*Rechtsstaat*, state socialism), as it were, backwards on to the Platonic worldview, these historians were to become constant references – which is not to say 'uncontested authorities' – for Russian specialists of antiquity, historian-philologists, as well as philosopher-philologists writing after the turn of the twentieth century and into the 1920s. The historian, V. Buzeskul, for example, took up the theme of antiquity in terms of its relation to modernity not just to account for the heritage of the former, but also to uncover the 'modern', i.e. that which is normally considered as belonging to 'our times', in antiquity. This twofold ambition allowed him to highlight, if not exaggerate, a set of neat parallels between Plato's idea of communism and contemporary political theories. Accordingly, Plato's 'republic' may be likened to 'state socialism', Plato's criticism of oligarchy is comparable to latter-day criticism of capitalism, the Athenian poor are today's proletariat. The political struggle, which Plato bore witness to in his day, was not entirely unlike the class struggle marking so much recent history.[22] And, despite what Buzeskul recognized to be glaring differences between the ancient and the modern social orders (the notion of the 'city-state', the practice of slavery), he nevertheless argued for general points in common between their respective political worldviews. For the ancients and the moderns alike, the state should be grounded in the principles of 'truth' (*pravda*) and in justice, and both, he added, conceived of the state as the best means to realize the good of the citizen in his relation to the state.

The philologist, Faddei Zelinskii, also adopted a modernizing approach to his presentation of the Greek conception of the state. But, unlike Buzeskul, Zelinskii did not go so far as to speak of a 'Greek modernity', his underlying concern being, as I suggested in an earlier chapter, to vindicate an unhampered instruction in classical philology in Russian schools and universities. Accordingly, his emphasis lay on the scientific, cultural and educational significance of the ancient world for contemporary society. Greek culture, Zelinskii argued, is the seedbed of all modern European culture. Therefore studying this distant past is, in the first place, a means to grasp our own reality at the level of that which is the most enduring (*prochnoi*) and vital.[23] This perspective, in turn, guided Zelinskii's presentation of Greek political theory and practice as a concern to conjugate the interests of both the individual and the state, a concern which, of course, was of central importance for Russian liberal thinkers writing in the early twentieth century. Zelinskii was, surely, alluding to the reform process in Russia, beset with its attendant hopes for modernization, when he chose to consider the development of Greek political understanding in light of the following leading questions: how should the state be constructed so as to afford the person the greatest possible moral perfection? If one is to affirm the moral significance of the state, what should its relation to the person be? 'Embedded in these questions',

Zelinskii wrote, 'are elements of a struggle between two ideas, which are equally valuable and equally important for cultural progress – the idea of statehood (*gosudarstvennost'*) and the idea of individual freedom.' In addition, he reminded his audience of their own immediate reality, observing that 'the Athenians endeavoured to emancipate the person without, so far as it was possible, diminishing the strength of the state'.[24]

Interpreting the *Republic*

In order to furnish a typology of interpretations of the *Republic* in nineteenth and early twentieth-century Russia, it is first of all necessary to highlight two main stages in the history of its interpretation more generally. An important initial phase, reflected in the writings of Redkin and Karpov, concerned endeavours to uncover the underlying meaning of the dialogue. Was it an exposition of a theory of justice, or a treatise about the state as an institution? How coherent, unified was the content of the dialogue, how much subject to contradictions? This initial, 'hermeneutic' phase gradually gave way, in the closing decades of the century, to a plethora of vying interpretations in which broader socio-political factors, but also the constant refinements in historical method, were brought to bear in assessing the significance, or lack thereof, of Plato for contemporary society. But even here, despite the diversity of appraisals that appeared in the literature, one could argue that these originated in a choice between two main viewpoints on the matter. Interpreting the *Republic* was either motivated by attempts to actualize Plato in varying degrees, seeing in him a distant precursor of, say, socialism, and, indeed, sometimes going even further, claiming him as a useful interlocutor with respect to specific socio-political issues in the contemporary world. Or, on the contrary, interpretations of the dialogue were governed by a refusal to admit any relevance at all for a post-Enlightenment society, with its cornerstone principles of the rights of the individual and the citizen.

Both phases of interpretation, the 'hermeneutic' and the 'historical-philosophical', were, of course, the fruit of a constant interplay with Western scholarship. In addressing the question as to whether Plato was essentially concerned with issues of a political or of a moral nature, Karpov and Redkin were explicitly picking up an issue inaugurated through the philological and philosophical perspectives of early to mid-nineteenth century German scholarship, associated with the names of Schleiermacher, Ast, Morgenstern, but especially Hegel. Karpov took both Morgenstern and Scheiermacher to task, but for opposed reasons. While the former had exaggerated the importance of the historical context as a means to uncover the meaning of the dialogue, the latter had underestimated the political dimension of the dialogue, seeing its place as tributary to Plato's main concern, the virtue of justice.[25] Worse still, the next generation of German scholars, and here Karpov referred to Eduard Munk and Karl Steinhart, had treated the dialogue almost exclusively as an account of the idea of the good, a form of reductionism which, for Karpov, bore the hallmark of contemporary German philosophy with its 'one-sided subjectivism and logical formalism'.[26] Against this, Karpov advanced his own opinion, insisting on a balanced unity between the two dimensions of the dialogue: 'Plato's aim', he wrote, 'was to sketch an image of perfected human virtue', to conceive of this 'both in the souls of individual human beings, and in the society of citizens (*grazhdanskoe obshchestvo*).' Not only did he set out to demonstrate the 'force and excellence' of virtue, 'but also to teach that the vile and the shameful can insinuate themselves into social life, and that human happiness is destroyed by this evil'.[27] In short, Karpov had only praise for 'the unity of form in this superb composition, and the perfect "balanced unity" (*tselost'*) of its content'.[28]

In his introduction to the *Republic*, Redkin also referred to Steinhart (one of Karpov's main targets for criticism), addressing the same issue of whether or not the dialogue betrayed a conflict of interests between the moral and the political.[29] According to Steinhart, as Redkin read him, if the dialogue is regarded as a defence of the triumph of the supreme good, then the difficulties of assessing the dialogue as an account either of justice or of the state exclusively are removed.[30] Redkin himself finally withheld his views as to whether Plato (or his German interpreter) had succeeded in affording a unity to the dialogue. Given that his own underlying aim was to situate the dialogue within the context of the history of the philosophy of law, it is perhaps no surprise that he should call on, and sympathize most with, Hegel's reading of the dialogue (in his *Lesson on Philosophy of History*, and his *Philosophy of Right*). Redkin believed that Hegel's understanding of the *Republic* went deeper than Morgenstern and Schleiermacher, or even the next generation of philologist-philosophers, with Karl Hermann and Godofredus Stallbaum at the forefront. It was Redkin's opinion that Hegel had made a significant contribution to the problem how best to understand the dialogue by introducing the term *Sittlickheit*, the sense of which was to show that morality is borne by political and social structures.[31] Redkin echoed this idea when he claimed that:

> Plato wanted to show that truth and justice (*pravda i spravedlivost'*) exist only in the state, only in this objective reality of the actuality of law (*real'nost prava*), where 'law' is understood in the broadest terms, meaning 'right' (*pravo*), morality/ethics (*moral'nost'*) and morals/moeurs (*nravstvennost'*). The upshot of this view is that every individual subject has as his aim the universal (*vseobshchee*). Uniquely, from and within this spirit of the universal does the individual strive to act and to live.[32]

This prompted Redkin, following Hegel, to speak of a *vozvyshenie* (literally, a movement upwards) in Plato's thinking, that is, a passage from morality/ethics (*moral'nost', Moral, Sittenlehre*) to morals (*nravstvennost' Sittlichkeit*). It is a passage moving from the moral (*moral'noi*) virtue of individuals, which comes to expression in the accomplishment of specific objectives, towards that supreme virtue which lives and acts for the state. Consequently, at one level, Hegel, according to Redkin, came close to Plato's first interpreters, the ancients themselves, for whom the dialogue was fundamentally about the idea of the state, while, at another level, he had also succeeded in rehabilitating the ethical content of the dialogue in both its subjective and objective nature, together with the corresponding distinctions between the private and public spheres, between morality and moeurs.[33]

Besides his reconstruction of the dialogue along Hegelian lines, Redkin gave some consideration to Plato's predilection for the Spartan practice of rule. His point here was to show that Plato was somehow caught between two models – one, historical, the Spartan, the other, a model derived from his philosophy as such. The upshot was a curious radicalization of the Greek concept of the state; the personal freedom of the individual is entirely engulfed by it. For Redkin, this was strangely at odds with another Plato, namely the one who had 'urged that, by means of true philosophical knowledge, the inner spiritual life of the citizens ascend to hitherto unheard of heights, such that individuality may also be freed from its finitude, to become infinite, just as the universal (*vseobshchnost'*) is infinite'.[34] How could Plato explore the spiritual depths of man, then deny him freedom?

Notwithstanding Redkin's valiant attempt to make Plato a positive reference for nineteenth-century juridical science and philosophy, what in the end still went begging, for both himself and Hegel, was some recognition by Plato of the right to individual freedom within the polis. It was a question which was to preoccupy the next generations of Russian scholars, writing in the late nineteenth and early twentieth centuries. By that time, of course, the practice of combining historical, philological and philosophical, even psychological, considerations in their appraisals had become *de rigueur*. And the upshot of these combined approaches, as I suggested earlier, was to nuance the 'Plato problem' in a whole variety of ways. Some critics drew attention to Plato's 'life drama', his disenchantment with the world in which he lived. Others endeavoured to reconstruct the 'logic' of the *Republic* as an application of the Platonic theory of ideas, of the good, and of the virtues to a conception of the state and ideal legislation. Correspondingly, differences in interpretation (or, alternatively, the interplay of several) largely depended on whether Plato was regarded as a man of his times, or a philosopher for all times. Moreover, the choice of a theoretical, or a historical and biographical accent in these interpretations was generally unaffected by the nature of the discipline a given commentator was supposedly representing. In his lecture course, *The History of Ancient and Modern Philosophy of Law* (Kiev,

1899), Evgenii Trubetskoi paid virtually no attention to the underlying political and juridical significance of the dialogue, but focused instead on what he deemed to be the ethical – inchoately religious – impulse in Plato's idea of a well-organized state. The philosopher of law, Pavel Novgorodtsev addressed the difficulties inherent in analysing the dialogue from a combined philosophical and historical viewpoint, where the latter optic, moreover, could be understood in two ways. While, on one level, the historical viewpoint simply meant a description of the political disintegration forming the immediate background to the dialogue, on another, Novgorodtsev also used the term to remind his readers of the historical dimension (meaning 'backward looking') embedded in Plato's 'philosophical' projects for a future ideal political and social order. According to Novgorodtsev, Plato's philosophical, or theoretical, impulse mixed poorly with his evident nostalgia for a Golden Age, for a patriarchal society in which the communitarian principle was practised only at the level of material wealth. Plato's fondness for an idealized past explained his radical, reactionary rejection of all existing forms of government, together with his criticism of an emergent capitalism, the seeds of which he detected in the ever widening gap between the rich and poor. Yet Novgorodtsev did give credit to those elements of the *Republic* which, to his mind, derived from Plato's theoretical views – the division of society into three classes, his ideas relating to education, his arguments that property rights be based on a communitarian principle. Though strongly tainted with the spirit of utopianism, for Novgorodtsev these elements constituted the most original part of Plato's thought. But even here, Novgorodtsev was a long way from blind admiration. To his mind, Plato's project for an ideal legalisation failed, and on two counts – both in terms of the objectives he had set himself, as well as from the perspective of modern society with its, loosely speaking, liberal principles which Novgorodtsev so evidently shared, and which he brought to bear in his concluding remarks. Even if the project were judged exclusively on Plato's own terms, the contradiction between ends and means would be nonetheless glaring. For, despite his high ideals to combat the evils he saw in contemporary society, the solution Plato proposed was little more than a retrograde autarchy. From a modern perspective this 'autarchic ideal' was 'run through with such distrust for the efforts of individual people, and by such a conviction in the infallibility of the plan he conceived, that its realization is just incomprehensible'.[35] In answer to Plato, Novgorodtsev summarized his own personal credo:

> Society is first of all a union of individuals (*lits*), and is precisely that which is denied. Instead of the free person, it is the infallible authority of the Philosopher-ruler which forms the keystone of society. This may be understood in light of the theoretical presuppositions of the Platonic ideal, but it becomes totally unthinkable once brought into practice as a norm of life.[36]

Confronting Western Scholarship: 'Classical' versus 'Modernizing' Trends

In their evaluations of the *Republic*, most Russian scholars referred to contemporary and recent Western literature on the subject. The problem here, though, was the number of interpretations available, with seemingly little, if any, coherence among them. Russian readers found themselves before the 'classical' Hegelian-inspired reading of Zeller, who saw and criticized the absence of individual liberty in the Platonic conception of the state, while the 'modernizers' Pöhlmann (and later Wilamowitz-Möllendorff) endeavoured to update Plato, making him a viable interlocutor in more recent discussions on the idea of a rule of law state. To this one should add the perspective of the social-democrats, Karl Kautsky and Georg Adler, who depicted Plato as a distant parent of socialism.[37] Where did Russian Plato specialists situate themselves with respect to this range of interpretations?

While the most widely used text in university courses, right up to the October Revolution, continued to be Zeller's *Die Philosophie der Griechen*, by far the most widely discussed, and disputed, interpretation – both before and after the Revolution – was undoubtedly Robert Pöhlmann's *Geschichte des antiken Kommunismus und Sozializmus* (Munich, 1893–1901[38]). Pöhlmann's thesis marked a challenge to the still dominant Hegelian interpretation of the Platonic state, according to which the individual has virtually no intrinsic value, but is rather absorbed into and subordinated to the all-inclusive nature of the state. On these grounds, Hegel had opposed Plato's exclusion of private property from the ideal city, his destruction of the family bond and his refusal to grant choice of rank within the city. On the contrary, for Hegel, property is indispensable as a means to affirm the person within society, and he believed that the family, although it has limits in the sense that it is by nature private, had to be recognized as 'the primordial unit of civil society'. Granted, Hegel did view more positively Plato's conception of justice as an organizing force, and he applauded Plato's division of classes on the grounds that it provided the best guarantee of an harmonious distribution of tasks within the state. But, it remains, that the lasting image of Plato the social thinker, which Hegel contributed to, was one in which the individual was entirely subordinated to the interests of the state.[39]

Pöhlmann's efforts to combat the persuasive nature of this kind of criticism were in many respects an uphill battle. His appeal to a 'soft line' Plato focused on a series of counter-arguments to the Hegelian image of a muscular Plato demanding loyalty to a 'like-mindedness' (*edinomyslie*).[40] First, Plato's conception of a just state was one in which 'the rights of the person' were, in fact, recognized, he said. The state administers to her needs in harmonious exchange for the share the individual brings to the common weal:

> The Platonic state does not at all seek to turn its citizens into automatons, subjugated to an alien will. It is not Plato's intention to constrain them by state force, to turn them into chains in a great wheel. The citizen's will draws its content and orientation as much from itself as it does from the whole. The subjective and objective moment (...) should also exist in harmonious reciprocity. This tendency is already discernible in the fact that, alongside the idea of society, as that which determines the whole, and which places the requirements of the whole above any claims of a partial nature, another idea of a quite different nature runs like a leading thread through the entire project for the ideal state. It is the idea of justice which grants each person her due.[41]

Pöhlmann's line of argument was designed to create a portrait of Plato as a thinker who admitted of the individual's natural right to freedom and equality, as well as to the full development of her specific gifts or qualities. Evidently, the underlying point in all this was to bring Plato fully into line with modern-day political principles. Indeed, Pöhlmann's text contained a number of remarks on the pertinence of the Platonic conception of the state to contemporary Germany.[42] One might reasonably imagine that this line of argument would find a note of approval among Russian scholars. Yet, while perhaps sympathizing with Pöhlmann's aims, they nevertheless tended to be cautious of the conclusions he came to. The historian, Mikhail Rostovtsev, one of the editors of the Russian translation of Pöhlmann's book (and after the Revolution a renowned authority in the West in ancient history) summed up neatly the opinion of many scholars who saw Pöhlmann's 'erroneous interpretations' as the consequence of a misguided desire to study the ancient world through the prism of contemporary literature on social questions. The upshot was to 'force his point of view and occasionally risk being somewhat hackneyed in the process'.[43]

As a rule, Russian philosophers and historians tended to opt for a more 'traditional' critique which stressed the incompatibility between the Platonic and modern worldviews. Against Pöhlmann, most Russian readers contested the claim that the Platonic communitarian principle did, in fact, extend to the 'dark masses', the third class of artisans and labourers. For Evgenii Trubetskoi, Pöhlmann had exaggerated Plato's individualism, in the sense that he failed to account for an important aspect of Plato's metaphysics, the theory of forms, or ideas. 'For Plato', Trubetskoi riposted, 'the absolute, that which saves human life and affords it a divine content, is not the living person, but the impersonal generic idea (*rodovaia ideia*) which, by its very nature, is hostile to the individual.' In short, individuality did not fit into Plato's metaphysical system: 'The individual is on a par with the material. It is evil.'[44]

Despite what seems to have been a fairly widespread rejection of Plato's relevance to modern society, many readers did, nevertheless, use him as a foil in endeavours to tackle contemporary issues. Uncovering the 'modern' in the ancient past (the case of Buzeskul) was as much a design to pass comment on the present, as it was an academic exercise in historical method. As a metaphor for absolute state control, an account of the Platonic worldview was occasionally intended as an implicit – sometimes open – criticism of the autarchic nature of Russian nineteenth-century bureaucracy. There was a trace of 'original Platonism', it was noted, in the ban imposed on those in state service to practice profit-making private commerce, the spirit of which, in neither case, 'had nor has, much to do with the idea of the economic restructuring of society'.[45] As for Marxist interpretations intent on legitimating the present and future course by referring to (or recasting perceptions of) past models, it was clear that Plato could not, for all his elitism, be excluded from the gallery of distant precursors of socialism. His vindication of values such as equality between men and women, social justice, his expressed hopes for an alternative way of life based on communitarian principles, were arguably too close to the ideals of modern socialists to permit rejecting his philosophy outright as anachronistic. Marxist interpretations, or those that could be identified with Marxist trends, were to become particularly prominent in the 1920s, at a time when at issue was the need to provide the historical foundations for a political-cultural tradition in the making. But even prior to the Revolution, the works of Kautsky and Adler found, curiously enough, perhaps more sympathy among Russian non-Marxists than did, finally, Pöhlmann's more innovative views. Despite their Marxist, even 'utopian' tendencies, or the way they sometimes exaggerated the importance Plato attached to socio-economic factors, these authors nonetheless cleaved, *grosso modo*, to a 'classical' interpretation based on recognizing the limits of compatibility between Platonic and modern worldviews. The points Kautsky raised, which were to be repeated innumerable times in the early Soviet period – and this, despite Lenin's denunciation of him as renegade for having criticized the October Revolution[46] – focused on Plato's criticism of social and sexual inequality (the latter incidentally, corroborated by the sentiments expressed in the *Communist Manifesto*), of private property, and his ideas on education. In short, for Kautsky, Plato was the first thinker to have given a systematic defence of communism. The outstanding problem was that its reach did not extend to the workers, but was confined to the guardians and the soldiers. Indeed, it was the fundamental difference between Platonic and post-Enlightenment conceptions of communism that prompted Kautsky, and Adler after him, to qualify this prototype version as 'aristocratic', and as 'consumer' communism, a label which was to crop up time and again in subsequent Russian Marxist literature. Ironically, it was precisely Kautsky's insistence on the limits of affinity that brought him closer to the 'traditional criticism' to which most Russian commentators of the *Republic* seemed to subscribe, even though, between socialists and liberals, the significance each side attached to Plato's communitarian principles differed quite radically. Whereas, for the former, it signalled a promise of hope that human relations might be based on mutual respect, for the latter it amounted to an outright rejection of individual liberty.

The Actuality of the *Republic*: Education and the Woman Question

Two themes which were central to Plato's construction of the ideal state and which caught the attention of Russian and European commentators alike, were those of education and sexual equality. Both these issues gained in importance in the aftermath of the October Revolution. Lenin, for one, understood the age-old wisdom that education represents the best means to ground a (communist) state. Education was surely the most effective way to inculcate the populace with a sense of order, group ethics, self-discipline, in short, military values. For Lenin, the school was the place in which the seeds of social division, that is, the nefarious bourgeois values of self-interest, could best be destroyed.[47] Plato, who advocated that children be removed from the influence of their parents to be trained in the laws of the state, was arguably not alien to the spirit of new educational experiments in Soviet schools such as the 'brigade' system of collective study and examination, even if their immediate models were contemporary American and European theorists (John Dewey, W.H. Kilpatrick, Helen Parkhurst's 'Dalton Plan'), rather than Books Three and Seven of the Platonic dialogue. But, in any event, Plato's concept of an ideal education was sufficiently actual to be the object of monographs and commented translations in the opening decades of the twentieth century as well as in revolutionary Russia.

Plato, the Teacher (Nastoiashchii Uchitel')

In the pre-Revolutionary period appeals to Plato's role as a 'real teacher' (*nastoiashchii uchitel'*) were, in part, made within the much broader perimeters of a long-standing quarrel between proponents of a classical versus a technical education, and partly in light of recent developments in pedagogical science, especially in Germany. An image of Plato, defender of knowledge for knowledge's sake, helped ward off what 'humanists' feared as the threat to moral and intellectual values which they saw encapsulated in the pragmatic 'school for life' motto. Recall, they said, Plato's comments on the charms of the science of arithmetic and 'the many ways it is conducive to our desired end, if pursued in the spirit of a philosopher, and not of a shopkeeper!' (*Rep.* VII 525). Professor at Warsaw University, N. Novosadskii, wrote:

> For Plato, the aim of education is, first and foremost, to master theoretical problems – an ability which broadens the intellectual horizons of the person – rather than proficiency in problems of a practical nature. Plato believed in the supremacy of 'knowledge for the sake of knowledge' over knowledge for the

sake of expediency. He did not regard schooling in terms of a preparation for the practical requirements of life. Education should, first of all, provide the state with good, upright (*khoroshchii*) people. The highest aim of education is knowledge of the idea of *blago* meaning the moral and intellectual well-being of the person, because it is precisely the idea of *blago* which lies at the source of all other ideas (in the Platonic sense).[48]

Interestingly, while virtually all Russian readers recognized how intertwined the moral-individual and social dimensions of education were for Plato, certain commentators, like Novosadskii, focused predominantly on the personal improvement to be had from education. One major exception in this regard was Evgenii Trubetskoi, who sharply opposed the educational dimension of the ideal state on the grounds that it was constructed 'to stamp out all that is individual, personal in man, to eradicate any sign of one's own will'.[49] Incidentally, Trubetskoi's views unwittingly prefigured Soviet attitudes towards Plato on this point, the difference between them being that, what Trubetskoi considered inadmissible, was, for the early Soviets, highly commendable.

For commentators, like Novosadskii, their selective reading of Plato, 'the true teacher', arguably allowed them to suspend the doubts they might otherwise have had about Plato, the political programmer, who was usually accused of neglecting the individual. Of course, Novosadskii was aware of the fact that Plato did not develop his pedagogical ideas in a vacuum, that these were inextricably bound with questions of social order and the state.[50] But this did not, in his eyes, diminish the contemporaneity of Plato's ideas, and the reinforcement they brought to the 'neo-humanist' approach to schooling. With its underlying conviction that the aim of education is knowledge and the good, the call to cultivate humanist values through education also carried with it an appeal to recognize innate talents and the individual gifts of the pupil. Plato, Novosadskii and like-minded thinkers argued, wanted people to be nurtured on moral principles from a very early age, so that these should somehow be part of the very flesh and blood of citizens. As for those destined to occupy the highest posts in the state, Plato urged 'that they liken themselves, as far as this is humanly possible, to the gods'.[51]

Besides invoking Plato – the protector of moral values – for the sake of defending classical education against the incursion of more technically oriented schooling, attempts were made by educationalists and psychologists to uncover Plato's relevance as a social pedagogue, an approach surely inspired by contemporary West European literature.[52] According to one commentator, Plato was the first author of 'scientific social pedagogy', a term inspired by recent German pedagogical theories, associated with Döring, Paul Bergemann and Paul Natorp, to designate the combined ethical and social functions of education.[53] M.M. Rubinshtein openly deferred to Natorp when he remarked that Plato constructed his social-pedagogical theory on the basis of his psychology, 'together with frequent recourse to his own, personal, extremely valuable psychological-pedagogical observations. We are therefore justified in calling his pedagogy "philosophical-psychological", thereby updating him to modern times'.[54] But, for Rubinshtein, whose monograph was published twice – at the outbreak of war and towards the close of War Communism – at issue was not merely the actualization of Plato's pedagogical theories for the sake of advancing contemporary science. In insisting on the way Plato's innovative theories had marked a radical break with the Greek practice of his day, Rubinshtein also had in mind their potential relevance to the major social and political upheaval that Russia was then in the midst of. Little surprise, then, that Rubinshtein should present Plato as a challenge to the existing system, and, unlike Novosadskii, highlight his contribution to the social, practical foundations of education. The aim of education, he contended, is to forge a new social order, and a *homme nouveau*. To this end, children were to be removed from the influence of their parents and, under the guidance of the state, trained for future practical purposes, schooled in the qualities of courage and usefulness as citizens (*Rep.* VII 540–541).[55] The means Plato proposed ran counter to the existing social and economic fabric, which, to his mind, was responsible for the social inequality and malaise in the world around him, the destroyed morale in some, unwarranted pride and unjust behaviour as a consequence of the spoils of wealth in others. Against this, the abolishment of private property, *obshchnost'* (community) of women and children were devised as the most propitious means to eradicate parental and personal egoism, and to provide the greatest possible leeway for the 'selection of the best.' 'It is precisely this idea that we would like to stress', Rubinshtein wrote, 'because, nowadays, it is also this question which is becoming an extremely crucial one for human culture (...). Turning to the past at a time of spiritual ferment may spare us unnecessary mistakes'.[56]

Sexual Equality, Solidarity, or 'Stud Farm'?

Rubinshtein's appeal to the actuality of Plato was echoed in a remark that Bertrand Russell made in 1920 after a recent visit to Soviet Russia. 'No historical precedent', he wrote, 'makes us think of the Bolshevik regime as much as Plato's Republic'.[57] For even the most casual observer, the spirit of early Soviet propaganda and party pronouncements were alarmingly reminiscent of Plato's scheme of organization. For instance, the Party Code of Conduct (1919) stipulating the duties of the Communist, his obligation to 'set an example in the observance of labour and state discipline' was not unlike the rigorous behaviour Plato demanded from his state guardians:

And they will have to be watched at every age in order that we may see that they preserve their resolution, and never under the influence, either of force or enchantment, forget or cast off their sense of duty to the state. (*Rep.* III 412).

The Bolshevik party member, for his part, was to set an example 'in the observance of labour and state discipline, to master the techniques of his work and continually raise his production and work qualifications.'[58] Or the first Family Code of 1918, which included articles on the eventual transfer of children to the state (by forbidding adoption into individual families), recalled the preconditions Plato believed necessary to ensure equality between members of the guardian and warrior classes. In the Soviet state, children were to benefit from a collective upbringing. The family, stripped of its previous social function, would gradually wither away, leaving in its place fully autonomous, equal individuals, free to choose their partners on the basis of love and mutual respect:

> The worker mother who is conscious of her social function, will rise to a point where she no longer differentiates between yours and mine, she must remember that there are henceforth only 'our' children, those of the communist state, the common possession of all workers.[59]

> Is that not the best state in which the greatest number of persons apply the terms 'mine' and 'not mine' in the same way to the same thing? (*Rep.* V 465).

Both Plato and the Bolsheviks placed 'solidarity' in close relation to a cult of physical exercise. Gymnastics was not just a means to assure harmony between the body and the intellect, but also had a strategic function, namely to inculcate, through strict disciplinary, militarized drills, a sense of group cooperation, and a readiness to defend the Fatherland in times of war. Perhaps going further than Plato's original intentions, some early Soviet enthusiasts, also took 'solidarity' to mean licence to 'healthy, free and natural sex'. As Commissar for Public Health, Alexandra Kollontai for one, pledged herself to instruct the people in collectivist amorous behaviour. Based on love, passion and comradeship, this new sexual attitude was summed up in one famous slogan of the period – make way for the winged Eros!ized[60] Granted, this *mot d'ordre* had little to do with Plato's own views when he imagined a new community between men and women, but it certainly captured rather well the spirit of the proletarian revolution where, for a while at least, social and sexual equality were almost interchangeable notions.

Marx and Engels had bequeathed to early Soviet enthusiasts a view on marriage as an institution to legalize offspring, nothing more. But Plato was possibly a useful ally here as well. As one Soviet author, writing at the beginning of the NEP period, put it:

> Plato's bourgeois commentators (...) could in no way manage to reconcile themselves with such a blasphemous encroachment on the sacred foundations of monogamy, which today, to a greater degree than in Plato's time, is summoned to strengthen, in the form of wedlock, certain property based relations.[61]

A useful ally maybe, if only by default. According to the historian of socialist doctrines, Viacheslav Volgin, between Plato and Marx there was certainly a happy coincidence of minds on this matter, but in Plato's case it was not because he challenged the reigning practice or *moeurs* of his times, as was the case of Marx. On the contrary, Plato's views bore witness to the attitudes of the privileged, 'enlightened' circle in which he lived:

> Plato defends the absolute equality between the sexes. It is perhaps the most amazing aspect of his entire composition (...). His appeal to equal rights in no way corresponds to what might be called the general social tone of the *Republic*. One would rather expect Plato's aristocratic leanings to have guided his views on the relation between the sexes (...). But that Plato did not take this line in resolving the question of the relation between the sexes may only be explained by the attitudes of his immediate intellectual milieu in which women already enjoyed a fairly prominent role.[62]

While it might be tempting to think that treatment of the *Frauenfrage* in Russia before and after the Revolution underwent a radical change, corresponding to a rejection of 'bourgeois morality' as the new Soviet era consolidated itself, this was, in fact, not such a clear-cut issue. Granted, in the late nineteenth century, Plato's ideas did shock and disgust some readers, but others rallied to defend him, and not necessarily because their sympathies lay with Engels' critique of the family as the bastion of bourgeois self-interest and perpetrator of class divisions. Solov'ev and Karpov expressed in no uncertain terms a sense of revulsion. While Solov'ev remarked that Plato's account of sexual relations made one think of a 'stud farm',[63] Karpov sharply criticized Plato for advocating equality between the sexes:

> Our philosopher has taken his idealization of human virtue too far, seemingly having no idea of the irreparable damage he risked doing to human nature. In preparing women for responsible posts in society alongside men, he did not separate the first from the second, even within the walls of the gymnasium where both sexes ran about naked. Platonic philosophy omitted to study the psychical factors which determine the differences between the sexes, and which also demonstrate, irrefutably, that the place of each on earth, the temperament and gifts of each are very different. Even if we were to accept that the body can be trained like an instrument, tailored to a given physical task, this is not at all the case when it comes to the soul. If you would like a woman to be the same as a man, you would be vesting her with male qualities in vain. Any success would necessarily entail the deprivation of her womanly

qualities. Having lost her feminine qualities she would become an object of suspicion in the eyes of men, and hateful to women.[64]

Sergei Trubetskoi and Aleksei Kozlov took a different view on the matter, each defending Plato against the charge of promiscuity. In destroying the family in the class of the guardians Plato was not, they argued, proposing free sexual cohabitation, any more than he was promising the emancipation of women. Trubetskoi:

> In order to eliminate the family and private property the woman had to be transformed into an Amazon. Plato remains true to himself even with respect to the 'woman question'. His insistence on equality between men and women was not in the interest of women as such, as for the sake of his ideal state to which everyone, men and women alike, were to be subordinated.[65]

Kozlov suggested that Plato's ideal of equality betokened not so much free sex, as abstinence. In this sense his ideas prefigured the Christian ideal/ practice of self-denial. It should not be forgotten, he remarked, that:

> In no way did Plato's communism and his rejection of the family take their cue from the arbitrary passions of individuals – something which, incidentally, we come across all too often in modern-day theories which reject the family in the name of free sexual relations. Indeed, the underlying motivation for such theories has less to do with communism as it does with *promiscuité*. Faced with Platonic communism, which demands the sacrifice not only of an *individualized feeling of love,* but also of *individualized sexual arousal* (...), many of those today seeking to banish the family in their call for free sex would recoil. By his idea of communism Plato not only did not encourage uncontrolled passion and sexual promiscuity, but, on the contrary, was placing perhaps the highest sacrifice on males before the state altar of Moloch – to give up free individual choice in love, and on women – to deny their natural maternal instincts.[66]

In defending Plato against the charge of promiscuity Kozlov was pointing an accusing finger at Marxist-inspired rejections of bourgeois prudery. Yet, paradoxically, in this quarrel over 'new' versus 'old' *moeurs* there were points of implicit, unavowed agreement. It was precisely the *Frauenfrage*, and not extramarital sex, that Karl Kautsky had in mind when he brought Plato and passages from the *Communist Manifesto* together. In both cases, he argued, education, the abolishment of the family, and especially equality between the sexes, were devised in the best interests of women. That this notion of sexual equality extended to women's participation in wars was for Kautsky eloquent proof that Plato's women were anything but the *Hausfrauen*, confined to the foyer, that they were to become in the modern world, a 'mere instrument of production' – a wife – for the bourgeois mind.[67] On this point, he said, for all the advantages to be had from industrialization, modern society was simply regressive. Thus, whatever misgivings Kautsky may have had with respect to Plato as one of the forefathers of communism, his sympathy for Plato the feminist figures undeniably as one moment, against which the specific development of modern industrialized society, fell sadly short. In modern society, answers to the woman question were still far from satisfactory, and, as such, could not be used as a criterion to disqualify Plato's actuality.[68] It was, moreover, especially this view of Plato which, initially, assured him a degree of esteem among his Soviet readers. Certainly, in the immediate aftermath of Revolution Plato's views on sexual equality (irrespective of his own reasons) corresponded well with ambitions to turn bourgeois values upside down. Unfortunately (or ironically), with the return in the thirties to traditional codes of conduct – meaning culture, good manners and, above all, the restoration of family values, the fine example of sexual equality and sexual liberation that had earlier been enthusiastically accredited to Plato no longer served any purpose.

Plato's idea of solidarity stemming from a communitarian principle (*obschina, obshchinnost'*) was interpreted in a variety of ways, serving any number of worldviews, whether they be grounded in sexual, social, economic equality, or inspired by the promise of spiritual communion. But, it was precisely because of its flexibility, the fact that it could be assimilated to fairly remote contexts, that Plato himself had ultimately little or no place in these worldviews at all. He was 'everywhere' and 'nowhere'. Early Soviet attempts to legitimate Plato as a distant precursor of socialism were quickly obliged to address the issue of a fundamental irreconcilability between the Platonic and Marxist conceptions of communism. I shall discuss this in more detail in the next chapter. Suffice it to say for the moment that it was a confrontation which solicited fidelity to one or another master, and so, inevitably, precipitated the demise of Plato, his expulsion from the pantheon of Soviet literature. Obviously, the stress in Russian Marxist literature on the process of production and distribution on 'social bases' had very little to do with Plato's project for an harmonious social order, where material well-being was assured by the class of artisans who, otherwise, were not included in his ideal community. In other words, as one commentator put it, Plato's concerns about 'the mechanisms of governance' mixed poorly with the Marxist debate on the importance of socio-economic factors.[69]

Between the ideal city and Communist dreams, there was also the Romantic Slavophile nostalgia for a 'spiritual brotherhood' (*sobornost'*), an idea which was anchored in an idealized account of Russia's spiritual and cultural specificity in her pre-Petrine past. Thanks to the existence of the '*obshcina*' in ancient Russia, a form of social organization in which common use of land was practised, with 'juridical' decisions taken by mutual agreement in light of traditional community customs, Russia, it was believed, had been able to protect a sense of spiritual solidarity. The religious beliefs of the Russian people, Kireevskii argued, had not been contaminated with pagan rationalism, nor by the secular ambitions of the Roman Catholic Church. On the contrary, the combined notions of *sobornoe* and *obshchina*, the two central underpinnings of the Slavophile worldview, formed the dominant colours in a portrait of Russian pre-Petrine life where society connoted, in the first place, a 'moral bond'. Russia, it was believed, had resisted the 'pernicious rationalization and formalization of vital social bonds' which, in Western Europe, had brought about a rift between the private and the public spheres, reducing human relations to a form of social contract.[70]

The Slavophile longing for an ideal past, or the Bolshevik reverie for an ideal future were arguably uncomfortably similar to one another, even as the underlying premises on either side were radically different. Moreover, both invite parallels with specific details of Plato's original project for an ideal city. The Slavophile rejection of the theory of 'gens' (viz. that primitive communities in Russia were based, like everywhere else, on blood ties) for an account of social relations governed by a bond of moral convictions as exemplified in the *obshchina* is comparable to Plato's ideas that man's natural egoism may be overcome by breaking down the family unit: 'Mutual aid is not charity, but a social obligation, rooted in the friendly association among members of the *obshchina*, and conditioned by mutual benefit.'[71] These words of Khomiakov could be as much a Platonic motto, as they unwittingly prefigured the spirit of so many Bolshevik '*mots d'ordres*' to come. Nor is it difficult to 'translate' Konstantin Aksakov's definition of the *obshchina* into either Platonic or Bolshevik language. The *obshchina* 'provides the right conditions for the fulfilment of Christian love. It is not a contract, not a transaction, but an expression of the national spirit (*narodnyi dukh*), a union of people, who have chosen to forsake all personal gains in the name of true Christian love'.[72] But for all the parallels that one could list between them, the contexts in which Slavophiles and Marxists developed their views owed very little to Plato's original project for an ideal city. Arguably, what similarities there were, was less the result of a close reading of the *Republic* itself, as a response to more recent interpretations such as these were fixed by acknowledged authorities. In other words, an image of the Platonic 'community' depended on its history of interpretation which obscured as much as it reaccentuated his original intentions. As I suggested in an earlier chapter, the Platonic impulse in the writings of the Slavophiles should be best understood in terms of the latter's greater affinity with Plotinus and the Church Fathers. Likewise, for early Russian Marxists, the notion of 'solidarity' they subscribed to was, in the first place, accredited to Marx in his battle with the Utopian socialists, as well as to Kautsky. But, behind all that, the Platonic conception was, nevertheless, still lurking.

A Question of Utopia-nism

It was perhaps fairly inevitable that, in discussing the *Republic*, the notions of 'utopia' and 'utopianism' should be addressed. By the mid- and late nineteenth century, however, the connotations attached to the term had become almost universally pejorative, the most characteristic descriptions consisting in dismissing utopias as a pell-mell of fantasy, of non-critical, idealized relations between members of the state, and usually little more than the product of a given author's hostility towards the social and political reality in which he happened to live.[73] Chicherin presented the matter in the following rather curt manner:

> In the *Republic*, Plato sketches an ideal state as the incarnation of the eternal ideas of truth and the good. It is the first so-called utopia, a description of a political order which is not only unrealizable, but also impossible. His idealism comes to the fore in all its hues, denying autonomy to anything living. It follows that social orders (*obshchestvennii byt*) devised along these lines are always unrealizable.[74]

Writing a few years earlier than Chicherin, the 'Nihilist', Dmitrii Pisarev, produced a brilliant diatribe against the Platonic ideal. Plato's quest for harmony simply blinded him to the differences which actually exist between individual human beings. He ignored the fact that it is precisely such differences which make the empirical, earthly world below so rich and colourful: 'Surely you agree, gentlemen, that the time has come to admit that the universal ideal makes as much sense as the production of uni-sized spectacles, or uni-sized boots.'[75] Novgorodtsev echoed this sentiment – albeit without the same expressive verve as the talented young literary critic – calling Plato's pursuit of an ideal of pure harmony between men, freed from danger and insecurity 'unrealizable and undesirable for both politics and philosophy.' Solov'ev, for his part, criticized the Platonic ideal from the standpoint of his Christian beliefs, claiming that 'for all the boldness of his conception, and the beauty of its overall structure, Plato's so-called ideal city is tarnished by those weaknesses from which humanity will one day be delivered, not just as an idea, but as a reality as well'.[76]

While, in practice, the degree to which Russian religious and liberal thinkers actually resisted utopian reverie themselves is open to question, in theory, neither the Christian nor the liberal perspectives on the idea of the state could be said to accommodate easily the utopian version of perfect harmony. According to the Christian faith, man cannot achieve perfection on the strength of his own unaided efforts: divine grace alone can save him. For liberal-minded thinkers, the state should not be an all-embracing authority, but should acknowledge as sovereign things such as the foyer, family, private property, and the like. Moreover, these negative connotations found more fuel once Marx had introduced his famous distinction between 'scientific' and 'utopian' socialism. Thereafter, for virtually any mid- and late nineteenth-century social reformer and political philosopher Plato's claim to fame was to be first in line in a rogues' gallery.[77]

Besides their differences, these various liberal, Marxist, nihilist, as well as Christian perspectives on 'utopia' and 'utopianism' did have at least one point in common: the meaning they attached to 'ideal' actually had little, if anything, to do with the way the term was first intended in Plato's metaphysics.[78] Indeed, it was perhaps its ordinary language connotations that prompted some critics to remind their readers of Plato's original distinction between the ideal and the real, a distinction which, in turn, motivated a reflection about the appropriateness, or inadequacy of the term utopia itself. Sergei Trubetskoi (not unlike Hegel) asked rhetorically whether the *Republic* should be read as a utopia or as a project, one that is situated squarely within the logic of his philosophy as a whole:

> We should not forget that, in Plato's eyes, the true ideal was more real than false reality. It possesses in and of itself the supreme truth, irrespective of whether it is brought to fruition in reality, or remains only 'in the heavens'. (...) If real states are out of kilter with this ideal, then *tant pis* for them. To the degree that they are in conflict with reason, indeed, oppose man's nature, such states are condemned to destruction.[79]

So, while most readers adopted a negative, sometimes hostile attitude towards Plato's utopianism, some did, like Trubetskoi, attempt to spare him the accusation by rejecting this label, or at least urge that it be requalified. Nikolai Grot followed suit, and, rather than accuse Plato of idle reverie, went so far as to criticize contemporary nations for neglecting the foundations of what he called a social morality, namely, the principles of truth and justice – precisely those principles which Plato's philosophy, as a whole, stood for.[80]

Attempts of a different kind to, so to say, 'save' Plato's utopia consisted in shifting the frame of reference from that of an ideal to be realized in some Golden, but terrestrial, age to come, to one situated beyond time, in the eternal heavenly kingdom. Plato's original project was reread in light of the Christian ascetic principles of self-denial as a path to salvation. In this vein it was argued that Plato was first and foremost guided by his belief in the supra-sensible divinity, and that it was his hope of salvation which brought him to insist on the renunciation of individual will, earthly happiness, and all base material interests. Thus, for some Russian commentators, the ideal city should best be understood as residing 'beyond the grave'.[81] Otherwise, where readers were less willing to think about the afterlife in terms of Plato's vision of social organization, they drew attention to the scores of neat parallels between the pagan 'ideal city' and the historical Christian medieval state. In this vein it was argued that

Plato's concept of the Greek city-state could be interpreted as a philosophical theocracy.[82]

The different perspectives governing readings of Plato's *Republic* as an earthly or celestial utopia are instructive in a number of ways. The first highlights not only a fundamental conflict of priorities between ancient and modern political worldviews, it also brings to view the range of meanings that Russian liberals and social-democrats attached to some of the key concepts of political philosophy at that time: the issues raised in the *Republic* served as a springboard, allowing them to reflect on the sense and role of the state, society, individual and the citizen in the contemporary world. Somewhat differently, the second, 'other worldly' perspective, may be said to highlight a 'utopian' dimension in Russian thought itself. If viewed as a pagan 'kingdom of God', Plato's project was not unlike the 'Christian Republics' of Solov'ev, Dostoevskii, or Fedorov, even as the latter owed their immediate inspiration more to the Slavophile nostalgia for a 'Russian Golden Age', located in the peasant commune, rather than in an idealized Athenian city-state.[83] Taken together, the two perspectives are also rather telling of the ways Russian intellectuals perceived their own current situation in late nineteenth-century Russia. For example, depicting the *Republic* as a model for the medieval worldview may be regarded as an eloquent way of dismissing Plato's relevance to a country which saw itself in the process of modernization. But it might also be seen as a tacit criticism of the pre-modern (perhaps 'anti-modern') nature of nineteenth-century Russian society itself.

Terrestrial Utopia

For some nineteenth and early twentieth-century critics, Plato's ideal city not only clashed with modern-day principles of social and political organization, it also, unfortunately, foretold of the dangers embedded in contemporary ideologies. Chicherin did not hesitate to pair the Platonic and Utopian Socialist conceptions of the state, and, with one blow, knocked down both as terrifying examples of the consequences of sacrificing individual freedom to an imaginary collective purpose. To his mind it was idealism taken to extremes:

> By 'utopia' we mean a pure ideal in which all the partial, discrete constitutive elements of reality are rejected in the name of a supreme unity. At this point idealism ceases to be a 'union of opposites' (*soglashenie protivopolozhnostei*); it becomes a simple 'accord' (*soglasie*), denying any opposition whatsoever. The autonomy of anything discrete, apart, disappears into the whole. Individual persons are absorbed into the universal substance and become its passive tools. And since this kind of one-sidedness is contradicted by reality, all such ideal constructions are merely the fruit of pure fantasy.[84]

For Novgorodtsev, the relation that Plato described between the state rulers and its members was no less than retrograde:

> Like care-worn fathers, they watch over their citizens as if they were children. In this respect Plato reminds us of the patriarchal order of the ancient Greek state, from which, incidentally, his own programme differs only by a greater absolutization of power.[85]

As Novgorodtsev saw it, Plato's project for an ideal city combined a nostalgic eye to an irretrievable past with unwitting, yet frightening, predictions of future forms of social organization:

> Plato's bold imagination mixes up the following elements: the simplicity of the earliest times in Greek history with the full blossoming of philosophical thought, the harsh regime of a military barracks borrowed from Sparta, the profound sincerity of moral-religious strivings, which make us think of the discipline in the Church of the Middle Ages. To this we should add, that with respect to economic questions Plato was a socialist, albeit an aristocrat. This is all rather complex and colourful![86]

All this had to be understood as the outcome of a fundamental incompatibility between Plato's metaphysics and his social ideas: Plato was the dupe of his philosophical dualism. For Novgorodtsev, the problems which undermined Plato's social philosophy originated in the particular significance he attributed to generic concepts (*rodovie obhchie poniatiia*). Only the world of ideas is real, true. The partial, the individual, having no real significance, cannot be morally justified. For this reason the actualization of a social ideal could not be conceived of as a task which individual people, freely come together in the act of social progress, might gradually fulfil. Rather it required a general plan, devised, for the sake of the people, by a higher wisdom symbolizing the stable order of the community (*obshchenie*) as a whole. As a reflection of the universal *rodovoi*, impersonal idea of justice, this order is likewise vested with the same *rodovoi* impersonal character. Just as, in the realm of ideas, the impersonal order of truth-justice is immutable and steady, so too, on earth it must remain unmoving, unshakeable. Individual people have no autonomous significance, but are merely links in the general plan. They may attain to the good once they are brought together in union, but, even here, everything is subordinated to the prescribed order. The smallest deviation immediately results in a fateful exclusion, a fall which then threatens society in its entirety. Clearly, such a social ideal which seemed to eliminate any hope of development and progress, or deny human beings the possibility of gradually attaining to the supreme principle of life, could only be an anathema.[87] For so-called 'thinking realists', such as Pisarev, the consequences of aspiring to a perfect society from the murky perspective of real-life imperfections were all too obvious: perfection would inevitably be tarnished by human foibles.

Regardless of the criticism and outrage it provoked, Plato's envisaged ideal city unwittingly highlighted an unresolved problem in late nineteenth-century Russian social and political reality. For the 'conservative-liberal', Chicherin and other, more moderate liberals, the Platonic ideal lent an ironic twist to their endeavours to combine the autocratic power of the Russian tsar, watching over the prosperity of his subjects, with a legality that would restrict arbitrary rule and secure law and order. At issue here was a question of the relation to establish between civil and political freedom and rights. For intellectuals living and working in a society, which did not, as yet, have any legally admitted political parties, it was especially important to admit of civil rights. They believed that, without the freedom of the citizen, as the prerequisite of human freedom, there could never be talk of political rights.[88] So, when they opened the pages of the *Republic* they came across a situation which was diametrically opposed to the hopes they nurtured, but which was uncomfortably reminiscent of the situation that they actually found themselves in. Reading Plato, Russian liberals – not to speak of the radical intelligentsia – quickly saw that the priority they themselves attributed to political and civil freedom stood in inverse proportion to Plato's. For Plato, freedom was the privilege of the philosopher-rulers governing according to their own will, their own reason, with every citizen subjugated to their unlimited rule. For most Russians this meant an outrageous discrepancy between the governors and the governed. Regardless of whether Plato's means were honourably intended to justify the ends, for his modern-day Russian audience all it boiled down to was the total liberty of the rulers to do as they liked (including lying and cheating, as Pisarev put it), while the ruled were bound by the letter – not the spirit – of a strictly devised code of moral behaviour. Granted, some recent Western commentators have suggested that, despite this discrepancy, Plato did admit a degree of political freedom, though, of course, not civil freedom. In the sense that the citizen is called to participate in the general affairs of the state to which he entirely belongs he may be said to be vested with political agency. But precisely because all actions are subordinated to the interests of the state, to speak of civil liberty would be utter nonsense.[89] Writing long before the time of Russia's constitutional experiment in the opening decade of the twentieth century, Chicherin had warned that metaphysical idealism, if taken to extremes, lay at the source of theories of the omnipotent state, and he spoke out against absolutizing lofty ideals for the sake of some general purpose. All too often these merely endangered the autonomy of the private spheres of individual human life.[90] That said, however, this awareness of the dangers in constructing globalizing views of political and social organization did not necessarily resolve the problems that Chicherin and others faced in their repeated appeals to reconcile civil rights with a paternalistic conception of the state, irrespective of whether the latter was understood positively, or accepted for want of anything better. As a conservative liberal, Chicherin's views amounted to a defence of an enlightened autocracy. Autocratic power was to be the only force capable of realizing reforms and safeguarding law and order. 'Society', he wrote, is a 'union of people, conjoined by shared principles of law and profit.' It is 'governed by a supreme power for the sake of the common good' – arguably a view not so very different from what he claimed to despise in Plato.[91]

Discovering the Kingdom of God: The Republic *as a Celestial Utopia*

For Novgorodtsev, the future Kadet, however, matters presented themselves differently. To avoid discrediting Plato altogether in ongoing attempts to speak of constitutionalism, it was judicious to argue that a distinction be made between the political and apolitical levels of the dialogue. This was possibly the only way to cope with the potential damage embedded in Plato's socio-political views. Plato's ultimate aim, Novgorodtsev reminds us, was to establish a harmony between the life of the state with the idea of divine justice. By drawing attention to Plato's fundamentally apolitical nature, Novgorodtsev was endorsing an argument already familiar to Russian readers of Sergei and Evgenii Trubetskoi, or Solov'ev, who treated Plato as a precursor of the Christian theocratic ideal:

> Several times in the dialogue [Plato] repeats the idea that the most important thing for man is to save his soul, and that this may be done only in such a state (...). Clearly, it was this, his deepest philosophical conviction, which resulted in a political reflection with strongly accented theocratic motifs. The aristocratic ideal of a strong state takes on a marked theocratic and ecclesiastical colouring.[92]

From this perspective, Plato's plan of social organization offered convenient formal parallels between the Republic and medieval European society. The severe rules he imposed on the members of the city-state were likened to the ascetic communism of monastic life. Accordingly, denial of the individual will and earthly happiness could be interpreted as the necessary preconditions for eternal salvation.

Evgenii Trubetskoi developed this point at some length in a number of essays on theories of the state. Referring to Ferdinand Baur, who had compared the Platonic state as a moral (*sittliches*) communitarianism with the Christian Church, Trubetskoi characterized the three classes in the *Republic* in light of the virtues espoused in medieval Christianity:

> Just as the Platonic state mixes in undifferentiated unity the functions of the Church and the state (i.e. the moral and the political care of its members), or, to put it another way, does not distinguish between them, so too, in the Middle Ages, we see that the Church had the function of the state (even today

nowhere do we see a clear dividing line between these two opposed spheres).[93]

The all-powerful class of philosophers in Plato's *Republic* corresponded to the despotic clergy of the Catholic Church (who combined both spiritual and secular authority). The second class made one think of the class of knights, who, like Plato's warriors, crusaded for the 'kingdom of God' in the belief that their vocation was to protect the divine order against enemies – the heretics and barbarians. Lastly, Plato's class of artisans were the future serfs (*krepostnie*), the fruits of whose labour ensured the free classes with everything necessary for their material well-being.

Trubetskoi's underlying point here was to present Plato as a proponent of theocracy:

> For how else might we call this society which, both in its basic principles, as well as in the most minute details of its organization, is determined by a 'beyond the grave' ideal, – this state, which aims to be a mirror-image of supra-sensible reality? How else might we characterize a political ideal which professes total self-denial – both by the person and by society as a whole – for the sake of eternal life in the divine?[94]

Karpov offered similar conclusions by attempting to recast the Platonic notion of the state in terms of Divine Providence and the Fall. Commenting on the myth (in *Politicus*) according to which God seemingly abandons the world to watch over it from afar, Karpov assured his reader that, although God relinquishes the helm of the world, it is not to watch over it helplessly. Rather he watches over it in case of real need. True, in this respect, one might rightfully claim that the world does indeed manage alone, without Divine Providence:

> but, to this we would reply that the world is abandoned by God only when the soul implanted within it pays no heed to the divine commandment, when, instead, it falls prey to its innate weaknesses, forsaking the law of reason for the dominion of the flesh (which, incidentally, does not prevent Divine Providence from caring about the soul's salvation ...). And so, by his myth, Plato, in our opinion, shows that the world once lived blissfully in the total dominion of the Supreme God, that the omnipresent authority of Divine Reason did not allow the world to be corrupted by innate matter.[95]

Karpov then transferred this idea to the philosopher-ruler in the *Republic*. In the best-governed state, the principle of governance must be that of divine reason itself, which comes to expression in the political wisdom of the ruler. If, on the contrary, the ruler's wisdom 'succumbs to the whimsy of a complacent soul, then he will lead his state away from the rule of divine reason, plunging it downwards into a wretched existence'.[96]

Certain Russian commentators of the dialogue – including Evgenii Trubetskoi in his *Sotsial'naia Utopia Platona* (1908) – set out to reread the utopian traits of the *Republic* in light of Christian eschatology. Trubetskoi contributed to this image when he paired Plato with Solov'ev, paying tribute to their shared, albeit, in his opinion, unfulfilled ideal, namely, the realization of the Kingdom of God on earth. In projecting Solov'ev's theocratic ideas on to his own reading of Plato, Trubetskoi wanted to show that Plato's underlying motivation in the *Republic* was a dream of 'the universal salvation of the collective body', and that, as such, this foreshadowed the Christian social ideal of 'rebirth'/regeneration (*pererozhdenie*). If, as Trubetskoi argued, the *Republic* is read as a treatise on *truth-justice*, and if one accepts that the essence of truth resides in the fact that both in the human soul and in society as a whole the immortal principle governs over the mortal one, then at issue is the need for the total regeneration of life.[97]

Solov'ev grounded his own personal 'Republic', as a free theocracy, in the (neo-) Platonic motifs of unity, oneness and the good. Yet, in accommodating this tradition, he was just as much 'completing' Plato as he was paying tribute to him. As I suggested earlier, his idea of Godmanhood which he projected onto his reading of the Platonic Eros was intended as a solution to the dualism that Plato had never convincingly overcome. For Solov'ev, Godmanhood is that principle which recognizes the absolute moral value of man and human life. It is the God-man who is coming into the world to save it, to regenerate it and to make it the Kingdom of God. Only then may the person in her perfection fulfil herself in a perfect society: 'The absolute moral significance of the human person requires perfection or the plenitude of life.' For Solov'ev, this requirement could only be satisfied by Christianity which, alone, affords 'the real presence and realization of man in and through the wholeness of human life'.[98]

Salvation unites people into a single whole, meaning that no one individual can be saved in isolation. To save any one person, the resurrection (*vozrozhdenie*) of the entire social milieu is required. In this regard, Trubetskoi believed, Plato came close to the Apostle Paul in his letters to the Corinthians:

> Plato made the same demand that St. Paul would later make on the members f the Church, as the body of Christ. It is not enough that one man regain his own imperishable (*netlennoe*) essence. What is needed is that, with him, all of society achieve such heights or total transformation (*pod'em, povorot*). It is *in general* necessary to bring divine content into human forms, to make human life 'Godlike and divine'. For, in the words of St. Paul: 'If one part is suffering, all the rest suffer with it; if one part is treated with honour, all the rest find pleasure in it. And you are Christ's body, organs of it depending on each other'. (Corinthians: I, xii, 26).[99]

Trubetskoi was of course aware that drawing parallels between the Christian and Platonic worldviews did have its limits. One significant difference between them concerned what was respectively understood by the term 'rebirth' itself. Whereas Christian rebirth was understood in spiritual terms, Plato's designs to reorganize society went no further than an idea of natural-physical rebirth. Whereas Christianity teaches us that the 'godmanhoodly life is the fruit of the immaculate conception', and requires that 'all mankind be born in the image of the Heavenly father (*nebesnyi rodonachal'nik*) – of the second Adam', all that Plato wanted to achieve was 'a new species of ideal citizens generated from human sperm'.[100]

Solov'ev had made a similar point when recasting the Platonic Eros into the ideal of Christian salvation. Though one might consider the Platonic Eros as a distant ancestor of the Godman, Plato had failed to exploit the potential of his idea, namely the double, spiritual-corporeal nature of Eros corresponding to what Solov'ev called 'the resurrection of mortal nature in view of eternal life'. Plato's poignant personal tragedy, was that having failed to accomplish the task he had set himself, namely to bridge two worlds (a task, which as the philosopher-poet, he had described so brilliantly), he 'remained on earth with empty hands (...), on an empty earth where there is no truth'.[101] As for Trubetskoi's closing remarks in his monograph on Plato, he gave over to unabashed Christian pathos, finding a Christian solution to the *Republic* in the notions of Divino-humanity and the metaphysics of all-unity, notions which, by the time he was writing, bore the recognizable stamp of Solov'ev's thought:

> When God appeared in the flesh, was crucified and risen, a mystery was revealed to Christian consciousness, which the very greatest of ancient thinkers was unable to unravel. The path downwards and its upward return, about which Plato dreamed so much yet failed to achieve, was finally traversed. That God was made man meant that the abyss separating the earth from the heavens was filled. The world came to understand that there is no insurmountable barrier between the spiritual and the corporeal. For God was born in matter, transfigured it by bestowing spirit upon it. Likewise, the 'celestial city' (*Vyshchnii gorod*) was to be grounded in an eternal, unshakeable foundation. For, the *Vyshchnii gorod* is neither heaven nor the earth, but the perfect reconciliation of both, their indestructible and indissoluble unity.[102]

*

Irrespective of the accent they placed on their readings of the *Republic*, for these Russian philosophers of law and religious thinkers Plato's ideal city, to be appreciated at all, had to be understood as residing 'beyond the grave' – anything but a political programme which most found repugnant. Indeed, to mitigate charges of 'conservative', or 'reactionary', they would draw attention to Plato's strengths as a philosopher and a poet. For Solov'ev, the problem in presenting Plato as a political thinker was the glaring absence of a moral foundation in his conception of society and of relations between men. The consequence was to preclude any thought of real amelioration within social and political institutions. From this Solov'ev concluded that, in the end, the political problem had little to do with what really interested Plato. Plato cared but little as to how men were to organize themselves on earth, where the truth did not reside, nor would ever do so.[103] Novgorodtsev, too, rejected Plato's political programme both from the perspective of the importance he himself attached to a 'personal principle', but also in view of the inconsistencies he, and others, had pointed to between Plato's metaphysical idealism and his project for an ideal city. 'But for all that', he concluded, 'we cannot help but feel an elevated moral spirit running through the dialogue as a guiding and grounding motif. This moral spirit enthrals us by its great power, and because of this we suffer all the more from disappointment'.[104]

In the end, despite the obvious difficulties in accommodating the Platonic worldview to nineteenth-century 'liberal' conceptions of the state – not to mention more radically oriented political thought – certain Russian readers were nonetheless willing to vindicate Plato's teaching on the grounds of his good intentions. Plato's main concern, they said, was to uncover the meaning of life. They portrayed a Plato whose main task was, like theirs, to answer the question 'how should we live?' In the opening lines of *The Justification of the Good*, Solov'ev stated that the aim of his enquiry was to understand what the sense or purpose of our lives should be. In *Plato's Social Utopia*, Evgenii Trubetskoi paid tribute to both Plato and Solov'ev for having understood that the key to grasping the sense of our lives was to acknowledge the divine source of human existence:

> Life in fact supposes that good (*dobryi*) meaning which Plato once attributed it. Otherwise, if this goes wanting, life cannot be justified. Whence the enormous importance of the Greek thinker's teaching about the life path that both the person and society should pursue. A closer analysis of Plato's social doctrine shows (...) how the temporal and spatial, the here and now, are lit with supranational, universal values.[105]

In a sense, as Trubetskoi suggests, Plato could be a philosopher 'for all times', even though by paying him this tribute Trubetskoi was far from turning a blind eye to the cultural and social differences dividing the ancient past and the modern world. Indeed, for Trubetskoi to have done otherwise would not have passed muster, given that many commentators went to such lengths to situate Plato 'in his times'. But, whether a philosopher 'for all times', or 'of his times', Plato was, paradoxically, a foil allowing Russian intellectuals to pass comment on 'their own times', too. Again and again, careful historical analyses of Plato's ideas came up against the temptation to provide a sideways look at the more proximate contexts of cultural and social reality in late nineteenth-century, and pre-Revolutionary Russia. Elements of these were constantly being refracted through what were otherwise scholarly appraisals of Plato's dialogues.

This tendency became all the more prevalent in the immediate post-Revolutionary period. For the historian, the role and fate of Plato as a social thinker are instructive not only for understanding the nature of utopian thought in its Sovietized form, but also for highlighting some of the vicissitudes in Soviet intellectual and political reality. Assessments of Plato's *Republic* on Soviet soil bring to view the many discrepancies between ideology and political practice in the latter culture, as well as help sharpen the reader's sense of the cruel ironies to which generations of people were subjected under Soviet rule. Whereas, during the first waves of Revolutionary fervour – at a time when many were suffering the ravages of war, famine and disease – the spirit of Platonic social ideals were welcomed as attainable future realities, in the space of a few years, as Soviet daily life under NEP gradually became more tolerable, they were to be rejected as non-scientific, worse, as aristocratic and elitist. Yet, ironically, what were deemed 'distasteful features' in Plato's ideal legislation became part and parcel of Soviet life once Stalin consolidated his power. Plato's dogmatism, his belief in the all-commanding power of the guardians as the holders of truth, and thereby, a fairly disparaging attitude towards the potential competence or initiative of the *hoi polloi*, his caste-system (as Marx called it), his arguments in favour of censorship in the arts were, no doubt, for certain readers in the decade of Stalin's purges, chilling reminders of the reality they found themselves in.

By the late twenties Plato would be denounced as a social thinker for his views in the *Republic*. But he would be partially rehabilitated as author of the *Laws*, just at the time when the Soviet Constitution of 1936 was being drafted and revised.[106] Otherwise, as the 'Father of Idealism', aspects of Plato's philosophy (his theory of knowledge and dialectic) were to form an important, if problematic, paragraph in Soviet historiography of philosophy. This ambivalence invites us to reassess the usual tendency of ascribing positive appraisal of Plato to his nineteenth-century readers, and hostility as a matter of course to his Soviet interpreters.

Notes

1 D. I. Pisarev, 'Idealizm Platona. Obozrenie filosofskoi deiatel'nosti Sokrata i Platona, po Tselleru; sostavil *Klevanov*' (1861) in *D.I. Pisarev: Sochineniia v shesti tomakh*, t.1 (SPb., 1894), p.276.
2 'Dorogu krylatomu Erosu!' – a slogan launched by Alexandra Kollontai, Commissar for public health. See L. Heller-M. Niqueux, *Histoire de l'utopie en Russie* (PUF, Paris, 1995), pp.205-206.
3 Evg. Trubetskoi, *Sotsial'naia utopiia Platona* (Moscow, 1908), p.26.
4 K.A. Kuznetsov, *Platon. Vvedenie v analiz 'Gosudarstva', 'Zakonov'* (Odessa, 1916). The original, anonymous, 1805 publication appeared as 'Platonova Respublika', *St.Peterburg Zhurnal*, 5-6.
5 Selected extracts were published in anthologies. For example: *Drevnii mir v pamiatnikakh ego pis'menosti* (Gosizdat, Moscow, 1921), II: 11-12, III: 20-22, V: 11 & 18, VI: 4; V.P. Volgin, *Predshestvenniki sovremennogo sotsializma v otryvkakh iz proizvedenii* (M.-L., 1928), II: 369-376, III: 412-417, IV: 419-423, V: 451-464. These extracts were translated by A.I. Rubin, I.B. Rumer and V.S. Sergeev; *Antichnyi sposob proizvodstva v istocnikakh* (Leningrad, 1933), excerpts from books. I, II, IV, V, VIII, IX; *Antichnie mysliteli ob iskusstve* (Moscow, 1938), excerpts from books III & X, translated by P.S. Popov. Other translations of the dialogues included the projected fifteen-volume translation by the 'Old Professors', S.A. Zhebelev, E.L. Radlov and L.P. Karsavin. See above, Chapter One.
6 S.V. Melikova, *Pedagogicheskie vozzreniia Platona i Aristotelia* (Pg., 1916), translated parts of bks III and VII (together with *Laws*, extracts from bk VII). Another case in point was the publication of *Arhitektura anticnogo mira* (Moscow, 1940), edited by V.P. Zubov and F.A. Petrovskii. Some of the extracts were taken from the Karpov and Solov'ev translations. Other re-edited pre-Revolutionary literature on the *Republic* includes: M.M. Rubinshtein, *Platon-Uchitel'* (Irkutsk, 1920) first published under the title 'Pedagogicheskie idei Platona', *VFP*, kn.124 (1914), and V.P. Buzeskul, *Antichnost' i sovremennost'. Sovremennie temy v antichnoi Gretsii* (Moscow, 1924), first published in 1913.
7 See, for example, N.I. Kareev, *Gosudarstvo-Gorod antichnogo mira* (SPb., 1903); S.A. Zhebelev, 'Grecheskaia Politicheskaia Literatura i *Politika* Aristotelia', op. cit. Both historians relied considerably on works by Solov'ev and S.N.Trubetskoi. Among the more renowned historians to teach students majoring in classical philology were M.S. Kutorga and F.F. Sokolov at St. Petersburg University. See M.N. Tikhomirov, M.A. Alpatov and A.L. Sidorov (eds), *Ocherki istorii istoricheskoi nauki v SSSR*, 3 vols. (Moscow, 1955).
8 S.N. Trubetskoi, *Kurs istorii antichnoi filosofii*. Originally a lecture course, it first appeared in lithograph form in 1894-95, and was published posthumously in 1906. References are taken from the 1997 edition (Vlados, Moscow). See also A.A. Kozlov's, *Metod i napravlenie filosofii Platona*, originally a course given at Kiev University, and N.Ia. Grot's *Ocherk filosofiia Platona*, also, initially a lecture course read at Moscow University during the winter semester of 1891. Like Kozlov and Trubetskoi, Grot's outline focused on the metaphysical aspects of Plato's thought, and, with respect to *Republic*, he followed the usual procedure, concentrating on the moral dimension of the dialogue. Grot also discussed in some detail the Platonic communitarian principle, and the pivotal role of education as a means to achieve Plato's ultimate aim of realizing the common good.

9   For example, see the anonymous *'Platon' po knige Windelbanda. Otvety na dva pervykh bileta po istorii filosofii prava Prof. P.I. Novgorodtseva* (Moscow, 1909). The second 'question card' analysed Plato as a 'social politician'.
10 P. Redkin, 'O Platone voobshche' in *Istoriia filosofii prava...*, vol.4, p 335, p.339.
11 B.N. Chicherin, *Istoriia politicheskikh uchenii*, vol.1 (Moscow, 1869), p.50.
12 The same is true for less well-known authors such as Ar. Fateev, Professor of Law at Kharkov University. See his *Istoriia obshchikh uchenii o prave i gosudarstve*, 2nd. ed. (Kharkov, 1909), pp.44-49; also N.M. Korkunov, *Lektsii po obshchei teorii prava* (SPb., 1904).
13 M.M. Kovalevskii, *Ot priamogo narodopravstva k predstavitel'nomy i ot patriarkhal'noi monarkhii k parlamentarizmu: Rost gosudarstva i ego otrazhenie v istorii politicheskikh uchenii*, vol.1 (Moscow, 1906), p.45.
14 K.A. Kuznetsov, *Platon. Vvedenie v analiz...* , p.10. (Kuznetsov based his argument on *Republic* II, 369). In this monograph, Kuznetsov referred quite extensively to the 'modernist' historian, Wilamowitz-Möllendorff's work *Staat und Gesellschaft der Griechen und Römer* (Berlin & Leipzig, 1910).
15 Ibid., pp.25-28.
16 Ibid., p.28.
17 Ibid., pp.16-17.
18 For example: N.I. Kareev, *Vvedenie v kurs istorii drevnego mira* (Warsaw, 1882), also his *Gosudarstvo-gorod antichnogo mira. Opyt istoricheskogo postroeniia politicheskoi i sotsial'noi evoliutsii antichnykh grazhdanskikh obshchin* (SPb., 1903); P.I. Alandskii, 'Lektsii po istorii Gretsii' in *Kievskie Universitetskie Izvestiia* (Kiev, 1884); R.Iu. Vipper, *Lektsii po istorii Gretsii* (Moscow, 1905), and his *Istoriia Gretsii v klassicheskuiu epokhu, IX-IV vv* (Moscow, 1916); V. Buzeskul, *Vvedenie v istoriiu Gretsii* (Kharkov, 1903) and his *Istoriia Afinskoi Demokratii* (SPb., 1909).
19 M.S. Kutorga, *Osnovy Afinskoi grazhdanskoi obshchiny* and his *Afinskaia Politeia. Eja sostav, svoistvo i vsemirno-istoriheskoe znachenie*, in *Sobranie sochineniia*, 2 vols. (SPb., 1894-1896); 'Vvedenie v istoriiu drevnei grecheskoi obrazovannosti', *ZhMNP*, pt.CXXXIII (1867); Evgenii Trubetskoi wrote his very first memoir on the practice of slavery in the ancient Greek world, seeing it as a crucial phenomenon if one was to grasp the Greek world outlook as a whole: 'Rabstvo v drevnei Gretsii' (Iaroslavl', 1886).
20 'Dve intelligentsii' (1912). Cited in V. Buzeskul, *Vseobshchaia istoriia i ee predstaviteli v Rossii v XIX i nachale XX veka*, vol.2 (Leningrad, 1931), pp.188-189.
21 'Drevnii filosof na sovremennye temy, the title of an article by Evgenii Trubetskoi in *Moskovskii Ezenedel'nik*, 16 (1907).
22 Given that Buzeskul legitimated the class struggle by pointing to its distant origins, it is unsurprising that this monograph fared quite well in the early Soviet period.
23 F.F. Zelinskii, 'Drevnyi mir i my', *ZhMNP*, Oct. (1903), p.79.
24 Ibid., pp.78-79.
25 Vl. Karpov, 'Politika ili Gosudarstvo. Vvedenie', in *Sochineniia Platona*, vol.3 (SPb., 1863), p.10 ff. On Schleiermacher's reading of the *Republic*, see U. Zimbrich, 'Un Etat étrangement imaginé' in André Laks and Ada Neschke (eds), *La Naissance du paradigme herméneutique*, Cahiers de Philologie, 10 (Presses Universitaires de Lille, 1990), pp.225-244.
26 Karpov, Ibid., p.10.
27 Ibid., p.21. Interestingly, Karpov distinguishes between the terms 'state' and 'society', suggesting that the latter is wider reaching; it applies to the 'entire human species', whereas 'state' implies the 'national'. Karpov's point in making this distinction is that, although Plato may have been cosmopolitan in intention, many of his views betray their confined, historically determined, Greek national origins. Ibid., p.23.
28 Ibid., p.21.

29 Redkin, op. cit., vol.4, pp.119-163.
30 Ibid., p.143; p.147.
31 Cf. J.L. Vieillard-Baron who writes: 'Le sens de la *Sittlichkeit* est de montrer qu'avant même d'être individuelle, la morale est portée par la structure politique et sociale, et qu'en même temps l'Idée se réalise dans l'histoire à travers les actions et les institutions des hommes.' J.L. Vieillard-Baron, *Platon et l'idéalisme allemand (1770-1830)* (Paris: Beauchesne, 1979), p.358.
32 Redkin, op. cit., pp.141-142.
33 Ibid. Cf. Vieillard-Baron, who comments on Hegel's attempts to rehabilitate the dialogue in light of his own *Rechtsstaat* theory. Op. cit., p.351.
34 Redkin, Ibid., p.137.
35 P. Novgorodtsev, *Politicheskie idealy drevnego i sovremmenogo mira*, vol. 2 (Moscow, 1913), p.75.
36 Ibid.
37 While, it is no doubt true that Kautsky became more of a celebrity reference in early Soviet Plato scholarship, until, that is, his demise in 1927, when the publication of his *Die materialistiche Geschichtsaufassung* provoked the wrath of Communist Party leaders, it should be noted that several of his works dealing with antiquity had been translated into Russian long before the Revolution: *Iz istorii kul'tury. Platonovskii i drevne-khristianskii kommunizm*, trans. G.F. L'vovich (SPb., 1905); *Iz istorii obshchestvennikh techenii*, vol.1: 'Predtechi noveishchego sotsializma', trans. E.K. and I.K. Leont'evyi (SPb., 1906). A second edition (SPb., 1907), published in the series *Istoriia. Sotsializma v Monografiiakh*, included a foreword by Kautsky himself written especially for his Russian readers. A third edition appeared in 1919. Also, G. Adler, *Iz istorii obshchestvennyh uchenii* (SPb., 1909), especially chapter two on the socialistic ideals in Athens, and chapter three, a critical evaluation of Plato's communism. Speranskii, in his preface to the Russian translation of Adler's works, suggested that although Adler was striving for a *'vnepartiinyi'* interpretation, and that, philosophically, he subscribed to a neo-Kantian, criticist point of view, his Marxist, and he adds, 'Utopian' tendencies are, nevertheless, visible to the reader (pp.v-vi).
38 Published in Russian translation in 1910 (*Istoriia antichnogo Kommunisma i Sotsializma*) as part of a series under the general title *Obshchaia istoriia evropeiskoi kul'tury*, edited by Professors M.M. Grevs, F.F. Zelinskii, N.I. Kareev and M.I. Rostovtsev (SPb: Brokgaus/Efron).
39 According to Vieillard-Baron, Hegel also supported the Platonic idea of an elite as a class apart: 'Dans ses *Principes de la philosophie du droit* de 1821, Hegel distingue (...) trois classes sur le modèle platonicien: la classe substantielle (celle des paysans), la classe des industrielle (artisans, fabricants, commerçants) et la classe universelle (celle de la réflexion, chargée des intérêts généraux de la société) – der dritte, denkende Stand.' In other words, Plato's class of warriors became the modern-day bourgeoisie. Vieillard-Baron, op. cit., p.368.
40 Term used by Novgorodtsev in op. cit.
41 Pöhlmann, 'On the coexistence of individualism and socialism in Plato', op. cit., p.183. (This and following quotations are taken from the Russian translation.)
42 Ibid., pp.186-187.
43 Rostovtsev, foreword to *Istoriia antichnogo....*
44 E.N. Trubetskoi, *Sotsial'naia utopiia Platona*, p.71.
45 Kuznetsov, op. cit., pp.47-48. Zeller had also suggested parallels between Plato's leaders and guardians with contemporary bureaucrats in state service in Germany. Cf. Buzeskul, *Antichnost'....*, p.24.
46 Cf. L. Kolakowski, *Main Currents of Marxism*, vol.2 (Oxford: Clarendon Press, 1978), p.31.

47 Cf. George S. Counts, foreword, in G. Kline (ed.), *Soviet Education* (London: Routledge, 1957), p.ix. See also: John Dunstan and Avril Suddaby, 'The Progressive Tradition in Soviet Schooling to 1988', in J. Dunstan (ed.), *Soviet Education under Perestroika* (Routledge, London-New York, 1990), pp.1-13; Wl. Bérélowitch, *La Soviétisation de l'école russe, 1917-1931* (l'Age d'homme, Lausanne, 1990); S. Fitzpatrick, *The Cultural Front. Power and Culture in Revolutionary Russia* (Cornell University Press, 1992).
48 N.I. Novosadskii, 'Pedagogicheskie Idealy Platona', *Varshavskie Universitetskie Izvestiia*, 1 (1904), p.4. See also F. Zelinskii, 'Antichnaia Gumannost' in *Vestnik Evropy*, 1 (1898), pp.195-229; also his 'Antichnost' i klassicheskoe obrazovanie', *Germes*, 1 (1918), pp.17-34. During the war and Revolution the issue of classical education was still considered actual. See, for example, a certain 'Ja. B.', 'Tsennost' klassicheskogo obrazovaniia s tochki zreniia sotsialista', *Germes*, 1 (1918), pp.34-38. This author defended the place of Latin and Greek in schools, arguing that these subjects in no way conflicted with the principles of socialism.
49 E.N. Trubetskoi, *Sotsial'naia utopiia....*, p.75.
50 Novosadskii, op. cit., pp.13-14; pp.21-22.
51 Novosadskii, op. cit., pp.21-22. Some thirty years earlier, Iurkevich had applauded Plato for his ideas concerning education through music. Music, he believed, develops the individual child's capacities of will and moral strength. P. Iurkevich, *Kurs obshchei pedagogiki*, 1869. (Cf. A. Sostyn, 'Nravstvenno-vospitatel'noe znachenie muzyki po vozreniiam Platona i Aristotelia'. Rech', proiznechennaia v sokrashchenii na publichnom akte MDA, 1 x 1898 [Sergiev Posad, 1899]). That said, both Iurkevich and Sostyn were, of course, aware of the social relevance of Plato's views on education, notably the importance he attributed to gymnastics as an occasion to develop a knowhow with weapons of war.
52 Western authors cited in Russian literature include: Döring, *System der Pädagogik im Umriss* (Berlin, 1894); Paul Bergemann, *Sozial-Pedagogik auf erfahrungswissenschaftliche Grundlage und mit Hilfe der induktiven Methode als universalistische oder Kultur-Pädagogik* (1900); Paul Natorp, *Sozialpädagogik: Theorie der Willenserziehung auf der Grundlage der Gemeinschaft* (Stuttgart, 1904); Paul Tannery, 'L'education platonicienne', *Revue philosophique*, XI (1881); A. Mazarakis, *Die platonische Pädagogik*, (Zurich, 1900).
53 G.G. Zorgenfrei, 'Sotsial'naia pedagogika Platona', *ZhMNP*, Dec. (1906), pp.188-201. Also I.D. Narbekov, 'Idealy vospitaniia i obrazovaniia u drevnikh grekov po sochineniiam filosofa Platona, *Politik ili Gosudarstvo*, i *Zakony*', *Pravoslavnyi Sobesednik*, 7-8 (1912), pp.130-163.
54 M.M. Rubinshtein, *Platon-Uchitel'*, (Irkutsk, 1920), p.118. This monograph was a slightly revised version of an article first published in 1914 under the title 'Pedagogicheskie Idei Platona', *VFP*, 124 (1914), pp.400-461.
55 Rubinshtein, ibid., (1914), p.408.
56 Ibid., p.435; p.459.
57 B. Russell, *The Practice and Theory of Bolshevism* (1921). Cited in Heller-Niqueux, op. cit., p.200.
58 Cited in Theodore H.von Laue, *Why Lenin? Why Stalin? A Reappraisal of the Russian Revolution, 1900-1930*, (New York, 1964), p.187.
59 Cf. Wendy Z. Goldman, *Women, the State, and Revolution: Soviet Family Policy and Social Life, 1917-1936*, (Cambridge University Press, 1993), pp.1-58.
60 *Dorogu krylatomu Erosu* [pamphlet] (Moscow, 1923.)
61 K.P. Novitskii, *Platon*, published in a series entitled 'Ancestors of Utopian Communism' (Moscow, 1923), pp.16-17.
62 V. Volgin, *Sotsialism v drevnei Gretsii* (Moscow, 1925), p.159. Volgin also edited a commentary and translated extracts of utopian literature in several volumes

(*Predshestvenniki sovremennogo sotsializma v otryvkakh iz ikh proizvedenii* (M.-L., 1928). The first volume contained passages from book V of the *Republic* (451-464) concerning the social equality, and differences between men and women in society.

63 Solov'ev, *La Justification du bien*, p.244. Sil'vestr Gogotskii made the same point almost as bluntly: 'Plato sanctifies those relations between people which are repulsive to the moral aims of society.' See his 'Platon' in *Filosofskii Leksikon*, vol.IV, pt.1 (Kiev, 1872), p.126.

64 Vl. Karpov, commentary to *Politika ili Gosudarstvo* in *Sochineniia Platona*, vol.3 (SPb, 1863), pp.35-36.

65 S.N. Trubetskoi, *Kurs istorii drevnei Filosofii*, p.389.

66 A.A. Kozlov, *Metod i napravlenie filosofii Platona*, p.182.

67 '...ein blosses Produktionsinstrument. Er hört, dass die Produktionsinstrumente gemeinsam ausgebeutet werden sollen und kann sich natürlich nichts Anderes denken, als dass das Moos der Gemeinschaftlichkeit die Weiber gleichfalls treffen soll.' K. Kautsky, *Vorläufer des neuen Sozializmus* (Stuttgart, 1895), p.13.

68 'Die Grundlage der gesellschaftlichen und politischen Gleichstellung der Frau mit dem Manne bildet ihre Befreiung von den Arbeiten des Haushaltes. Im platonischen Staat geschieht dieses dadurch, dass diese Arbeiten den arbeitenden Klassen zugewiesen werden. So lange es nicht möglich war, zum mindesten die schwersten dieser Arbeiten von der Maschine besorgen zu lassen, konnte eine Emanzipation der Frau auf anderer Grundlage nicht erreicht werden.' Ibid.

69 Kuznetsov, *Platon. Vvedenie v analiz ...*, pp.47-49.

70 I. Kireevskii, 'Deviatnadtsatyi Vek' (1832), and his 'V otvet A. S. Khomiakovu' (1839).

71 Khomiakov, cited in the entry 'Pozemel'naia obshchina', in Brokgaus and Efron (eds), *Entsiklopedicheskii Slovar'*, vol.xxiv (1898), p.213.

72 Ibid. For literature concerning the history and ideology of the Russian commune see, for example: C. Goehrke, *Die Theorien über Entstehung und Entwicklung des 'mir'* (Wiesbaden, 1964); M. Malia, 'Herzen and the Peasant Commune', in E.J. Simmons (ed.), *Continuity and Change in Russian and Soviet Thought* (Cambridge, Mass., 1955), pp.197-217; N.D. Kazantsev, *Utopicheskii i nauchnyi sotsializm o pereustroistve sel'skogo khoziaiistva (Politiko-iuridicheskii aspekt)* (Moscow, 1969).

73 See the entry 'Utopii' in Brokgaus and Efron (eds), *Entsiklopedicheskii Slovar'*, vol.xxxv (SPb., 1902), pp.76-77. See also B. Baczko, *Lumières de l'Utopie* (Payot, Paris, 1978); L. Heller-M. Niqueux, op. cit.

74 B.N. Chicherin, *Istoriia politicheskikh uchenii*, vol.1 (Moscow, 1869), p.43.

75 Pisarev, op.cit., p.267.

76 V.S. Solov'ev, *La Justification du bien*, p.244.

77 For a detailed discussion of the distinction, and overlaps, between scientific and utopian socialism see B. Baczko, op. cit.

78 Typical of this sentiment are, for example, the following comments by a certain I.I. Ivanov, for whom the terms 'ideal' and 'idealism' are synonymous with 'unrealizable'. 'Plato', he says, 'betrayed Socrates, in the sense that he abandoned the *real'nyi put'* paved by his spiritual master for the sake of 'otherworldly ideals.' I.I. Ivanov, 'Filosofiia bez faktov', *RM*, 2 (1893), pp.37-60. See also S.S. Gogotskii's entry 'Platon' in *Filosofskii Leksikon*, p.126.

79 S.N. Trubetskoi, *Kurs istorii drevnei...* p.393. The Professor of Philosophy of Law, Fateev, took yet another view on the matter, suggesting that Plato's etatist communism was intended for the well-being of a utopian state and not for the well-being of living people. But, he added, Plato was aware of this, and as a means to correct what he himself recognized to be an error went on to write the *Laws*. Ar. Fateev, *Istoriia obshchikh uchenii...*, p.48.

80 N.Ia. Grot, *Ocherk filosofii Platona*, p.165.

81 E.N. Trubetskoi, *Istoriia drevnei i sovremennoi filosofii prava* (Kiev, 1899), pp.58-59. See also his 'Politicheskie idealy Platona i Aristotelia v ikh vsemirno-istoricheskom znachenii', *VFP*, 4 (1890), pp.1-36.
82 Aristotle, on the contrary, was treated as the precursor of the 'contemporary European cultural state'. Evg. Trubetskoi, ibid., pp.64-65. Novgorodtsev also developed the same point of contrast between the two thinkers.
83 Cf. Heller-Niqueux, op. cit.
84 Chicherin, *Istoriia politicheskih uchenii*, vol.5, pp.55-56.
85 Novgorodstev, *Socrat i Platon* ...., pp.58-59.
86 Ibid., pp.46-47.
87 Novgorodstev, *Politicheskie idealy*..., Vol.2 (1913), p.34.
88 In his pamphlet 'Konstitutsionnyi vopros v Rossii', printed in manuscript form in 1878, and published in 1906 (SPb.), that is, at the time of the constitutional experiment, Chicherin wrote: 'Freedom ranks as perhaps the most essential factor – both in terms of social well-being, and also with respect to political power. Moreover, freedom necessarily connotes the participation of the people in deciding matters of state' (p.5).
89 Cf. Vieillard Baron, op. cit., p.366.
90 Cf. Walicki, *Legal Philosophies*..., p.142.
91 Chicherin, 'Gosudarstvo' in *Filosofiia Prava* (Moscow, 1900), pp.301-326.
92 Novgorodstev, *Sokrat i Platon*, pp.72-73.
93 Evg. Trubetskoi, *Istoriia filosofii prava* (Kiev, 1899), p.75. Trubetskoi was referring to Ferdinand Baur's *Das Christliche des Platonismus, oder Sokrates und Christus. Eine religionsphilosophische Untersuchung* (Tübingen, 1837).
94 Ibid., p.64. Cf. P. Iurkevich: 'The state is an objective body, the reality of which is determined by the divine understanding of the world (*bozhestvennoe miroponimanie*), and not by the fact that we require its existence', *Istoriia filosofii Prava*... (1872-1874), p.64. In his course 'Encyclopaedia of Law' (1917 version) E.N.Trubetskoi advanced a more moderate view of the state 'on earth': 'In fact, the state is far from being the 'supreme realization of the moral idea. It aspires neither to the common good, nor to the happiness of all its subjects. In reality, the state pursues a whole range of aims, so any attempt to reduce it to a single overriding aim inevitably fails to account for its multifaceted character' (p.223).
95 Karpov, op. cit., Vol.6 (1879), pp.54-55.
96 Ibid.
97 Evg. Trubetskoi, *Sotsial'naia utopia Platona*, p.32.
98 *La Justification du bien*, pp.247-248.
99 Evg. Trubetskoi, op. cit., p.61.
100 Ibid., pp.65-66.
101 Solov'ev, *Le Drame de la vie de Platon*, p.162.
102 Trubetskoi, op. cit., p.110.
103 Solov'ev, *Le Drame*..., p.164; *La Justification du bien*, p.244.
104 Novgorodstev, *Politicheskie idealy*..., Vol.2 (1913), pp.95-96.
105 E.N. Trubetskoi, *Sotsial'naia utopiia Platona*, pp.10-11.
106 Excerpts from books III, IV, VI, VIII were translated by A. Egunov in *Antichnyi sposob proizvodstva v istochnikakh* (Leningrad, 1933), pp.54-55, pp. 536-560. See also *Antichnie mysliteli ob iskusstve* (Moscow, 1938), pp.106-130. Noteworthy in this regard is the coincidence, in 1936, between the drafting of the definitive version of the new Soviet Constitution and the publication of a translation and commentary of Aristotle's *Politeia! Afinskaia Politiia. Gosudarstvennoe ustroistvo Afinian*, translated and with commentary by S.I. Radtsig (IFLI, Moscow, 1936).

Chapter 5

A Question of Russian Platonism

Like that of so many cultural emblems identified with the pre-Revolutionary world, Plato's fate on Soviet soil was, in most respects, but not entirely, a foregone conclusion. Whereas in the nineteenth century, for a seminarist to be granted the name of Plato was a token of high reward for his academic achievement,[1] in the decades following the October Revolution, 'Plato', 'Platonic' and 'Platonism' were labels which quickly became weighted with disparaging connotations. Plato, that prime enemy of a classless society, turned out to be a little more than a parasite proposing that the privileged classes alone benefit from the labours of the artisans and of those who toiled the soil.

At the most immediate level, the pendulum swing in attitudes from hero to rogue, together with isolated attempts at a partial rehabilitation in the post-Stalinist years, are, if anything, instructive of the changes taking place in Soviet political reality, and of their effects on intellectual culture. A first, significant downwards turn in Plato's demise from 'divine' to *'persona non grata'* came in the year 1923, when Lenin issued a decree ordering the removal from public libraries of philosophical works deemed unsuitable for mass consumption. Plato and his companions, Descartes, Kant, Schopenhauer and Nietzsche, were destined to become the more exclusive objects for 'specialized research in academic institutions'. But, far from being silenced altogether, or simply forgotten, Plato was to be brought before an informed public in Soviet histories of philosophy and social thought. Henceforth, in this more restricted context, he was duly treated as a mystic, reactionary, and even as a plagiarist depending on the degree of allegiance to party ideology that happened to be required. In other words, familiarity with Plato's philosophy became subject to the ideological underpinnings of Soviet scholarship, the origins of which, in its crudest form, was little more than a hollow elaboration on some random comment once uttered by Marx and Lenin. Accordingly, the Platonic ideal state was described, after Marx, as 'an Athenian idealization of the Egyptian caste system', while his theory of knowledge and metaphysics – the seedbed of all idealist philosophy in ancient and modern times – was coined in shorthand, after Lenin, as 'the line of Plato'.[2] With the introduction of the New Economic Policy (1921–1928), these references gradually became the cornerstones in official Soviet assessments of Plato's works. No surprise, then, to see that his role as a 'social' thinker was initially important in early endeavours to uncover the solid foundations of modern socialism, and that he would ultimately be rebuked for his utopianism as Soviet reality woke up from its own utopian dream of the immediate post-Revolutionary years. Somewhat differently, Plato's dubious status as the 'father of idealism', whose *raison d'être* was to combat the materialist 'line of Democritus', was destined to become a lasting hallmark of Soviet historiography of philosophy.

Plato's *Republic* in a Soviet Utopia

In the immediate aftermath of war and Revolution, the process of undermining Plato's reputation had not yet begun. Indeed, during its initial phase of War Communism (1918–1921), possibly the most 'utopian' period in Soviet history, explicit reference to Plato as author of the *Republic* tended to draw attention to his actuality, and the pertinence of his original 'communist' project to Bolshevik ambitions. Re-edited translations and commentaries, as well as newly edited anthologies with carefully selected extracts from this dialogue promoted a portrait of Plato congenial to the needs of the new leaders in their endeavours to construct a new state.[3] In this vein, it was argued that Plato's communism was a communism 'for all', an 'economic democratism'.[4] Others took sides with Pöhlmann in his quarrel with Zeller as to whether Plato's views of a communitarian life could be said to extend to the class of artisans, or whether it was confined, as Zeller had argued, to the classes of soldiers and guardians. Like Pöhlmann, early Soviet scholars sought passages in the dialogue confirming their claim that the workers were, indeed, included in the ideal city. One A. Rozhdestvenskii, for example, cited passages from books VII 519 and IV 421 on happiness residing in the state as a whole. Happiness comes about when each and every member carries out the particular task or role assigned to him, and it lasts only if the extremes of wealth and poverty are avoided.[5]

These very early appraisals in favour of Plato's actuality as a proponent of a non-elitist communism were, however, short lived. As the new Bolshevik ideology began to consolidate itself, and, particularly, as NEP became *de rigeur*, Soviet social and political policies underwent a discernible shift, moving away from an initial 'spontaneous' utopianism, together with its incumbent optimism of a future-oriented history, towards a more critical – albeit ideological – review of the past in order to legitimate not so much the future as the present. Correspondingly, more 'scholarly' works also began to appear about the historical development of socialism from its utopian through to its scientific phase.[6] It was criticism of the former that had prompted the Marxist distinction between 'utopia' and 'science', and even though this opposition was far from being clear-cut, in the sense that the Marxist concept of history, with its belief in 'progress', finality, or the distinction made between 'pre-history and 'true history' grounded in true beginnings, was, itself, not entirely free of utopian traits, it did mean that the extent to which Plato could be presented as a forefather of communism was subject to the Marxist optic on historical development.[7] It is in this context that the name of Plato began to appear more frequently, only, unfortunately, no longer to be glorified as a distant parent of socialism. Rather, he was found guilty of utopianism, conservative reaction and, by the end of the decade, with the gradual consolidation of Soviet historiography of philosophy, was scorned as the villainous leader of idealism.

Declarations of allegiance to the Marxist-Leninist perspective on intellectual traditions not only resulted in the downfall of Plato himself, but brought with it a host of his nineteenth and early twentieth-century 'bourgeois' liberal, as well as 'non-Orthodox Marxist' interpreters, all of whom had played a considerable role in forging the beginnings of Russian Plato scholarship prior to the war and Revolution. First, among the 'authorities' to be toppled were the so-called 'modernizers' in historical research, like Robert Pöhlmann, and 'religious' philosophers as well, such as Evgenii Trubetskoi and Novgorodtsev. All had addressed the vexed question of Platonic communism, and all had endeavoured to discover some redeeming features in it. By the end of the decade they were joined by other, newly designated '*persona non grata*' – Karl Kautsky, Georg Adler and Max Beer – the latter severely criticized for his *Allgemeine Geschichte des Sozialismus und der sozialen Kämpfe* (1919).[8] Evidently, the process of turning more and more past masters into outcasts stood in direct proportion to the degree of fidelity expected from scholars to Marxist-Leninist ideology as it began tightening its reins. A rapid comparison of monographs published in 1923, 1925–1928, and 1929 – those by K.P. Novitskii, Viacheslav Volgin, and S.L. Lur'e respectively – shows that Plato's own demise was just as much part of a more complex process of discrediting the political and ideological allegiances of his latter-day interpreters.[9]

Both Novitskii and Volgin singled out for approval themes of Plato's *Republic* which Kautsky, as we saw in the previous chapter, had found praiseworthy. These included repeated vindications of values such as equality (between men and women), freedom, social justice, hopes for a future way of life based on communitarian principles, sympathy for the oppressed masses. Novitskii interpreted the revolt of the poor in Plato as proof of the social instability of the materially well-endowed classes. To his mind, the wealthy lived under the permanent threat of a social revolution. Volgin applauded Plato for pointing out that the accumulation of wealth is evil, because it inevitably leads to the breakdown of society. In this sense, he argued, Plato may be said to admit of the class struggle. If so, it also provided persuasive arguments to the effect that Plato's *Republic* was a prototype for present-day constructions of socialism. According to Volgin, these 'not only took from Plato the abstract idea of *obshchnost'* (communitarianism) as a radical means to combat the idea of private property, but also a significant part of his argument in defence of communism, and his attacks on the evils of money grabbing'.[10]

Such attempts to legitimate Plato as a distant precursor of socialism were nevertheless obliged to confront the issue of a fundamental irreconcilabilty between the Platonic and Marxist conceptions of communism. Accordingly, Novitskii and Volgin regretted Plato's neglect of the workers, claiming, moreover, that his interest in the communitarian principle had little to do with the 'means of production', rather that it referred merely to the distribution of consumer goods among the guardians and the class of soldiers. Conceived of as a means and not as an end, it was more appropriate, they concluded, to join Marx in labelling Plato's communism, 'consumer' (*potrebitel'skii*) and not 'production communism'. Volgin listed other related issues which, for adherents of modern-day communism, could at best be a cause for unease, at worst, grounds to disqualify Plato as a precursor of communist ideals:

> We have before us an enemy of capitalism, but one who does not deny private property, an enemy of extreme wealth and poverty, but who regards total equality as undesirable. Hostile to plutocracy, he is nonetheless hostile to democracy and the revolutionary impulses of the '*cherny*' (mob/rabble).[11]

Novitskii, for his part, criticized the blind trust Plato put in his 'philosopher-tsar'. It betrayed, he said, the Greek philosopher's political naivety, a naivety which he unwittingly bequeathed to his successors, the nineteenth-century Utopian socialists:

> Like Plato, they were also guilty of associating the communist system not with the movement and the struggle of the working masses, but with the good will of wise monarchs and kindly bankers (*dobrodetel'nie bankiry*) (...). Alone, the scientific communism of K. Marx and F. Engels turned the question of how to achieve a communist system on its head. Unlike the belief in the good works of the dictator, the authors of scientific communism openly declared that 'the liberation of the workers should be a matter to be taken in hand by the workers themselves', and that the objectives that the proletariat sets itself may be attained uniquely by a violent overthrow of the entire contemporary social order.[12]

Even though their critical – and sometimes rather disparaging – remarks might lead us to think otherwise, in the end, neither Novitskii nor Volgin seemed prepared to dismiss Plato's relevance for modern socialism altogether. Insofar as Plato criticized social injustice, and spoke about the class struggle, he should, they believed, deservedly be regarded as the precursor of communism. As for many nineteenth-century interpreters, so too for Novitskii and Volgin, Platonic communism was elitist, aristocratic, the stuff of pure invention, with little anchorage in reality for the project to be feasible. But that said, they welcomed his vision of a way of life based on the principles of equality between the sexes, equal share in material goods and the breakdown of the private family unit.

While the underlying point for virtually all Soviet commentators was to vindicate the October Revolution, the means available to do so became increasingly limited as the consolidation of power by the Bolsheviks took its toll on scholarship. One consequence of imposing a rigorous fidelity to the principle of *partiinost'* meant that, besides producing highly schematic and heavily idealized accounts of philosophy and social thought, the choice of authorities who might be cited in this task became more and more restricted. Between Novitskii, Volgin and Lur'e, the demise of Kautsky as a legitimate reference serves as one telling example of the mechanisms of Soviet scholarship such as these were practised under Stalin's rule. Despite Lenin's attack against him – already prior to the Revolution – as 'renegade', Kautsky's book, *Vorläufer des neuen Sozialismus* (1895), continued to have pride of place in early Soviet scholarship. In terms of the way they structured and weighted their appraisals of the *Republic,* both the Novitskii and Volgin monographs bear witness to this. It was only with the publication of his *Die materialistiche Geschichtsauffassung* in 1927, which caused the wrath of Communist Party leaders, that Kautsky's name and works were finally banned altogether. Accordingly, as the Soviet Union was led out of NEP and into a programme of 'socialism in one country', attempts to vindicate Plato as a precursor of socialism, an interpretation popularized by Kautsky and, as we saw, echoed in early Soviet scholarship, were declared anathema.

This shift is readily perceptible in Lur'e's monograph, *A History of Ancient Social Thought.* Taking as his starting point the definition of 'scientific socialism', Lur'e set out to uncover examples in antiquity of 'the workers' movement, aimed at the immediate improvement of the material lot of the working class; second, traces of the idea of the socialization of production'.[13] In view of these priorities alone, it is pretty clear that Plato had little chance of being accepted into the pantheon of socialist literature:

> Platonic communism was in no way a reaction in the name of the oppressed 'Demos'. It merely subscribed to the principles of the pre-existing aristocratic state, albeit in an ennobled form which Plato took as the basis of his social ideal. From this, it follows that ancient and contemporary socialism, despite the name, have nothing in common.[14]

In view of his outright rejection of Plato as a precursor of modern-day socialism, Lur'e may be said to mark the 'end point' in a process in rendering Plato redundant, a process which initially involved paying greater tribute to Marx and Engels in their quarrel with St. Simon, Fourier and Owen, and which was finally capped by the ever-tightening controls over what, apart from Marx and Lenin, could pass as respectable authorities for Soviet science. Lur'e dotted the 'i's and crossed 't's in eliminating any non-orthodox interpretations – those of Kautsky, Pöhlmann and Beer. Any attempt to modernize Plato, to portray him as a prototype of social democracy, was, in his terms, 'sheer rubbish':

> There can be no greater mockery of the scientific method, than to compare Plato with contemporary socialism. While we may speak of Plato as a precursor of medieval Christianity, as a precursor of 'Jesuitism', as the precursor of the Holy Alliance, in no way may he be said to be the precursor of socialism.[15]

The image of Plato as a social thinker that predominated between 1923 and 1927 was far from being unique to Soviet scholarship. He was cast in a similar light as National Socialist propaganda in Germany began to hold sway. Not unlike their Soviet enemies, Nazis also applauded Plato as the first to have argued for a communitarian principle and for rejecting the family unit. They also regretted Plato's aristocratic brand of communism because of its neglect of the working masses.[16] As I suggested in Chapter Four, it is not difficult to find parallels between passages of the *Republic* and specific items of early Soviet legislation and propaganda, particularly those bearing on education and sexual equality. Similarly, in Germany, commentators of the dialogue were quick to see points of comparison between Platonic ideals and their own new reality in the making.[17] But, it remains that, in both cases, the parallels in question were superficial, if not unintentional. Kollontai's disquisition on sexual liberty, for example, was far more indebted to Engels than to Plato, even as she provocatively defied her fellow comrades to make way for the 'winged Eros'. Indeed, to suggest that early twentieth century politics or ideology of a totalitarian kind was consciously drawing on Plato as a model to copy would be misleading. Rather the image of Plato that both Nazis and Soviets promoted was a convenient strategy, among others, for forging, as one recent critic accurately coined it, 'an organic society, free of all undesirable elements'.[18] Moreover, it is highly probable that Soviet commentators were aware of these Platonic traits in National Socialist propaganda, and that it was the need to mark their differences with an enemy ideology that prompted them to discredit Plato's social views as virulently as they did. 'In Fascist Germany', Mikhail Dynnik wrote, 'an entire series of so called studies about Plato has been published, where, in the guise of analysing Platonism, the man-hating ideology of German Fascism is being propagated.'[19] In other words, by the early thirties, disqualifying Plato was not only part of a bigger project to debunk bourgeois scholarship generally, it had also become an issue of immediate political and ideological relevance. Moreover, such explicit denunciations of the kind voiced by Dynnik were, arguably, as much a tacit admission that, in the twenties particularly, both Soviet and German popular culture had actually shared a similar 'Hellenistic obsession' – that, indeed, both had been tempted to use Plato's project as a strategy for consolidating their own promises of an harmonious and well-ordered state.

Plato, the 'Father of Idealism' and Soviet Historiography of Philosophy

By the mid-1930s, textbook presentations of the main lines of Platonic idealism had been structured according to a codified account of the overall historical development of philosophy, namely, as a battle between idealism and materialism, as well as in light of the requirement to determine the political commitment (*partiinost'*) of a given philosophical system. Accordingly, Plato's 'reactionary' philosophy was interpreted as the direct outcome of the socio-political and ideological battle between aristocratic and democratic parties in fifth-century Athens. Plato had propagandized geometry in the hope of 'enslaving the people', and thereby to defend the interests of the aristocracy of his times. The phrase 'god always geometrizes', it was suggested, should, in fact, be read as 'god is the enemy of democratic fair share'.[20]

Validated authorities to which authors of these summary accounts referred were, as I suggested above and as one would expect, Marx and Lenin. But also Aristotle insofar as Lenin had claimed that Aristotle's criticism of Plato's 'ideas' amounted to a criticism of idealism in general. Taking his cue from Aristotle's objections to Plato, Lenin concluded:

> Platonic ideas are empty abstractions. They do not help explain the sense perception of things, nor do they constitute the essence of things. The doctrine of ideas not only distracts us from a study of the cognitive process of the world of things, it also has nefarious consequences on the development of scientific knowledge.[21]

That said, Lenin was prepared to recognize Plato's importance for advancing the dialectical method, even though his assessment was filtered through haphazard notes and jottings on Hegel's 'Lectures on the History of Philosophy', rather than on the strength of a direct response to Plato himself. It remains, however, that possibly the most fateful remark Lenin ever uttered about Plato was his comment to the effect that, as a battle between idealism and materialism, the entire history of philosophy describes the 'tendencies' or 'lines' of Plato and Democritus. Henceforth the 'line' or 'tendency' of Plato designated all philosophical systems which *grosso modo* fell into the province of idealism.²² By the same token, Lenin had guaranteed a place for Plato – albeit as an anti-hero – in Soviet scholarship.

These somewhat random observations became the cardinal points to be included in all accounts of Platonic philosophy, the upshot of which was a highly reductionist portrait. When his reputation in Soviet Russia reached its lowest ebb (corresponding roughly to the decades under Stalinist rule) Plato was uniformly treated as a political reactionary, and anti-scientific. (Witness, it was argued, his cosmological views in the *Timaeus*.) Plato's theory of ideas (in *Theaetetus*) was primarily devised so as to combat materialism, even though he had taken over much of his enemy, Democritus', terminology – 'idea', 'logos', 'synthesis' – to do so. Granted, this view that Plato had 'stolen from Democritus' had actually been put forward earlier in the mid-1920s,²³ but it was to become part of standard practice in discrediting both Plato's philosophy and his person by the 1930s and later. In this spirit, it was argued that Plato had developed his theory of ideas solely to combat the reigning philosophy of nature (natural science and materialism). But his own 'teleological understanding of nature' was non-scientific, mystical, and out of touch with the scientific achievements of his times such as these were exemplified in the work of Democritus: 'All of Plato's childishly naive contradictory, and scientifically unfounded system is directed against Democritus' mechanistic comprehension of the world.'²⁴

Writing after the publication of Stalin's *Short Course*, the historian of philosophy, Georgii Aleksandrov, gave an assessment of Platonic philosophy, respecting all these canons of Marxism-Leninism.²⁵ His catalogue of the main points of Plato's idealism in view of the battle with materialism led him to the following, highly unsurprising conclusions. Plato's theory of ideas betrays a religious worldview. It is opposed to science, indeed, did much to hinder the development of scientific conceptions of nature. His social views, such as they emerge from a reading of *Politicus, Republic* and *Laws*, show him to be backward looking and reactionary. Positive evaluation of Plato's thought concern, once again, those points which Lenin, and, now more recently, Stalin, had singled out for approval. Plato's greatest achievement was his contribution to the dialectical method, even though he had worked on this from a blatantly idealistic standpoint. It is interesting to note that, in order to pay tribute to the last, but not the least, in line of dialectical materialists – Josef Stalin - Aleksandrov chose a quotation from the latter's *Questions of Leninism*, and did not, on this particular point, refer to Lenin at all.²⁶ Given the period he was writing in (the early 1940s), this 'literary device' was, of course, anything but surprising.

Generally speaking, it was only after the death of Stalin that a return to Lenin's original view on the matter, together with a more comprehensive appreciation of Plato's 'real' contribution to the development of the dialectic became possible. Beginning in the mid-1950s, it became, once again, usual to suggest that, even if it was intended to serve his idealist philosophy, 'to the degree that Plato's dialectic consisted in confronting opposed opinions in the process of knowledge, it played an important part in the development of dialectic in the ancient world'.[27] Dated 1957, this comment by the historian of ancient philosophy, Mikhail Dynnik, was wholly in line with the by now standardized 'Soviet Plato' which had been restored after the very low ebb in scholarship under Stalin. The argument was virtually always the same. Although Plato's entire philosophy was devised in order to combat materialism, and to hinder the development of science, his discovery of the dialectic merited a place in the history of philosophy.

Dynnik's portrait of Plato appeared in the newly revised first volume of the *History of Philosophy*. The fate of this six-volume publication, and particularly the volume on ancient philosophy, first edited in 1940 (indeed, to which Dynnik had contributed[28]) is not without interest, given that the original paragraph on Plato had deviated slightly from the prescribed canons. In its original draft, emphasis had been placed on a progression in Platonic thought, allowing the authors to break down his production into four main periods, and thereby draw on existing philological findings. Attempts had also been made to minimize the frequent charge of dualism, and to centre the discussion on Plato's contribution to the dialectic instead. To this end, much attention was given to the problem of the 'one' and the 'many' in *Parmenides*, a dialogue which was largely ignored in more standard Soviet accounts of the Stalinist period. Obviously, because of its more 'lenient' views, this edition was quickly withdrawn from circulation, with its authors and editors severely reprimanded for their tactical errors. Yet, the fact that it was written at all, let alone published, invites us to reconsider for a moment the stereotyped image of Plato that 'official' Soviet historiography of philosophy seemed so intent on creating. Paradoxically, the open pillory of Plato sanctioned the publication of new and revised translations of individual dialogues. Generally speaking, it was, of course, a question of those dialogues that could be used in support of the dialectical method as a principle of science (for example: Book VII of the *Republic, Sophist,* or *Symposium, Phaedo* and *Philebus* which Lenin had referred to in his *Philosophical Notebooks*[29]), or those considered of crucial importance – albeit ostensibly for the purposes of refutation – in consolidating the historical-philosophical foundations of dialectical materialism. In this regard *Theaetetus, Timaeus*, in particular, were dubious favourites. They were seen as a challenge to the Soviet theory of sense perception in knowledge, and, as a challenge, they required a counter-argument.[30]

Textbooks, encyclopaedia entries, or commentaries to translations are also quite telling of the subtleties involved in Soviet scholarship, even in periods when it was most expected to cower before ideology. Lengthy extracts of Platonic dialogues were sometimes quoted in textbooks, perhaps to give a taste of the forbidden fruit, but certainly enabling the reader to judge for him- or herself how far the quotation corresponded to the interpretation proposed by a given author. Anthologies on art, or 'means of production' were also an occasion to include 'relevant' passages from a Plato dialogue.[31] In addition, the identity of some of the translators themselves is telling of the haphazard development of Soviet science. Some were long since dead translators of pre-Revolutionary editions (an anthology dating from 1940 comprised extracts from *Gorgias*, *Republic*, *Laws*, *Critias*, *Theaetetus*, *Philebus*, using Karpov and Solov'ev's translations). Others were classical scholars, whose education pre-dated the Revolution, and who otherwise, because of an assumed hostility to the Soviet regime, were not granted any work at all.[32]

Continuity and Change in Perceptions of Plato

The question ultimately arises whether there were any significant changes in perceptions of Plato before and after the October Revolution. In some respects, Russian and Soviet assessments remind us of Florenskii's use of 'plus' and 'minus' signs when he set Kant off against Plato. Similarly, between the Russian and Soviet Plato, while the terms of reference remained more or less the same, their meaning appears to have altered radically. But not altogether: much depends on whether, at issue, was Plato, the father of idealism, or Plato, the Utopian thinker. Though, between nineteenth century liberals and twentieth-century communists, political and ideological perspectives differed considerably, each voiced a reluctance to accept Plato's project for an ideal city.[33] There were a number of formal parallels between certain nineteenth-century and Soviet perceptions of Plato, the idealist, too. Presenting Plato's philosophy as a system was a trait common to different generations of scholars. Both for Silvestr Gogotskii, author of a *Philosophical Lexicon* (1857–1873), and for the editors of the *Shorter Soviet Encyclopaedia* (1939), 'Platonism' implied an all-inclusive philosophy made up of organically linked bits – dialectic, theory of ideas, physics, ethics, and capped by his socio-political views. Moreover, a major sticking point for both pre- and post-Revolutionary interpreters was that of Plato's dualism. Granted, they tended to tackle the problem from quite different perspectives. Solov'ev, we saw, situated the problem in the context of Plato's cosmology, which he then coloured with his own, personal Christian beliefs: although the Eros had been conceived as a bridge bringing the ideal and real worlds together, Plato tragically failed in the task he had set himself. Somewhat differently, Plato's Soviet critics approached the issue from an epistemological perspective. The usual claim was that Plato's radical dualism was the outcome of his having ignored the role of sense perception in knowledge of matter, all for the sake of keeping sacrosanct his theory of ideas.³⁴ The one major exception to this criticism, however, was the aforementioned 1940 volume, which attempted to minimize the charge of dualism by enhancing Plato's contribution to the dialectical method. Moreover, as I have said, the authors of this edition combined a philosophical and philological approach to the dialogues, thereby pointing – more sympathetically perhaps and in a way which recalls the approach adopted by nineteenth-century commentators earlier – to an evolution in Plato's thought.³⁵

On the whole, though, it is true to say that it was the reductionist, codified portrait of Plato which dominated throughout the first three decades of Soviet period. One would have to wait for Khrushchev's thaw for a more complete, official, revival of his thought with all the accompanying paraphernalia of new translations, monographs, colloquia, and so on.³⁶ This new wave of interest was, to a considerable degree, initiated by the historian of philosophy, Valentin Asmus, together with the classical scholar, Aleksei Losev, whose endeavours to nuance Plato's 'objective idealism' as 'ancient objective idealism' were an important gesture towards rehabilitating the fallen idol. To this end, Losev drew on factors of a historical-cultural kind. His bibliographical references, moreover, suggest a discreet post-Stalinist rehabilitation, not only of Plato, but also of his nineteenth-century Russian interpreters.³⁷ Albeit paying lip service to certain well-established 'turns of phrase' of his times, such as the notorious 'caste system' and 'dialectic', Losev rejected the accepted criticism of Platonic dualism. Basing his comments on the *Phaedrus*, he argued that, thanks to the dialectic as a method dividing the 'one' into the 'many', and vice versa – reducing the 'many' to 'one', Plato resoundingly put paid to any such suspicion of dualism. Losev gave additional fuel to his argument by appealing to a view of Plato as a 'typical ancient Greek'. If one bears in mind the ancient world outlook with its pagan gods, the squabbles between them, and the drama of religious rituals, the opposition between the ideal and real world that Plato speaks of in his philosophy is less stark than it might first appear to the modern reader:

> For him, matter was, in the end, something beautiful, like an ideally ensible cosmos. The ideal world was filled with the very same things – people natural and social phenomena – except that they were depicted as prototypes (like the gods), eternal, imparting meaning to the material world.³⁸

And again, to drive his point home:

> If the ideal world is eternally immutable, while the material world is forever in flux, changing, this opposition is possible for Plato only because of a principle which is at once immutable and mobile. This principle is the soul of the cosmos. It is ideal, yet it also imparts life to all of existence.³⁹

It is tempting to say that, thanks to Losev, Soviet scholarship came full circle with Russian nineteenth-century research, ready to move on where the latter had been brought to an abrupt halt. Certainly, like Solov'ev, Giliarov, Novgorodtsev and others, Losev expressed sympathy for the 'drama of Plato's life', and welcomed his role as a moral force. Prior to that, during the Stalinist period, the idea of Plato as a moral example to follow in quest of the good was, of course, laughable. If anything, only his theory of the dialectic might have had some bearing on contemporary views concerning the construction of knowledge and a theory of science, but not to the extent of undermining the prevailing image of Plato as father of idealism and precursor of utopianism. Between nineteenth-century readers and scholars working in the Stalinist and post-Stalinist periods, these two labels had been attached to Plato's name countless times. The only difference was that, with few exceptions, the connotations attached to these labels passed from positive approval to negative or mitigated criticism.

Conclusion: Was there a 'Russian' Platonism?

Was there a 'Russian Platonism' in some way distinct from the interpretations produced by, say, the early Christians, the Renaissance, the Cambridge School, German Idealism, or indeed, neo-Kantianism, but which might be rightfully included in such a list of Platonic revivals? As I suggested in the Introduction to the present study, Plato reception in nineteenth and early twentieth-century Russia passed through several phases. A first wave of interest in the wake of the Napoleonic wars was followed by a second one in the decades of Reform and Counter Reform, a period which, as I have said, corresponded to the real consolidation of Plato scholarship in Russia, and which has been the main topic treated here. Soviet readings of Plato, as I have described above, consisted largely in discrediting his philosophy, but also in safeguarding those elements which Lenin had once singled out, even though Lenin's own appreciation actually owed more to his quarrel with Hegel than it did to a reading of the dialogues themselves.

As I argued in the Introduction and Chapter One, in nineteenth-century Russia the problem of education played a central role in a process of modernization which was constantly hindered by more conservative measures to sustain an ideology of national identity grounded in Orthodox spirituality. Vindicating Plato for the purposes of education produced a number of stereotypes. For his nineteenth-century readers, Plato was the philosopher-poet *par excellence*, a humanist, and a moral force. Widely regarded as an emblem of the culture of antiquity, his thought, and the person of Plato himself hidden in the dialogues, seemed to fit well with the values that certain intellectuals and university professors wanted to promote through a solid classical education. For bureaucrats confronted by the quickening pace of modernization which threatened to undermine autocratic rule, an exercise in Greek (and Latin) grammar was seen as a useful way of keeping the tempo in check.

Yet the image of Plato to emerge here was not so much 'Russian' as 'Everyman's Plato'. During much the same period, renewed interest for Plato in France, and particularly in Germany – often for the sake of ensuring a solid classical education – frequently fell back on the same stereotypes.[40] Uvarov's conception of schooling had several points in common with the Humboldtian notion of *Bildung*, in which the study of poetry and antiquity were, of course, key factors. The Greek idea of aesthetics, as a harmony of forms, brought with it the promise of moral perfection. Uvarov, like Humboldt, conceived secondary and university education as the supreme expression of the moral culture of a nation, and both of them appealed to the ancients for its most appropriate anchorage. Moreover, while the classical world was believed to exemplify the universal characteristics of mankind, it did not seem to hinder the idea of national identity which both Humboldt and Uvarov advocated.

Between German, French (in the combined scholarly work and official functions of Victor Cousin and François Guizot), and Russian vindications of the classical world for the sake of advancing modern-day education there were, of course, some differences, the most obvious one having to do with religious confessions. Indeed, at times of more severe censorship, which often went hand in hand with an exaggerated sense of nationhood (under Nicholas I and Alexander III), Plato enjoyed pride of place because of the supposed pertinence of his thought to Byzantine-Russian Orthodoxy, a claim which could scarcely be made in Germany or France. The irony, however, was that, despite occasional hostilities expressed towards the 'Latin' (rationalist, Catholic) origins of West European culture, in practice, schooling in the ancients in Russia, like everywhere else, tended to focus on Latin grammar and Roman authors, rather than on the more difficult subject of Greek, which placed more demands on the pupil.[41]

I have suggested that Russian conservative thinkers fostered an image of Plato in order to inculcate a sense of Russia's spiritual and traditional differences with the rest of Europe. However, to say that this betokened a 'Russian Platonism' would, to my mind, be unconvincing. It is perhaps more fitting to regard it as an 'ideological' assimilation of past images of Plato, of age-old polemics concerning his thought, caring but little for the original, specific context in which these polemics and past revivals first took place.[42] Moreover, as I have suggested, this image of Plato, as the guardian of moral values against dehumanizing science, was not confined to Russia, but was one which cropped up everywhere. That said, the outstanding question remains whether or not it is possible to reconstruct readings of Plato which are inscribed in the cultural and historical circumstances peculiar to Russia. Can it be shown that interpretations were – sometimes, if not always – motivated by some crucial problem of Russian actuality, and that, in turn, this was brought to bear on the way they assimilated certain aspects of Plato's thought, while rejecting others?

In Chapter Three I discussed the emergence of a juridical consciousness in Russia, and a reading of Plato by certain jurists and religious thinkers which privileged his theory of justice and the good as a distant prototype of the theory of natural law/justice. Lecturing on the philosophy of law professors would almost inevitably draw their students' attention to the distinction to be made between codified laws (*zakon*) and law as a normative principle (*pravo*). Some went further to explore the moral dimension of the latter, if not its relation – positive and negative – with morality. In doing so, it was not unusual to backtrack to past philosophies – notably to Kant and Plato (although both Redkin and Chicherin also referred extensively to Hegel). Beginning with Iurkevich in the early seventies, then in the writings of Novgorodstev, Solov'ev, and Evgenii Trubetskoi at the turn of the century and after, there were repeated attempts to fill out the theoretical framework provided by Kant with 'the moral impulse' bequeathed by Plato. Plato (and Aristotle), they believed, had taught that abstract principles of equality and freedom alone are not enough to establish harmonious social forms. To attain to the ideal of social justice meant having to complement the abstract principle of justice with a new moral content. True, the Russian philosophers of law discussed in this study were well aware of the restricted relevance that Plato's thought could have for modern-day preoccupations. But for all that, they did occasionally try to accommodate him to a more modern worldview, even at the risk of inventing a Plato of their own in the process. Plato was coupled with Solov'ev for his 'justification of the good'. He also became an acclaimed defender of the 'inalienable rights of man' under all conditions and in every situation, despite what was otherwise admitted as his evident neglect of the individual in the ideal city-state.

With respect to what might constitute 'Russian Platonism' these kinds of readings are rather telling. Might we understand by 'Russian Platonism' questions of a moral nature in the life of the individual, but also society, whence its pertinence for a philosophy of law? It is, of course, an open question. We should take into account, for example, the revived interest in natural law in Germany which was taking place at roughly the same time, and the way the neo-Kantians, Hermann Cohen and Paul Natorp, brought Plato and Kant together in their attempts to revise aspects of Kantian philosophy. Nevertheless, the fundamental reasons prompting certain Russian juridical thinkers to return to Plato were, I suggest, different. For some educators, drawing attention to the moral dimension of law – indeed, occasionally appealing to religious pathos as in the case of Iurkevich – was possibly the most effective way of bringing a nation, traditionally suspicious of the judicial procedure, to appreciate the real meaning of civil rights and duties. To a degree, Plato embodied the values that they were themselves keen to advocate. These considerations, together with the fact that the Plato taught in schools was precisely the one of those dialogues in which the moral dimension of his thought was privileged, arguably facilitated the creation of what we might call a 'Russian juridical Platonism'. Certainly, the mechanisms at work here are not unlike the selective readings of Plato that previous revivals produced in order to meet more immediate needs, such as the Christian or aesthetic principles that Plato's early Christian or Renaissance readers had once sought to defend.

In the end, though, it might be best to ask just how many Platonisms there were in nineteenth and twentieth-century Russia? We may count several. First, there was a Platonism born out of a conception of education, and which matched the more general return to the classical world in French and German educational practice at that time. Then came the Platonism of Jena, meaning the presence of Plato in the philosophy of Schelling, but also Hegel, whose impact on the Russian Slavophiles and their successors was so important. Alongside this strictly philosophical revival we should, of course, place neo-Platonism, such as this was handed down through the writings of the Church Fathers, ultimately to become highly significant for the cultural identity of the Slavophiles and the young Solov'ev. In this list of Platonisms one should also include images of Plato which were fixed in more popular statements about his philosophy, and of course, Lenin's Plato, which was largely compiled from his reading of Hegel, and which became a central point of discussion for Soviet commentators. Finally, we should note a 'Russian juridical Platonism', a reading which saw in Plato a vindication of natural law. Failing to find satisfactory solutions in contemporary Western juridical science to the problems that Russian philosophers of law had to confront, and, no doubt, owing to the tradition of censorship in Russia – a situation which Plato tended to profit from – it is perhaps this particular 'Platonism' which corresponded well to the salient features of Russian juridical thought towards the end of the nineteenth century. Both the moral dimension of Plato's concept of natural law/justice, and his ambitious project to improve the Athenian social order were mirrored in the concern among certain Russian intellectuals about how best to address social and political problems in a country on its long and difficult path towards modernization, a country caught, as it were between two conflicting dynamics of progress and tradition.

Notes

1 The case, for example, of the philosopher and *publitsist*, Giliarov-Platonov (the father of the Professor of Philosophy who has figured in the present study), or the Metropolitan Levshin (1737-1812) who took monastic orders under the name of Plato. Voltaire, incidentally, referred to him as the 'Russian Plato'.
2 The reference to Marx comes from *Das Kapital*, while Lenin's remarks were made in the context of sharp polemics with the revisionist Marxists, Iushkevich and Bazarov. See

his *Materializm i Empiriokrititsizm* (Moscow, 1909). My reference is taken from the 1989 edition (Politizdat', Moscow), p.140.
3   On translated extracts see Chapter four, Note 5.
4   V.P. Pertsov, 'Sotsial'no-politicheskoe mirovozzrenie Platona' in *Trudy Belorusskogo Gosudarstvennogo Universiteta*, 2-3 (Minsk, 1922), pp.50-73.
5   A. Rozhdestvenskii, 'Polozhenie tret'ego sosloviia v *Gosudarstva* Platona', in *Sbornik Iaroslavskogo Gosudarstvennogo Universiteta*, vyp.1 (1918-1919), pp.35-59.
6   Indications of this new development towards more 'scientific literature' on the phenomenon of utopia is suggested by the publication, in 1923, of a guide to utopian classics, *Katalog Utopii*, compiled by a certain V. Sviatlovskii. Cf. Baczko, *Lumières de l'Utopie*, who describes this edition as '(une) sorte de guide bibliographique raisonnée pour les militants', p.25.
7   Cf. Baczko, op. cit., pp.22-23, p.205.
8   All these works appeared in Russian translation. R. Pöhlmann's book was published in Russian in 1910, Adler's in 1909, Kautsky's in several editions (1906, 1907, and again in 1919), Beer's in 1927. See above, Chapter Four, notes 37 and 38 for exact references. Indigenous pre-Revolutionary, though still 'kosher' authorities in the early twenties included the historian, V. Buzeskul, and S.A. Zhebelev.
9   K.P. Novitskii, *Platon* (Krasnaia nov', Moscow, 1923), published in a series entitled 'Ancestors of Utopian Communism'; V.P. Volgin, *Sotsialism v drevnei Gretsii* (M.-L., 1925). Also his commentary to the first volume of an anthology of utopian literature, *Predshchestvenniki sovremenogo sotsializma v otryvkakh iz ikh proizvedenii* (M.-L., 1928), pp.14-38, pp.43-49; S. L. Lur'e, *Istoriia antichnoi obshchestvennoi mysli* (M.-L., 1929).
10 Volgin, *Predshchestvenniki...*, 1928, p.13.
11 Volgin, *Sotsializm v drevnei Gretsii*, p.141.
12 Novitskii, op. cit., pp 25-26.
13 Lur'e, *Istoriia antichnoi obshchestvennoi mysli*, p288.
14 Ibid., p.338.
15 Ibid., p.310.
16 See, for example, J.J. Wunenburger, 'Platon, ancêtre du totalitarisme? Quelques interprétations contemporaines', in Nesckhe-Etienne (eds), *Images de Platon....*, pp.435-450.
17 See Ulrike Zimbrich, *Bibliographie zu Platons Staats*.
18 J.J. Wunenburger, op. cit., pp.441-442.
19 M. Dynnik, 'Za Marsistkoe izuchenie antichnogo materializma', *Vestnik drevnei istorii*, 4 (1948), p.13.
20 S. L. Lur'e, 'Platon i Aristotel' o tochnykh naukakh' in *Arhiv Istorii Nauki i Tekhniki*, vyp.9 (M.-L., 1936). Cited in F. Kh. Kessidi (ed.), *Platon i ego epokha* (Moscow, 1979), p.251.
21 Lenin, *Filosofskie Tetrady* (1915). This remark was very frequently incorporated into Soviet readings of Plato.
22 See note 2 supra.
23 See, for example, M. Vygodskii, 'Platon kak matematik', in *Vestnik Kommunistiskoi Akademii*, kn. XVI (1926) pp.192-215); G.Bammel' 'Demokrit i Platon' in *Arhiv K. Marksa i F. Engel'sa*, kn.3 (M.-L., 1927), pp.470-479.
24 V. Serezhnikov, *Ocherki po istorii filosofii*, vol.1 (M.-L., 1929), p.141, cited in Kessidi, op. cit., p.257. For a more moderate view, however, see Serezhnikov's commentary to his translation of *Theaetetus* (1936), also his 'Sokrat. Osnovnye problemy filosofii Platona' (MIFLI, Moscow, 1937).
25 G. Aleksandrov, *Bor'ba materializma i idealizma v antichnoi filosofii* (Gospolitzdat, Moscow, 1941).
26 Alexandrov quoted the following, rather empty phrase: 'By dialectic, the ancients understood the art of attaining to the truth by means of exposing and resolving

contradictions in the opponent's statements. In Antiquity, certain philosophers contended that exposing contradictions in thought, and the confrontation of opposite opinions are the best means to uncover the truth.' Stalin, *Voprosy Leninizma*, cited in ibid., p.47.

27 M. Dynnik, 'Materializm V v. do n. e. i ego bor'ba s idealizmom ('liniia Demokrita' i 'liniia Platona')' in *Istoriia Filosofii*, vol.1 (Moscow, 1957), p.108.

28 Together with Valentin Asmus, Orest Trakhtenberg. Aleksandrov was one of the main editors. On the controversy provoked by the 1940s edition, see G. Batygin and I. Devyatko, 'The Soviet Philosophical Community and Power: Some Episodes from the Late Forties', in *SEET*, vol.46, no.3, (Sept. 1994), pp.223-245.

29 Soviet translations of *Sophist* date from 1936 (Dovatur). Translations of the *Symposium* appeared in 1935, 1939, 1940, 1947, and excerpts from book VII of the *Republic* on the nature of the dialectic in 1938 and 1940.

30 *Theaetetus* was translated in 1935, 1936 (by Serezhnikov), 1940; *Timaeus* in 1935.

31 Aleksandrov, for example, quoted in disproportionate length, from the *Theaetetus*. It was not uncommon for long extracts of Plato's dialogues to be included in anthologies with titles such as 'Ancient Means of Production', or 'Views of Ancient Thinkers on Art'.

32 A case in point was the classical scholar, A.I. Dovatur, and the poet and classical scholar, A.N. Egunov. Dovatur translated the *Philebus* and *Sophist* (1936). Egunov's translation of the *Laws* was published in the 1920s 'Academia' edition. His translation of the *Republic* appeared in the Asmus and Losev's *Complete Works* in 1971. On Egunov, see G.S. Knabe, *Grotesknyi epilog klassicheskoi dramy: Antichnost' v Leningrade 20-x godov* in 'Chteniia po istorii i teorii kul'tury', vyp.15 (RGGU, Moscow, 1996).

33 Other 'constant' features between pre-Revolutionary and Soviet interest in Plato concern discussions of socio-economic factors such as these are depicted in the *Republic*. For example: L.V. Fedorovich, 'Istoriia politicheskoi ekonomii s drevneishikh vremen do A. Shmidta', *Zapiski Novorossiiskogo Universiteta*, vol.79 (Odessa, 1900), pp.77-85; D.F. Shcheglov, 'Istoriko-Ekonomicheskie Ocherki. Gosudarstvo Platona', kn.1 (1866), pp.490-511; A.V. Mishulin, 'Utopicheskii Plan Agrarnoi Magnezii (po 'Zakonam' Platona)', in *Vestnik Drevnei Istorii*, 3 (1938), pp.92-116. Examples of German scholarship on this question include S. Lauffer, 'Die platonische Agrarwirtschaft' in *Vierteljahrschrift für Sozial-u. Wirtschaftsgeschichte*, 29 (1936), pp. 233-269. See U. Zimbrich, op. cit.

34 Cf. Serezhnikov, Aleksandrov and Dynnik in op. cit. Also Dynnik in *Ocherk istorii filosofii klassicheskoi Gretsii* (Moscow, 1936), pp.186-216.

35 For example, Solov'ev in his *Brokgaus-Efron* entry. Also Ernst Radlov in his *Filosofskii Slovar'*, 2nd ed. (Moscow, 1913).

36 This revival included, in 1968 a new three-volume 'Complete Works' translation, edited by Asmus and Losev.

37 In his entry on Plato in the *Philosophical Encylopedic Dictionary* (1967) Losev organized his materials in a way not unlike Solov'ev's *Brokgaus-Efron* entry of 1898. Having argued for a passage from 'negative' to 'positive' idealism, Solov'ev took these markers to guide his account of what he considered to be the salient features of Plato's philosophy. He listed these as theory of knowledge and dialectic (which he based on a discussion of *Theaetetus* and book VII of the *Republic*), theory of ideas; cosmology (with reference to *Philebus* and *Timaeus*), psychology, ethics and politics, the last three grouped together. Losev, for his part, began with a discussion of the three main ontological substances (one, mind and [world]-soul), then addressed the question of matter. A third paragraph dealt with gnoseology, logic and dialectic, a fourth with psychology, ethics and politics, a fifth on aesthetics, with a concluding section on religion and mythology.

38 Losev, op. cit., vol.4, pp.267-268. This point was taken up by Asmus in his own monograph on Plato. See V.F. Asmus, *Platon* (Moscow, 1976).
39 Losev, ibid., p.268.
40 On the history of education in nineteenth-century France see, for example: M. Vaughan and M. Scotford Archer, *Social Conflict and Educational Change in England and France, 1789-1848* (Cambridge, 1971); F. Mayeur, *De la Revolution à l'Ecole républicaine* in *Histoire générale de l'Enseignement et de l'Education en France*, vol.3 (Nouvelle Librairie de France, Paris, 1981). On Germany, see, among others: H.J. Frank, *Geschichte des Deutschunterrichts, von den Anfängen bis 1945* (Munich: Carl Hanser Verlag, 1973); W. Schmale and N.L. Dodde (eds), *Revolution des Wissens? Europa und seine Schulen im Zeitalter der Aufklärung (1750-1825)* (Verlag Dr. Dieter Winkler, Bochum, 1991) which treats the majority of European countries in the given period, with the exception of Russia.
41 See, for example: F. Nethercott, 'L'établissement du système scolaire en Russie (1800-1850) : référence française ou référence allemande?' in Katia Dmitrieva and Michel Espagne (eds), *Philologiques IV. Transferts culturels triangulaires. France-Allemagne-Russie* (Editions de la Maison des Sciences de l'Homme, Paris, 1996), pp.187-204.
42 For an analysis of the polemics between partisans of scholasticism and the early Humanists, see James Hankins, *Plato in the Italian Renaissance*, 2 vols. (Leiden, 1990). Concerning the debates in Byzantium between the tenth and fifteenth centuries, together with the influence of the 'Platonists', Psellus and, especially Maxim the Greek, on the development on Russian spiritual culture, see A. Abramov, 'Otsenka filosofii Platona v russkoi idealiticheskoi filosofii', in F. Kessidi (ed.), op. cit., pp.212-237.

Biographical Profiles

Below are brief descriptions of the university careers of those scholars whose works have been discussed in the present study. Without claiming to be exhaustive, these accounts are designed to highlight the place that Plato occupied in their careers as teachers and researchers. In some cases, working on Plato reflected a deep personal interest. This is especially true with respect to Karpov, Giliarov, Florenskii, and Sergei Trubetskoi. For others, however, it was clearly only a marginal concern, and, no doubt, in answer to governmental and ideological constraints. Regardless of a scholar's main field of research in the humanities, knowledge of some aspect of ancient culture remained a *sine qua non* of being 'well educated'. A grounding in the classics was also essential if one was to 'educate well'. More generally, reconstructing these professional *curricula vitae* highlights the progression, but also the setbacks, in Russian science. While it is true that, as the nineteenth century drew to a close, research became more specialized, a cursory look at the individual itineraries presented here, shows just how uniform teaching programmes in different institutions continued to be throughout the period studied.

The authors are grouped according to the main university they taught in, and they are listed chronologically, that is, in function of the year of their professorial nomination, or nearest equivalent. Information has been drawn from a variety of pre-Revolutionary materials including Biographical Dictionaries published under the auspices of Moscow, Kiev and St. Petersburg Universities, the Brokgaus and Efron 'Encyclopaedical Dictionary', obituary notices, personal memoirs, Programmes of Courses, together with some Soviet and post-Soviet encyclopaedical dictionaries. Exact references are given in the Select Bibliography. Unfortunately, not all the sources consulted correspond with respect to certain specific details about a given author. Where discrepancies occur I have usually opted for the information given in nineteenth-century accounts, which, not infrequently, were drafted by close colleagues or former students. More detailed monographs concerning the main authors treated in the present study are indicated in the main bibliography.

University of Moscow

Petr Redkin (1808–1891)
Professor of State Law Codes (1835–1848)

Redkin began studying law at the University of Moscow in 1826. In 1828, he was sent to Dorpat for two years to complete his studies in law (in particular, Roman law, encyclopaedia of law, history of law and Prussian law), together with history (Russian and general history). This initial period of training in the subject was immediately followed by a four-year study period (1830–1834) in Berlin. Here Redkin attended lectures by Friedrich Savigny (to whom Redkin and other students were officially assigned by the Russian authorities) in Roman law and Prussian law, Eduard Gans (philosophy of law, philosophy of history and contemporary history), Friedrich von Raumer (politics and modern history), and Hegel (logic, and history of philosophy). On his return to Russia, Redkin was named Professor in '*Zakonovedenie*'. In this capacity he taught the 'Fundamental Laws' of the State, and 'Laws on State Service', courses which were ostensibly destined for first and second-year students. For more advanced students, Redkin read a special course in 'philosophy of law and its history', an Hegelian-inspired programme which formed the beginnings of his seven volume work published some fifty years later. In 1842 and 1843 Redkin travelled widely throughout Europe (England, France, Germany, Italy and Spain) in order to familiarize himself with the contemporary state of legal practice and court procedure abroad. In the early 1840s, he launched two major publication series: *Juridical Notes* (1841), and *Library for Education* (1843).

In this period Redkin was very much associated with the first wave of Westernizers – Belinskii, Granovskii and Herzen. He is also noted for being the first to have published an article in the Russian language on Hegel ('An overview of Hegel's logic', *Moskvitianin*, 1841).

In 1848 Redkin was forced to resign from his post, for reasons which remain obscure, but probably because of his 'liberal' views, and the relatively 'free-thinking' way in which he reputedly taught his subject. Thereafter he concentrated on pedagogical problems, and worked as a school inspector. In 1859 he founded, and presided, the St. Petersburg Pedagogical Society. The Society was closed down in 1879 on the orders of the Minister of Education, Tolstoi, on the grounds that Redkin's society had opposed a statute passed by the government concerning the strict ways and means of teaching classical languages in schools.

Pamfil Iurkevich (1827–1874)
Professor of Philosophy (1861), Dean of the Historical-Philological Faculty (1869–1873)

With the chair of philosophy reopened (1861) in the universities after their closure on Nicholas I's instructions, one of the major problems facing the authorities was how to fill the newly available posts, given the obvious dearth of candidates from within the university itself. Iurkevich was among a number of theological academy professors to be invited to take up the charge of teaching philosophy. Although he had originally specialized in German and Greek philosophy, at the university, Iurkevich lectured on a variety of subjects 'traditionally' covered by the discipline – logic, psychology, history of philosophy, and, during his mandate as dean, pedagogy. Additionally, from 1872 to 1874, he gave courses in the philosophy of law. Under his guidance student groups in philosophy translated several works of Western scholarship, one noted example being A. Schwegler's *Geschichte der Philosophie im Umriss* (Moscow, 1864).

Boris Chicherin (1828 – 1904)
Professor of State Law (1861– 1868)

From 1845 to 1849, Chicherin studied law at the University of Moscow, attending Redkin's and Kavelin's courses (history of Russian law codes), together with courses in European and Russian history read by Granovskii and S.M. Solov'ev. In 1853, he presented his Master's dissertation on regional institutions in seventeenth-century Russia, but it was refused by the Dean on the grounds that the portrait he drew of the Russian past was too unfavourable. (The thesis was eventually accepted in 1857.) In this period, Chicherin published a number of articles on combined historical-juridical themes aiming to show how the state in modern Russian had consistently played an all-determining role.

In 1861, Chicherin was offered the position of Extraordinary Professor of State Law by the Academic Council of Moscow University, but collegial conflicts provoked his 'ostentatious resignation' (Walicki) in 1868. During his period as professor he also tutored the Heir Apparent, Nikolai Aleksandrovich in state law. He completed his doctoral dissertation, 'On Popular Representation', in 1866.

Chicherin's disputes with his peers largely stemmed from the legal and political principles that he rigorously defended. A case in point concerns his brief episode as the Mayor of Moscow (1881–1883). His forced resignation from this post was due to a public appeal to encourage local self-government which he included in his speech given on the occasion of Alexander III's coronation.

Once retired from professorial activities, Chicherin dedicated much of the rest of his life writing an impressive number of scholarly works on law and philosophy, as well as on political issues. His publications in law served as the basis of courses taught by several generations of law professors. They include: *History of Political Doctrines*, 5 vols (Moscow, 1869–1902); *A Course of Political Science*, 3 vols (Moscow, 1894–1898); *Philosophy of Law* (Moscow, 1900).

Nikolai Grot (1852–1899)
Professor of Philosophy (1886–1899)

Grot took his first degree at the University of St. Petersburg in 1875, and after a period of study in Germany, began teaching philosophy at the Nezhinskii Historico-Philological Institute (1876). His Master's dissertation at St. Petersburg (1880) dealt with the question of psycho-physiology, and his doctoral research (Nezhin, 1882) was in logic. After a brief period as Professor of Philosophy at Odessa University (1885–1886), Grot took the chair of philosophy at Moscow University where he remained until his death. His teaching here involved reading and commentary of works by Plato and Aristotle, psychology and some history of philosophy. In Moscow, Grot was president of the 'Moscow Psychological Society', and edited the first major philosophical journal in the Russian language, *Questions of Philosophy and Psychology*. In his philosophical trajectory Nikolai Grot passed from an interest in positivism to idealism, a passage which is reflected in some of his main publications, notably *Giordano Bruno and Pantheism* (Odessa, 1885), and *On the Soul in Light of Contemporary Theories of Free Will* (Odessa, 1886).

Veniamin Khvostov (1868–1920)
Privat-Docent in Roman Law (1895–)

Khvostov studied law at Moscow University, where he received both his Master's (1895) and Doctoral (1898) degrees in Roman law. In 1895, he began teaching Roman law at the same university, and from 1917, offered courses at the Courses of Higher Education for Women, the Advanced Law Courses for Women Courses, as well as at the A.L. Shaniavskii University (a popular, 'alternative' university, accepting both men and women, which functioned between 1908 and 1918). His *Outline of the History of Ethical Doctrines* (published 1912) was a course which he originally read at the Courses of Higher Education for Women.

Sergei Trubetskoi (1862–1905)
Professor in Ancient Philosophy (1900–1905)

Having taken his first degree at Moscow University (Faculty of History and Philology), Trubetskoi passed his Master's exam in 1886, and presented his Master's dissertation, 'Metaphysics in Ancient Greece', in

1890. As a *Privat-Docent*, he gave courses in the history of modern philosophy, psychology, and also ran seminars on Aristotle and Plato. After defending his doctoral dissertation in 1900 (on the doctrine of the logos, and its history), Trubetskoi was appointed Professor of Ancient Philosophy. After Grot's death, he also took over the editorship of the journal *Questions of Philosophy and Psychology*.

Publication of lecture courses: *History of Ancient Philosophy* (Moscow, 1906).

Pavel Novgorodtsev (1866–1924)
Professor of Encyclopaedia of Law, and History of the Philosophy of Law (1904–1906)

Having completed his first degree in law at Moscow University (1888), Novgorodtsev was sent to Berlin and Paris, to prepare for a professorship. In 1894, he passed his Master's examination, obtaining the grade of *Privat-Docent*. In 1897, he presented his Master's dissertation (on the Historical School of law), and thereafter began teaching regularly, giving courses in encyclopaedia of law, and the history of the philosophy of law. In 1902, Novgorodtsev was granted the degree of doctorate for his dissertation on Kant and Hegel as philosophers of law. In 1903 he was named Extraordinary Professor, and following year, Full Professor.

Like many of his contemporaries, Novgorodtsev also gave courses in other institutions of further education, notably the Courses of Higher Education for Women, and, from 1906, following his dismissal from the University for political reasons, at the Higher Institute of Commerce. Novgorodtsev was the Institute's director between 1906 and 1918. In 1921, he emigrated to Prague, where, with the support of the Czech government, he set up a 'Russian Juridical Faculty'.

Publication of lecture courses: *A History of the Philosophy of Law* (Moscow, 1897); *Socrates and Plato. Lectures given at the Courses of Higher Education for Women* (Moscow, 1901); *A Synopsis of Lectures in the History of Philosophy of Law* (Moscow, 1908); *Political Ideals in the Ancient and Modern Worlds*, 2 vols (Moscow, 1910–1913); *An Introduction to the Philosophy of Law* (1922).

Evgenii Trubetskoi (1863–1920)
Named Professor of Encyclopaedia of Law, and Philosophy of Law in 1906

Having taken a first degree in law from the University of Moscow (1885), Trubetskoi began his teaching career (1886) at the Iaroslavl Juridical lycée. In 1892 he presented his Master's dissertation to the University of Kiev, and in 1897 obtained his doctoral degree there. Both his dissertations dealt with the question of theocracy in early and medieval Western Christianity.

First named Professor of Law at Kiev University, Trubetskoi transferred to Moscow after Novgorodtsev's dismissal.

Publication of lecture courses: *A History of the Philosophy of Law: Ancient and Modern* (Kiev, 1899); *Synopsis of Courses in the Encyclopaedia of Law* (published in several revised editions, Moscow 1913-1917).

Matvei Rubinshtein (1878–1953)
Professor of Philosophy at Moscow University (1918), and the first Rector of the 'East-Siberian University' (Irkutsk) from 1918 to 1920

In 1905, Rubinshtein completed his studies in philosophy at the University of Freiburg (Germany). In 1912, having passed his Master's exam, he was named *Privat-Docent* at the University of Moscow, and, only some six years later, Professor, teaching philosophy and psychology. Rubinshtein also lectured at the Courses of Higher Education for Women, and at Moscow's Shaniavskii University. During the 1920s and 1930s, he taught in various institutions for further education in Moscow. In 1941, he was named head of department at the Krasnoiarsk Pedagogical Institute, and, in 1943, finally obtained the post of Professor of Psychology at the Moscow State Pedagogical Institute.

Viacheslav Volgin (1879–1962)
Named Professor at Moscow University in 1919

In 1908, Volgin completed his first degree (majoring in history) at the Historical-Philological Faculty of Moscow University. Named Professor in the immediate aftermath of the Revolution, he taught the history of socio-political systems, concentrating in particular on the ancient world. In this period he also took an active part in organizing the 'Socialist' (later renamed 'Communist') Academy, as well as its Institute of History. Between 1921 and 1925, Volgin occupied the post of Rector of the University. Nominated Academician in 1930, he served as the secretary of the Academy of Sciences from 1930 to 1935, and was its Vice-President from 1942 to 1953.

Mikhail Dynnik (1896–1971)
Researcher, Professor of the History of Philosophy

Dynnik completed his first degree in philosophy at the University of Kiev in 1919. Thereafter he taught philosophy in various institutions of further education, and from 1930 to 1950 lectured on ancient philosophy at Moscow State University and the 'elitist' Moscow Institute for History, Philosophy, and Literature (MIFLI).

Much of Dynnik's career was dedicated to research, particularly in the history of ancient philosophy. In 1958, he was elected to the Academy of Science as a corresponding member. He was also very much involved in the organizational side of scientific production, and, in this capacity, occupied a number of important posts – as 'head of department' for the History of Philosophy at the Academy of Social Sciences (affiliated to the Communist Party Central Committee), and as a researcher in the Institute of Philosophy (of the Soviet Academy of Sciences) in the sector of the History of West European and American philosophy. In 1968 he was named director of the sector.

Textbook publications include: *An Outline of the History of Philosophy in Classical Greece* (Moscow, 1936). Edited volumes include *Materialists in Ancient Greece. Translated Fragments from Heraclitus, Democritus, Epicurus* (Moscow, 1955).

Moscow Theological Academy

Pavel Florenskii (1882–1937)
Extraordinary Professor in the History of Philosophy, and Lecturer in Theology (1914–1919)

In 1900, Florenskii enrolled at the Faculty of Physics and Mathematics of Moscow University, where he passed his first degree. During his studies he also took part in the Student Historical-Philological Society, founded at the initiative of Sergei Trubetskoi, and under whose guidance Florenskii drafted an essay entitled 'The Idea of God in Plato's Republic'. In 1904, Florenskii registered at the Moscow Theological Academy, and in 1908 was named *Docent* to the chair of History of Philosophy. In 1911, he was ordained priest.

Florenskii's teaching career at the Academy spanned roughly a decade (1908–1919), first as a *Docent,* then as Professor, his main courses being in the history of ancient philosophy, philosophy of culture and theology. In 1912 he took up the editorship of the Academy's journal (*Bogoslovskii Vestnik*), a post which he occupied until 1917.

With the closure of the Academy in 1918 by the Bolshevik government Florenskii's teaching 'career' became progressively restricted. His publications in the 1920s bore on subjects as far afield as as electro-technology and the fine arts. Granted, the fact that he engaged in this type of literature was largely a consequence of the ideological pressures being put on him. But it also clearly reflected the wide scope of his talents which he could draw on in an atmosphere where 'idealist' philosophy was looked upon with increasing suspicion. Arrested and exiled in 1933, Florenskii was executed in 1937.

Publication of Courses: *The Limits of Gnoseology* (Moscow, 1913); *The Meaning of Idealism* (Sergiev Posad, 1915), a course on the history of

Platonism read to first-year students at the Academy; *First Steps in Philosophy* (Sergiev Posad, 1917).

University of St. Petersburg

Petr Redkin (1808–1891)
Ordinary Professor in Encyclopaedia of Law (1863–1878), University Rector (1873–1876), Member of the State Council (1882)

Redkin's biographers generally note that, in the 1860s Redkin shifted from an early enthusiasm for Hegel towards positivism. However, the degree to which this is reflected in his main seven volume publication, is, actually, fairly marginal. According to Redkin's successor to the chair of Encyclopaedia of Law, Nikolai Korkunov, Redkin was never able to abandon fully his Hegelian training.

Vladimir Solov'ev (1853–1900)
Privat-Docent (1880–1882) in Philosophy

In 1869, Solov'ev enrolled at the Faculty of Mathematics and Physics of Moscow University in order to study natural science. In his third year he transferred to the Faculty of History and Philology. At the same time (1873–1874), he also attended lectures in philosophy as an unregistered student at the Moscow Theological Academy. In 1874 he presented his Master's dissertation, 'The Crisis of Western Philosophy'. In 1875, he was engaged to teach the history of modern (German) philosophy at the university, but spent much of 1875 and 1876 travelling abroad (England, France, Italy and Egypt). In 1877, he was named *State-Docent* to the Chair of Philosophy, and during the next three years prepared two major works, *The Philosophical Principles of Integral Knowledge* and *A Critique of Abstract Principles*. The latter work was presented as a doctoral dissertation at the University of St. Petersburg in 1880. During the next two years Solov'ev lectured on metaphysics and philosophy of history. He also read courses in the history of ancient philosophy at the St. Petersburg Courses of Higher Education for Women. Solov'ev ultimately abandoned a university career (for one primarily as a *publitsist* and poet) as an indirect consequence of the stand he had taken against the execution of Tsar Alexander II's assassins in 1881.

Faddei Zelinskii (1859–1944)
Ordinary Professor in Classical Philology (1890–1922)

Zelinskii took his first degrees (1876–1880) in ancient history and classical philology at the University of Leipzig where his main tutor was Otto

Ribbeck. In 1880, he also defended, in Leipzig, his first doctoral dissertation (on the history of the second Punic wars). In 1884, after a period of further study in Munich and Vienna (where he studied Roman epigraphy), and travels in Greece and Italy, he began teaching, as a *Privat-Docent*, at the University of St. Petersburg. In 1886, he presented a second doctoral dissertation to the University of Dorpat (on late Attic comedy). Named Extraordinary Professor at the University of St. Petersburg in 1887, he was upgraded to Full Professor in 1890. He occupied this position uninterruptedly until 1922, combining his scholarly work (particularly on Cicero) with popular lectures and articles about the ancient world, but also about Russia's educational system, destined for a wider audience. In 1922 Zelinskii emigrated to Poland (he was, in fact, of Polish origin) where he took the Chair of Classical Philology at the University of Warsaw. He remained in this post until 1939.

Sergei Zhebelev (1867–1941)
Professor of Classical Philology (1904–), Academician (1927)

Having taken his first degree in classical philology at the University of St. Petersburg, Zhebelev began teaching there as a *Privat-Docent* (1899). Both his Master's dissertation ('On the History of Athens', 1898) and his Doctoral research (*'Akhaika'*, 1903) reflected his combined interest in philology and socio-political history. Other examples of this double undertaking include his translation of Aristotle's *Politeia*, which he published together with a detailed account of political thought in Greece. Besides teaching at the university, Zhebelev also lectured on the history of ancient Greek art at the Academy of Fine Arts, and was responsible for the section on classical philology in the government run *Journal of the Ministry of Education*.

After the Revolution, Zhebelev undertook a new translation of the Plato dialogues, together with Ernst Radlov and Lev Karsavin, but only very few of the prepared fifteen were ever actually published. In the Soviet period, Zhebelev gave the greater part of his attention to archaeological work in the Black Sea area.

St. Petersburg Theological Academy

Vasilii Karpov (1798–1867)
Professor of Philosophy (1835–1867)

After his schooling (1814–1821) at the Voronezh Seminary, Karpov was hired at the Kiev Seminary to teach ancient Greek and German (1821–1825). In 1829, he obtained a 'baccalaureate' in French from the Theological Academy, and in 1832 a second 'baccalaureate' in philosophy.

In 1833, he transferred to the Theological Academy in St. Petersburg, where, two years later, he was named Professor of Philosophy. Karpov's courses covered a wide range, including mathematics, physics, logic, psychology, and philosophy. In the 1840s, he began working on the translation of Plato's dialogues and writing commentaries.

Between 1834 and 1854, Karpov was responsible for the Academy library, and also served as an inspector of theological institutions in the St. Petersburg region. Among his other 'extra-curricular' charges, Karpov was a member of the censorship committee in religious affairs (1855–1857), and a state councillor (1859).

Several of Karpov's publications were originally courses read in the Academy. These include an *Introduction to Philosophy* (1840), a *Systematic Outline of Logic* (1856), *On Self-Knowledge* (1860), *On Moral Principles* (1867) and *An Introductory Lecture in Psychology* (1868).

University of Kiev

Orest Novitskii (1806–1884)
Professor of Philosophy (1837), several times Dean of the Faculty (1835–1850)

Having completed his first degree at the Kiev Theological Academy (1831), Novitskii began his career teaching philosophy (first, at the Poltavsk Seminary, then at the Academy in Kiev itself). In 1835, he also began lecturing, as Extraordinary Professor, in the newly founded university (1834), shortly thereafter to become its first Full Professor in philosophy. During the 1830s and 1840s, Novitskii taught a wide variety of subjects including logic, 'experimental psychology', moral philosophy and history of philosophy (the latter based to a large extent on works by Victor Cousin, Heinrich Ritter, F. Fischer, Ernst Reinhold, among others). After a second clampdown on the university in 1848, and the closure of departments of philosophy throughout the Empire, Novitskii worked as a censor. His major work on the history of Greek religions and philosophy, which he published in the 1860s, grew out of lectures given two decades earlier in which he sought to bring out the reciprocal relation between philosophy and theology in ancient European, but also Indian and Chinese cultures.

Publication of textbooks include one in psychology (1840), and a second in logic (1844) which ran into several editions.

Silvestr Gogotskii (1813–1889)
Professor of Philosophy at the Kiev Theological Academy (1848),
Professor of Philosophy and Classical Philology at Kiev University (1850),
Dean of the Faculty (1862–1863)

Having completed his early schooling as a seminarist at the Kiev Theological Academy (attending, among others, Karpov's lectures), Gogotskii began teaching Polish and German. In 1841, his interests turned to philosophy and pedagogy. He received his first degree in this subject at the University in 1845 and his Master's degree there in 1848. As *Privat-Docent*, Gogotskii was attached to the Chair of Modern Philosophy until its suspension on Nicholas I's orders later the same year. In 1850, he was promoted to the post of Full Professor, and, for the most part taught didactics and pedagogy, as well as Latin. During the academic year 1861–1862, Gogotskii was abroad (Berlin, Dresden, Cracow and Lemburg), and after a brief mandate as Dean, gave up teaching altogether in order to 'concentrate' (as contemporary accounts put it) on various research projects. His scientific output in this period includes a philosophical lexicon, a history of philosophy, monographs on Kant and Hegel, and studies in pedagogy. He resumed teaching in 1867.

Lectures published include *17th and 18th Century Philosophy Compared with 19th Century Philosophy, and the Relation of Each to Education.*

Aleksei Kozlov (1831–1901)
Professor of History of Philosophy (1884)

In 1857, Kozlov completed his first degree in political economy at Moscow University. Thereafter he worked as a teacher of Russian language in various schools in the Moscow area, publishing articles on financial and economic issues. At that time, however, his main interests were political, and, in 1866, he was expelled from Moscow for his active involvement with the populist movement. It was only in this period, in exile, that Kozlov really began studying philosophy seriously. First, he worked on positivist theories, but quickly moved on to authors such as Schopenhauer and Eduard von Hartmann, a choice which reflected Kozlov's growing disillusionment with populism and its attendant materialist worldview. In 1876, Karpov obtained the grade of *Privat-Docent* in philosophy at the University of Kiev, and shortly thereafter began teaching logic, together with some history of philosophy. Beginning in 1878, he also lectured on psychology at the Kiev Courses of Higher Education for Women, and offered a course in pedagogy at the Institute for Women of Noble Birth (1879–1880). In 1880, he obtained his Master's degree (for his 'Philosophical Studies', published in two volumes, the second of which concerned the philosophy of Plato), and in 1884 was made Full Professor after defending a doctoral dissertation (on the genesis of Kant's theory of time and space). In his courses in the history of philosophy, the authors who attracted his attention most included Plato, Giordano Bruno, Kant and Schopenhauer.

Karpov retired in 1887 because of poor health. He settled in St. Petersburg where he drafted his philosophical autobiography, 'Conversations with the Socrates of St. Petersburg', *In My Own Words* (1888–1898).

Vasilii Modestov (1839–1907)
Professor of Classical Philology (1869–1877)

Modestov completed his first degree in classics at St. Petersburg University, and thereafter worked in a gymnasium teaching Latin and ancient history. After a study period in Bonn (1862–1864), he took a Master's degree (with a dissertation on Tacitus) at St. Petersburg University, and was named *Privat-Docent* for Latin at the Novorossiiskii University (Odessa). From 1867 to 1869, he taught at Kazan University, before being named Professor of Latin at Kiev University. From 1871 to 1876, he also lectured at the Theological Academy.

In 1878, Modestov transferred to St. Petersburg where he held a professorship at the theological academy for a mere two years, being forced to quit teaching on the grounds of having published seditious articles against the government policy in education. He resumed an academic post some years later, first teaching as *Privat-Docent* at St. Petersburg University (from 1886), and as Full Professor at the Novorossiiskii University (1889–1893). Throughout, he managed to combine a double role as a scholar and public figure, tirelessly campaigning for a more flexible system of education. One of his main scientific works, *An Introduction to Roman History*, 2 vols (1902–1909), combined linguistic and archaeological findings.

Aleksei Giliarov (1856–1938)
Professor of Philosophy (1891–)

In 1876, Giliarov completed his first degree in classical philology and philosophy at Moscow University. In 1885, he obtained the post of *Privat-Docent*, but in 1887 transferred to Kiev, where, the following year, he presented his Master's dissertation on the theme of the Sophists in light of their political and cultural role in ancient Greece. During this period Giliarov also studied abroad (Berlin, Munich, Paris and London). A year after his nomination to the post of Professor at Kiev in 1891 (replacing Kozlov), he completed his doctoral dissertation, once again on the Sophists, and the role of Plato as an 'historical witness'. As Professor, Giliarov taught the history of ancient philosophy primarily, but also lectured on medieval and modern philosophy. His seminars concentrated, in the main, on close readings of works by Aristotle and Plato.

After the Revolution, Giliarov was elected to the sector of socio-economic questions in the All-Ukrainian Academy of Science (1922). In this period he produced a two-volume 'history of philosophy from the perspective of historical materialism'. A seminar, which he ran under the auspices of the department, was attended by, among others, Dynnik and Asmus, both future historians of philosophy with a special interest in ancient Greek philosophy.

Publications based on lectures and textbooks intended for teaching purposes include: *An Introduction to Philosophy. Lectures read at the Women's Higher Courses 1906–1907* (Kiev, 1907); *A Handbook of Philosophy* (Kiev, 1916).

Kiev Theological Academy

Pamfil Iurkevich (1827–1874)
Professor of Philosophy (1861)

Having studied at the Academy (1847–1851), Iurkevich obtained his Master's degree there in 1852. Beginning in 1854 he served as adjunct to the Academy Inspector, but, in 1856, asked for permission to give up this function in order to concentrate entirely on his research and teaching. From 1857 he taught philosophy (psychology, logic, metaphysics and history of philosophy), and the German language. Named Extraordinary Professor of Philosophy in 1858, he was upgraded to Full Professor in 1861 by a decision of the Holy Synod which had noted his remarkable qualities as a teacher. In the same year, however, Iurkevich transferred to the University of Moscow to teach a broad programme in philosophy (see above).

Other

Ivan Kireevskii (1806–1856)

Like many sons of the gentry, Kireevskii was educated at home, taking lessons from a number of Moscow University professors in a variety of subjects including Latin, Greek and English. In 1824, he qualified as a documentalist and translator in the Moscow State Archives for Foreign Affairs, but his main preoccupation here was his involvement in the famous 'Society of Wisdom Lovers', which he formed with his colleagues. In 1830, Kireevskii travelled abroad to 'complete his education'. In the various university towns he visited (Berlin, Dresden, Munich, principally), he attended lectures given by some of the most renowned scholars of the day – Heinrich Ritter, Gans, Schleiermacher, Savigny, Hegel and Schelling. On his return to Moscow he founded the journal, *The European*, for which he was quickly censored by Tsar Nicholas I.

Vladislav Buzeskul (1858–1931)
Professor of History at Kharkov University (1890–1914) and Petrograd University (1914–1920)

Buzeskul completed his first degree in history at Kharkov University in 1880. He began teaching ancient history there as *Privat-Docent* in 1885. In 1889, he presented his Master's dissertation (a study of Pericles), and, in 1895, his doctoral thesis on the theme of Aristotle's *Politeia* as a source for the study of the history of the Athenian state. In 1890, at the age of 32, he was named Professor, and shortly thereafter was also made Dean of the Faculty. Prior to the revolution, Buzeskul published a number of monographs on the history of ancient Greece, intended for teaching purposes. These include: *An Introduction to the History of Greece* (in three editions Kharkov, 1903, 1904, Pgd., 1915); *A History of Athenian Democracy* (SPb., 1909). In 1910, Buzeskul published a shorter, revised version of his 'Introduction', originally a series of lectures given at the Kharkov 'Courses of Higher Education for Women'. He was also the author of chapters on medieval and modern history in a major four-volume 'Lectures in General History'.

After the Revolution, Buzeskul was elected to the Academy of Sciences (1922) and in 1925 to the Ukrainian Academy of Sciences. At the end of his life, he published a two-volume 'directory' of Russian historians.

Pavel Miliukov (1859–1943)
Historian, founding member of the Liberal Kadet movement

Miliukov took his first degree in Russian history at Moscow University in 1882. Kept on by the then head of department, Vasilii Kliuchevskii, to prepare for a professorship, he spent the following years (1886–1895) carrying out research and teaching. Besides his courses at the university, Miliukov also taught in a gymnasium for women, and at the Higher Women's Pedagogical Courses. In 1892 he obtained his Master's degree (on state administration during the reign of Peter the Great). His lectures in Russian history, which he read at the university as *Privat-Docent* were published in lithograph form in 1895. Among his other 'pedagogical' activities at this time was his presidency (1894) of the Moscow-based commission set up to deal with the problem of illiteracy, and a Summer School in England (1894). However, already, during this period, Miliukov was starting out on his political career. This soon led to his arrest and exile to Riazan. It was here that he began working on his famous three-volume cultural history of Russia (1896–1903). During the next decade, Miliukov travelled widely, invited to give lectures in history in different countries across the world. Among these were talks given at the Institute for Further Education, Sophia, in 1897, a lecture series in the United States on 'Russia and her crisis' in 1903, and a second series in England in the winter of the same year. Between 1906 and 1917, Miliukov invested the major part of his energies in political activities, serving as a Deputy in the third and fourth State Dumas, and, briefly, as Minister of Foreign Affairs in the Provisional Government (March–April, 1917). Miliukov emigrated in 1920.

Robert Vipper (1859–1954)
Historian, with a special interest in methodology, Professor of Moscow University (1899–1922), and again in 1941

Vipper took his first degree in history at Moscow University (1876–1880). After a period of study in Switzerland, he presented a dissertation on Calvinism in Geneva, and the relation between Church and State (1894) which was honoured with the degree of Doctor. Thereafter (1894–1897), he taught general history at the Novorossiiskii University (Odessa), and, in 1897, took up the post of *Privat-Docent* at the University of Moscow. He was named Professor at the same university two years later. Prior to the Revolution, Vipper published two lecture courses on the socio-political aspects of ancient Greece: *Lectures on the History of Greece* (Moscow, 1905); *A History of Greece in the Classical Period IX–IV BC* (Moscow, 1916).

In 1922, Vipper emigrated to Latvia. He pursued his career as Professor of History at the University of Latvia (Riga) until 1940. In 1941, he was invited to take up the post of Professor at Moscow State University. Vipper was named Academician in 1943.

Aleksander Kizevetter (1866–1933)
Historian and *Publitsist*

Having taken his first degree in history at Moscow University (1888), Kizevetter was kept on to prepare for an eventual professorship. Named *Privat-Docent* in 1900, he began teaching history at Moscow's Lazarevskii Institute of Oriental Languages, and at the L.F. Rzhevskaia Gymnasium. In 1903, he completed his Master's dissertation (on the *obshchina* in eighteenth-century Russia), and in 1909, his Doctoral dissertation (on the Russian town during the reign of Catherine the Great). Prior to the Revolution, Kizevetter published numerous articles on history and current events in the journal *Russian Thought*.

Aleksei Losev (1893–1988)
Professor of Classical Philology at Nizhne-Novgorod University in 1919, Professor of Classical Philology at the Moscow State Pedagogical Institute in 1944

In 1915, Losev completed his first degrees in classical philology and philosophy at Moscow University. After a very short-lived professorship in the provinces, he took up various teaching posts in Moscow (Professor at the Moscow Conservatory, and head of the department of aesthetics at the State Academy for the Arts /GAkHN/). Arrested in 1930 on suspicion of defending philosophical idealism, Losev spent ten years in forced labour camps, where his health seriously deteriorated. Finally released after the personal intervention of the wives of Gorky and Lenin, he was allowed to return to Moscow, and to teach (although virtually blind) in provincial institutes for further education. From 1942 to 1944, he was granted permission to teach at the Moscow State University, but was soon after dismissed, once again on grounds of his suspected philosophical 'idealism'. Two years later, he received the post of Professor in Moscow's Pedagogical Institute, where he worked alongside figures such as the aforementioned Rubinshtein.

Select Bibliography

Main Bibliographies Consulted

Drozdov, N. (1878), *Literatura po klassicheskoi filologii v Rossii*, Kiev.
Jashchenko, A. (1915), *Russkaia bibliografiia po istorii drevnei filosofii*, Iurev.
Voronkov, A.I. (1961), *Drevnaia Gretsiia i Drevnii Rim. Bibliograficheskii ukazatel' izdanii vyshedshikh v SSSR (1895-1959 gg)*, Moscow.
(1980) *Sovetskaia nauka ob antichykh avtorakh (1960-1975). Izdanie i issledovanie*, Moscow.
Zimbrich, Ulriche (1994), *Bibliographie zu Platos Staat. Die Rezeption der Politeia im deutschsprachigen Raum von 1800-1970*, Frankfurt.

Russian Plato Scholarship

Translations

Indicated below is the frequency with which certain individual dialogues were translated and re-edited. Where possible, the name of the translator (and edition) is given in brackets. Also listed are anthologies of selected excerpts. I have not included the 'Complete Works' editions, details for which are given in Chapter One of the present study.

Without claiming to be an exhaustive list, the general picture to emerge is one of a preference, in the nineteenth century, for those dialogues in which Plato's ethical views are expounded, with, by contrast, little or no tendency suggesting itself in the Soviet period. Granted, the reasons for translating dialogues such as *Theaetetus* and *Timaeus* may be understood against the background of contemporary ideology, but the quantity of anthologies, often made up of existing, pre-Revolutionary translations, suggests, on the contrary, that ideological designs on science were never as complete as some may have wished.

Apology	1861, 1870, 1875 (A. Ellinskii), 1880, 1884 (K. Danil'chenko, 1892 – 2nd edn), 1890 (Postynyi), 1893 (A. Iakimakh), 1897 (4th ed. of A.F. Pospishil's trans.), 1898 (D. Lebedev), 1899, 1904, 1912, 1913 (S.I. Rumer), 1915.
Crito	1832, 1870, 1876, 1879, 1884, 1885 (twice: O. Petruchenko, Moscow; V. Paskhalov, Kiev, 1890 – 2nd edn., 1898 – 3rd edn., 1903 – 4th edn.) 1895, 1896 (Pospishel'), 1898 (Lebedev), 1899, 1900 (S.V. Myshetskii), 1901 (Shlosberg), 1910 (E.V. Kisel'nikova), 1913.
Euthyphron	1888 (K. Gil'bershtadt), 1893 (A. Iakimakh).
Laches	1884, 1887 (A.F. Pospishil'), 1886 (B.M. Krauze), 1890, 1891 (N. Vinogradov), 1894, 1900.
Protagoras	1890 (twice: A. Dobiash; E.D.).
Gorgias	1857 (Karpov).
Meno	1868 (Skvortsov), 1879 (Riabets).
Euthydemus	1872, 1878 (Skvortsov).
Hippias I	1859 (Karpov).
Hippias II	1858 (Karpov).
Symposium	1893 (Nechaev, 1904²), 1905 (A. Press, 1910 – 2nd edn.), 1908 (Gorodetski, Moscow, 1910 – 2nd edn.), 1910 (St. Petersburg), 1935, 1939, 1940, 1947.
Phaedo	1804, 1861 (Klevanov), 1874 (Lebedev, 1896 – 2nd edn.), 1887 (V. Kel'tuial), 1892 (N. Vinogradov), 1893, 1895, 1898, 1899, 1900.
Republic	1805, 1916 (K. Kuznetsov).
Phaedrus	1858 (Karpov), 1895, 1904 (N. Murashov).
Theaetetus	1867 (Skvortsov), 1891 (A. Dobiash), 1936 (V. Serezhnikov).
Parmenides	1873 (F.A. Zlatoustovskii).
Sophist	1905, 1906, 1907 (S. A. Anan'in).
Philebus	1936 (Dovatur).
Timaeus	1883 (G. Malevanskii), 1935 (V. Serezhnikov).
Critias	1883 (G. Malevanskii).
Laws	1827 (V. Obolenskii), 1898–1899 (G. Ianchevetskii).
Theages	1777 (Novikov), 1857 (M. Kastorskii).
Alcibiades I	1857 (Karpov).
(1861)	Klevanov, A. (trans. and ed.), *Filosofskie besedy Platona v russkom perevode. Evtifron, Apologia Sokrata, Kriton, Fedon* (with a short account of Plato's life), Moscow.
(1895)	Kumskoi, P.A., *Drevnaia istoriia v otryvkakh iz istochnikov: Apology, Phaedo, Crito*, Tbilisi.
(1896)	Leper, R.Kh., *Otryvki iz grecheskikh pisatelei: Phaedo*, SPb.
(1900)	*Scythica et Caucasia*, vol.1: *Phaedo, Laches, Euthydemus, Gorgias, Menexenus, Laws*, SPb.
(1903)	Glebovskii, B., *Drevnie pedagogicheskie pisateli: Meno, Laws*, SPb.

(1916)   Melikova, S.V. and Zhebelev, S.A., *Pedagogicheskie vozzreniia Platona i Aristotelia* [*Republic*: III, VIII; *Laws*: VII], Pgd.
(1921)   *Drevnii mir v pamiatnikakh ego pis'mennosti*, vol.2: *Apology, Protagoras, Republic* [II, III, V, VI], Moscow.
(1928)   Volgin, V.P., *Predshestvenniki sovremennogo sotsializma v otryvkakh iz proizvedenii: Republic* [II, III, IV, V], M.-L.
(1933)   *Antichnyi sposob proizvodstva v istochnikakh: Gorgias, Protagoras, Republic* [I, II, IV, V, VIII, IX], *Laws* [II, IV, VI, VIII] (Egunov), Leningrad.
(1935)   Suslin, M.I. (ed.), *Antichnie Filosofy: Symposium, Republic, Theaetetus, Timaeus*, Moscow.
(1936)   *Antichnie teorii iazyka i stilia: Cratylus, Sophist, Philebus* (Dovatur), Leningrad.
(1938)   *Antichnie mysliteli ob iskusstve: Ion, Hippius I, Philebus, Republic* [III, X], *Laws*, Moscow.
(1939)   *Khrestomatia po antichnoi literature*, vol.1: *Symposium*, Moscow.
(1939)   *Grecheskaia literatura v izbrannykh perevodakh: Symposium, Phaedrus* (Zhebelev), Moscow.
(1940)   Aleksandrov, G. (ed.), *Antichnaia Filosofiia. Fragmenty i svidetel'stva: Symposium, Theaetetus, Phaedo* (Karpov), Moscow.
(1940)   *Arkhitektura antichnogo mira: Gorgias, Republic, Laws, Critias, Theaetetus* (Solov'ev, Karpov), Moscow.

Commentaries

(NB. In order to illustrate the development of Plato scholarship, this section and the following section, 'Russian Science of Antiquity' are arranged chronologically.)

(1841-1842) Karpov, V., 'O socheneniakh Platona'; *Protagoras, Euthydemus, Laches, Charmides, Hippius Minor, Euthyphron, Apology, Crito, Phaedo, Meno, Gorgias, Alcibiades I, Alcibiades II*, in *Sochineniia Platona perevedennye s grecheskogo professorom Karpovym*, 2 vols, SPb. A second revised edition in 6 volumes (SPb., 1863-1879) contained commentaries to all the dialogues, except *Laws* and *Letters*.
(1847)   Tkhorzhevskii, K., *De Politia, Timaeo, Critia, ultimo Platonico tenione, librorum de legibus praecipua ratione habita*, Kazan.
(1850)   Basistov, P.E., 'Ob istoricheskom znachenii Platonova *Simposiona*', *Otechestvennye Zapiski*, 9, pt. 2, pp. 53-63.
(1854)   Menshikov, A., 'Fileb, dialog Platona', *Propilei*, vol.1, pp. 311-349, Moscow.
(1866)   Shcheglov, D.F., 'Istoriko-Ekonomicheskie Ocherki. Gosudarstvo Platona', *Otechestvennye zapiski*, kn.1 (June), pp. 490-511.
(1866)   Skvortsov, N., '*Protagor, dialog Platona*', *ZhMNP*, 9, pt.3, pp. 330-366.
(1868)   Skvortsov, N., *Menon, dialog Platona* (Greek text and commentary), Moscow.
(1871)   Skvortsov, N., *Platon o znanii v bor'be s sensualizmom i rassudochnym empirizmom. Analiz dialoga Feetet*, Moscow.

(1872) Zakharbekov and Gaichman, *Evtifron. Dialog Platona s primech. i slovarem*, Moscow.
(1874) Lebedev, D., 'Platon o dushe. Analiz dialoga *Fedon*', *Zapiski Novorossiiskogo universiteta*, vol.14, pp. 27-274.
(1878) Skvortsov, N., *Evtidem, dialog Platona* (Greek text with commentary), Moscow.
(1879) Riabets, F., *Dialog Platona 'Menon'. Otnoshenie etogo dialoga k 'Protagoru' i podlinost' ego*, Odessa.
(1880) (1880) Pospishil', A.O., *Izbrannye sochinenia Platona. Lakhet* (Greek text with commentary and introduction), Kiev (1887 – 2nd edn.).
(1883) Malevanskii, G.B., *Platon. Dialogi. Timei, ili o priropde veshei, i Kritii* (trans. and comm.), Kiev.
(1884) Pospishil', A.O., *Izbrannye sochinenia Platona. Apologia Sokrata, Kriton* (Greek text with comm. and intro. on Greek philosophy), Kiev (1890 – 2nd edn., 1891 – 3rd edn.).
(1885) Krauze, Vl., *Lakhet, dialog o muzhestve* (Greek text with intro., comm., and lexicon), Kazan.
(1886) Nikitin, P.B., 'Zametki k tekstam grecheskikh pisatelei', *ZhMNP*, no. 2.
(1889-1891) Redkin, P., *Ion, Hippius Major, Hippius Minor, Alcibiades I, Laches, Protagoras, Meno, Apology, Crito, Georgias, Politicus, Republic*, and *Laws*, in *Letsii po istorii filosofii prava v sviazi s istorii filosofii voobshchee*, vols. 3-5, SPb.
(1890) Solonikio, A., 'Analiz dialoga Platona *Kharmid*', *Gimnazia*, 11, pp.8-15.
(1890) Zhitetskii, P.I., 'Dialog Platona *Kratil* (analiz)', *ZhMNP*, 12, pp.307-318.
(1896) Pospishel', A., *Kriton*, vol.2, SPb. (2nd edn.).
(1897) Georgievskii, L. and Manshtein, S. (eds), *Illiustrirovannoe sobranie grecheskihkh i rimskikh klassikov s ob'iasnitel'nymi primechaniiami* (4th edn.; 1912 – 5th edn.).
(1899) Solov'ev, V.S.,*Theages, Alcibiades I, Alcibiades II, Ion, Laches, Charmides*; 'O pervom otdele platonovykh tvorenii', in *Tvorenie Platona*, vol.1, Moscow.
(1899) Solov'ev, V.S., 'Iz zametok o dialogakh Platona' (on *Laches*), *VFP*, 47, pp. 146-159.
(1900) Solov'ev, V.S., 'Ob avtore dialoga Protagora', *VFP*, 53, pp. 357-380.
(1901) Pospishil', A.O., *Kriticheskie zamechaniia k tekstu Platonovoi Apologii Sokrata*, Kiev.
(1901) Shlosberg, A. and Knauf, A., *Crito*, Riga.
(1901) Trubetskoi, S.N., 'Protagor Platona v sviazi s razvitiem ego nrastvennogo ucheniia', *VFP*, kn.58, pp. 207-228.
(1903) Solov'ev, V.S., *Hippias Major, Protagoras*, in *Tvorenie Platona*, vol.2, Moscow.
(1903) Trubetskoi, S.N., *Protagoras, Euthydemus, Apology, Crito, Euthyphron*, in *Tvorenie Platona*, vol.2, Moscow.
(1904) Murashov, N., *Phaedrus*, Moscow.

(1912)   Narbekov, I.D., 'Idealy vospitaniia i obrazovaniia u drevnikh grekov po sochineniiam filosofa Platona, Politik ili Gosudarstvo, i Zakony', *Pravoslavnyi Sobesednik*, 7-8, pp. 130-163.
(1913)   Iakovenko, B. (foreword), *Apology* and *Crito*, Moscow.
(1915)   Bokobnev, P., 'Filosofskie ucheniia Platona v dialoge *Fedon*', *Germes*, xx, pp. 492-504.
(1915)   Pospishel', A.O., *Apologia Sokrata*, 2 vols., SPb. (6th edn.).
(1916)   Kuznetsov, K.A., Platon. *Vvedenie v analiz 'Gosudarstvo' i 'Zakonov'*, Odessa.
(1918-1919) Rozhdestvenskii, A., 'Polozhenie tret'ego sosloviia v Gosudarstva Platona', in *Sbornik Iaroslavskogo Gosudarstvennogo Universiteta*, vyp.1, pp. 35-59.
(1926)   Egunov, E., 'Zamechaniia k pervoi knige Zakonov', in *Sbornik v chest' S.A. Zhebeleva*, Moscow, pp. 253-259.
(1928)   Volgin, V.P., *Predshchestvenniki sovremenogo sotsializma v otryvkakh iz ikh proizvedenii*, M.-L.
(1936)   Serezhnikov, V., *Theaetetus*, Moscow.
(1938)   Mishulin, A.V., 'Utopicheskii Plan Agrarnoi Magnezii (po 'Zakonam' Platona)', in *Vestnik Drevnei Istorii*, 3, pp. 92-116.

Monographs and Articles on Plato's Philosophy

(1855)   Tkhorzhevskii, K., 'Izsledovanie o kosmicheskoi sisteme Platona', in *Uchenie zapiski Kazanskogo universiteta*, III, 3, pp. 123-172.
(1859)   Iurkevich, P.D., 'Ideia', in *P. D. Iurkevich. Filosofskie Proizvedeniia*, Pravda, Moscow (1990), pp. 9-68.
(1861)   Pisarev, D.I., 'Idealizma Platona. Obozrenie filosofskoi deiatel'nosti Sokrata i Platona, po Tselleru; sostavil Klevanov', *Sochineniia v shesti tomakh*, t.1, SPb. (1894), pp. 257-280.
(1864)   Karpov, V., 'Sochineniia Platona, perevedennye s grecheskogo i ob'iasnennye professorom Karpovym', *Strannik*, t.2, 6, pt. 3, pp. 73-114.
(1866)   Iurkevich, P., 'Razum po ucheniiu Platona i opyt po ucheniiu Kanta', in *P. D. Iurkevich: Filosofskie Proizvedeniia*, Pravda, Moscow (1990), pp. 466-526.
(1867)   Linitskii, P.I., 'Obshchii vzgliad na filosofiiu Platona', *TKDA*, 10, pp.52-88.
(1868)   Linitskii, P.I., 'Platon-predstavitel' idealizma v drevnei filosofii', *TKDA*, 7 and 9, pp. 48-108, pp. 419-467.
(1872)   Gogotskii, S.S., 'Platon' in *Filosofskii Leksikon*, vol.IV, pt.1, Kiev.
(1874)   Platonov, *O Platonickeskoi troichnosti Bozhestva pered svetom khristianskogo i Bogootkrovennogo ucheniia o Presviatoi Troitse* (no place of publication given).
(1876)   Linitskii, P.I., *Uchenie Platona o bozhestve*, Kiev.
(1878)   Riabets, F., *Iskusstva muz i gimnastika, kak vospitatel'nye sredstva po Platonu*, Kishinev.
(1880)   Kozlov, A.A., *Metod i napravleni filosofii Platona*, Kiev.
(1882)   Orlov, M.A., *Vopros o sud'be dushi po smerti v filosofskoi sisteme Platona*, Odessa.

(1883) Malevanskii, G.V., 'Muzykal'naia i astronomicheskaia sistema Platona v sviazi s drugimi sistemami drevnosti', *TKDA*, 2, pp. 278-313.
(1886) Kalenov, P., 'Liubov' po Platonu', *Russkii Vestnik*, 11, pp. 121-139.
(1887) Giliarov, A.N., *Platonism, kak osnovanie sovremennogo mirovozzreniia*, Moscow.
(1887) Shostyn, A., 'Uchenie Platona o materii', *Vera i Razum*, 14, pp. 82-109.
(1889) Amfiteatrov, E.V., 'Istoricheskii obzor uchenii o krasote i iskusstve. Iz akad. chtenii. Uchenie o krasote i iskusstve v klassicheskoi filosofii. 1. Sokrat i Platon', *Vera i Razum*, 15, pp. 79-105.
(1889-1891) Redkin, P., 'O Platone voobshche', in *Letsii po istorii filosofii prava v sviazi s istoriei filosofii voobshche*, vol.3, SPb., pp. 244-391.
(1890) Zelenogorskii, F., 'Ideia i dialetika po Platonu', *Vera i Razum*, 7-8, pp. 285-312, pp. 327-339.
(1891) Giliarov, A.N., *Istochniki o Sofistov. Platon, kak istoricheskoi svidetel'. Opyt istoriko-filosofskoi kritiki*, Kiev.
(1893) Ivanov, I.I., 'Filosofiia bez faktov', *RM*, 2, pp. 37-60.
(1896) Grot, N.Ia., *Ocherk filosofii Platona*, Moscow.
(1896) Orlov, E., *Platon. Ego zhizn' i filosofskaia deiatel'nost'*, SPb.
(1897) Bogdashevskii, D.I., 'Uchenie Platona o znanii', *TKDA*, 12, pp. 557-579.
(1897) Guliaev, A., 'Kak Platon ponimal svoiu filosofiiu?', *Vera i Razum*, 13, pp. 1-27.
(1898) Shostyn, A., 'Nravstvenno-vospitatel'noe znachenie muzyki po vozreniiam Platona i Aristotelia'. Rech', proiznechennaia v sokrashchenii na publichnom akte MDA, 1 x 1898', *Bogoslovskii Vestnik*, 10, pp. 48-74.
(1898) Solov'ev, V.S., 'Platon' in Brokgaus and Efron (eds), *Entsiklopedicheskii Slovar'*, SPb., vol. xxiii (a).
(1898) Solov'ev, V.S., *Zhiznennaia drama Platona*, SPb.
(1899) Khalippa, I., 'Sistematicheskii ocherk gnoseologicheskikh vozzrenii Platona i kriticheskaia otsenka ikh', *Vera i Razum*, 4, pp. 101-108.
(1899) Solov'ev, V.S., 'Zhizn' i proizvedeniia Platona. Predvaritel'nyi ocherk' in *Tvoreniia Platona*, vol.1, Moscow.
(1903) Muretov, M.D., 'Novozavetnaia pesn' liubvi sravnitel'no s *Pirom* Platona, i *Pesn'iu Pesnei*', *Bogoslovskii Vestnik*, 11-12, pp. 461-499, pp. 555-612.
(1904) Novosadskii, N.I., 'Pedagogicheskie idealy Platona', *Varshavskie Universitetskie Izvestiia*, 1, pp. 1-20.
(1906) Zorgenfrei, G.G., 'Sotsial'naia pedagogika Platona', *ZhMNP*, Dec., pp. 188-201.
(1908) Trubetskoi, E.N., *Sotsial'naia utopia Platona*, Moscow.
(1909) Florenskii, P., *Obshchechelovecheskie korni idealizma*, Sergiev Posad.
(1912) Novgorodtsev, P., 'Uchenie Platona o estestvennom prave', in *Filosofskii Sbornik*, Moscow, pp. 282-290.
(1913) Radlov, E., 'Platon', *Filosofskii Slovar'*, Moscow (2nd edn.).
(1914) Rubinshtein, M.M., 'Pedagogicheskie idei Platona', *VFP*, kn.124, pp. 400-461.

(1916)	Zelinskii, F.F. (intro.), *Pedagogicheskie vozzreniia Platona i Aristotelia*, Shkola i Zhizn', Pg.
(1918)	Florenskii, P., 'Kul't i filosofiia', in *Bogoslovskie Trudy*, 17 (1977), pp. 119-135.
(1920)	Rubinshtein, M.M., *Platon-Uchitel'*, Irkutsk.
(1922)	Pertsov, V.P., 'Sotsial'no-politicheskoe mirovozzrenie Platona', in *Trudy Belorusskogo Gosudarstvennogo Universiteta*, 2-3, Minsk, pp. 50-73.
(1923)	Novitskii, K.P., *Platon*, Krasnaia nov', Moscow.
(1923)	Zhebelev, S.A. and Radlov, E.L. (foreword), *Polnoe sobranie tvorenii Platona v 15 tomakh*, vol.1, Pbg.
(1926)	Vygodskii, M., 'Platon kak matematik', in *Vestnik Kommunistiskoi Akademii*, kn.xvi, pp. 192-215.
(1927)	Bammel', G., 'Demokrit i Platon', in *Arhiv K. Marksa i F. Engel'sa*, kn.3, M.-L., pp. 470-479.
(1930)	Mishulin, A.V., 'Platon protiv Marksa', in *Revoliutsiia i Kul'tura*, 21-22, pp. 125-128.
(1936)	Lur'e, S.L., 'Platon i Aristotel' o tochnykh naukakh', in *Arhiv Istorii Nauki i Tekhniki*, vyp.9, M.-L.
(1937)	Serezhnikov, V., 'Sokrat. Osnovnye problemy filosofii Platona', MIFLI, Moscow.
(1942)	Petritsi, I., *Rassmotrenie platonovskoi filosofii i Prokla Diagokha*, Tbilisi.
(1957)	Dynnik, M., 'Materializm Vv. do n.e. i ego bor'ba s idealizmom ('liniia Demokrita' i 'liniia Platona')', in *Istoriia Filosofii*, vol.1 Moscow.
(1967)	Losev, A., 'Platon' in *Filosofskaia Entsiklopediia*, vol.4, Moscow, pp. 262-269.
(1975)	Asmus, V.F., *Platon*, Moscow.
(1979)	Kessidi, F.Kh. (ed.), *Platon i ego epokha: k 2400-letiiu so dnia rozhdeniia*, Moscow.

Western Literature Translated, Adapted or Cited by Russian Scholars

(Titles are listed according to the date of the Russian publication. For translations, the date of the original publication is given in square brackets, and, where possible, the name of the translator is included. Works which were not translated are listed according to the edition most frequently cited in Russian literature.)

(1804-1810)	Schleiermacher, F., *Platon. Werke (mit Anmerkungen)* [Berlin].
(1816)	Ast, F., *Platon's Leben und Schriften* [Leipzig].
(1826)	'Fileb ili razgovor Platona o vysochaishchim blage: analiz iz *Journal des savants*', *Moskovskii Teleskop*, nos.1-2.
(1836)	Ritter, Heinrich, 'Platon und die ältere Akademie' (O zhizni i tvoreniiakh grecheskogo filosofa Platona'), trans. V. Lisitsyn, in *ZhMNP*, pt.10, pp. 486-512 [Hamburg, 1829-1834].
(1837)	'Vzgliad Platona na nauku filosofii (po Ritteru)', *ZhMNP*, pt.13, pp. 265-301.

(1837) Baur, Ferdinand, *Das Christliche des Platonismus, oder Sokrates und Christus. Eine religionsphilosophische Untersuchung* [Tübingen].
(1854) Eichhoff, 'Razbor trekh dialogov Platona: *Menon, Kriton, Fedon* v logicheskom otnoshenii (Logica trium dialogum Platonicorum explicatio)', in Zapol'skii, N., 'K voprosu o prepodovanii logiki', *ZhMNP*, pt.167, pp. 67-90.
(1861) Klevanov, A., *Obozrenie filosofskoi deiatel'nosti Platona i Socrata (po Tselleru)*, Moscow.
(1869) Fouillée, Alfred, *La Philosophie de Platon, exposition, histoire et critique de la théorie des idées*, 2 vols. [Paris, 1894 – 2nd edn.].
(1876) Rezener, F. (trans.), *Platon, v izlozhenii K-na K-za* (Collings), SPb.
(1876) Po Deutshle (Deuschle), *Disposit. der Apologie*....[Leipzig, 1867].
(1878) Hoelbe, A., 'De Pietatis, quae sit in Platonis Euthyphrone, ratione', *ZhMNP*, 10, pt.V, pp. 127-141.
(1881) Tannery, Paul, 'L'education platonicienne', *Revue philosophique*, XI.
(1883) Luniac, 'Miscellanea critica', *ZhMNP*, 11, p. 267 ff.
(1894) Dobiash, A.V., *Etiudy po Platonu*. Vol.1. *Razbor vzgliada Sharshmidta (Schaarschmidt) na Platona*, Kiev.
(1894) Stelletskii, N., 'Neskol'ko kriticheskikh zamechanii po povodu mneniia nemetskogo filosofa F. A. Lange o sravnitel'nom znachenii dlia razvitiia nauki vzgliadov Protagora i Platona na poznanie', *Vera i Razum*, 16, pp. 156-180.
(1895) Natorp, Paul, 'Platos Staat und die Idee der Sozialpädagogik'.
(1898) Fouillée, A., *Liubov' po Platonu*, trans. and foreword N. Gerasimov, Moscow [Paris].
(1898) Struve, G.E., 'O logike Platona v sviazi s khronologiei i stilometrieiu ego sochinenii' (on W. Lutoslawski's *The Origin and Growth of Plato's Logic*), *VFP*, kn.43, pp. 187-205.
(1900) Mazarakis, A., *Die platonische Pädagogik* [Zurich].
(1900) Windelband, *Platon*, trans. Al. Grombakh, SPb. (1904 – 2nd edn.); 2nd trans. I.V. Postman, with a foreword by Prof. K. Zhakov, SPb., (1909) [Stuttgart, 1899].
(1912) Deussen, Paul, *Vedânta und Platonismus im Lichte der Kantischen Philosophie,* trans. M. Sizov, Moscow [Berlin, 1904].

Other Works Cited or Consulted

Abramov, A. (1997), 'Filosofiia v dukhovnykh akademiiakh (traditsia platonizma v russkom dukhovno-akademicheskom filosofstvovanii)', *VP*, 9 pp.138-155.
Copenhaver, Brian and Schmidt, Charles (1992), *Renaissance Philosophy* in *A History of Western Philosophy*, vol.3, Oxford.
Hankins, James (1990), *Plato in the Italian Renaissance*, 2 vols., E. J. Brill, Leiden, New York.
Jayne, S. (1995), *Plato in Renaissance England*, Kluwer, Dordrecht.
Neschke-Hentschke, A. (1995), *Platonisme politique et théorie du droit naturel : contributions à une archéologie de la culture politique européenne*, Editions de l'Institut supérieur de Philosophie, Louvain.

Neschke-Hentschke, Ada and Etienne, Alexandre (eds) (1997), *Images de Platon et lectures de ses oeuvres. Les interprétations de Platon à travers les siècles*, Editions de l'Institut supérieur de philosophie, Louvain.
Novotny, Frantisek (1977), *The Posthumous Life of Plato*, Martinus Nijhoff, The Hague.
Vieillard-Baron, J.L. (1979), *Platon et l'idéalisme allemand (1770-1830)*, Beauchesne, Paris.

Russian Science of Antiquity

Ancient Philosophy and its History

(1841-1842) *Istoriia drevnei filosofii, prisposoblennaia k poniatiiu kazhdogo obrazovannogo cheloveka*, 2 vols., Moscow.
(1860-1861) Novitskii, O.M., *Postepennoe razvitie drevnikh filosofskikh uchenii*, 4 vols., Kiev.
(1870-1872) Linitskii, P.I., 'Nravstvennye i religioznye poniatiia drevnikh grecheskikh filosofov, *TKDA*.
(1871) Gogotskii, S.S., *Vvedenie v istoriiu filosofii*, Kiev.
(1878) Ostroumov, M., *Obzor filosofskykh uchenii*, Tambov (Moscow, 1880).
(1880) Markov, N., *Obzor filosofskykh uchenii*, Moscow (1881 – 2nd edn.).
(1880) Sokolov, M.E., *Kratkaia istoriia filosofii*, Simbirsk.
(1888) Giliarov, A.N., *Grecheskie Sofisty, ikh mirovozzrenie i deiatel'nost' v svazi s obshchei politicheskoi i kul'turnoi istoriei Gretsii*, Moscow.
(1889) Karinskii, M.I., *Lektsii po istorii drevnei filosofii, chitannie studentam SPb. Dukhovnoi Akademii v 1888/9 g*, SPb.
(1890) Trubetskoi, S.N., *Metafizika v drevnei Gretsii*, Moscow.
(1893) Strakhov, N., *Ocherk istorii filosofii s drevneishikh vremen filosofii do nastoiashchego vremeni*, Kharkov (1910 – 2nd edn.).
(1894) Bezobrazova, M.V., *Kratkii obzor sushchestvennykh momentov istorii filosofii*, Moscow.
(1895) Nazar'ev, I., *Kratkaia istoriia filosofii*, Voronezh.
(1895-1896) Filippov, M.M., *Filosofiia deisvitel'nosti. Istoriia i kriticheskii analiz nauchno-filosofskykh mirosozertsanii ot drevnosti do nashikh dnei*, 2 vols., SPb.
(1901) Obolenskii, L.E., *Istoriia mysli. Opyt kriticheskoi istorii filosofii*, SPb.
(1902) Linitskii, P., *Ocherki istorii filosofii, drevnei i novoi*, Kiev.
(1903) Filippov, M.M., *Istoriia filosofii s drevneishikh vremen*, SPb. (1910 – 2nd edn.).
(1906) Trubetskoi, S.N., *Istoriia drevnei filosofii*, 2 vols., Moscow (1912 – 2nd edn.).
(1908) Zelenogorskii, F., *Ocherk iz istorii drevnei filosofii*, Kharkov.
(1912) Vvedenskii, A.I., *Lektsii po drevnei filosofii*, SPb. /lithograph/.
(1913) Solov'ev, I.P., *Kurs istorii filosofii*, SPb.
(1925) Volgin, V.P., *Sotsialism v drevnei Gretsii*, M.-L.
(1926) Lur'e, S.L., *Predtechi anarkhizma v drevnem mire*, Moscow.
(1926) Vol'gin, V.P., *Ocherki po istorii sotsializma*, Moscow.

(1929) Lur'e, S.S., *Istoriia antichnoi obshchestvennoi mysli*, M.-L.
(1929) Serezhnikov, V., *Ocherki po istorii filosofii*, vol.1, M.-L.
(1930) Losev, A., *Ocherki antichnogo simvolizma i mifologii*, Moscow.
(1933) Dynnik, M., *Bor'ba materializma i idealizma v antichnom mire*, Baku.
(1936) Dynnik, M., *Ocherk istorii filosofii klassicheskoi Gretsii*, Moscow.
(1938) Dynnik, M., 'Bor'ba materializma idealizma v antichnom obshchestve', *Pod Znamenem Marksizma*, 5, pp. 124-185.
(1941) Aleksandrov, G., *Bor'ba materializma i idealizma v antichnoi filosofii*, Moscow.
(1948) Dynnik, M., 'Za Marsistkoe izuchenie antichnogo materializma', *Vestnik Drevnei Istorii*, 4, pp. 3-13.
(1965) Asmus, V. F., *Istoriia antichnoi filosofii*, Moscow.

Western Literature Translated, Adapted or Cited by Russian Scholars

(1831) Ast, F., *Obozrenie istorii filosofii*, adaptation Vershinski, SPb.
(1837) Nadezhdin, F., *Ocherk istorii filosofii po Reingol'du (Reinhold)*, SPb.
(1864) Drechsler, Ad., *Kharakteristika filosofskikh sistem*, trans. R. Ul'ianinskii, Moscow.
(1864) Schwegler, A., *Geschichte der Philosophie im Umriss*, trans. and ed. P.D. Iurkevich, Moscow, [Stuttgart, 1848].
(1866) Bauer, W., *Geschichte der Philosophie für gebildete Leser, zugleich als Einleitung in das Studium der Philosophie*, trans. and ed. M. Antonovich, SPb. [Halle, 1863].
(1866) Lewes, George Henry, *The History of Philosophy from Thales to Comte*, SPb. (rev. trans. V. Chuiko, 1892) [London, 1857, 1868 – 2nd edn., 1872 – 3rd edn.].
(1867) Grote, George, *Plato and the other Companions of Socrates* [London].
(1881) Lange, F.A., *Geschichte des Materialismus und Kritik seiner Bedeutung in der Gegenwart*, trans. N.N. Strakhov, SPb. (trans. and ed. V.S. Solov'ev, Kiev-Kharkov, 1899-1900) [1866].
(1882) Weber, Alfred, *L'histoire de la philosophie européenne*, trans. by I. Linnichenko and Vl. Podvysotskii, ed. A.A. Kozlov, Kiev [1872].
(1883) Mahaffy, John-Pentland, *A History of Classical Greek Literature*, trans. Aleksandra Veselovskaia, Moscow [1880].
(1886) Zeller, E., *Die Philosophie der Griechen*, 3 vols., trans. M. Nekrasov, ed. M. Karinskii, SPb. [Tübingen, 1844-1852].
(1892) Burnet, John, *Early Greek Philosophy* [London].
(1893) Windelband W., *Geschichte der alten Philosophie*, trans. ed. A. Vvedenskii, SPb. (1898 – 2nd edn., 1902 – 3rd edn.) [1888].
(1894) Fouillée, A., *Histoire de la Philosophie*, trans. P. Nikolaev, Moscow, (1898 – 2nd edn.) [Paris, 1875].
(1895) Kirchner, Fr., *Katechismus der Geschichte der Philosophie. Von Thales bis zur Gegenwart*, trans. V.D. Vol'fson, SPb. [Leipzig, 1877, 1884 – 2nd edn., 1896 – 3rd edn.].

(1898) Rehmke, J., *Grundriss der Geschichte der Philosophie, zum Selbststudium und für Vorlesungen*, trans. N.O. Losskii, SPb. [Berlin, 1896].
(1902) Tannery, P., *Pour l'histoire de la science hellène*, trans. N.N. Pol'nova and S.I. Tsereteli, eds, E. Radlov and G.F. Tsereteli, foreword, A. Vvedenskii, SPb. [Paris, 1887].
(1907) Laas, Ernst, *Idealismus und Positivismus* (3 vols.), vol.1 trans. and ed. S. N. Eberling, Moscow [1879-1884].
(1910) von Arnim, Hans, *Die Europäische Philosophie des Altertums*, trans. S. I. Povarnin, SPb. [Leipzig, 1909].
(1910-1912) Wundt, W., Oldenburg, G., et al., *Obshchaia istoriia filosofii*, 2 vols., trans. I.V. Postman and I.V. Iashunskii, ed. A.I. Vvedenskii and E.L. Radlov, SPb.
(1911) Vorländer, K., *Geschichte der Philosophie*, trans. and ed. V.A. Sabal'skii, SPb. [Leipzig, 1903].
(1911-1913) Gomperz, Th., *Griechische Denker. Eine Geschichte der antiken Philosophie*, 2 vols., trans. E. Gertsyk and D. Zhukovskii, ed. S. Zhebelev, SPb. [1895, 1903 – 2nd edn., 1912 – 3rd edn.].
(1912) Gomperz, Th., *Die Lebensauffassung der griechischen Philosophen and das Ideal der inneren Freiheit* (trans. as *Zhizneponimanie grecheskikh filosofov*), SPb. [Jena, 1904].
(1913) Brasch, M., Die *Klassiker der Philosophie. Von frühesten griechischen Denkern bis auf die Gegenwart*, 3 vols., SPb. [Leipzig, 1884-1885].

Ethics, Law and Social Philosophy in Antiquity

(1869-1902) Chicherin, B.N., *Istoriia politicheskikh uchenii*, 5 vols., Moscow.
(1870) Shcheglov, D., *Istoria sotsial'nykh sistem ot drevnosti do nashikh dnei*, vol.1, SPb. (1891 – 2nd edn.).
(1872-1874) Iurkevich, P.D., 'Istoriia filosofii Prava. Vvedenie' (lectures given at Moscow University).
(1886) Derevitskii, A., 'Iz Istorii grecheskoi etiki: literaturno-filosofskie ocherki', *Vera i Razum*, Kharkov.
(1889-1891) Redkin, P., *Lektsii po istorii filosofii prava v sviazi s istoriei filosofii voobshche*, 6 vols., SPb.
(1890) Bershadskii, A., *Lektsii po istorii filosofii prava*, SPb.
(1890) Trubetskoi, E.N., 'Politicheskie idealy Platona i Aristotelia v ikh vsemirno-istoricheskom znachenii', *VFP*, 4, pp. 1-36.
(1895-1897) Kovalevskii, M., *Proizkhozhdenie sovremmenikh demokratii*, 4 vols., Moscow.
(1897) Chicherin, B.N., *Politicheskie mysliteli drevnego i novogo mira*, Moscow.
(1899) Trubetskoi, E.N., *Istoriia drevnei i sovremennoi filosofii prava*, Kiev.
(1901) Novgorodtsev, P., *Sokrat i Platon. Iz lektsii po istorii filosofii prava, chitannykh na Vysshikh Zhenskikh Kursakh i v Moskovskom Universitete*, Moscow.
(1904) Korkunov, N. M., *Lektsii po obshchei teorii prava*, SPb.

(1906) Kovalevskii, M.M., *Ot priamogo narodopravstva k predstavitel'nomy i ot patriarkhal'noi monarkhii k parlamentarizmu: Rost gosudarstva i ego otrazhenie v istorii politicheskikh uchenii*, 2 vols., Moscow.
(1908) Novgorodtsev, P., *Konspekt k lektsii po istorii filosofii prava*, Moscow.
(1909) Fateev, Ar., *Istoriia obshchikh uchenii o prave i gosudarstve*, Kharkov (2nd edn.).
(1910-1913) Novgorodtsev, P., *Politicheskie idealy drevnego i sovremmenogo mira*, 2 vols., Moscow.
(1911) Zhebelev, S., 'Grecheskaia politicheskaia literatura i 'Politika' Aristotelia', in *Politika Aristotelia*, Moscow.
(1912) Khvostov, V.M., *Ocherki istorii eticheskikh uchenii*, SPb.
(1913) Speranskii, V.N., *Obshchestvennaia rol' filosofii. Vvedenie v istoriiu politicheskykh uchenii*, SPb.

Philosophy of Law: General Questions

Chicherin, B.N. (1900), *Filosofiia Prava*, Moscow.
Novgorodtsev, P. (1901), *Kant i Hegel' v ikh ucheniakh o prave i gosudarstve: dva tipicheskikh postroeniia v oblasti filosofii i prava*, Moscow.
Novgorodtsev, P. (1902), 'Nravstvennii idealizm v filosofii prava: k voprosu o vozrozhdenii estestvennogo prava', in *Problemy Idealizma*, Moscow.
Novgorodtsev, P. (1904), 'Gosudarstvo i Pravo', *VFP*, 74-75 pp. 397-450, pp. 508-538.
Novgorodtsev, P. (1909), *Krizis sovremennogo pravosoznaniia*, Moscow.
Novgorodtsev, P. (1922), *Vvedenie v filosofiiu prava*, Moscow.
Petrazickij, Lev (1905), *Vvedenie v izuchenie prava i nravstvennosti*, SPb.
Petrazickij, Lev (1909-1910), *Teoriia prava v sviazi s teoriei nravstvennosti*, SPb.

Western Literature, Translated, Adapted or Cited by Russian Scholars

(1860) Hildenbrand, Karl, *Geschichte und System d. Rechts und Staatsphilosophie* [Leipzig].
(1870) Stahl, F.J., *Geschichte der Rechtsphilosophie* [1829 – 1st edn.].
(1871) Janet, Paul, *Histoire de la philosophie morale et politique, dans l'antiquité et les temps modernes*, 2 vols., trans. A. Vasil'ev, SPb. (1878 – 2nd edn.) [Paris, 1858 – 1st edn.].
(1880) Fouillée, Alfred, *La science sociale contemporaine* [Paris].
(1885) Gumplowicz, Ludwig, *Grundriss der Soziologie*.
(1895) Michel, Henry, *L'idée de l'Etat. Essai critique sur l'histoire des théories sociales et politiques en France depuis la révolution*, [Paris].
(1897) Pollock, F., *Kurze Geschichte der Staatslehre*, SPb. [Leipzig, 1893].

Ancient History

(1848) Kutorga, M.S., *Istoriia Afinskoi Respubliki*, SPb.
(1867) Kutorga, M.S., 'Vvedenie v istoriiu drevnei grecheskoi obrazovannosti', *ZhMNP*, no. cxxxiii.

Select Bibliography 219

(1869) Vasilevskii, V.G., *Politicheskaia reforma i sotsial'noe dvizhenie v drevnei Gretsii v period ee upadka*, SPb.
(1882) Kareev, N.I., *Vvedenie v kurs istorii drevnego mira*, Warsaw.
(1884) Alandskii, P.I., 'Lektsii po istorii Gretsii', in *Kievskie Universitetskie Izvestiia*, Kiev.
(1886) Trubetskoi, E.N., 'Rabstvo v drevnei Gretsii', Iaroslavl'.
(1894-1896) Kutorga, M.S., *Afinskaia grazhdanskaia obshchina. Afinskaia Politeia. Eia sostav, svoistvo i vsemirno-istoricheskoe znachenie* in *Sobranie Sochineniia*, 2 vols., SPb. (Posthumous publication of texts drafted in 1885-1886).
(1900) Fedorovich, L.V., 'Istoriia politicheskoi ekonomii s drevneishikh vremen do A. Shmidta', *Zapiski Novorossiskogo Universiteta*, vol.79, Odessa.
(1903) Buzeskul, V.P., *Vvedenie v istoriiu Gretsii*, Kharkov.
(1903) Kareev, N.I., *Gosudarstvo-gorod antichnogo mira. Opyt istoricheskogo postroeniia politicheskoi i sotsial'noi evoliutsii antichnykh grazhdanskih obshchin*, SPb.
(1903) Zelinskii, F.F., 'Drevnii Mir i My', *ZhMNP*, Aug., Sept., Oct., pp. 1-45, 17-47, 65-114, SPb. (1905 – 2nd edn. as separate monograph).
(1905) Vipper, R.Iu., *Lektsii po istorii Gretsii*, Moscow.
(1909) Buzeskul, V.P., *Istoriia Afinskoi Demokratii*, SPb.
(1913) Buzeskul, V.P., *Antichnost' i sovremennost'. Sovremennye temy v antichnoi Gretsii*, SPb. (Pgd., 1924 – 2nd edn.).
(1916) Vipper, R. Iu., *Istoriia Gretsii v klassicheskuiu epokhu, IX-IV vv*, Moscow.

Western Literature Translated, Adapted or Cited by Russian Scholars

(1867) Fustel de Coulanges, N.D., *La cité antique*, trans. E. Korsh, Moscow (SPb., 1906) [Paris, 1864].
(1890) Pöhlmann, Robert, 'Grundzüge der politischen Geschichte von Griechenland', in J. Müller (ed.), *Handbuch der klassichen Altertumswissenschaft*, vol.3, Moscow (SPb., 1908, 1910 – 2nd edn.) [1889].
(1897-1905) Belloch, K.J., *Griechische Geschichte*, 2 vols., trans. M. Gershenzon, Moscow [1893-1897].
(1905) Kautsky, Karl, 'Der platonische und der urchristliche Kommunismus', trans. G. F. L'vovich, SPb. [1895].
(1906) Kautsky, Karl, *Die Vorläufer des Neueren Sozialismus*, vol.1, trans. E.K. and I.K. Leont'evyi, SPb. (1907 – 2nd edn., 1919 – 3rd edn.) [Stuttgart, 1895].
(1907) Adler, G., *Geschichte des Sozialismus und Kommunismus von Platon bis zur Gegenwart*, vol.1, trans. SPb. (1913 – 2nd edn.), [Leipzig, 1899].
(1910) Pöhlmann, Robert, *Geschichte des antiken Kommunismus und Sozialismus*, trans. and eds, M.M. Grevs, F.F. Zelinskii, N.I. Kareev and M.I. Rostovtsev, preface by M. Rostovtsev, SPb. [Munich, 1893-1901].
(1911) Meyer, Eduard, *Platons Staatsideal in geschichtlicher Beleuchtung* [Berlin].

The Science of Antiquity: The Current State of Research

(This section does not include short review notices of Western publications, many of which appeared in the specialized journals, such as *Zhurnal Ministerstva Narodnogo Prosvesceniia, Filologicheskoe Obozrenie, Voprosy Filosofii i Psikhologii, Germes*. References may be located by consulting the 'general bibliographies' listed above).

(1896)   Giliarov, A.N., 'Trudy po istorii grecheskoi filosofii (za 1892-1896)', *Kievskie Universitetskie Izvestiia*, 6 and 12, pp. 53-72, pp.211-226.
(1900)   Buzeskul, V.N., 'Kharakternie cherty nauchnogo dvizheniia v oblasti grecheskoi istorii za poslednee tridtsatiletie', *RM*, 2, pp. 58-79.
(1924)   Buzeskul, V.N., 'Razrabotka grecheskoi istorii v Rossii', *Annaly*, 4, pp. 139-153.
(1929-1931) Buzeskul, V.N., *Vseobshchaia istoriia i ee predstaviteli v Rossii v XIX i nachale XX veka*, 2 vols., Leningrad.
(1955)   Tikhomirov, M.N., Alpatov, M.A. and Sidorov, A.L. (eds), *Ocherki istorii istoricheskoi nauki v SSSR*, vol.2, Moscow.

Education and Research in Nineteenth and Early Twentieth-Century Russia

Primary Materials

Obozrenie Prepodovaniia (1840-1917) for the faculties of History and Philology, and Law in the Universities of Moscow, St. Petersburg, Kiev, and *Obozrenie predmetov, naznachaemykh dlia otkrytogo ispytaniia studentov* (Theological Academies).
Zhurnal Ministerstva Narodnogo Prosveshcheniia (1840-1917).
Biograficheskii Slovar' professorov i prepodavatelei Imperatorskogo St.-Peterburgskogo Universiteta za istekshuiu tret'iu chetvert veka ego sushhcestvovaniia (1868-1894) (1896-1898), SPb., 2 vols.
Biograficheskii Slovar' professorov i prepodavatelei Imperatorskogo Moskovskogo Universiteta. 1755-1855 (1855), 2 vols., Moscow.
Biograficheskii Slovar' professorov i prepodavatelei Imperatorskogo Universiteta Sv. Vladimira. 1834-1884 (1884), Kiev.
Chistovich, I. (1857), *Istoriia Sankt-Peterburgskoi Akademii*, SPb.
Emel'ianov, Iu.N. (ed.) (1989), *Moskovskii Universitet v vospominaniiah sovremennikov. 1755-1917*, Sovremennik, Moscow.
Filippov, M.M. (1901), *Reforma gimnazii i universitetov*, SPb.
Glinskii, B. (1900), 'Universitetskie ustavy (1755-1884)', *Istoricheskii Vestnik*, Jan-Febr. pp. 324-351, pp. 718-742.
Ia. B. (1918), 'Tsennost' klassicheskogo obrazovaniia s tochki zreniia sotsialista', *Germes*, 1, pp.34-38.
Izgoev, A. (1909), 'Ob intelligentnoi molodezhi', in *Vekhi*, Moscow.

Kizewetter, A. A. (1927), *Moskovskii Universitet i ego traditsii: Rol' Moskovskogo Universiteta v kul'turnoi zhizni Rossii*, Den' russkoi kul'tury, Prague.
Miliukov, P. (1902), 'Universitety v Rossii', in Brokgaus and Efron (eds), *Entsiclopedicheskii Slovar'*, Vol.xxxiv (a), pp.788-803.
Modestov, V. (1889), 'Mesto klassicheskoi filologii sredi nauk istoriko-filologicheskogo fakul'teta i eia prepodavanie', *ZhMNP*, 12, pp. 1-16.
Novgorodtsev, P. (1929), 'Institutions of Higher Education before the War', in *Russian Schools and Universities in the World War*, Yale University Press, New Haven.
Shmid, E. (1878), *Istoriia srednyh uchebnikh zavedenii v Rossii*, SPb.
Solov'ev, V.S. (1885), 'Gosudarstvennaia filosofiia v programme Ministerstva Narodnogo Prosveshcheniia', in *Sobranie Sochineniia*, vol.2, Moscow, (1989), pp. 175-184.
Vernadskii, V.I. (1901), *Ob osnovaniiakh universitetskoi reformy*, Moscow.
Zelinskii, F.F. (1898), 'Antichnaia gumannost', *Vestnik Evropy*, 1, pp. 195-229.
Zelinskii, F.F. (1918), 'Antichnost' i klassicheskoe obrazovanie', *Germes*, 1, pp.17-34.

Other Works Cited or Consulted

Alston, P. (1969), *Education and the State in Tsarist Russia*, Stanford University Press, Stanford.
Archpriest Vl. Mustafin (1986), 'Filosofskie discipliny v S.-Peterburgskoi Dukhovnoi Akademii', in *Bogoslovskie Trudy. Iubileinyi Sbornik*, Moscow, pp.186-191.
Bérélowitch, Wl. (1990), *La Soviétisation de l'école russe, 1917-1931*, l'Age d'homme, Lausanne.
Besançon, A. (1974), Education et société en Russie dans le second tiers du XIXè siècle, Mouton-Paris-La Haye.
Dunstan, John and Suddaby, Avril (1990), 'The Progressive Tradition in Soviet Schooling to 1988', in J. Dunstan (ed.), *Soviet Education under Perestroika* Routledge, London-New York, pp. 1-13.
Eklof, Ben (ed.) (1993), *School and Society in Tsarist and Soviet Russia*, St. Martin's Press, New York.
Fitzpatrick, S. (1992), 'Professors and Soviet Power', in *The Cultural Front: Power and Culture in Revolutionary Russia*, Cornell University Press, Ithaca and London.
Hans, N. (1931), *The History of Russian Educational Policy*, London.
Kassow, S.D. (1989), *Students, Professors and the State in Tsarist Russia*, University of California Press.
Kline, G. (ed.) (1957), *Soviet Education*, Routledge, London.
Mathes, W.L. (1968), 'The Origins of Confrontation Politics in Russian Universities: Student Activism, 1855-1861', *Canadian Slavic Studies*, 11, no. 1, Spring.
Mathes, W.L. (1972), 'N. I. Pirogov and the Reform of University Government, 1856-1866', *Slavic Review*, vol.31, March.
Maurer, Trude (1998), *Hochschullehrer im Zarenreich: Ein Beitrag zur russischen Sozial-und Bildungsgeschichte*, Böhlau, Köln.
McClelland, J.C. (1979), *Autocrats and Academics. Education, Culture and Society in Tsarist Russia*, Chicago.

Nethercott, F. (1996), 'L'établissement du système scolaire en Russie (1800-1850): référence française ou référence allemande?', in K. Dmitrieva and M. Espagne (eds), *Philologiques IV. Transferts culturels triangulaires. France-Allemagne-Russie*, Editions de la Maison des Sciences de l'Homme, Paris, pp.187-204.
Nosov, A.A. (1996), 'K istorii klassicheskogo obrazovaniia v Rossii (1860-nachalo 1900-x godov)', in G.S. Knabe (ed.), *Antichnoe nasledie v kul'ture Rossii*, Moscow, pp. 203-229.
Tolz, V. (1997), *Russian Academicians and the Revolution. Combining Professionalism and Politics*, Macmillan, London.
Whittaker, C.H. (1984), *The Origins of Modern Russian Education. An Intellectual Biography of Count Sergej Uvarov 1786-1855*, Northern Illinois University Press.

Russian Thought and Culture (1840-1930)

Primary Materials

'Pozemel'naia obshchina', in Brokgaus and Efron (eds) (1898), *Entsiklopedicheskii Slovar'*, SPb., vol. xxiv.
Arsen'ev K.K. (ed.) (1904), Glavnye deiateli i predshestvenniki sudebnoi reformy, SPb.
Arsen'ev, K.K. (1915), 'Tsarstvovanie imperatora Aleksandra III-go', in *Za Chetvert' Veka (1871-1894). Sbornik Stat'ei*, Pgd.
Chicherin, B. (1862), *Neskol'ko sovremmenikh voprosov*, Moscow.
Chicherin, B. (1878), Konstitutsionnyi vopros v Rossii, Moscow.
Chicherin, B. (1897), 'Sushchestvo i metody idealizma', *VFP*, 37, pp. 185-238.
Chicherin, B. (1900), 'Rossiia nakanune dvatsatogo stoletiia', in *B.N. Chicherin: Filosofiia Prava*, Nauka, SPb. [1998].
Ern, V. (1910), 'Nechto o Logose, russkoi filosofii i nauchnosti: po povodu zhurnala *Logosa*', *Moskovskii Ezhenedel'nik*, nos. 29-32.
Karpov, V. (1856), 'Vzgliad na dvizhenie filosofii v mire khristianskom i na prichiny razlichnikh eia napravlenii', *ZhMNP*, vol.92, 11, pp. 167-198.
Karpov, V. (1860), 'Filosofskii ratsionalizm noveishchego vremeni', *Khristianskoe Chtenie*, kn. 3, 4, 5, 6, 12.
Kireevskii, I. (1852), 'O kharaktere prosveshcheniia Evropy i ego otnoshenii k prosveshcheniiu Rossii', in *I.V. Kireevskii: Kritika i estetika*, Iskusstvo, Moscow [1979], pp. 248-293.
Kireevskii, I. (1856), 'O neobkhodimosti i vozmozhnosti novykh nachal dlia filosofii', in *I.V. Kireevskii: Kritika i estetika*, Iskusstvo, Moscow [1979], pp.293-332.
Lenin, V.I. (1909), *Materializm i Empiriokrititsizm*, Moscow.
Novgorodtsev, P. (1903), *Nravstvennaia problema filosofii Kanta*, Moscow [pamphlet].
Solov'ev, V.S. (1894), 'Idealism' in Brokgaus and Efron (eds), *Entsiklopedicheskii Slovar'*, SPb., vol. xii (a).
Solov'ev, V.S. (1895), 'Kant' in Brokgaus and Efron (eds), *Entsiklopedicheskii Slovar'*, SPb., vol. xiv.
Solov'ev, V.S. (1896), 'Mirovaia dusha', in Brokgaus and Efron (eds), *Entsiklopedicheskii Slovar'*, SPb., vol. xix (a).

Solov'ev, V.S. (1897), *La Justification du Bien*, trans. T.D.M., intro. Patrick de Laubier, Slatkine, Genève [1997].
Trubetskoi, S.N. (1890), *O prirode chelovecheskogo soznaniia*, in *S.N. Trubetskoi: Sochineniia*, Mysl', Moscow [1994].
Trubetskoi, S.N. (1894), 'Istoriia filosofii' in Brokgaus and Efron (eds), *Entsiklopedicheskii Slovar'*, SPb., vol. xiii (a).
Trubetskoi, S.N. (1896), *Osnovaniia Idealizma* in *S.N. Trubetskoi: Sochineniia*, Mysl', Moscow [1994].
Trubetskoi, S.N. (1897), 'V zashchitu idealizma', *VFP*, 37, pp. 288-327.

Monographs and Articles on the Main Russian and Soviet Scholars Cited

Asmus, V.F. (1990), 'Filosofiia v Kievskom universitete v 1914–1920' /Iz vospominanii studenta/, *VF*, 8, pp. 90-108 [on Giliarov].
Bohachevsky-Chomiak, Martha (1976), *Sergej N. Trubetskoi. An Intellectual Among the Intelligentsia in Prerevolutionary Russia*, Notable & Academic Books, Belmont.
Gaidenko, P.P. (1994), 'Konkretnyi Idealizm' S.N. Trubetskogo', in *S.N. Trubetskoi: Sochineniia*, Mysl', Moscow.
Grot, N.Ia. (1904), *Filosofiia i eia obshchie zadachi. Sbornik Statei*, SPb. [Introduction].
Gurvitch, G. (1922-1923), 'Die zwei grössten russischen Rechtsphilosophen: Boris Tchitcherin und Wladimir Solowjeff', in *Philosophie und Recht*, vol.2.
Gurvitch, G. (1924), 'Prof. P.I. Novgorodtsev, kak filosof prava', *Sovremennye zapiski*, vol.20, Paris.
Hamburg, Gary M. (1992), *Boris Chicherin and Early Russian Liberalism. 1828-1866*, Standford.
Isaev, V.I. (1991), 'V.P. Buzeskul. Istorik, politolog, prosvetitel'. (Analiticheskii obzor)' in *Istoria Evropeiskoi Tsivilizatsii v russkoi nauke. Antichoe Nasledie*, Moscow, pp. 106-127.
Losev, A.F. (1990), *Vladimir Solov'ev i ego vremiia*, Progress Press, Moscow.
Müller, E. (1966), *Russicher Intellekt in Europaïcher Krise. Ivan V. Kireevskij*, Köln-Graz.
Nemeth, T. (1993), 'Karpov and Jurkevic on Kant: Philosophy in Service to Orthodoxy?', *SEET*, vol. 45, no.3, pp. 169-211.
Novgorodtsev, (1901), 'Ideia prava v filosofii Vl. S. Solov'eva', *VFP*, 6, pp. 112-129.
Pamiati V.N. Karpova zasluzennogo professora Sanktpeterburgskoi duhovnoi akademii (1868), SPb.
Rouleau, F. (1990), *Ivan Kiréievski et la naissance du slavophilisme*, Namur.
Solov'ev, V.S. (1874), 'O filosofskikh trudakh P. D. Iurkevicha' in *P.D. Iurkevich: Filosofskie Proizvedeniia* (1990), Moscow, pp. 552-577.
Tol'stoi, I.I. (1940), 'Akademik Sergei Aleksandrovich Zhebelev v razvitii russkoi istoriografii po antichnosti', *Vestnik drevnei istorii*, 1.
Trubetskoi, E.N. (1913), *Mirosozertsanie V.S. Solov'eva*, 2 vols., Moscow.
Trubetskoi, E.N. (1921), *Vospominaniia*, Sofia.
Zhukov, V.N. (1994-95), 'The Social Philosophy of P.I. Novgorodtsev', *Russian Studies in Philosophy*, vol.33, no.3, Winter.
Zork'in, V.D. (1984), *Chicherin*, Iuridecheskaia Literatura, Moscow.

Background Reading

Abramov, A. (1994), 'Kant v russkoi dukhovno-akademicheskoi filosofii' in *Kant i Filosofiia v Rossii*, Moscow.
Abramov, A. (1994), 'O russkom kantianstve i neokantianstve v zhurnale *Logos*' in *Kant i Filosofiia v Rossii*, Moscow.
Abramov, A.I. and Kovalenko, A.V. (1987), 'Filosofskie Vzgliady G.S. Skovorody v krugu ego istoriko-filosofskikh interesov' in *Nekotorie ocobenosti russkoi filososkoi mysli XVIII v*, Moscow.
Akhutin, A.V. (1991), 'Sophia and the Devil: Kant in the Face of Russian Religious Metaphysics', *Soviet Studies in Philosophy*, Spring.
Baberowski, Jörg (1996), *Autokratie und Justiz. Zum Verhältnis von Rechsstaatlichkeit und Rückständigkeit im ausgehenden Zarenreich 1864-1914*, Klostermann, Frankfurt am Main.
Baczko, B. (1978), *Lumières de l'Utopie*, Payot, Paris.
Batygin, G. and Devyatko, I. (1994), 'The Soviet Philosophical Community and Power: Some Episodes from the Late Forties', *SEET*, vol.46, no.3, September, pp. 223-245.
Berman, H. (1992), *Justice in the USSR*, rev. ed., New York.
Bezrodnyj, M. (1992), 'Zur Geschichte des russischen Neukantianismus. Die Zeitschrift *Logos* und ihre Redakteure', *Zeitschrift für Slawistik*, 37, pp. 489-511.
Billington, James H. (1966), *The Icon and the Axe*, New York.
Bollack, Mayotte and Wismann, Heinz (eds) (1983), *Philologie et herméneutique au XIXe siècle*, Göttingen.
Charle, Christophe (1996) *Les Intellectuels en Europe au XIXe siécle. Essai d'histoire comparée*, Paris.
Chervel, A. (1986), *Les auteurs français, latins et grecs aux programmes de l'enseignement secondaire de 1800 à nos jours*, Paris.
Clowes, E.W. (ed.) (1991), *Between Tsar and People: Educated Society and the Quest for Public Identity in Late Imperial Russia*, Princeton University Press.
Copleston, F. (1986), *Philosophy in Russia: From Herzen to Lenin and Berdyaev*, University of Notre Dame Press, Notre Dame, Indiana.
Eklof, B., Bushnell, J. and Zakharova, L. (eds) (1994), *Russia's Great Reforms, 1855-1881*, Bloomington.
Florovsky, G. (1987), *Ways of Russian Theology*, Part Two (trans. Robert L. Nichols), Notable and Academic Books.
Frank, H.J. (1973), *Geschichte des Deutschunterrichts, von den Anfängen bis 1945*, Carl Hanser Verlag, Munich.
Glatzer Rosenthal, Bernice (ed.) (1995), *Neo-Kantianism in Russian Thought*, *SEET*, vol.47, December, 3-4.
Goehrke, C. (1964), *Die Theorien über Entstehung und Entwicklung des 'mir'*, Wiesbaden.
Goldman, Wendy Z. (1993), *Women, the State, and Revolution: Soviet Family Policy and Social Life, 1917-1936*, Cambridge University Press.
Haumann H. and Plaggenborg, S. (eds) (1994), *Aufbruch der Gesellschaft im verordneten Staat. Russland in der Spätphase des Zarenreciches*, Frankfurt am Main.
Heller, L. and Niqueux, M. (1995), *Histoire de l'utopie en Russie*, PUF, Paris.

Select Bibliography

Isaev, V.I. (ed.) (1991), *Istoria Evropeiskoi Tsivilizatsii v russkoi nauke. Antichoe Nasledie*, Moscow.

Judge, E.H. and Simms, J.Y. Jr. (eds) (1992), *Modernization and Revolution. Dilemmas of Progress in Late Imperial Russia. Essays in Honor of Arthur P. Mendel*, New York.

Kazantsev, N.D. (1969), *Utopicheskii i nauchnyi sotsializm o pereustroistve sel'skogo khoziaiistva (Politiko-iuridicheskii aspekt)*, Moscow.

Knabe, G. S. (1996), *Grotesknyi epilog klassicheskoi dramy: Antichnost' v Leningrade 20-x godov. Chteniia po istorii i teorii kul'tury*, Vyp.15, RGGU, Moscow.

Kolakowski, L. (1978), *Main Currents of Marxism*, vol.2, Clarendon Press, Oxford.

Koyré, A. (1929), *La philosophie et le problème national en Russie au début du XIXe siècle*, Paris.

Koyré, A. (1950), *Etudes sur l'histoire de la pensée philosophique en Russie*, Vrin, Paris.

Laks, André and Neschke, Ada (eds) (1990), *La Naissance du paradigme herméneutique : Cahiers de Philologie, 10*, Presses Universitaires de Lille.

Léontovitch, V. (1986), *Histoire du libéralisme en Russie*, Fayard, Paris [1957].

Lincoln, B.W. (1990), *The Great Reforms. Autocracy, Bureaucracy, and the Politics of Change in Imperial Russia*, DeKalb.

Losskii, N.O. (1952), *History of Russian Philosophy* (trans. N. Duddington), London.

Mayeur, F. (1981), *De la Revolution à l'Ecole républicaine, in Histoire générale de l'Enseignement et de l'Education en France*, vol.3, Nouvelle Librairie de France, Paris.

Pares, B.A. (1926), *History of Russia*, Jonathan Cape, London [rpt. Methuen, University Paperbacks, 1965].

Raeff, M. (ed.) (1966), *Russian Intellectual History. An Anthology*, Harcourt, Brace & World, Inc, New York.

Raeff, M. (1984), *Understanding Imperial Russia* (trans. Arthur Goldhammer), New York.

Riasanovsky, N. A. (1963), *History of Russia*, New York.

Schmale, W. and Dodde, N.L. (eds) (1991), *Revolution des Wissens? Europa und seine Schulen im Zeitalter der Aufklärung (1750-1825)*, Verlag Dr Dieter Winkler, Bochum.

Schneider, U.J. (1992), 'Bibliography of Nineteenth Century histories of philosophy in German, English and French (1810-1899)', in *Storia della Storiografia*, 21, pp. 141-169.

Schneider, U.J. (1993), 'The Teaching of Philosophy at German Universities in the Nineteenth Century', *History of Universities*, vol XII, Oxford, pp. 197-338.

Shpet, G. (1922), *Ocherk razvitiia russkoi filosofii*, Petrograd [rpt. in *Russkaia Filosofiia*, Moscow, 1991].

Silnizki, Michael (1997), *Geschichte des gelehrten Rechts in Russland. Jurisprudencija an den Universitaten des Russischen Reiches 1700-1835*, Vittorio Klostermann, Frankfurt am Main.

Simmons, E.J. (ed.) (1955), *Continuity and Change in Russian and Soviet Thought*, Camb. Mass.

Solomon, Peter H. Jr. (ed.) (1997), *Reforming Justice in Russia, 1864-1996. Power, Culture, and the Limits of Legal Order*, M.E. Sharpe, New York and London.

Stites, Richard (1989), *Revolutionary Dreams. Utopian Vision and Experimental Life in the Russian Revolution*, Oxford.

Troitskii, N. A. (1979), *Tsarizm pod sudom progressivnoi obshchestvennosti 1866-1895 gg.*, Moscow.

Vanchugov, V. (1994), *Ocherk istorii filosofii, samobytno-russkoi*, Moscow.

Vaughan M.N. and Scotford Archer, M. (1971), *Social Conflict and Educational Change in England and France, 1789-1848*, Cambridge.

Walicki, A. (1975), *The Slavophile Controversy: History of a Conservative Utopia in Nineteenth Century Russian Thought*, Oxford.

Walicki, A. (1980), *A History of Russian Thought from the Enlightenment to Marxism*, Oxford.

Walicki, A. (1987), *Legal Philosophies of Russian Liberalism*, Clarendon Press, Oxford.

Wartenweiler, David (1999), *Civil Society and Academic Debate in Russia 1905-1914*, Clarendon Press, Oxford.

Wcislo, F. W. (1990), *Reforming Rural Russia. State, Local Society, and National Politics, 1855-1914*, Princeton.

Wortman, R. (1976), *The Development of a Russian Legal Consciousness*, Chicago, London.

Zenkovskii, V.V. (1991), *Istoriia Russkoi Filosofii*, 2 vols., EGO, Leningrad [Paris, 1948-1950].

Index

absolutism 73, 109, 125
Adler, Georg 145, 147, 175
Akhutin, Anatoly 86
Aksakov, Konstantin 100, 155
Alcibiades I 44
Aleksandrov, Georgii 180
Alexander I 21, 77, 78
Alexander II 20, 35, 96, 198
    see also Reforms and Counter Reforms
Alexander III 20, 98, 185, 193
    see also Reforms and Counter Reforms; Russification
all-unity
    in Hegel 66
    in Solov'ev 64, 73, 164
ancient world
    Russian depictions of 20, 23, 35, 70, 116, 136, 139, 185
    see also education, ideology of; history
antiquity, science of
    in Russia 2, 6, 8, 26, 35, 140
    compared with Western Europe, 51n14, 53-54n44&45
    and modernity 7, 34, 35, 139, 140, 147
Apology 37, 107, 135
Arakcheev, Alexis 77
Aristotle 7, 9, 37, 41, 43, 68, 132n85, 172n82, 179, 194, 195, 199, 203, 204
    and Plato compared 36, 37, 40, 59, 67, 70, 74, 116, 123, 136, 186

Aristotelianism 3, 13, 36
Asmus, Valentin 49, 183, 203
Ast, Friedrich 42, 141
autocracy 3, 10, 24, 126, 185
    enlightened 160-161
    and nationhood 6, 20, 78

Baur, Ferdinand Christian 32, 161
Beer, Max 175, 178
Bely, Andrei 8
Berdiaev, Nikolai 59
Berlin, Isaiah 14
Billington, James 77
Bouterweck, Friedrich 76
Briusov, Valery 8
Bulgakov, Sergei 79, 82
Burnet, John 34, 49
Buzeskul, V. 140, 146, 204

categorical imperative 106, 110, 113, 119, 120
    see also Kant; Solov'ev
censorship
    in pre-Revolutionary Russia 3, 5, 77, 79, 100, 122, 185, 187
    in Soviet Russia 49, 166
Chernyshevskii, Nikolai 33
Chicherin, Boris 10, 13, 23, 41, 90, 99, 101, 102, 103, 106, 110-113, 118, 121-126, 134, 137, 156, 158, 160, 186, 193
Church Fathers 12, 24, 36, 37, 39, 61, 64, 68-70, 80, 187
Cicero 24, 26, 41

citizen, citizenship 16, 103, 122, 123, 137, 138, 140-143, 146, 149, 150, 168, 160, 164
  see society and individual; freedom, individual; state, conceptions of
classical studies, in Russia 6, 7, 8, 20, 23-27, 35-38, 76, 136, 140
  compared to Germany and France 7, 24, 26, 185, 187
  see also ancient world; antiquity; education; schools; universities, theological academies
Cohen, Hermann 87, 186
Comte, Auguste 28, 41
constitution, constitutionalism 77, 101, 102, 123, 126, 138, 160, 161
  see also liberalism
Courses of Higher Education for Women 48, 112, 194-196, 198, 201, 204
Cousin, Victor 42, 70, 185, 200
Cratylus 46
Critias 47, 182
Crito 37, 107, 135

Decembrist uprising, impact on higher education 21
Delianov, I.D. 24, 36
democracy
  Athenian, Russian perceptions of 12, 179
Democritus 174, 180, 197
Descartes 68, 79, 173
dialectic
  in ancient philosophy 12, 30, 31, 42, 58, 82, 166, 180-184
  see also materialism, dialectical; Hegel
Dorpat, University of 26, 192, 199
dualism,
  Platonic 45, 46, 113, 133, 159, 163, 181-183
Dynnik, Mikhail 178, 179, 181, 196, 203

education (humanities and law)
  and state measures 6-9 17n15, 21, 20, 23, 24, 26, 27, 36, 37, 77, 78, 99, 100, 101, 140
  and pedagogy 135, 136, 148-150
  ideology of 2, 4, 35-38
  see also schools; universities
Engels, F. 134, 152, 176, 178
Enlightenment philosophy 77, 109, 119, 138, 139
  see also Kant; natural law
Ern, Vladimir 61, 79, 88, 89,
Eros 46-48, 57n90, 89, 163-165, 182
ethics
  in Plato 37, 41, 42, 105, 135-137, 182, 189, 190n37
  'objective' 3, 41, 99, 105, 115-117, 120, 121
  see also categorical imperative

Faculty
  of Law 96, 100, 101, 135, 137
  of Philology and History 6, 9, 16, 25, 51n8, 101, 128n9, 136, 137, 193-196, 198
Fet, Afanasii 43
Fichte 66
Florenskii, Pavel 1, 61, 79, 80-83, 85-87, 89, 182, 191, 197
Florovsky, George 76
Fouillée, Alfred 9, 29
Frank, Semën 65, 88
freedom,
  Platonic 116, 118, 135, 138, 139, 143, 146, 158, 160, 175, 186
  Kantian 103, 116, 118, 119, 120
  in Slavophile thought 62, 65, 91n10, 99, 100
  in Russian legal thought 102, 110, 111, 113-116, 121-127, 158, 160
Fustel de Coulanges, N.D. 34

Giliarov, Aleksei 1, 31, 33, 87, 184, 191, 202
Godmanhood 40, 48, 163-165
Gogotskii, Silvestr 30, 182, 201
Golitsyn, Prince A. 77-79

Gomperz, Theodor 28, 29, 31, 34
good, the 16, 33, 39, 40, 42, 45, 47, 58,
    62, 64, 90, 96, 105-118, 121, 122,
    124, 127, 138, 142, 143, 149, 186
  common 23, 90, 99, 113-115, 118,
    125, 127
  social 16, 97, 106, 126
Gorgias 37, 46, 105, 107, 108, 182
Granovskii, Timofei 7, 11, 26, 192, 193
Grot, Nikolai 9, 59, 87, 157, 194
Grote, George 34, 45
Guizot, F. 185

Hegel, Hegelian 12, 21, 23, 28, 29, 30,
    33, 41, 59, 60, 66, 68, 69, 71-74,
    79, 87, 89, 112, 121, 128, 136,
    141-145, 157, 179, 184, 186, 187,
    192, 195, 198, 201, 204
  Hegelianism 28, 41, 67, 72
Hermann, Karl 142
Hessen, Sergei 88
history
  ancient Greek 7, 8, 23, 26, 34, 35,
    53n44, 101, 136, 139, 140, 146,
    147, 167n7, 191, 198, 199, 202,
    204, 205
  Russian 103, 128, 192, 193, 204
historiography 11, 34, 166, 174, 175,
    179, 181
humanism 2
  'Russian' 35
humanities
  see education; schools, universities;
    theological academies
Humboldt, W. 185

idea
  Platonic doctrine of 31, 46, 58, 60,
    74, 81-84, 87, 133, 143, 180
idealism
  'concrete' 59, 67, 71, 72, 75
  German 12, 21, 28, 40, 59, 61, 69, 73,
    76, 87, 184
  'negative' and 'positive' 45-48
  'objective' 67, 88, 183

and materialism 33, 174, 179-181
and realism 65-67, 74, 86, 91n5
Russian, compared with German 59,
    60, 71-74, 79, 80, 86, 88
ideal-realism 82, 91n8,
see also Hegel and Hegelianism;
    Slavophilism; philosophy, history
    of
ideology
  Bolshevik 34, 166, 173-175, 178-182
  Tsarist 3, 5, 20, 26, 38, 77, 78, 184
  see also education
integral knowledge 58, 61, 63-65, 89
intelligentsia, 'academic'
  (self-) perception of 8, 14-15
  and the state 4-6
  and West European scholars 5, 27, 31-
    33, 36, 49
  professionalization of 11, 27
Iurkevich, Pamfil 13, 61, 64, 79, 80, 82-85,
    89, 101, 103-105, 118, 186, 193,
    203
Ivanov, Viacheslav 8

Jacobi, Friedrich 58
Jashchenko, A. 49
justice 11, 16, 23, 33, 41, 43, 90, 96-98,
    104-110, 116, 118, 124, 137, 141,
    142, 145, 146, 163, 186

Kant, Kantian, 9, 15, 16, 46, 60, 61, 63, 66,
    68, 71, 73-90, 97, 103, 106, 110-
    122, 173, 182, 186, 195, 201, 202
Kantianism 88
  see also Neo-Kantianism
Karinskii, Mikhail 29, 31
Karpov, Vladimir 13, 35, 38-42, 61-64, 78,
    79, 106, 136, 141, 142, 152, 162,
    163, 182, 191, 199, 201
Karsavin, Lev 13, 44, 49, 199
Katkov, Mikhail 8
Kautsky, Karl 34, 136, 145, 147, 153, 154,
    156, 175, 177, 178
Kavelin, Konstantin 23, 103, 193
Khomiakov, Aleksei 155

Khvostov, Veniamin 112, 113, 194
Kireevskii, Ivan 61, 67-74, 89, 155, 203
Kizewitter, Alexander 126, 205
Kollontai, Alexandra 151, 178
Korkunov, Nikolai 41, 101, 102, 123, 198
Kovalevskii, Maxim 138
Kozlov, Aleksei 31-33, 65, 87, 134, 153, 201, 202
Kroner, Richard 88
Kuznetsov, K. 135, 138, 139

law
   philosophy of, 11, 15, 23, 38, 39, 41, 96, 101-108,113, 137, 192, 195
   and morality 11, 16, 90, 96, 99, 103, 104-106, 111-115, 121-124, 142
   natural, 38, 99, 105, 107-109, 116, 118, 123, 186, 187
   Roman 100, 192, 194
   syllabus and state measures 20, 41, 100, 104
   'encyclopaedia' 15, 22, 100, 101, 192, 195, 198
   law codes 23, 100, 192, 193,
   see also education; Faculty; legal system; reform; state, conceptions of; universities
Laws 44, 47, 109, 166, 180, 182
legality 97, 98, 106, 107, 122, 126
legal system 97, 98, 104
Leibniz 64
Leipzig, University of 26, 198-199,
Lenin 173, 179, 181, 206
Levitskii, Sergei 85
Lewes, George Henry 32
liberals, liberalism 4, 16, 124, 125
   in Russia 125, 127, 144, 156, 158, 160
   see also constitution
lichnost' 73, 99, 102, 104, 112, 119
   see also personhood
Lipsius, Justus H. 26
logic 7, 9, 18n15, 22, 76, 189n37, 192-194, 200, 203
logos 79, 80

Losev, Aleksei 49, 67, 88, 183, 184, 206
Losskii, Nikolai 60, 65, 67
Lur'e, S. 175, 177

Magnitskii, Mikhail 21, 77-79
Marx, Marxist 134, 147, 152-157, 166, 173-176, 178, 179
   Marxism-Leninism 134, 175, 180
materialism 36, 59
   dialectical, 179, 180, 181
   see also idealism
Mehlis, Georg 88
metaphysics
   Platonic 2, 31, 46, 83, 85, 116, 127, 133, 135, 137, 146, 159, 165, 167
   Kantian 110
   Russian 62, 86, 88, 92n47
Metner, Emil 88
Meno 37, 46
Meyer, Eduard 34
Miliukov, Pavel 100, 101, 204
modernization
   and traditionalism 3-6, 15, 20, 184-187
Modestov, Vasilii 8, 202
morality 41, 46
   see also ethics
Morgenstern, C. 141
Müller, Hieronymos 42
Munk, Eduard 142
mystical, mysticism 58-60, 64, 73, 75, 77, 80, 88, 91n8, 122, 173, 180

Nadezhdin, Nikolai 76, 78
Napoleon III 24
nationalism
   see autocracy; Russian culture; Russification
Natorp, Paul 87, 88, 150, 186
Neo-Kantianism 119, 184, 186
   and Neo-Slavophiles 79, 87, 88
   and Platonism 87
Neo-Platonic, Neo-Platonism 2, 12, 43, 80, 88, 187
Neschke, Ada 3, 108
New Economic Policy (NEP) 174, 177

Nicholas I 3, 11, 21, 22, 24, 78, 79, 100, 101, 185, 193, 201, 204
nihilism, nihilist 24, 25, 30, 99-101, 134, 156, 157
  see also Pisarev, Dmitrii
Novgorodtsev, Pavel 8, 10, 13, 41, 48, 90, 101-128, 134, 138, 144, 156, 159, 161, 165, 175, 184, 186, 194
Novitskii, K. 175, 176, 177
Novitskii, Orest 30, 33, 200
Novosadskii, N. 148, 149, 150

obshchina
  in ancient Greece 139, 154
  in Russia 205
  see also Slavophilism
Orthodoxy
  and philosophy 20, 63, 78, 79
  and the state 6, 11, 20, 21, 77, 78, 184
  see also education; Plato and Russian Orthodoxy

Pares, Bernard 25
Parmenides 80
Parmenides 46, 181
Pavlov, M.G., 22
pedagogy 192, 193, 201
personal principle 165
personhood 65
  see also *lichnost'*
Phaedo 37, 46, 135, 136, 181
Phaedrus 47, 136, 183
Philebus 47, 136, 181, 182
philosophy
  syllabus, university 7, 9, 22, 37, 43, 91n12
  and state measures 20, 22, 76
  history of, in Western Europe 28, 29, 30, 32,
  history of, in Russia 7-9, 15, 22, 23, 30, 41, 51-52n22, 70, 73, 74, 79, 83, 89, 120, 173, 179, 181, 192, 194, 196, 197, 200, 201, 202, 203
  Russian 'national' 21-22, 40, 59, 60, 62, 65, 67

  see also education, ideology of; universities; theological academies
Pirogov, Nikolai 4
Pisarev, Dmitrii 30, 134, 156, 160
Plato
  and communism 134, 135, 147, 151, 153-155, 174-177
  and fascism 178
  and liberalism 16, 41, 27, 28, 144, 148, 156-158, 160, 165, 182
  and the Communist Manifesto 147, 153
  and Russian Orthodoxy 2, 10, 21, 36-40, 185
  as a 'moral example' and educator 35, 37, 117, 135, 136, 149, 184
  as a 'Russian' philosopher 1, 10
  and sexual equality 134, 147
  Plato scholarship in Russia 25, 26, 37, 46-49, 56n72&77, 57n84, 65, 141
  compared with Western Europe 11, 21, 31-34, 42-45, 50, 56-57n81, 141, 146, 149, 185
  Plato scholarship in Soviet Russia, 49, 134, 136, 174, 175, 179-184, 189n32, 33, 37
  see also education
Platonism
  definitions 12, 58, 59, 62, 65-66, 82, 89, 147, 173, 178, 182, 187
Plotinus 12, 64, 65, 155
Pogodin, Mikhail 100
Pöhlmann, Robert 34, 136, 140, 146, 147, 174, 175, 178
Politicus 162, 180
positivism 28, 32, 33, 36, 41, 59, 194, 198, 201
  legal 102-103
Protagoras 44, 121
Protestant, Protestantism 69, 78, 79, 81
psychology 7, 9, 18n15, 22, 79n12, 193, 194, 195, 196, 200, 201, 203
  pedagogical 149, 150
  and Plato 39, 189n37

Radlov, Ernst 13, 44, 49, 65, 199

rationalism 21, 61, 65, 68, 74, 77, 88, 100
Redkin, Petr 15, 23, 26, 38, 40, 41, 42,
    101, 104, 106, 107, 141, 143, 186,
    192, 193, 198
Reformation 67
Reforms
    and Counter Reforms 3, 27, 59, 96,
        97, 98, 101, 104, 122, 126
    see also education; schools;
        universities
Renaissance 2, 35, 67
Republic 16, 37, 44, 47, 105, 109, 133-
    172, 180-182
Riasanovsky, Nicholas 77
Rickert, Heinrich 88
Ritschl, Friedrich Wilhelm 26
Rostovtsev, Mikhail 146
Rouleau, François 48, 71
Rubinshtein, M. 150, 196, 206
Russian culture contrasted with the West
    3, 6, 13, 36, 39, 40, 60-70, 74, 86,
    88, 100, 125, 155, 185
Russification 6, 20

Savigny, Friedrich 102, 192, 204
Schelling, Friedrich 2, 12, 22, 61, 64, 66,
    69, 70, 76, 187, 204
Schleiermacher, Friedrich 12, 42, 43, 45,
    58, 70, 141, 142, 204
scholasticism 40, 68, 70
schools, *gimnasia*
    curricula (Latin and Greek), 6, 8, 23,
        24, 25, 37
    Realschule 25
    private 17n11
    see also education; universities
Schopenhauer, Arthur 173, 201, 202
Schwegler, Albert 32
Shevyrev, Stepan, 100
Shtern, Ernest 26
Skovoroda, Grigorii 14
Skvortsov, I.M. 79
Slavophilism 62, 73, 100, 155, 187
    critique of Western philosophy 60-70

    see also integral knowledge; *obschina*;
        Schelling; Solov'ev
social democrats 136, 145, 158, 178
socialism
    scientific 157, 175, 177
    utopian 157, 158, 175, 176
society
    and the individual/citizen 99, 103, 110,
        118-127, 137, 142, 144
    see also state, conceptions of; freedom,
        individual
societies, scholarly 5, 44, 126, 192, 194,
    197
Socrates, Socratic 39, 42-48, 63, 75, 88,
    139
Solov'ev, Vladimir 13, 38, 61-67, 73, 79,
    87, 90, 99, 105, 117-125, 128, 134,
    138, 152, 156, 158, 161-165, 182,
    184, 186, 187, 198
    on law and morality 113-115
    and Slavophilism 43, 63, 64, 113, 127
    as a translator of Plato 43-47
Sophist 46, 181
Sophists 44, 107-109
Spencer, Herbert 28
Speranskii, Mikhail 77
spiritualism, spiritualist 9, 29, 32, 65, 66
    'concrete' 32
    'pan-spiritualism' 65
    see also Kozlov, A.A; Weber, A.
St. Paul 40, 110, 163
Stalin, Stalinist 166, 177, 180, 181, 184
Stallbaum, Godfredus 42, 142
state
    conceptions of, in Plato 41, 42, 47, 105-
        118, 124, 133-140, 143-146, 153,
        156, 161
    in modern Western thought 73, 113
    in Russian nineteenth and twentieth-
        century thought 23, 100, 103, 113,
        117, 120-127, 134, 138, 140, 141,
        156-161, 165
    rule of law 41, 102, 122, 123, 126, 138,
        145
Steinhart, Karl 42, 142

Stepun, Fedor 88
Stolypin, Petr 97
syllabus
　see schools; universities
Symposium 47, 181

Teichmüller, Gustav 45
Theaetetus 46, 82, 83, 85, 136, 180, 181, 182
theological academies, curricula 22, 76, 78
　Kiev 14, 38, 79, 199-201, 203
　Moscow 1, 36, 76, 197, 198
　St. Petersburg 29, 38, 62, 199-202
Timaeus 47, 65, 136, 180, 181
Tolstoi, D.A. 24, 36
Tolstoi, Lev 101, 127
translations, Russian
　of philosophy 29, 30, 32, 37, 38, 41-43, 48, 49, 76, 87
　of history 54n45, 140
　of law 129n16
Troitskii, M.M., 9
Trubetskoi, Evgenii 9, 13, 41, 48, 87, 101, 123, 138, 144, 146, 149, 161-165, 175, 186, 195
Trubetskoi, Sergei 8-10, 30, 38, 43, 67, 71-75, 86, 121, 137, 153, 157, 161, 191, 194, 197

Überweg, Friedrich 28, 136
universities
　Kiev 9, 18n30, 31, 37, 87, 195, 196, 200, 202

Moscow 8, 9, 14, 22, 23, 37, 41, 59, 87, 100, 126, 139, 192-198, 201, 204-206
St. Petersburg 9, 18n30, 30, 37, 44, 123, 144, 194, 198, 199, 202
　see also education; intelligentsia, academic; Reform and Counter Reform
utopia, utopianism 120, 122, 126, 128, 133, 135, 144, 147, 156, 158, 163, 174, 184
Uvarov, Sergei 23, 77, 79, 185

Vellanskii, D.M. 22
Vipper, R. 139, 205
Vladislavlev 9
Volgin, Viacheslav 152, 175, 176, 196
Vvedenskii, Aleksandr 9, 29

Walicki, Andrzej 64, 99, 100, 193
Weber, Alfred 9, 32
Wilamowitz-Möllendorff, Ulrich 34, 140, 145
Windelband, Wilhelm 9, 28, 29, 30, 33, 48, 87
World Soul 64, 65, 73-75,

Zelinskii, Faddei 26, 31, 33, 35, 140, 198
Zeller, Eduard 9, 28-33, 136, 145, 174
Zhakov, K. 48, 60, 87, 89
Zhebelev, Sergei 13, 44, 49, 199

For Product Safety Concerns and Information please contact our EU
representative GPSR@taylorandfrancis.com
Taylor & Francis Verlag GmbH, Kaufingerstraße 24, 80331 München, Germany

www.ingramcontent.com/pod-product-compliance
Lightning Source LLC
Chambersburg PA
CBHW071352290426
44108CB00014B/1514